Greenhill
Books

ZULU
VANQUISHED

This book is dedicated to the memory of the late
Colonel Joe Williams, representative of the Royal Regiment of Wales
in South Africa, 1991–2004.

and

The late Lieutenant-Colonel S. Bourquin,
acknowledged expert on Zulu history and language.

ZULU VANQUISHED

THE DESTRUCTION OF THE ZULU KINGDOM

RON LOCK AND PETER QUANTRILL

FOREWORD BY DAVID RATTRAY

Greenhill Books, London
Stackpole Books, Pennsylvania

Zulu Vanquished
The Destruction of the Zulu Kingdom

First published 2005 by Greenhill Books/Lionel Leventhal Limited
Park House, 1 Russell Gardens, London NW11 9NN
and
Stackpole Books, 5067 Ritter Road, Mechanicsburg, PA 17055, USA

British Library Cataloguing-in Publication Data
Lock, Ron
Zulu vanquished : the destruction of the Zulu kingdom
1. Zulu War, 1879
I. Title II. Quantrill, Peter
968.4'045

ISBN 1-85367-660-8

Library of Congress Cataloging-in Publication Data available

Edited and typeset by Donald Sommerville

Printed and bound in Great Britain by
MPG Books Ltd, Bodmin, Cornwall

Contents

List of Maps and Diagrams

List of Illustrations

(pages 177–208)

Authors' Note

Much confusion exists in the spelling of Zulu names. For example the River Tugela is also spelt Thukela or Thugela; the Umfolozi River is also spelt Imfolozi and Mfolozi. Kambula may also be spelt Khambula. The Zulu name for the Buffalo River is the Mzinyatha, and Koppie Allein may be spelt Koppie Alleen. In addition the spellings of Zulu personal and regimental names vary. Readers familiar with the Anglo-Zulu War will note that we have chosen to spell place names in contemporary style; that employed by writers of reports, journals, diaries and other primary source material.

The word 'kaffir' in common usage during the nineteenth century, is offensive, and has been used only in direct quotes.

Chapters 1–5 were written by Ron Lock; Chapters 6–8 and 10–12 were written by Peter Quantrill; Chapter 9 and Chapter 13 were a 'joint effort'. This is not to say that the manuscript was not a team production as, without close co-operation and interchange of ideas in an atmosphere of close friendship, this book would not have been written.

Acknowledgements

As with *Zulu Victory: the Epic of Isandlwana and the Cover-up*, this sequel could not have been written without help and encouragement from varied sources and friends many of whom are acknowledged experts in their own right in matters relating to the Anglo-Zulu War. In no particular order, we wish to offer profuse thanks to the following, who took both the trouble and time to share their expertise with us.

Nicki von der Heyde, whose knowledge of the Anglo-Zulu War, coupled with a degree in English literature, was invaluable in her role of chief critic and corrector of text; Elizabeth Bodill who with calm and expertise set out and typed the manuscript, miraculously transforming dog-eared and rewritten pages into pristine chapters; Miriam Vigar for her interest and sound advice; Marise Bauer of Pietermaritzburg for once again, as in *Zulu Victory*, exercising patience and skill in the production of the maps; Manfred Kramer, whose family has for generations owned the farm on which the Battle of Gingindlovu was fought, for guiding us over the battleground and pointing out the exact corners of the square formed by the British; Dr J. C. van der Walt, historian from Richards Bay, KwaZulu-Natal, and an acknowledged expert on the history of Eshowe, Gingindlovu and the Naval Brigade, for sharing his primary source material; David Rattray of Fugitives' Drift Lodge for his unflagging enthusiasm for all things Anglo-Zulu, but in particular for the expedition to Hlobane Mountain and pinpointing the location of the Frontier Light Horse rearguard – confirmed by the discovery of decaying cartridge cases, undisturbed for 125 years, and for his foreword to this book; Colonel Mike McCabe, Royal Engineers, who took the time to responded to a barrage of queries to guide us in the right direction, including the invaluable role played by the Corps of Engineers in 1879 and in the initial preparations during 1878. Major (Retd) Paul Naish, battlefield guide and Anglo-Zulu War expert who helped in the research and generously provided both anecdotes and primary source information; Ken Gillings, KwaZulu-Natal military historian and Zulu linguist, for sharing his deep knowledge, proof-reading certain chapters and for debating contentious issues; Alain Delvilani, owner of the Villa Prince Imperial, Vryheid, KwaZulu-Natal, for drawing our attention to a rare copy of Paul Deleage's book on the Prince Imperial published in French in 1879 and for translating controversial portions of the text; Arthur Konigkramer, Chairman of AMAFA (Heritage Council) for his interest and continual support and for allowing us access to AMAFA records at Ulundi; Barry Marshall, Chief Executive Officer of AMAFA, together with Alan Reid, Chief Administrative Officer AMAFA and Regina von Vuuren, Curator, Cultural Museum, Ulundi, for their generous help; Julian Whybra, for responding to our queries; Peter Robinson, whose continual interest in our work and further research, particularly relating to the Prince Imperial, has helped us immeasurably; Lieutenant-Colonel John Cross, Pokhara, Nepal, historian and acknowledged as the leading English/Nepalese linguist; Major Martin Everett, Curator of the Royal Regiment of Wales Museum, Brecon, for the detailed history of both battalions of the 24th Regiment of Foot during their service in South Africa; John Young, acknowledged as a leading authority on all aspects of the war, for sharing his expertise with us and from time to time guiding us in the right direction and also for generously allowing us access to his remarkable collection of illustrations; the cheerful and ever helpful staff of the Killie Campbell Africana Library, Durban, and likewise the staff of the Natal Archives, Pietermaritzburg; Lee Stevenson, who although busy with his own publications on the Anglo-Zulu War, generously tracked down elusive snippets at the UK National Archives; the late Fred Duke, who was always happy to walk over Hlobane Mountain and to share his vast knowledge of the battle; Shaun Friend of Vryheid, for his reassuring presence when the mist descended on Hlobane Mountain; Brian Thomas for providing a copy of Major Dennison's DSO citation; Jack Crutchley for his company on Hlobane and his photographs; Justin Young for his continual interest and the extract of the letter describing the retreat of Raaff's Rangers on Hlobane; Rob caskie for his company and support. The authors would also like to acknowledge the assistance given by Mrs Jill Kelsey, Deputy Registrar of the Royal Archives, Windsor. All quotations and photographs originating from materials in the Royal Archives are reproduced by gracious permission of Her Majesty Queen Elizabeth II. And, as proffered in *Zulu Victory*, we would like to offer a big nod of appreciation to the people of Zululand for their continual cheerfulness, ready smiles and great sense of humour.

Last, but of course not least, our thanks and appreciation go to our most patient and understanding wives, Brenda Lock and Jacqueline Quantrill, without whose loving support this book would not have been possible.

Glossary

amakhosi	In the context of 1879, chiefs of the Zulu nation.
Boer	Dutch-speaking white settler from the Cape.
Brevet	A document entitling a commissioned officer to hold temporarily a higher military rank without the appropriate pay and allowances.
donga	A dry watercourse or gully, derived from the Zulu word *u(lu)Donga* (plural *izinDonga*).
drift	A fordable point in a river.
ibutho	(plural *amabutho*) Age grade men formed into regiments.
ikhanda	(plural *amakhanda*) Military dwellings or barracks, comprising numerous individual huts generally circular or oval in shape, used to house regiments.
iklwa	(plural *amaKlwa*) A stabbing spear for close-quarter fighting.
impi	A military body of any size.
indaba	An important meeting or discussion.
induna	(plural *izinduna*) Officer in state or army, headman, councillor.
isiGodlo	(plural *iziGodla*). Woman selected as Zulu king's concubine.
iziNyanga	Healers and witchdoctors.
kloof	A cliff or small ravine.
kop	A prominent hill or peak.
kraal	A cattle enclosure located within or close to an *ikhanda* or *umuzi*. Considered by the Zulu to be a derogatory term when used by the British to describe an *ikhanda* or *umuzi*.
laager	A word derived from Boer usage. A defensive position made by the formation of wagons into a barricade.
nek	A saddle between two hills.
pont	Flat-bottomed boat used as a ferry at river crossings.
puggaree	An Indian turban. A coloured scarf tied around a sun helmet.
sluit	A deep gully eroded by rainfall. Also a narrow water channel constructed for irrigation.
spruit	A small stream.
trek	To make an overland journey.
umuzi	(plural *imizi*) A Zulu civilian homestead or village, under a single head.
voorlooper	A person who goes ahead, leading an ox wagon, usually wielding a long whip.

Foreword

Ron Lock and Peter Quantrill recently made their mark with *Zulu Victory: The Epic of Isandlwana and the Cover-up* (Greenhill, 2002). It is a remarkable book, thoroughly researched and beautifully written, and it will be a long while before a more substantial treatment on that great battle is published.

Few people would dispute the statement that the Anglo-Zulu War of 1879 enjoys a disproportionately high profile, but it is the opening battles that have caught the public eye. The enigma of Isandlwana will live on forever and authors will debate what really happened in those closing moments of the battle for the rest of time. Rorke's Drift must surely be one of the most famous battles Britain ever fought, and the sad reality is that for many people that is where the story ends. Few people have any knowledge or understanding of the rest of the campaign. Some may have heard of the death of the Prince Imperial of France, and fewer still of Ulundi, but, tragically, few footprints are to be found on the battlefields of Meyer's Drift, Hlobane, Kambula, Nyezane and Gingindlovu.

At last we now have a book that completes the tragic saga. *Zulu Vanquished* is a thorough examination of the destruction of the Zulu Kingdom.

Were it not for the drama of 22 January, I am sure that the other events of 1879 would still enjoy a high profile – only the focus would have shifted to the north of the territory where the war was played out in a region so spectacular in terms of topography that words fail. The brilliance of Mbelini wa Mswati at Meyer's Drift, the sheer magnificence of Hlobane and the stark desolation of the spot where the last Napoleon Bonaparte fell are just part of the story.

What I have really loved about the book is the confidence the reader feels because the authors know the ground. This fact sets these two men apart from the others. Recent years have seen a plethora of books, many of them well researched and most of them well written, but here we have a book written by two men who have travelled the region thoroughly. They are also military men who write giving a soldier's perspective and they see the ground with a soldier's eye.

I am delighted that Captain Dennison's version of what really did happen at Hlobane is given prominence. The resulting account of Hlobane is groundbreaking and all future commentators on that great fight will find it difficult to refute their hypothesis. It is absolutely riveting – but so is the rest of the book.

All who are interested in this campaign will find themselves racing through the pages towards the tragic battle of Ulundi and the capture of the awesome King Cetshwayo.

Ron and Peter established themselves as serious authors on the Zulu War with *Zulu Victory*. They have now taken this one step further and, given the research they have done, the ground they have covered, and the writing flair they have demonstrated, I believe this volume is their greatest contribution thus far.

I have spent many happy days with the authors on these great battle-fields. What a privilege it all has been and I am humbled that they should ask me to write these words.

David Rattray
Fugitives' Drift

Chapter 1

A Shaken Empire

Brevet-Colonel Evelyn Wood: 'Perhaps Cetshwayo will give us a fight?'
Sir Garnet Wolseley: 'No, Shepstone will keep him quiet until we are ready.'

Aldershot, England, 1877

Captain Alan Gardner, 14th Hussars, legged on his sweat-caked horse down the final slope towards the pudding-shaped hill that dominated the little settler hamlet of Utrecht. Gardner was the bearer of catastrophic news. The main column of a British invasion force, almost 5,000 strong, that had crossed the Buffalo River only eleven days earlier, intent on the conquest of the Zulu kingdom, had been defeated, shattered and dispersed. Some 850 British and colonial soldiers and some 500 of their black allies now lay in death and bloody mutilation around the base of a hill that, worn by time and wind, had taken the outline of a sphinx. Its name, Isandlwana, would now ever be synonymous – as far as the British were concerned – with humiliation and defeat. For the Zulu warriors who had been victorious, it marked the zenith of their martial power. Gardner had been there. Prior to the battle he had heard the boasts and had seen the swaggering over-confidence. Probably he had bragged himself, as had everyone in the column, from Lord Chelmsford, the General Officer Commanding HM Forces in Southern Africa, down to the common private soldiers. 'I am inclined to think that we may possibly induce him [Cetshwayo, the Zulu king] to attack us which will save us a great deal of trouble', Lord Chelmsford had declared.[1]

But, at dawn on 22 January 1879, Chelmsford had been decoyed into leaving the British camp at Isandlwana and, with a battalion of infantry – the 2nd/24th Regiment of Foot – four 7-pounder guns and most of the mounted men then on hand, he had marched out in the confident belief that he would shortly engage and defeat the Zulu Army. He left behind an unentrenched and virtually defenceless camp: the tents, horse lines and wagon parks strung out along the eastern base of the Isandlwana Hill for almost a mile. 'As defenceless as an English village', someone had remarked.

As Chelmsford and his column had marched south-east for ten miles, the Zulu Army had marched west, concealed in the undulations of the plain.

Less than four miles separated the two as they strode parallel to each other in opposite directions. Then, as Chelmsford's force split and floundered in the pursuit of elusive decoys, the Zulu army, over 22,000 strong and undetected, deployed to attack the British camp – even the Zulu skirmishers whose presence should have given early warning of the Zulu intent, were, when encountered, unrecognised for what they were. Gardner had the misfortune of being there. Having originally gone out with Chelmsford he had been sent back to Isandlwana carrying an order that the camp should be packed and made ready to move.

He had got into camp just before the Zulu encirclement was complete and suddenly found himself fighting for his life as the warriors came on, their advance later described as being like 'the Tugela River in flood'. Gardner had seen the futile attempts of the Royal Artillery gunners to halt and scatter the advancing tide with high explosive, but on they came; then, closer, the guns had fired shrapnel, but to no avail; and in the final seconds, the guns were loaded with canister, but too late, they were overtaken and many of the gunners slaughtered as they tried to get away with their guns. It had been much the same with the scattered companies of the 1st/24th Regiment, a regiment of tough mature redcoats, disciplined and confident, who had marched and fought their way up from the Cape. With disciplined volley fire, a company of eighty men could blaze off up to 800 rounds a minute of bone-shattering, man-stopping, 0.45-inch ammunition. Gardner had seen the devastating volley fire send the hyped and frantic young warriors to ground as many of their comrades were brought down in sprawling heaps. But not for long. Fearless remonstrating leaders strode amongst the momentarily cringing warriors and, by their example, the tide rose and never again faltered as the regiments sped on to claim the honour of being first into the British camp. Even Lord Chelmsford would later grudgingly remark that the Zulus were 'undoubtedly a very brave people'. HRH the Duke of Cambridge, the Commander-in-Chief of the British Army, was no less stinting in his praise:

> Nowhere, either in southern or central Africa did such a powerfully organised, well-disciplined and thoroughly trained force of courageous men exist as lay at the disposal of Ketchwayo [*sic* Cetshwayo, the Zulu king].[2]

In less than an hour of the guns opening fire, the battle of Isandlwana was over and the few Europeans that had so far survived were desperately fighting their way through a chink in the encirclement of warriors, an escape route that seemed to offer little more hope of survival than to await death amongst the turmoil of the camp. Only those fortunate enough to find a horse would survive as the fugitives, heedless of the direction of their flight, spurred over rocks and gulleys, down a six-mile-long gauntlet of warriors who were faster and fleeter than a horse over the ghastly terrain. Gardner had been amongst them and had reached the Buffalo River, the boundary between Zululand and the colony of Natal, where he gazed in horror at the river, ploughing and humping past in spate. The choice was between a likely death by drowning, or certain death at the hands of the enemy. He urged his horse, it frantic with fear, into the mill race. Minutes later Gardner, not really knowing how he had made it, arrived horseless and half-drowned on the Natal bank. He was one of only five regular officers to have survived the battle.

With other fugitives, Gardner had made his way on foot to the British base at Helpmekaar, eighteen miles distant and high up in the mountains. He had been well aware of a closer British post at a place called Rorke's Drift, where a hundred or so men of the 2nd/24th guarded regimental supplies and a makeshift hospital. But Rorke's Drift, so close to Isandlwana and logically the next place to be attacked, would, in all probability, have been overrun. Nevertheless, Gardner, the zealous staff officer that he was, had managed to scribble a note, warning those at Rorke's Drift, which he sent on by a mounted man of the Natal Native Horse (NNH).

Confusion, close to panic, reigned at Helpmekaar. In the gloom of a moonless night, makeshift defences were being thrown up in a fever of haste. A number of the colonials who had retained their horses volunteered to take warning of the disaster – and the expected flood tide of invading Zulus – to the villages and towns of Natal. An imperial officer, alarmed at the exodus of so many enthusiastic messengers, all eager to ride away to relative safety, threatened to have all the horses shot, which caused further panic and desertions. However, there were no volunteers applying to ride north, closer to the Zulu homeland, through the vast sprawling hill country, mostly uninhabited, that might well by now be a high road for an advancing Zulu army. And it was essential that someone should go, for in the north there was another British column, designated No. 4, that was completely unaware of the catastrophe and equally unprepared to receive the victorious Zulu army that could descend upon it at any moment. The column was commanded by Colonel Evelyn Wood VC and its purpose in the scheme of the British invasion was not to advance immediately towards the Zulu capital, but to contain a vast area, known as the Disputed Territories, that, long before the war had started, had been a seething hotbed of dispute between the immigrant Boers and local native chiefs.

Gardner, aware that Wood's column would be widely deployed and vulnerable, sought a volunteer to ride north. But even Gardner's offer of a cash reward could find no takers; the fear of what those desolate hills between Helpmekaar and Utrecht might contain outweighed the prospect of reward. So Gardner decided to go himself. Scribbling a note, a masterpiece of brevity, describing in 120 words what had happened, he prepared to ride to Utrecht where Wood's camp was located.[3] By now he had been on the go for twenty-four hours and was utterly exhausted. Nevertheless, in the half light of dawn he set out for Dundee, twenty-five miles distant, a small settlement on the way north. There he managed to secure a fresh horse and snatch a few hours sleep. Refreshed, but dirty and dishevelled, having lost his jacket and boots when swimming the Buffalo River the previous day, he rode without incident for another fifty miles through the deserted hills, coming within sight of Utrecht at four o'clock in the afternoon.

Wood's base was a crude fort, recently constructed by a detachment of the 90th Light Infantry (LI). Nevertheless, it was an effective defence with a moat seven feet deep and six feet wide, sloping parapets of sod and stone, a substantial gate and a drawbridge. Gardner arrived exhausted, looking more like a vagrant on a stolen horse than an officer of hussars. The NCO in charge of the guard later recorded Gardner's sudden appearance out of the hills.

> He was in a deplorable state, poor fellow, with an old shirt and something resembling britches. His horse was about done up. He desired to know who was in charge . . . and he shouted 'Up with your drawbridge, the General's camp is taken and every man slaughtered.' We at once put him down as mad . . .[4]

Closer examination revealed Gardner's identity. His scribbled note was entrusted to a gunner of the Royal Artillery who knew the whereabouts of Wood's temporary camp, close to Hlobane Mountain, fifty miles to the east. The note was finally delivered during the morning of 24 January, forty-eight hours after the camp at Isandlwana had been destroyed.

By now, and unbeknown to Wood, the situation was worse than Gardner's message described: not only had No. 3 Column ceased to exist as an effective force, No. 2 Column had suffered likewise and the majority of its black troops of the Natal Native Contingent (NNC) had either fled or had been disbanded. Worse still, No. 1 Column, under the command of Colonel Charles Knight Pearson, that had set out along the coast into Zululand 4,700 strong, would shortly be besieged. On the same day that the Battle of Isandlwana had been fought, Pearson's column had successfully engaged a Zulu army of 5,000. The warriors had lain in ambush close to the Nyezane River and had at first scattered the leading companies of Pearson's NNC. However, infantry, supported by a naval contingent from HMS *Active*, had pressed forward and, having taken a small hill, opened fire with a Gatling gun supported by volleys of musketry from the sailors and redcoats. The battle raged for some time, one British officer recalling 'They [the Zulus] slithered through the long grass and although they suffered severely, they came nearer and nearer.' Eventually, having taken heavy losses, the Zulu attack broke and the column continued its advance to Eshowe where Pearson set about fortifying an abandoned Norwegian mission station. He assumed that the other invasion columns had been equally successful as he, and that all were converging, as planned, on the Zulu capital at Ulundi. Yet, in two weeks Pearson was told of the Isandlwana disaster and consequently became besieged in his own fort.

Meanwhile, by the greatest good fortune, Lord Chelmsford and his decoyed column had not been cut off and destroyed. On the morning of the battle, they had marched out to engage the enemy without any reserve ammunition and with only one day's rations. However, by the time they had retraced their steps and reached the gory battleground of Isandlwana, the Zulu army had had enough and vacated the now smoking camp, taking with it a treasure trove of British rifles and half a million rounds of ammunition. There Chelmsford's column spent the night and, as the Zulu camp fires blazed on the nearby hills and the noise of incessant drumming carried ominously to the camp, Chelmsford and his men, surrounded by the corpses of their former comrades, waited in trepidation, expecting to be attacked at any moment.

Marching on the next day at dawn, still unmolested, they encountered more Zulus, an *impi* of considerable size but again, miraculously, the warriors were not inclined to fight. They were the remnants of the Zulu reserve that, against their king's orders, had gone on the previous day to attack the British post at Rorke's Drift. Some 3,000 in number they had, by yet another miracle, been kept at bay and finally defeated by little more than 100 British soldiers and a few colonials.

By the time Wood received Gardner's message, Lord Chelmsford had already left the remnants of his column, demoralised and camped in disarray amongst the charred ruins at Rorke's Drift, whilst he hastened on to Pietermaritzburg. He was anxious to confer with the High Commissioner, Sir Bartle Frere, whose plans for a confederation of southern African territories under the British flag were now as dead as the unburied bodies at Isandlwana. Two years earlier, in its quest for confederation, Britain had annexed, almost without bloodshed, the Boer Republic of the Transvaal, leaving only Zululand – deemed to be an archaic and savage kingdom, unsuitable for inclusion in a confederation – thwarting Britain's imperial plans. The warrior regiments of Zululand, numbering 40,000 men, could not be ignored, however. Bordering both the Transvaal and the Colony of Natal, the Zulu kingdom would always be seen as a threat to the vastly outnumbered white population and a deterrent to future white immigration.

The Disputed Territories

Amongst the many factors that aggravated peaceful relations between the British colonial government and the Zulu kingdom were the Disputed Territories whose boundaries were the furthest frontiers of both British and Zulu authority alike. Thirty years earlier they had been ruled by local chiefs who held allegiance to the Zulu king. Then immigrant Boers, attempting to find a 'promised land' in which to establish a republic beyond British jurisdiction, began to settle thereabouts. They occupied land, negotiated dubious treaties and later claimed equally dubious ownership. Cattle raids and bloodshed became common occurrences. More immigrants arrived: a Swazi clan, led by a warrior of royal birth named Mbelini wa Mswati, was given refuge by the Zulu king who received in return devoted allegiance. In

1860 more white people followed the Boers when a group of German Lutheran missionaries established an extensive agricultural centre that they named Luneburg. There they trained aspiring farmers, both black and white. Luneburg became a prosperous, but defenceless community, in a lawless land. There were also, long established in the territory, inhabitants of mixed race, high-cheekboned and of Hottentot appearance, led by their chief, Manyanyoba kaMagondo. They occupied a fortress-like mountain, Manyanyoba's Stronghold, and a large tract of grazing land that bordered the farms of the Lutheran missionaries. In addition there was the abaQulusi clan, of many thousand, liege people of the Zulu king.

At the time, the territory did not fall under British authority; the main protagonists and claimants were the Zulu kingdom and the fledgeling Boer Republic of Utrecht (the Boer Volksraad at Potchefstroom was unwilling to incorporate Utrecht into the greater Boer community due to the suspect nature of Utrecht's claim to its territory). In order to prevent more bloodshed and violence on its borders – that might well spill over into Natal – the British colonial government offered to act as an intermediary and a peacekeeping force while it impartially examined the claims of all the parties. It was agreed that the colonial government would then proclaim and demarcate the boundary lines of the territorial awards that were to be made by a committee appointed and approved by both the Boers and the Zulus. Both parties agreed to abide by the decision of what was to be called the British Boundary Commission. Three men were selected for the task, all honest and incorruptible: the Honourable M. Gallwey, Attorney-General of Natal, the Honourable J. Wesley Shepstone, Acting Secretary for Native Affairs, and Lieutenant-Colonel A. W. Durnford, the senior Royal Engineer officer in the colony. For months the commission assiduously pondered claims and counter-claims. By mid-November 1878 it had completed its findings, which included the award of 1,800 square miles of land to King Cetshwayo. It was an award that frustrated Frere's plans to tame and diminish the Zulu kingdom and, consequently, the ruling was not immediately made known. Instead, Cetshwayo was invited to attend a great *indaba* (conference) to be held on the Natal bank of the Tugela River at a place called the Lower Drift. There, on 11 December 1878, the Boundary Commission award would be made public. And so it was, much to the satisfaction of Cetshwayo's deputies. But there was more to come. The plans for war with Zululand that Frere had plotted for months were suddenly revealed.

It is likely that, amongst the higher echelons of the British Army and the Colonial Office, the war had been planned for several years, rather than months. Years later, Wood recorded a conversation that he had had at Aldershot, in November 1877, with Sir Garnet Wolseley and a Colonel William Butler. Sir Garnet, who was in anticipation of going to South Africa for the Ninth Frontier War, remarked how much he regretted that Wood would be unable to accompany him:

I [Wood] said, 'Perhaps Cetshwayo will give us a fight,' but he [Wolseley] replied, 'No, Shepstone will keep him quiet until we are ready.' Colonel Butler said, 'When we fight the Zulus, we shall want 10,000 men.[5]

The Ultimatum and the Consequences

The astonished Zulu deputies were given an ultimatum at the conference at Lower Drift. Frere was well aware that it would impossible for Cetshwayo to comply with its terms – that was the way the ultimatum had been designed. For instance, Cetshwayo could no more disband the Zulu army of 40,000 warriors, as demanded, than order the destruction of the national harvest. The terms of the ultimatum, utterly unexpected and incomprehensible to Cetshwayo, were to be fulfilled within thirty-one days, failing which a state of war would exist. The month of grace would also allow Lord Chelmsford to deploy his invasion columns along the Zulu border, ready to strike on 11 January as indeed they did, only to be halted within ten days by a defeat that shocked the British Empire.

The shock waves of that calamity, spread by the white couriers from Helpmekaar and the black deserters of the NNC, stampeded the inhabitants of Natal into a commotion of defensive activity. Across the Buffalo River, less than twenty miles from Isandlwana, Mrs Fynn, the wife of the resident magistrate of Msinga, a border hamlet, prayed all night as she and several other ladies watched the glow in the night sky from the burning mission at Rorke's Drift. Further along the road towards Pietermaritzburg at Greytown, it was later reported in the prose of the time, that the townsfolk had been, '. . . rather flustered, going into laager, which it was found required practice to ensure calmness and correctness necessary on such occasions.'

At Luneburg, perhaps the most vulnerable settlement of all, it was reported that tens of thousands of Zulus were assembling to attack; Colonel Wood, a phlegmatic soldier who could never be accused of panic, jocularly promised the citizens that the only thing he could offer with assurance was a decent burial. Closer to Pietermaritzburg, the little church at Weston was put into a state of defence and the citizens ordered to bring as much food and as many arms as they possessed. The stone fort at Estcourt allowed farmers to bring ox wagons within the laager itself – on condition there were no more than eight beasts per vehicle. The Pinetown defence, known as 'Fort Funk', was reported as being undoubtedly the best in the colony. It consisted of a double row of iron railway tracks sunk into the ground, with railway sleepers dropped in between, making a barricade 260 yards long, ten feet high and with flanking bastions to its rear. It was big enough to hold 1,500 people and was surmounted with a Union flag. The commotion also spread to far-off Durban where a redoubt was hastily thrown up to command the open ground above the port, and a gun mounted that had been kindly provided by the Royal Navy. The gunpowder from the town's magazine was transferred aboard a lighter, which was then moored in the bay, while stonemasons loopholed the court house walls. Furthermore, a

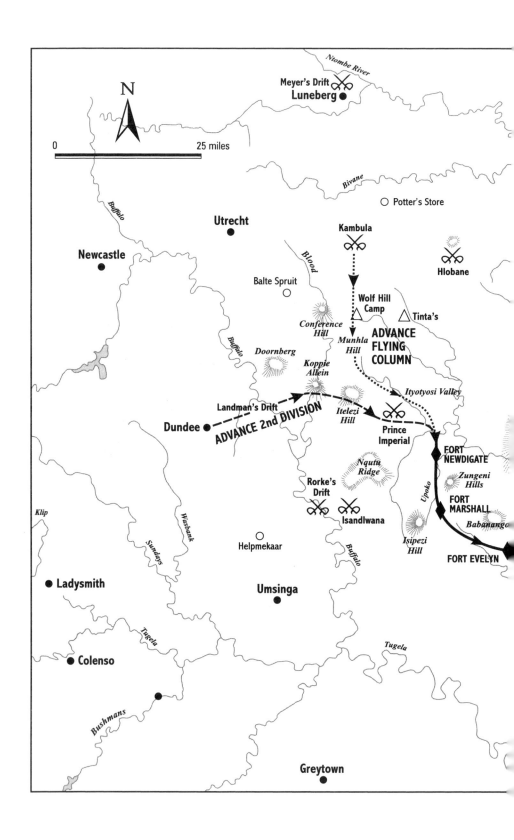

N

0   25 miles

Ntombe River

Meyer's Drift

Luneberg ●

Bivane

○ Potter's Store

Buffalo

Utrecht ●

Blood

Kambula

Hlobane

Newcastle ●

Balte Spruit ○

Wolf Hill
Camp △   △ Tinta's

*Conference
Hill*

Buffalo

Doornberg

*Munhla
Hill*

ADVANCE
FLYING
COLUMN

*Koppie
Allein*

Ityotyosi Valley

Landman's Drift

ADVANCE 2nd DIVISION

*Itelezi
Hill*

Dundee ●

Prince
Imperial

FORT
NEWDIGATE

*Nqutu
Ridge*

*Zungeni
Hills*

Klip

Rorke's
Drift

FORT
MARSHALL

Washbank

Isandlwana

Babanango

Buffalo

Upoko

*Isipezi
Hill*

○
Helpmekaar

FORT EVELYN

Ladysmith ●

Sundays

Umsinga ●

Tugela

Colenso ●

Tugela

Bushmans

Greytown ●

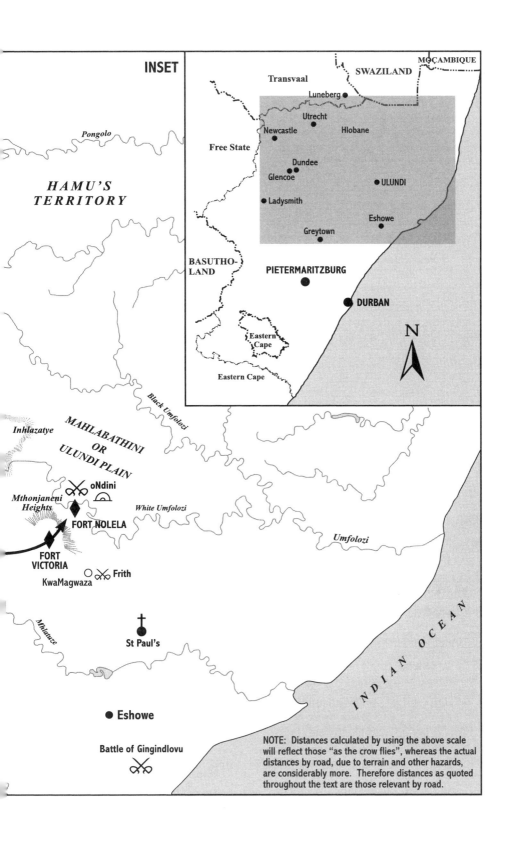

MOÇAMBIQUE

SWAZILAND

Transvaal

Luneberg

Utrecht

Hlobane

Pongolo

Newcastle

Free State

HAMU'S
TERRITORY

Dundee

Glencoe

ULUNDI

Ladysmith

Eshowe

Greytown

BASUTHO-
LAND

PIETERMARITZBURG

DURBAN

Eastern
Cape

N

Eastern Cape

Black Umfolozi

Inhlazatye

MAHLABATHINI
OR
ULUNDI PLAIN

oNdini

Mthonjaneni
Heights

White Umfolozi

FORT NOLELA

FORT
VICTORIA

Umfolozi

Frith

KwaMagwaza

Mhlatuze

St Paul's

INDIAN OCEAN

Eshowe

Battle of Gingindlovu

NOTE: Distances calculated by using the above scale
will reflect those "as the crow flies", whereas the actual
distances by road, due to terrain and other hazards,
are considerably more. Therefore distances as quoted
throughout the text are those relevant by road.

defence committee was formed under the presidency of the mayor and it was resolved:

> . . . that whilst the committee did not entertain any apprehension for the safety of the borough, it admitted that the communication from Lord Chelmsford, to the opposite effect, made it imperative for steps to be taken to guard against any remote consequences.

The town guard, sixty strong, was ordered to attend a church parade and the Durban volunteer artillery was sent off to the Umgeni River to guard the northern approaches to the borough.

By the time Lord Chelmsford reached Pietermaritzburg he found the town to be in panic and Sir Bartle Frere busy writing a communiqué, apprising HRH the Duke of Cambridge of the situation. Now, with Chelmsford able to give testimony – and seemingly unruffled and making to play down the disaster, Frere wrote:

> I had collected what [information] I could from the fugitives who came in here & from the few letters we got from the front, relative to the sad disaster on the 22nd, when Chelmsford was able to give, in a connected form, the latest & best information procurable, which has expressed what we had gathered in many cases from excited, exhausted & uneducated men. Your Royal Highness will, I am sure, be glad to hear that though greatly worn by all he has gone through, he [Chelmsford] is well in health & a few days comparative rest will, I hope, quite set him up. [Then came the first tentative feelers, seeking a scapegoat.] He feels the calamity the more because he is naturally averse, pending the result of the enquiry he has ordered, to express any opinion as to who of the poor fellows, who are gone, was to be blamed for the undoubted neglect of orders which led to the disaster.[6]

The 'poor fellows' who were subsequently blamed for Lord Chelmsford's own neglect, his disdain of advice, over-confidence and contempt for his adversaries, were conveniently both dead: Brevet Colonel Anthony Durnford and Brevet Lieutenant-Colonel Henry Pulleine.

On the same day Chelmsford also wrote to the Duke of Cambridge. One can almost glimpse Frere and Chelmsford collaborating in their correspondence, backing each other up. Attempting to justify Frere's invasion of Zululand (which had not been sanctioned by the British government), Chelmsford wrote:

> We have certainly been seriously underrating the power of the Zulu Army, and it is fortunate for Natal that Cetywayo [*sic*] never ordered it to cross the border when there was but one battalion in the colony and no colonial defence worth mentioning. From our present experience it is evident that one year ago the Zulu Army could have swept through Natal from one end to the other without any possibility of stopping it.[7]

Chelmsford then went on, with a touch of awe in his pen: 'The Zulus appear to have no fear whatever of death' and, seemingly, all confidence gone, he speculated hopefully on the prospects of No. 1 and No. 4 Columns, those of Pearson and Wood, not knowing at the time that Pearson was besieged at Eshowe:

> There is of course always the possibility of a success on their parts which may redeem our present misfortune but I am at the present moment inwardly inclined to view everything 'Au noir' although I need scarcely assure Your Royal Highness that I do not allow anyone here to perceive it.[8]

Frere had earlier advised London by telegram, via Cape Town, of the disaster. Lady Frere, his wife and confidante, being his intermediary. His daughter, Mary, had also been privy to his dispatches and was swift in coming to her father's defence. Only five days after Isandlwana Mary wrote an impassioned letter to Lieutenant-General Sir Henry Ponsonby, Private Secretary to Queen Victoria, knowing that her letter would be put before the queen as soon as it arrived:

> The Genl [Chelmsford] returned to P.M.B. [Pietermaritzburg] (wch it was feared wd be immediately attacked) and wch is in a hollow in a circle of hills & quite undefended. The object is to keep the Zulus if possible out of Natal itself. The fear is of the whole country being overrun, of its [black] population rising . . . & of a repetition at P.M.B. of the siege of Lucknow . . . The great need is of mounted men to break masses of infantry [warriors] & find out where they are. The Zulus travel nearly as fast as men on horseback. They are reckless of death . . . What my Father foresaw has occurred. Our present struggle is for national as well as personal existence . . . My Father is, you may be sure, doing in every way all that it is possible to do, to maintain confidence. The entire & absolute confidence felt in him & evidenced throughout the whole colony is the one human strength we have in this time of trial . . . But I must not disguise from you that the danger is very extreme. He may not be living when you receive this.[9]

However, Mary need not have feared for her father's life, any more than the rest of the white population need have feared that the black colossus of the Zulu army would appear rampaging out of the night. The Zulu army had, in fact, disbanded and fragmented itself; those who had survived the battles of Isandlwana, Rorke's Drift and Nyezane had returned to their homes after experiencing the solace of after-battle cleansing that only the rituals of their ancient culture could provide. In the days prior to the battle, the warriors had experienced fleeting contact with the spirit world when, in preparation for the violence to come and the evil that would manifest from many deaths, the war-doctors had administered ritual protective medicines. The cleansing rituals, which were as urgent in their need as the attention given to the wounded, had been performed within hours of the battle. It was, perhaps, only then, with the elation of victory dwindling, that the Zulu army began to count the cost of its triumph. The exact number of Zulu casualties will never be known, but it is unlikely that they were fewer than 2,000 and tragic enough for King Cetshwayo to lament that it was as though an assegai had been thrust into the belly of the Zulu nation. A young white man, a Boer trader by the name of Cornelius Vijn, well known in Zululand, had been marooned there when the war started and was later able to testify to the national grief:

> As they [the people of the village in which Vijn was staying] approached they kept wailing in front of the kraals, rolling themselves on the ground and never quietening down; nay, in the night they wailed so as to cut through the heart of anyone. And this wailing went on, night and day, for a fortnight; the effect of it was very depressing; I wished I could not hear it.[10]

Colonel Evelyn Wood and No. 4 Column

So for the moment Natal was safe, but neither Frere, Chelmsford nor the population of the colony was to know it. It was believed that only Wood's No. 4 column and the hastily erected civil defences stood between the colony and a Zulu onslaught. Consequently, the colonial government was desperate for reinforcements and not only reinforcements but also a man who could replace both Frere and Chelmsford in the event of their demise. On 4 February, Frere wrote to the Duke of Cambridge:

> We greatly need a competent second in command who can take Lord Chelmsford's, or my place, in case of a breakdown. The strain is enormous. There is no one except Colonel Evelyn Wood, well-fitted in all respects, and he is junior to several other men in the field.

On the following day he wrote again:

> After carefully weighing the position with Lord Chelmsford & Sir Henry Bulwer [Governor of Natal] I have come to the conclusion that reinforcements should be not less than 10 [? original unclear] Infantry Battalions in two Brigades with Brigadiers & all staff complete. One regt in each Brigade might be Indian . . . & Two regiments of good Indian Irregular Cavalry with their horses complete & fit for immediate service.

Shortly thereafter the infantry would be on their way but they would be all British and the hoped for 'good Indian Irregular Cavalry' likewise never materialised; instead irregular cavalry would be enlisted immediately from amongst the colonial population of adventurers and drifters. Within a short time these white and black horsemen, recruited from hundreds of miles around, would be as effective in winning the war for the British government as any of the imperial troops including the 1st (King's) Dragoon Guards and the 17th Lancers (Duke of Cambridge's Own) who would later arrive from England. Meanwhile, it fell upon Colonel Evelyn Wood and No. 4 Column to take the war to the enemy – even if Wood's activities were confined to the area of the Disputed Territories.

Wood had had a very active service career, one to be envied by any serious army officer. Born in 1838, he had initially joined the Royal Navy at the age of fourteen as a midshipman and was soon ashore with the Naval Brigade in the thick of the fighting at Sevastopol during the Crimean War. He was severely wounded during the assault on the Redan and only managed to prevent his shattered arm being amputated by arguing fiercely with several doctors who were keen to have it cut off. Having been invalided back to England, he decided to transfer to the army as the easiest way of returning to active service. Appointed a cornet in the 13th Light Dragoons, it was not long before he was back in the Crimea where he immediately contracted typhoid fever, complicated by pneumonia and came close to death. His mother hastened from England to nurse her son and found his condition so extreme that the bones of his hips were protruding through the flesh, and his feet so enlarged with dropsy that not a shoe or slipper would fit them. Thanks to her devoted nursing, Wood survived.

By the time of the Indian Mutiny three years later, he was fit enough to sail with his regiment for Bombay. He saw much action and had the distinction of raising and commanding a local regiment of cavalry. He also won the greatest distinction of all, the Victoria Cross. Subsequent service brought about a transfer to the 17th Lancers, and then years of soldiering at home, both in Ireland and at Aldershot. In 1871 he transferred to the infantry, obtaining by purchase, at a cost of £2,000, a majority in the 90th LI then stationed at Stirling Castle in Scotland. It was not until 1873 that Wood saw active service again. By then a brevet lieutenant-colonel, he was selected to accompany, as a special service officer, Sir Garnet Wolseley's punitive expedition against the Ashanti Kingdom on the west coast of Africa. It was a particularly unpleasant campaign, the climate being just as deadly as the missiles with which the Ashanti warriors bombarded the white invaders. Wood later recorded, in rather quaint prose, Sir Garnet's disregard for the lives of his special service officers:

> The special service officers were serving under the eye of Sir Garnet Wolseley, and apparently wishing to justify his choice in selecting them, adventured their lives freely.[11]

Wood was given the distinction of raising a native regiment, 500 strong, from the Fanti tribe, that would bear his name. They were fighting a fanatical, cruel and fearless enemy at close quarters in swamp land and bush that was so thick at times that an enemy could actually be touched but not seen. Wood was again wounded, but his Ashanti service would prove invaluable to his future career. It gave him entry to the exclusive 'Wolseley Ring', a pool of officers selected and gathered by Wolseley for special service, service that would undoubtedly lead to promotion.

It was during the Ashanti Campaign that Wood first met Redvers Buller, another member of the Wolseley Ring, who would become his great friend and second-in-command during the Zulu War yet to come.

Wood eventually returned home and took up various staff appointments at Aldershot. It was at this time that he received a proposition from a prosperous businessman who supplied equipment to the army. Their conversation is a Victorian cameo of the contempt that the gentry held for those in trade. The businessman, a Mr Thomas White, enquired obsequiously whether or not Wood would consider joining him in business and, if interested, the amount of remuneration Wood would require. Wood replied '£3,000 a year', whereupon Mr White:

> . . . jumped, nearly falling off his chair, and observed, '£3,000 a year is a large sum: pray may I ask what your pay is now, Sir?' '£664, including allowances.' 'The difference, you will allow me to say is great.' 'It is, yet not so great as the difference in service to Her Majesty, Queen Victoria, and Thomas White.[12]

Wood rejoined the 90th LI as commanding officer in January 1877 and was soon involved in fighting the Ninth Frontier War amongst the Amatola Mountains of the Eastern Cape. On the way out to South Africa he had found amongst his fellow passengers Lieutenant-General the Honourable Frederick Thesiger, who would soon inherit his father's title of Lord Chelmsford, and his old friend from the Ashanti Expedition, Major Redvers Buller. Shortly after arrival, the 90th LI was divided: five companies were to remain in the eastern Cape and three companies were to march to Utrecht, a distance of 450 miles as the crow flies.

In the campaign Wood worked closely with General Thesiger, operating in extremely difficult terrain comprising steep and wooded kloofs (ravines), and mountains. Continuous hard work, exposure to the elements and a pitiful diet, eventually left Wood too ill to move. The glands of his groin, armpits and neck became hideously swollen, his skin began to peel like 'that of a mummy' and chilblain-like cracks opened on his hands. He was carried out of the mountains in a hammock but, on being put on a diet of milk and eggs every four hours, soon recovered. Thesiger's campaign was successful and he was unstinting in his praise for Wood, writing in a despatch to the Duke of Cambridge:

> He has exercised his command with marked ability and great tact. I am of the opinion that his indefatigable exertions and personal influence have been mainly instrumental in bringing the war to a steady close.

Wood was soon riding north to Natal and to Zululand that lay beyond. Wood now held the prestigious position of column commander. Under his control were: a convoy of six guns of the Royal Artillery; five companies of the 90th LI; one company of mounted infantry; numerous armed wagon drivers and, bringing up the rear, Major Redvers Buller and the Frontier Light Horse (FLH), an imperial-paid but locally-recruited regiment. Buller was to be delayed for about a week whilst he recruited additional men to fill the ranks. The entire needs of the column were transported on forty-six wagons, hired locally at thirty shillings (£1.50) a day, each wagon, depending on weather and road conditions, being drawn by between ten and sixteen oxen. The men, having been on campaign for the best part of a year, fighting in harsh terrain and sleeping rough, looked more like tramps than soldiers. Most were heavily bearded and, with their once-smart uniforms tattered and patched with any material that had come to hand, they could have stood unnoticed beside a scarecrow. Their apparel had so diminished that Wood was obliged to ferret out locally made shirts. But like locally brewed beer at two shillings (£0.10) a bottle, the shirts were expensive, costing each man the equivalent of two weeks' pay. Nevertheless, scare-crows or not, they were fit, hard and self-reliant soldiers.

There was a similar column also making its way to Natal, commanded by Colonel Richard Glyn and manned mostly by the 1st/24th. Except for a fortunate few, these men were destined to die on the battlefield of Isandlwana a few weeks later.

Wood left King William's Town at the head of No. 4 Column on 26 June 1878 on the 500-mile march to Utrecht. It was midwinter but, although the night-time temperature occasionally plummeted to below freezing, the men were spared wet weather – most of southern Africa had been suffering drought conditions for some time. Covering an excellent average of almost ten miles a day, the convoy rolled across a barren undulating landscape that was virtually roadless. However, it was not all easy going for, as Wood recorded, no fewer than 120 streams or rivers, some as wide as the Thames, had to be crossed. It was the first time that a British army had come this way, although thirty-six years earlier, in 1842, a detachment of the 27th Regiment, only 260 strong, had marched a parallel course, along the coastal beach, thirty miles distant to the east. The detachment had left Fort Mgazi, the remotest British outpost in Africa, to do battle with the newly established Boer Republic at Port Natal (later Durban). The engagement that followed – the first of many future battles between Britain and the Boers – and the subsequent amphibious landing of additional British forces from a naval frigate, were the beginnings of British expansion north of the Eastern Cape.

No doubt Wood, like others before him, had experienced the temptation of following a coastal rather than an inland route, taking advantage of long stretches of flat white sand, reasonably able to support traffic when hard shortly after an ebbing tide. It would also have been easy to become intoxicated with the breathtaking beauty of the coastal path with its exotic vegetation – not to mention the feasts of mussels and oysters, easily gathered at low tide. It was (and still is) amongst the most beautiful coast-lines in the world. It was called the Wild Coast – and for good reason. It was the graveyard of many vessels, amongst the most famous the *São Bento*, a Portuguese treasure galleon that was wrecked in 1554. Two hundred years later the *Grosvenor*, a British East Indiaman, rumoured to be carrying the jewel-entrusted peacock throne of Persia, went aground and was lost. And, further south, the most famous wreck of all, HMS *Birkenhead*, a British trooper, carrying reinforcements to Port Elizabeth, struck a rock in 1852 and sank in shark-infested waters. As the vessel slowly went down, the troops stood on deck as if on parade. They set an example that thereafter became unwritten maritime law: 'women and children first'. It became known as 'The *Birkenhead* Drill', and a legend of bravery was born as over 450 men stood firm and paid the price. The coast further south would shortly claim another victim: HMS *Clyde*, carrying arms, ammunition and reinforcements to Lord Chelmsford, would also fall victim to the rugged South African shore.

Prelude to War

On 31 August, eight weeks after leaving King William's Town, No. 4 Column marched into Pietermaritzburg. The two companies under Brevet Major Cornelius Clery that had earlier gone ahead to Luneburg had found the area in a state of turmoil with the German settlers, in fear of their lives, ready to abandon their farms and flee. On two occasions they had been forced, under Zulu attack, to form a laager around their church. However, the arrival of the 90th and the subsequent construction of Fort Clery, complete with drawbridge and moat, stopped the exodus. Wood came under a certain amount of jocular criticism from Lord Chelmsford for occupying Luneburg and thus splitting his force. But later Wood's action was approved, Chelmsford acknowledging that, without the presence of Clery and his men, Luneburg and its valuable agricultural industry would have been destroyed. However, it was not long before the two companies of the 90th were withdrawn to rejoin the rest of No. 4 Column and were replaced at Luneburg by the Kaffrarian Rifles, who had also marched up from the Cape.

The new arrivals were a volunteer unit, 100 strong, drawn from the German community around East London and were former members of the German Legion that Britain had raised to fight on its behalf in the Crimean War. The war over, in 1857 the legionnaires had been offered the opportunity to migrate as settlers to the Cape. They were now led by Commandant Frederick Xavier Schermbrucker, a fiery fifty-three-year-old ex-officer of the Bavarian Army, who boasted that he could trace his ancestry through fourteen generations of German blood. He had entered the ranks of the Bavarian Army as a private with privileges of a gentleman cadet and was commissioned as a lieutenant in 1852. He was also credited with having been a Latin scholar, a newspaper proprietor, a public auctioneer, a butcher, a political agitator, a diamond prospector, and a member of the Cape Legislative Assembly. Schermbrucker immediately got a grip at Luneburg, with typical Teutonic authority striking fear into malingerers, rumour mongers and all who bucked his discipline. The worst of his wrath was reserved for drunkards and those who peddled grog. They could expect, and would receive, a sound flogging. Schermbrucker had also fought in the recent Cape War and was regarded as a good soldier and frontiersman.

Luneburg for the time being could be left safely in his hands despite a Zulu chief demanding on his king's behalf that all the settlers vacate the area immediately as it was Zulu territory.

Meanwhile, Wood had been busy establishing his lines of supply from Durban to Utrecht via Pietermaritzburg and Balte Spruit (Spartle Spruit). He had also pressed on to Luneburg from where, on or about 20 October 1878, accompanied only by his native interpreter and armed with nothing more than a riding crop, he rode on for five miles, crossed the Ntombe River and finally arrived at the village of Chief Manyanyoba, previously mentioned as an aggressive opponent of the German settlers. The village was situated below the fortress-like mountain of Manyanyoba's Stronghold and Wood, feigning nonchalance, but surrounded by over a hundred warriors, requested the presence of the chief. At first none would admit to his presence but, as Wood prepared to depart, declining to talk to anyone other than Manyanyoba, the chief suddenly appeared, surrounded by a strong bodyguard, all of whom were heavily armed. On being asked by Manyanyoba why he had brought soldiers to Luneburg, Wood replied that they were there merely to protect the farmers, not to invade Zululand. However, it is no more likely that Manyanyoba believed Wood, than Wood believed himself. Eventually Wood and his man rode away unmolested.

During Wood's home service at Aldershot he had – amongst his many other interests and activities – taken to the study of law. Rising each morning at 4.00 a.m., whilst the rest of the house slept, he read for three hours a day and eventually qualified as a barrister. With this background he was well equipped to dispense justice in the lawless Disputed Territories. He had a keen awareness of the value of political alliances and he made it his business to seek support from the local truculent Boers, many of whom still simmered with resentment at past British policies and conflicts. Both Frere and Chelmsford, disappointed at the home government's refusal to despatch additional troops in the numbers requested, looked and hoped for support from the local frontier community. Every Boer from childhood had been taught the necessary survival skills: horsemanship, marksmanship, the ability to find the way in often featureless territory, to track, to handle oxen and to endure in a hostile land. Wood's first attempt to recruit amongst these dour adherents to the Old Testament met with little success. Even his salesman-like appeal that their farms would increase in value once the Zulu menace was resolved fell on deaf ears. Wood was told that he would get little support until the Transvaal was returned to the Boers. In fact, because of the relatively meagre forces that had been assembled to conquer Zululand, the Boers predicted a Zulu victory and deemed it prudent to sit on the fence and await events. Unperturbed, Wood set about organising a public meeting, inviting all the farmers for miles around to attend. The meeting was called for 4 December 1878, a week prior to the findings of the Boundary Commission being made public, its conclusions, as we have heard, being greatly in favour of the Zulus. In fact, many of the Boers attending the meeting found, a week later, that the land that they held to be theirs now officially belonged to the Zulu king. However, it is highly improbable that Wood – unlike Frere and Chelmsford – had prior knowledge of the Boundary Commission's awards. Had he been apprised of the details, he would not naively have gone ahead with his enthusiastic recruiting campaign.

The meeting was held in the Utrecht courthouse, some of the assembled having travelled from distant Middleburg, 150 miles away in the Transvaal. There was an air of eager excitement and willing cooperation – rare between Boer and Briton. A chairman and committee were elected and Wood, speaking through an interpreter, put forward his proposals and conditions of service. The colonial government would supply arms, ammunition, rations and pay at five shillings (£0.25) per day; in return the Boers, mounted and equipped for immediate service, would remain enlisted until the close of operations against the Zulus. The burgers (citizens, entitled to vote) were to be:

> . . . commanded by their own officers according to their own laws but under the orders of the officer commanding the operations, whose orders must be obeyed.[13]

There was only one condition that caused some discord, that of the distribution of booty. The Boers could not agree that the cattle captured by them should go into the common bag but said they should be theirs alone. The majority of the burgers had been motivated by the prospect of being legally permitted, under British authority, to loot Zulu cattle – and as they were perfectly equipped and mounted for the role of rustlers, they deeply resented the notion that loot should be shared equally with the plodding British infantry. However, there was nothing that they or Wood could do in the matter as Lord Chelmsford had already issued an order stating:

> Cattle and other prize. The following rules, having reference to the capture of cattle, or other prize, will be adhered to by all forces serving under the orders of the Lieutenant General commanding. On any cattle or other prize being taken, the officer commanding the capture or party making the same, will at once report the circumstances and number or nature of the prize, to the officer in charge of the operations, who will thereupon determine what troops will share, and will appoint prize agents to arrange for the disposal of the cattle, and etc. and to distribute the proceeds according to the following scale, *viz*:

Trooper or private	= 1 share
NCO	= 2 shares
Captain or subaltern	= 3 shares
Field officer	= 4 shares
Officer in command of the operations	= 6 shares
Officers of the staff	= shares according to their rank.[14]

The disgruntled Boers had no option but to accept and Wood hopefully anticipated that as many as 2,000 mounted men, to be known as the Burger Force, would join him as soon as operations commenced. He told the Boers that he 'rejoiced to find that there is practically accord between us', and they in turn replied that the burgers would cooperate to bring 'the common foe to obedience and civilization'.[15]

Wood wrote enthusiastically to Chelmsford of his success but Chelmsford, knowing the allocations of the boundary awards, anticipated a furious Boer reaction. He waited until 10 December, the day prior to the awards being made public, before warning Wood that he should prepare the burgers for the shocking news that much of the territory that they held to be theirs had been awarded to those they considered to be the common foe.

As it happened, the calamity of the Boundary Commission was followed, within a month, by the British catastrophe of Isandlwana and the 2,000 horsemen that Wood had optimistically anticipated evaporated into the high veld, there to guard their farms, sit tight and await events.

Chapter 2
Holding the Fort

'MacLeod is to offer the Swazi king 50 horses with saddles and bridles and 200 cows if his men move to the Pongola and keep the Zulus out of the Transvaal. Try to get this done for half this price.'

Colonel Evelyn Wood, Utrecht, 1878

—⇒•⇐—

Wood was actively engaged with elements of the Zulu Army when he received Alan Gardner's scribbled note informing him of the events at Isandlwana. No. 4 Column at the time was scattered over a wide area and had skirmished with warriors of the local abaQulusi clan on several recent occasions. Three days earlier, after a brief encounter with a force estimated at 1,000 warriors in the wild country surrounding the Zunguin and Hlobane mountains, forty miles east of his main base of Utrecht, Wood and his men had the unique experience of observing from concealment, 4,000 warriors at drill, executing various movements and formation changes with great precision. During the early evening of 22 January, as Wood and some of his officers sat around a camp fire, they had heard the distant rumble of guns. Unbeknown to them, it was the guns of Chelmsford's stricken column, firing in the dark at the unseen enemy as the column approached the wrecked Isandlwana camp. The sound of the guns had travelled fifty miles through the stillness of the African night. Wood was questioned by his officers as to the possible reason for guns firing so late in the day. Wood sensibly replied that cannon fired after dark indicated an unfavourable situation.

Once apprised of the Isandlwana disaster and having assessed his now vulnerable situation, Wood gathered his scattered forces, abandoned the advance camp that he had formed at Tinta's Kop, thirty-five miles from Utrecht, *en route* for the Zulu capital at Ulundi, and retired. He made his new headquarters at a place called Kambula, more or less equidistant from the now extremely vulnerable settlements of Utrecht and Luneburg. Kambula had many advantages: not only was it centrally situated, it had an abundance of firewood that could be gathered from the wooded kloofs of the nearby hills, and water was plentiful from the White Umfolozi River that had its source near the camp. The dominant feature of Kambula was a low rampart-like mound from which the surrounding country of rolling hills swept to far horizons of wide and endless skies. Its only drawback was a shallow valley a short distance from the rampart mound, steep sided in part, that could provide a foe with concealment to within attacking distance of the mound itself. But on closer inspection the exit slopes of the valley could be dominated from above, causing any attack to expose itself to defensive volley fire from a distance of around 200 yards.

Wood was a good housekeeper, much dedicated to the welfare of his men, the condition of the horses and oxen and the upkeep of the column's wagons and equipment, so it was not long before he had field ovens in operation, providing the whole column daily with fresh bread.

The size of No. 4 Column had steadily increased, Wood being lavished with reinforcements as Chelmsford's confidence in his ability grew.

It was originally intended that No. 5 Column, commanded by Colonel Hugh Rowlands VC, would also invade Zululand from the Transvaal where it had been assumed Rowlands would have successfully dealt with Sekhukhune, the king of the baPedi nation. With the annexation of the Transvaal, Britain had inherited a conflict between the Boers and the baPedi in which the Boers had come off second best. Now Rowlands had done no better. Sekhukhune, secure in his fortress-like town, had proved to be a nut too difficult to crack. One imperial infantryman wrote:

> One thing the attack taught us – the uselessness of pouring lead into the strongholds of natural formation. Fortresses in themselves, from 300 to 500 feet high, formed in places where boulder towers on top of boulder, with massifs forty feet high, affording sufficient cover for hundreds of men.

The main body of Rowlands's force had numbered some 1,200 men. It was the height of a blazing summer, the land still in the grip of a drought without precedent – and the scourge of horse sickness had begun to reap a deadly toll amongst the cavalry. If, by some military miracle, Rowlands had overcome Sekhukhune, he and the whole of his column would likely have died of thirst as they attempted the return journey. Rivers and waterholes had dried up and, as Rowlands continued to advance, it only became possible to obtain water by digging, usually to find that before a third of the column's livestock had drunk, the hole, laboriously dug in the searing heat, had run dry.

Lieutenant C. E. Fenn of the FLH recalled, early on in the campaign, their plight and the lack of water:

> We found a stream of water trickling through the rocks. It was at the best a thread of water, but it was all that there was to supply the wants of about 500 thirsty men, to say nothing of the horses, mules and oxen. I found a small basin in the rocks and, kneeling down, I drank copiously and gratefully an enormous quantity of warm, thick, brackish water.

As the advance continued Fenn described how the drought got worse:

The water-hole was but a puddle at the best and by the time my horse came to drink the water was about the consistency of pea soup. Although I knew well that such filth would only tend to make me thirstier, I could not refrain from swallowing about a quart. By the time our poor horses had a turn at the puddle there was nothing left to mark its previous existence but a mass of slimy mud.

Fenn also noted that the plight of the infantry was even worse than that of the horsemen:

> I shall never forget the shocking sight some of the men of the 13th [Light Infantry] presented owing to their having been so long without water. The tongues of some of them were dreadfully swollen and black. Some of the volunteers seemed to have gone off their heads from the same cause and went about among our men offering fabulous sums for a mouthful of water.[16]

Rowlands, with the agreement of his senior officers, decided to retreat. It would be left to Sir Garnet Wolseley, with the good rains of 1879 and with 9,000 men, to conquer Sekhukhune.

Rowlands irrationally blamed himself for the failure and offered his resignation but was consoled by Chelmsford and persuaded not to resign, Chelmsford wrote:

> I have every reason to believe that this officer had no option but to retire without attempting an assault on Sekhukhune's town and I concur with his view of the immediate necessity of withdrawing the mounted portions of his force now horse sickness has broken out.[17]

Sir Bartle Frere also commented: 'Colonel Rowlands exercised sound discretion in discontinuing active operations.'

Chelmsford then issued Rowlands with rather vague orders to bring his column nearer to Zululand, but Chelmsford gave no firm view as to its actual disposition, other than suggesting that it be concentrated along the two existing roads that led to Pretoria. Rowlands made the mistake, believing it to be the best solution for the protection of the civilian inhabitants in view of the unrest in the territory, of deploying his 80th Regiment as six separate companies, stationed miles apart, as garrison troops.

Meanwhile, weeks previously, Buller and his FLH, who it will be remembered had followed No. 4 Column up from the Cape, had been ordered on from Utrecht, had joined Rowlands and had taken part in the unsuccessful advance on Sekhukhune's Stronghold. It is uncertain whether or not Buller was present when Rowlands conferred with his senior officers and received their unanimous agreement that the advance should be aborted; either way, a disgruntled Buller left Rowlands's command, possibly without permission, and let it be known that he held Rowlands in contempt for his decision.

Perhaps to show his disdain, even after Rowlands had given the order to retreat, Buller took eighty men of the FLH and went off on a three-day 'patrol', later being joined by a party from the 13th LI, as Fenn recorded:

> In the afternoon the major [Buller] with the patrol returned. They had experienced some hot fighting, having with the 13th attacked, taken, and destroyed M'Soot's Kraal. The niggers made a determined stand, and were only driven back after about four hour's fighting with about 100 killed. The loss on our side was three men of the 13th killed and five wounded, and two men of the FLH wounded. They burnt the kraal and destroyed a large quantity of mealies.[18]

Eventually, back at Utrecht, Buller wrote to Wood who, apart from being his commanding officer, was also a close friend:

> You must allow me just once to say – Damn that Rowlands – There, I am better now, a little better . . . between you and me my dear Evelyn, please keep it dark, Rowlands is quite useless. He cannot make up his mind to do anything, sitting on his behind in this position . . . I even wish you had been here. Joking apart, I do wish you had. I feel sure we should have tried something and usually to try means to do, but this idiot didn't try – just sits on his behind, that's his form, a charming man he is too, so nice, but I would rather be cursed by someone who would do something.[19]

Chelmsford would shortly write to Wood:

> No two men [Wood and Buller] in my command have supported me more loyally; and I know that you are both sincere friends as well as trustworthy 'Lieutenants'.

It was hardly a coincidence that a few days after Wood had received Buller's letter, Chelmsford wrote to Shepstone saying he had heard that Rowlands 'sits in his tent and writes all day'.

Although Buller was junior both in rank and years to Wood and to Chelmsford he had the enviable standing of a well-connected and extremely wealthy man, whereas Wood was comparatively poor and Chelmsford was far from being well off. Buller came from a long line of Devonshire gentry whose lands carried the hereditary title of 'Squires of Downes'. His father, apart from being a benevolent squire, had also been a member of parliament whilst his mother was a niece of the Duke of Norfolk. Buller's eldest brother had died some years earlier and Buller had inherited the family's estate and wealth. But martial blood ran in his veins and he preferred a hard and dangerous military life to the comfort and, no doubt, dull routine of rural Devon. At school (which had included both Harrow and Eton – he was expelled from the former for reasons unknown) and in his early army life, he had been regarded by his peers as pugnacious, dogmatic and aggressive. He was a man not to be argued with, immensely strong, tough and, above all, seemingly fearless. In 1858 Buller had been commissioned into the fashionable and expensive 60th Rifles. He came to Sir Garnet Wolseley's notice during his service in Canada and took part in Wolseley's Red River Expedition, which was remarkable for its 1,200-mile march through the Canadian wilderness at the height of winter. Some 500 miles of the journey were completed in specially constructed boats down waterways of frightening rapids and rushing rivers. Buller's great strength and his ability to use his hands – an attribute learnt in the carpenter's workshops and at the blacksmith's forge in Devon – made him an indispensable officer. As previously mentioned, he was later chosen, again by Wolseley, for the Ashanti Expedition. After his return to England, Buller had been promoted to a Deputy Assistant Adjutant-General's post at Horse Guards where he served for four years before proceeding to South Africa. As far as the men he commanded were concerned, they saw in him an officer whose interests were identical to theirs and one who brought no barrier of class distinction between them. He could in fact, they said, do everything they could do only better. The men were also wary of his strength and temper. Chelmsford and Wood were equally aware of his qualities and there can be little doubt that his derogatory and insubordinate opinion of Rowlands's ability, convinced Chelmsford to strip Rowlands of his command. First he wrote sharply to Rowlands:

> I am not at all satisfied with your proposed distribution of the 80th Regiment . . . I object most emphatically to their being left in small detachments to occupy positions where they cannot act offensively . . . Abandon all idea of any further movements against Sekhukhune and his supporters and consider yourself at my disposal for work on the Zulu border.[20]

To Sir Theophilus Shepstone, the Administrator of the Transvaal, Chelmsford wrote:

> I feel that I have no right to keep from you what has been gradually forcing itself upon my mind *viz.* – that Colonel Rowlands does not possess the requisite qualifications of an independent commander of troops in the field . . . and has produced failure where I had every expectation of success.[21]

Over the weeks that followed most of the units that had accompanied Rowlands were allocated to Wood and No. 5 Column eventually ceased to exist, with Chelmsford advising Wood, despite his being junior to Rowlands:

> That I am writing to him today to say that he [Rowlands] must be guided entirely by the information and advice you send him as to his movements . . . Kindly send Rowlands full instructions and remember he's on no account to interfere with your independence, but may act to assist you in such a way as you may advise him . . . I should feel most uncomfortable if I thought you were in any way hampered by the presence of Colonel Rowlands . . . and I am quite prepared to order him away if you find him a nuisance.[22]

As it had made its way up from the Cape Wood's No. 4 Column had consisted of the 90th LI, six guns of the Royal Artillery, Buller's FLH and small detachments of the Royal Engineers, Army Hospital Corps, Commissariat Department and civilian transport personnel. However, at Pietermaritzburg N Battery, 5th Brigade, Royal Artillery (N/5 RA), under the command of Major Arthur Harness, had left Wood in order to join No. 3 Column and later to meet the Zulu army at Isandlwana. On reaching Utrecht, Wood's artillery component was restored by the addition of four 7-pounder horse-drawn, muzzle-loading guns and two guns drawn by mules of 11/7 RA, commanded by Major Edmund Tremlett.

By this time the 90th had been in southern Africa for just on a year. When the regiment had embarked at Southampton in the late autumn of 1877, the men had been described as: '. . . a more miserable, limp, half-grown, shambling bunch of boys as never left England inside Her Majesty's uniform', harsh words indeed.

Wood, who was to command them, ascribed the absence of 'old soldiers' to War Office economy; many of the rank and file were due for discharge within the year and it would be a saving of their passage money to keep them at home. Nevertheless, there was a good sprinkling of old sweats left who would teach the youngsters the fine traditions of the regiment. Still serving were some who had fought in the Crimea and Indian Mutiny. One such was Lieutenant and Quartermaster John Newman, who had served in both campaigns and, as a young colour sergeant at the relief of Lucknow, had saved the life of Sir Garnet Wolseley, who was then a captain in the same regiment. Having been through the dangerous rough and tumble of the Ninth Frontier War for the last year, the 'boys' of the 90th who had embarked at Southampton were now men – perhaps not bearded but fit, eager and considered by Wood to be as good soldiers as any. When Wood was promoted to column commander, the command of the regiment had devolved upon Major R. M. Rogers VC, an officer of considerable combat experience who had fought in the Crimea and had won his Victoria Cross during the assault on the Taku Forts in China.

The Frontier Light Horse, although then in existence for only two years, had gained an enviable reputation. Originally raised in 1877 by Lieutenant Frederick Carrington of the 1st/24th, at King William's Town, unlike many other mounted units recruited from the local colonial population the FLH was financed by the home government. Initially, all ranks were issued with a cord uniform, ammunition bandolier, black riding boots, and a type of slouch hat complete with a burgundy-coloured puggaree. By the time the unit had fought and marched close on 2,000 miles up and down southern Africa, not much of the original uniforms remained and there were no replacements. But most men seemed able to procure a slouch hat of sorts complete with puggaree, and that would have to suffice as the unit's uniform for the rest of its existence. The colonial troopers, who signed on for periods of six months at five shillings (£0.25) a day, required a tough commanding officer to control them and in Buller they found a man equal to their toughest troopers.

Two additional regular regiments, the 13th and 80th, would also join Wood.

The 13th (1st Somersetshire) Prince Albert's Light Infantry, commanded by Lieutenant-Colonel Philip Gilbert, had been stationed in the Transvaal since marching from Pietermaritzburg to Pretoria in April 1877. Its role had been to support Shepstone's annexation of the territory. Thereafter, the battalion had been fragmented with detachments stationed in Pretoria and at various outposts. Three companies were in fact sent back to Utrecht to reinforce the garrison as, even as early as December 1877, the local settler population was in daily dread of a Zulu assault. Four months later, having completed a round march of 450 miles, the detachment returned to Pretoria in preparation for Rowlands's assault on Sekhukhune's Stronghold. The hardships they encountered were later described:

> The suffering of the 13th Light Infantry on their march was painful to witness and Colonel Rowlands might well say that the gain was not worth the candle. Hostilities consisted of marching under a broiling hot sun at the foot of steep mountains whence Basutos fired with such weapons and skill as they possessed.

Their appearance was later described by Private Edward McToy:

> Red, patched with black; black patched with white; with their helmets all torn, dirty, daubed with yellow clay and bootless in many instances . . .

At Kambula they were met by the band of the 90th who preceded them into camp, later giving them a rare feast of fresh bread, sardines, cheese and a glass of rum. McToy commented that this last was obtained with some difficulty as 'Colonel Wood did not exactly allow this sort of thing.'

Utrecht was quite changed from the place it had been earlier in the year. McToy again commented:

> On entering Utrecht we found an extensive camp, everybody busy storing goods, unloading wagons with ammunition, and etc. You could scarcely imagine the changes that had come over the place in twelve months. All was bustle and confusion, where once nothing had reigned but quiet.

Captain Waddy of the 13th later recalled the contrast between the relatively spick and span 90th and:

> . . . our rugged ruffians who were in rags; some without boots, helmets of the old Indian pattern, covered with old shirts to keep the cotton wool [for insulation] on the bamboo frames, belts and rifles dirtied by order. Hard-bitten, muscular men who looked the fighters they were. The 80th, like ourselves, were old hands. We had our Christmas dinner, such as we could muster, in a regular downpour.

However, the 13th would soon resemble smart solders again as they would be refitted before marching on into Zululand.

The 80th Regiment, now making its way down from the Transvaal in small detachments, was of ancient origin being able to trace its lineage to 1705. In battles past it had fought in many parts of the world including the West Indies, Spain, India, the Crimea, Burma and China. Of all the regiments in southern Africa, the 80th had been there the longest; three companies had been stationed on the Zulu border as early as May 1876. The rest of the regiment had arrived by sea a little less than a year later with some of the wives and children on board. Unfortunately, because some of the children had contracted measles, the whole ship was put into quarantine. Eventually the regiment was allowed ashore but confined to a narrow strip of beach where, at high tide, the sea came into the tents. Their first fourteen days ashore, like most of their service in southern Africa, must have been spent in vile conditions. They, too, had marched close on 2,000 miles since arrival and were the first to work on the construction of the Utrecht fort. Major Charles Tucker now commanded the regiment and would continue to do so for the next five years.

Within a few weeks of Isandlwana, No. 4 Column would also be joined by No. 1 Squadron, Mounted Infantry, of whom more later.

So much for Wood's imperial troops. They were a mixed bunch but the units of colonial volunteer horse were almost exotic by comparison. Apart from the FLH, there were elements of the Lydenberg Rifles, now riding under the name of Raaff's Transvaal Rangers, raised by their leader Commandant Pieter Raaff who, although born a Boer, would spend most of his adventurous life fighting for the British Empire. Slight and small of stature, he was a man of sterling qualities and courage. Now thirty years of age, Raaff had been engaged in frontier wars since his early teens. In most respects his attire was that of a country gentleman except for an incongruous spiked helmet made of brass. After taking leave of Rowlands, he had hastened to Kimberley, there to enlist men from the diamond diggings. His recruiting poster, carrying at its head the royal coat of arms, declared:

Volunteers!
Volunteers Required for Active Service in Captain Raaff's Horse.
Transvaal Rangers.
All booty shared by the volunteers only.

As we know from Chelmsford's edict on the distribution of booty, Raaff was making, perhaps unwittingly, a promise he would be unable to keep. Nevertheless, close on a hundred tough brigand-like ex-diggers, some of mixed blood, well armed and mounted, followed him up from Kimberley. Wood would later write of him that:

> Commandant Raaff, Transvaal Rangers, is a perfect type of border soldier.
> Brave, indefatigable and deeply versed in African warfare, I have profited
> equally by his assistance and advice.

And an officer of a rival unit commented maliciously on Raaff's troopers:

> . . . a forbidding lot of mixed Hottentots and scum of the diamond fields
> as was never collected together outside a prison wall.

Baker's Horse, who were also to perform first-rate service, had been recruited from men of a more genteel background. Commanded by Captain Frances Baker, late of the Ceylon Rifles and the Royal Anglesey Militia, the unit had been recruited from colonials of the Eastern Cape. It had fought in the recent Ninth Frontier War but had been disbanded in East London at the close of hostilities. Then came the shock of Isandlwana and, hardly had the men dispersed, when Baker was earnestly requested by Chelmsford to reform the unit and hasten to Northern Natal where equipment and horses would be waiting. Baker's Horse was evidently regarded as somewhat elegant and elite by East London society, one correspondent reporting with pride that they were '. . . men of the proper class, being strong young fellows, admirably suited for the work before them.'

Their courage was immediately put to the test as, in drafts of fifty men, they were put aboard an open lighter and towed by a tug through storm-tossed seas to their waiting vessel. The screws of the tug were frequently out of the water as it plunged madly through the waves. 'However, the brave young fellows managed to board the steamer eventually,' the local paper reported with relief. But there was no correspondent to record the progress of the 200 volunteers as they subsequently made their way on foot from Durban to Utrecht, a march of over a month covering 170 miles. One trooper later wrote of their ordeal in which the men slept rough alongside the road each night without tents or protection:

> As everywhere, the weaker went to the wall, succumbed to climate; fever
> and dysentery and rheumatism thinned out the weakly . . . drenched with
> frequent thunder storms and then frozen, it will not be wondered that
> many sank.

Wood was to comment approvingly of Baker: 'Though not strong in health he is singularly happy when leading his men in action and controlling them in camp.'

The five troops of the Natal Native Horse (NNH), recruited from a mixture of clans living in Natal under the protection of the colonial government, had fought well at Isandlwana, and had later that day cleared and held the drift across the Buffalo River, allowing many fugitives from the battlefield to cross and survive. They had received the admiration of all. The battle over, they had dispersed, several of the troops never to reform. The Christian element, the Makolwas as they were called by their Zulu enemies, retired to their mission station close by Ladysmith and had then temporarily joined a locally raised unit of dubious colonials, called Carbutt's Border Rangers, who had the reputation of imbibing much rum. The black troopers were treated with such harshness that their sergeant-major, Simeon Kambule, led them away to find Wood's column where they received a warm welcome. News of their whereabouts spread and more black NCOs and troopers joined them until the unit, all Christians, was almost 120 strong. They were put under the command of Lieutenant William Francis Dundonald Cochrane, a special service officer of the 32nd (Cornwall) Light Infantry, who had been with the NNH previously and was one of the five regular officers to have survived the Battle of Isandlwana. Cochrane was later joined by two colonials of the NNH who had likewise survived the battle, namely Lieutenants Charles Raw and Richard Wyatt Vause.

Commandant Schermbrucker's Kaffrarian Rifles, who had earlier garrisoned Luneburg, had also marched all the way from Durban and would soon be ordered to Kambula to be mounted and re-equipped in preparation for No. 4 Column's march into Zululand. When Schermbrucker received the order to move he was apprehensive about such a small unit of foot soldiers marching alone between Luneburg and Kambula unescorted by mounted men. When Wood received Schermbrucker's request for an escort, he pompously replied that Schermbrucker need not fear whilst he was in command of the area. Not in the slightest intimidated by Wood, Schermbrucker retorted that his concern was that of a commander for his men and assured Wood that he had no fear for his own life and that he was prepared to ride alone 'from here to Cetshwayo's kraal at any moment I might be required to do so'.

In the event the 106 men of the Kaffrarian Rifles, with Schermbrucker at their head, were later played into Kambula by the band of the 90th having safely, if uncomfortably, completed their march from Luneburg. Schermbrucker, to embarrass Wood and to highlight the woeful state of his men, had the leading section of his ill-shod command stride into camp without as much as a sock or boot on their feet.

With the aid of a young political officer, Captain Norman MacLeod, the future MacLeod of MacLeod, hereditary chief of the MacLeod clan, Wood, as instructed by Chelmsford, had been attempting to provoke the whole of the Swazi kingdom to join in and fall upon their traditional enemies, the Zulu. MacLeod, who was also British agent to the Swazi kingdom, was confident that he could prevail on the Swazi king to send 5,000 warriors against the Zulu. In an undated letter addressed to Sir Bartle Frere, MacLeod described a visit to 'Umbandini', King of the Swazis:

> I commenced my reading of the High Commissioner's message to the Swazi King informing of my appointment to visit the Swazi border. I endeavoured to explain who the High Commissioner was and to tell the King what my duties would be. I then told him that the troops were now on their way to the Zulu border, that the dispute with Cetshwayo would be settled first peacefully if possible, by war if necessary, after which the solders would return and eat him up.
>
> The king answered that he would rather not talk about my

appointment as he had not received any message from Somtseu [Sir Theophilus Shepstone]. Somtseu had always been the door by which he entered the white man's house.

I said I would like an answer now whether he would allow me to raise 700 men from his people to act as a protective force on the border. He answered that he had no young men, as a great many of his people had been killed.

I replied 'I am glad I have come as I want to tell the King that the English are friends with the Swazis, as they always have been, and that if Cetshwayo will not let other people live in peace, but sends his people into country belonging to the Swazis or the Transvaal, the English will have to fight, and if they once begin fighting Cetshwayo will be eaten up.'

In the evening I had a private conversation with one of the most influential of the *indunas* and the man who spoke for the King at the interview when two or three other *indunas* were present. I told him of the power of England and that if the Zulus did fight, they would have no chance at all. He answered that what I said might be true, he hoped it was, but he had never seen the English fight. They were always talking, always going to fight but never had and he thought they never would. He did not believe we should fight the Zulus at all, but if we did we should be beaten. He had seen the Zulus fight. They were numerous and powerful, and until he saw the English fight the Zulus and beat them he could not believe it possible. The Swazis were afraid of the Zulus. They would not fight the Zulus until they saw them running away to their caves then they would all come and help the English to hunt them out . . .

From all I saw and heard I am convinced that the Swazis hate the Zulus, that nothing could make them join together but that they considered them to be the ruling power, quite invincible by either white men or black, and I think that nothing short of a war with the Zulus, an actual demonstration that the white man is the stronger, will ever convince them to the contrary. I believe that they would gladly join the English against the Zulus if they thought there was any chance of the united armies being successful.[23]

It was never clear quite how the Swazis would profit for their trouble. The promise of rewards varied from a large tract of Zululand alongside the Pongolo (or Pongola) River, to as little as some cows and horses. In December 1878, Wood wrote from Utrecht:

MacLeod is to offer the Swazi King 50 horses with saddles and bridles and 200 cows if his men move to the Pongola and keep the Zulus out of the Transvaal. Try to get this done for half this price.

In the event the Swazis never came on that occasion, but many individual warriors, tempted by cash and as much as they could eat, volunteered and were quickly formed into a levy 300 strong and, to Wood's delight, were designated by Chelmsford 'Wood's Irregulars' – the same title that had been given to Wood's native troops during the Ashanti campaign on the other side of Africa. The Swazis were every white man's idea of a 'noble savage'. Of spectacular physique and dramatically attired in leopard skins and with head-dresses of ostrich plumes, they were greatly admired. Colonel Wood, it was reported:

> . . . has great confidence in them. He encourages them in every possible manner, and while keeping a distinct difference between them and the Europeans under his command, imbues them with a full sense of the honour of being allowed to fight for the Government. During enforced inaction he encourages them to compete in all kinds of athletic exercises. And it is almost unnecessary to say that in their fleetness they far surpass the Redcoats and colonial troops. Some of them are armed with Schneider [*sic*] rifles, an honour which is only conferred upon those of exemplary conduct or distinguished birth, for 'blood' is with them the acme of human merit. The main body is armed with muzzle-loading rifles and all carry the assegai. This latter, notwithstanding their veneration for firearms, is what they most rely upon in battle. To come to close quarters is the highest anticipation of their lives, and in that 'glorious hour' all is cast away – clothes, fire arms and the shield – and relying upon the assegai as the British soldier relies upon his bayonet, their innate cruelty is rampant in its course of slaying, mutilating and disembowelling, which latter is to them indispensable. But at other times quiet and obedient, without fawning, if firmly and kindly dealt with. Blustering disgusts them, and renders the blusterer open to their manifest derision. They cannot quite understand having to work. Frequently they are sent out to cut wood which displeases them intensely, saying it is women's work and that they had come to fight.

MacLeod also described the swazis:

> During the day bands of friendly Swazis joined us. Every party has its chief. They are all armed with assegais and shields and many have rifles also. As they came up each party sang a war song. They sing in such admirable way and in perfect harmony – the notes are very deep – these dirges remind me of the best opera choruses. Then all of a sudden a man covered with skins of tiger and with feathers or the tails of animals stuck in his head rushes out of the ranks with wild gesticulations! Eyes starting out of his head and brandishing his assegai he prances over the ground stabbing towards the earth shewing how he will assegai a Zulu. When exhausted he takes his place in the ranks and another rushes out. Another party we met who had been attacked did not sing but made a long wailing sound which meant they were sad and bereaved.

Later Wood reported less favourably on some of their white officers: '. . . the gross and coarser element has vanished before real hard work.' Eventually Wood put the Swazis under the control of forty-five-year-old Major William Knox Leet of the 13th LI, an officer who had served with distinction during the Indian Mutiny. A strong and athletic soldier, Knox Leet was also a tennis player of note.

It had been hoped in vain that 2,000 Boers would join No. 4 Column. However, a few local farmers became Wood's strongest and most valuable allies. Led by fifty-two-year-old Petros Lafras Uys (nicknamed Piet Hlobane) the Burger Force ended up as little more than a family unit mostly of fathers, brothers, uncles and cousins and numbered only forty men. Uys was motivated by an uncompromising determination to fight for what he believed to be his land, to be rid of the Zulu menace as he saw it, and to wreak vengeance for the deaths of his father and elder brother. Forty years earlier his father, leading a punitive expedition against Dingaan, the Zulu king at that time, had been ambushed and mortally wounded. Whilst the rest of the Boer raiding party sped away, leaving Uys to his fate, his young son Dirkie rode back and valiantly stood over his father until both died under a flurry of assegais. As a result Dirkie became a legend and later a venerated national hero. Piet would never forget and had always felt the need to avenge the deaths of his father and brother. He also feared that his own four sons would fall victim to the Zulu. He was a religious man, physically strong and of high morals. He refused remuneration for his services to the British but did ask Wood that, in the event of his death, some provision be made for his family. His four sons followed him on campaign, the youngest, named Dirkie after his uncle, only thirteen years of age. Within days of joining the column, Dirkie was engaged in a skirmish with the Zulus of the abaQulusi clan, shooting one warrior during the encounter.

With his intimate knowledge of the frontier and the surrounding territory, Uys was invaluable. Wood described his burgers as '. . . averaging 14 or 15 stone, with enormous shoulders, knotted arms and hands like iron'. One of their number was accredited with remarkable aim and eyesight:

> Andreas Rudolph . . . could see a native at a mile distance and shoot him at two . . . We in our knowledge can speak of their [the Boers'] wonderful powers of vision and accuracy of marksmanship.

They could see, it was said, like the Zulu and other tribes, better with the naked eye than a European could with a telescope. Uys also had his own battle plan and, had the 2,000 burgers that had been originally promised materialised, the war might well have been over in weeks. His idea was to form fast-moving raiding parties of 150–200 mounted men carrying little more than arms, ammunition and, for sustenance, dried meat and coffee. They were to strike deep into Zululand, avoiding any contact with the Zulu army, burning villages, looting cattle and destroying crops in surprise attacks. Uys estimated that by using this method he could bring the Zulu nation to the brink of starvation and final surrender. In Buller he found a kindred spirit, as Buller would later confide to Wood, when discussing the war in Afghanistan:

I have, as you know, always held that in dealing with natives, you must make them fear you before you can afford to be kind to them – until we have depopulated a valley or two and killed the inhabitants, root and branch, we shall ever have to fear the inhabitants of all the other valleys.[24]

Buller and Uys could not have been further apart in birth, background, wealth, education and social standing, one an affluent Devonshire squire and the other a raw frontiersman of modest means. Nevertheless, a bond of mutual respect flourished between them and for a brief few weeks they became inseparable as, with similar powers of endurance, they daily rode patrols, either scouting or cattle-raiding into the surrounding territory.

In late January, Buller with seventy-five men of the FLH accompanied by Uys and twenty-two of his Burger Force attacked a military kraal, about half a day's ride from camp, close by Zunguin Mountain, where previously Wood and his officers had seen the regiment of the abaQulusi drilling and deploying. The kraal was guarded by about fifty warriors who took cover immediately in high ground amongst some rocks. Part of Buller's force dismounted and stormed the position and, in a fight at close quarters, twelve warriors were shot and one trooper of the FLH killed and another wounded – both by wounded warriors feigning death only to spring alive and suddenly deliver a deadly upward thrust with an assegai. As the war progressed, it was a Zulu tactic that British troops would fear and no doubt one that resulted in wounded Zulu being shot rather than captured. Buller remarked:

We found four guns and a good many assegais all of which I had broke, but I did not search the ground thoroughly as I did not think the risk of getting men stabbed by wounded kaffirs worth the result.

In the days that followed, Buller and Uys raided into the eastern corner of Zululand and, on 1 February, with a force of 148 mounted men, attacked the Makulusine barracks, their route having again taken them past the Zunguin and Hlobane mountains. They took the Zulu garrison entirely by surprise and the defenders fled, some to be overtaken by horsemen and shot down. The barracks were set on fire and entirely destroyed and 300 head of cattle taken. Could this have been a dress rehearsal for Uys's guerrilla war strategy? If it was, it was an indication of how ruthlessly successful it could have been, but it was not implemented. It is doubtful if Chelmsford would have agreed to such a method of war, affecting, as it would, the whole Zulu population. Such would certainly have been greeted by an outcry of condemnation by missionary groups in Britain. However, later in the campaign, as will be seen, every village and hut in the face of the British advance towards the Zulu capital was destroyed.

A spin-off for the British of these mounted forays was the astounding number of cattle that were captured and one suspects that the raiding was motivated in part by the prospect of bovine booty. As early as 2 January, a week before the ultimatum expired, No. 4 Column had captured 2,000 head from Sekethwayo kaNhlaka of the Mdlalose, a powerful chief and a member of the king's inner council. On 14 January, Wood wrote:

> I sent to tell Sekethwayo, a chief of considerable importance, who had been negotiating with me since the 2nd, that I could no longer herd the 2,000 head of cattle we had taken from his territory but if he would come in, he should have them. The matter was complicated, as a considerable number of the cattle belonged to Cetshwayo, or rather to the Royal House. The chief could not make up his mind, and having waited 5 days, I sent the cattle away to the Free State, where they were sold.[25]

One cannot help but wonder how this vast number of cattle was herded and by whom on the 150-mile trek to the Free State.

Earlier in the same month, prior to Isandlwana, Wood had met with Chelmsford on the Buffalo River. While Wood and the general discussed strategy, the FLH successfully scoured the countryside for cattle. Newspapers of the time contain many reports of cattle being captured: on 17 February, 355 head were taken by Major Knox Leet and his irregulars and on 15 March Commandant Raaff and his Transvaal Rangers lifted another 500. In all it was estimated that No. 4 Column had taken 7,000 head during the first four months of hostilities.

It is difficult to pinpoint the skulduggery that undoubtedly went on prior to the final distribution of prize money as laid down by Chelmsford. Many complained of unequal distribution, or of receiving nothing at all. It was asserted that the captured beasts were sold to prize agents at thirty shillings (£1.50) a head, and later sold on to meat contractors who in turn sold them back to the columns at £8 per head. As early as 16 January, a committee, seemingly of civilians, was appointed to sit at Wood's headquarters for the purpose of valuing some captured cattle. The sale price was set at £3 per head and an offer of £2,500 for 1,000 beasts was not accepted. Yet, despite all the accusations regarding the distribution of prize money, at the end of the campaign later in the year, Captain Edward Woodgate of Wood's staff went to considerable trouble to ensure that the families of four Tongas of Wood's Irregulars, who had been killed in action, received their fair share of the prize money amounting to £11 7s. 11d. (£11.39½). Woodgate went so far as to pay the prize money from his own pocket while waiting for the sum to be reimbursed.

Not unexpectedly, there was also a lively market in the horse trade. In 1878 a good weight-carrying pony could be bought for £3. Once the war started the average price for a reasonable mount went up to £25. Guy Dawnay, a civilian who had attached himself to Chelmsford's column, complained that prices doubled within nine days of his arrival in Natal. When the extreme need for mounted men was realised, officers were sent scurrying to the far corners of southern Africa to buy mounts, while some horses were obtained from as far away as Australia and the Argentine. South Africa had once had a fine horse-breeding industry of its own but, in the years prior to 1879, it was neglected in favour of ostrich farming, an industry that benefited from the then insatiable demand for feathers, albeit a brief one dictated by the whims of fashion. By April 1879 good horses were selling at £30 or more and 'salted horses', those that had survived the dreaded horse sickness, were changing hands at around £70. It was rumoured that the Boers had discovered a cure for the disease but, for obvious reasons of profit, were keeping it secret. It is most doubtful that they had a cure as horse sickness is still as common and as deadly today as it was then. Needless to say, the nags purchased at short notice and in great haste for the colonial units were as rough as they came. The method of allocation to individual troopers was a matter of luck – and a dangerous business:

> The mode of selection was primitive in the extreme. The horses were driven into a stone enclosure, called a kraal. Every man then went in with a halter and from the plunging, kicking mass, selected what suited himself. The result being with men who did not know about horses, absurd; some large men got small horses and visa versa . . . The knowing ones got ponies as a rule, short, wiry and thick little brutes that could wear down any big horse by sheer dint of superior prowess of endurance . . . The men, many of them knowing little about riding, had to be taught; they learnt by dint of falling off . . . The falls were many, riders were bad and the horses young and untaught.[26]

During the course of the campaign many other items, once plentiful and cheap, became rare luxuries that only the officers could afford; preserved meat, sold in England at one shilling a tin, fetched six times that price and a penny box of matches cost ninepence. One can sympathise with all over their concern for a fair share of the prize money.

The camp at Kambula had now become a receiving depot for many hundreds of men, horses and a couple of thousand oxen. Although the mounted colonials were continuously at work, the infantry, apart from camp chores – especially the collection of firewood – had little to keep them busy and Wood made it his business to occupy much of their time with sporting activities. For the officers, some of whom preferred to play whist in their tents, there was a roughed-out polo ground and an equally rough tennis court. Spear-throwing competitions between the white and black troops became popular with, surprisingly, the white men dominating the sport. Wood ascribed this to the throwing spear having being superseded years previously throughout Zululand by the stabbing assegai. Tug-of-war competitions between the various units were keenly contested and, despite the 90th LI having beaten all comers in recent times, they were pulled off their feet with ease by the Boers who, all the while, continued to smoke their pipes.

Although Wood had been unsuccessful in recruiting the 2,000 burgers he had hoped to enlist, the startling possibility of a new ally presented itself. In late February a ragged white man, carrying a flag of truce, rode into Kambula camp. He was an emissary from Prince Hamu kaNzibe, chief of the Ngenetsheni clan of 6,000 warriors, a son of King Mpande, a half brother to Cetshwayo, and the pugnacious ruler of a tract of Zululand highly valued for its splendid grazing. Hamu, as he presided over his people at his great homestead at kwaMfemfe, was every inch the Zulu king he believed by right he should have been. Although senior to Cetshwayo he could not become king due to the intricacies of the Zulu succession; and Hamu seethed with resentment. For years Cetshwayo had regarded him as a dangerous man and a potential usurper, ambitious to seize the throne. Nevertheless, twenty-three years earlier, Hamu had supported Cetshwayo and had fought at his side during the Battle of Ndondakusuku where, after Cetshwayo had killed his half-brother Mbulazi kaMpande and thousands of his followers, the Tugela River had run red and was choked for days with the corpses of the slain.

By Mbulazi's death Cetshwayo had established his succession, but he was not the absolute monarch that the British government and his colonial neighbours believed him to be; throughout his reign he had good cause to fear his royal brothers and also many powerful chiefs. Even his coronation ceremony of 1873 came close to erupting into a bloodbath and it is probable that, without the support of the Natal government, someone other than Cetshwayo would eventually have ruled the Zulu kingdom. Events leading up to and during the ceremony underlined his insecure position. Since he knew that he needed British support, he had an invitation sent to the Natal government. However, Cetshwayo had to be cautious not to offend his chiefs, many of whom would regard a foreign presence at a sacred national ceremony as demeaning and offensive. Cetshwayo had to balance matters by restricting colonial participation to a minor add-on – although the grandiose wording of the invitation would convince the British otherwise:

> The Zulu nation wishes to be more one with the government of Natal; it desires to be covered with the same mantle; it wishes Somtseu [Theophilus Shepstone] to go and establish this unity by the charge which he will deliver when he arranges the family of the king, and that he shall breathe the spirit by which the nation is to be governed.[27]

Cetshwayo knew that among the great chiefs who would be present, Hamu included, there would be several who harboured ambitions to seize the kingdom.

The ceremony was to take place in the sacred eMakhosini Valley and whilst a Natal contingent, led by Theophilus Shepstone, of 110 soldiers of various colonial units, two guns and numerous officials made its laborious way north from Durban, the Zulu nation began to assemble on the nearby Mhlabathini Plain. As Cetshwayo advanced with many thousands of warriors, he was met by a similar cavalcade, equally as strong, of chiefs who could yet contest his rule. He had by his side John Dunn, a white man but nevertheless a Zulu chief in his own right, commanding 200 trained Zulu gunmen. In a show of power that was thinly disguised as a gesture of jubilation, the gunmen were ordered to advance and fire a volley into the air. Cetshwayo's authority established, the combined forces proceeded towards eMakhosini but paused as they faced the advancing warriors of the Mandlakazi clan led by their chief, Zibhebhu kaMaphitha, the most powerful and belligerent of all Zulu noblemen. He approached with a vast following minutes before Cetshwayo was to be crowned. As Zibhebhu drew nearer, so his warriors become more and more excitable and truculent. Suddenly, they began to deploy in an alarming fashion intent, it seemed, on bloodshed. Cetshwayo and Dunn conferred and emissaries were sent forward to Zibhebhu. Finally, in the face of Dunn's gunmen, the Mandlakazi's advance faltered and stopped. Dunn later recalled:

> I firmly believe that it was owing to my advising Cetshwayo to send messengers to check Zibhebhu's party in their advance that a general massacre was avoided.[28]

Finally, Cetshwayo was crowned in the manner and traditions of the Zulu nation and without colonial participation; he had halted the British column some miles away – much to the fury of Shepstone – where it would not cause offence but where its presence would be known and felt. Shepstone was greatly annoyed and suspected Zulu treachery. The whole column became alarmed, guns were loaded and an attack expected at any moment. Eventually, with much apprehension, having been permitted to advance, the column arrived at the coronation rendezvous and erected a large marquee that had been brought along. Shortly, Cetshwayo arrived with an escort of 1,000 warriors and reluctantly entered the marquee alone, except for his body servant. Inside Shepstone placed a British 'crown' (a mantle especially made by the regimental tailor of the 75th Foot) upon Cetshwayo's head and proclaimed him king; the Durban Volunteer Artillery fired a regulation 17-gun salute; the band struck a lively tune and the soldiers cheered. Yet there was to be a final moment of potential catastrophe. Suddenly, in a traditional gesture of approbation, 10,000 warriors raised their shields and with their fighting sticks set up a furious drumming. The effect was terrifying; the petrified cavalry horses threw their riders and bolted, charging straight towards the newly crowned king. As Shepstone later recalled. 'It belonged to a class of accidents that sometimes produce disasters and for a moment one seemed likely to happen.'[29]

As a parting gift, Cetshwayo presented Shepstone with some fine elephant tusks and confided that he was aware that the gift was small and in no way a measure of what he felt; it was more an indication of the poverty of the country than the greatness of his obligation: it was '. . . an expression of thanks and a wish that on your way home your heart is white and that your path be prosperous.'[30] These were not the words of a monarch seeking conflict with the Great White Queen.

Cetshwayo had reigned for six years since his coronation. Now the astute Hamu could see that Cetshwayo might not reign much longer. Hamu had had more contact with white men than most Zulu chiefs. Three white traders had made their homes in his territory with their wives: Herbert Nunn, who ran a trading store, had been Hamu's advisor and friend for almost twenty years – he also supplied Hamu with gin to which the prince was particularly partial. There was also James Rorke, (a son of the James Rorke who had given his name to the now famous drift on the Buffalo River) and a man by the name of Calverley. As boys, Calverley and his brother had been apprenticed by their widowed mother as servants to the elder brother of Piet Uys and had been brought up as Boers. Calverley was now in his mid-twenties and it was he who had been instructed to deliver Hamu's message requesting surrender terms.

The correspondent of the *Natal Witness*, J. M. Rathbone, later reported that after Isandlwana, Hamu had conspired to assassinate Cetshwayo but had failed when the would-be assassin collapsed and confessed all to the king. In turn, Cetshwayo had tried to lure Hamu to his presence. Hamu now knew that he was a marked man and was no doubt advised by his white friends that, despite the defeat at Isandlwana, the red soldiers, whose numbers were limitless, would return. Hamu saw many advantages to his defection; it would undoubtedly save his life and likely see him crowned king once Cetshwayo was defeated. It was unfortunate for him that his emissary, Calverley, chose to ride into Wood's camp astride a horse that was immediately recognised as having belonged to Lieutenant Nevill Coghill who, having escaped from Isandlwana, was later killed at Fugitives' Drift attempting to save the Queen's Colour of the 1st/24th.

There was an uproar in the camp. Many wanted to drag Calverley from his horse and lynch him for he also carried a Martini-Henry rifle and a water bottle, both looted from the 1st/24th. Wood, realising the importance of his unsavoury emissary, immediately intervened, probably saving Calverley's life. But Wood's terms left no room for negotiation; unconditional surrender was the best on offer. Chelmsford had already given instructions to cover the possibility of Hamu's surrender:

> He who is not with us is against us and if he [Hamu] remains passively in his kraal whilst we are advancing, he must not be surprised if we take him for an enemy.[31]

Hamu was anxious to leave Zululand. Rumours of his possible departure had reached the king and Cetshwayo's warriors were already deploying to guard the drifts. Hamu wanted out and wished to flee with his warriors, numerous wives, and, perhaps most important of all, his cattle. Norman MacLeod, working from Derby, acted as go-between. On 4 March he wrote to Wood, though his concern about paying the Boers whom he had called upon for assistance seemingly outweighed the importance of the political coup that he was about to achieve:

I have the honour to report that uHamu [*sic*] is now in my house here. I found him at a Swazi Kraal on the border on the 2nd, brought him to another Swazi kraal yesterday and in a wagon today. He has about 300 men with him and a white man Rorke and a man who has his name as Fynn otherwise, I am told, Calverley. Mr Nunn joined me yesterday, and will bring uHamu with all possible despatch to your camp. uHamu is most anxious to get there, and to get his wives out. He says 2,000 of his people will come too. I was informed at first that there was an impi after him so not to run any risk of his being taken when almost in our hands, I called for volunteers and got all that could be got: four white men and a few kaffirs. I sent all at once to Field-Cornet Labuschagne to bring some Boers, promising them all 15 shillings a day. I also started a wagon at once to go as far as possible. This will altogether cost about £30 which I have to request authority to expend. The Boers only arrived at Derby as I came back today, but having started I am bound to pay them one day.[32]

The enlisted Boers, who were led by a Mr Ferreira, hurried to the border, met up with Hamu and his entourage and looted most of his cattle. MacLeod continued his tale of woe:

On my return today, having being away for three days, I found Mr Ferreira had left some 2/300 head for uHamu and had divided the rest, 7/800, amongst his friends, going so far as to brand them.[33]

MacLeod also discovered that all Ferreira's friends had, until a few days previously, been drawing government pay as interpreters.

Wood was well pleased with Hamu's defection and the effect it would have on Zulu morale. It was now essential to get the Zulu prince and what was left of his cattle to the security of Kambula camp before an *impi* could overtake him. Unfortunately, the wagon road – if it could be called a road – between MacLeod's Post at Derby and Luneburg was not only fraught with danger, but the physical difficulty of getting wagons through had become enormous. The rains had started after the prolonged drought, and the whole countryside was sodden. The wagon roads had become a morass of mud, in places a quarter of a mile wide, as each wagon sought to find firmer ground to either side of the original track.

Like all kin of the Zulu royal family, Hamu was an immense man with particularly massive thighs, and he was not given to walking far. Some conveyance would have to be found to carry him. The fastest vehicle available was Wood's personal Cape cart and it was sent along with Buller together with an escort of the Frontier Light Horse to bring Hamu in. He was rescued and, riding in style, was brought back to Kambula without incident. He was accompanied by 200 of his warriors, many of whom had fought at Isandlwana and had trophies of war to prove it. It was a quick about-face for the warriors and white men alike; they went from enemies to allies in a matter of two weeks. But as they all trudged back to Kambula together, they seemed to have philosophically accepted that they were now comrades-in-arms.

The wheel of fortune was at last beginning to spin in Britain's favour with Wood and No. 4 Column being largely responsible for the favourable turn of events. Through the courage and perseverance of MacLeod, Hamu and many of his warriors had capitulated – it was as good and as effective as if a great chief had been captured and an *impi* defeated. Wood was well pleased with himself as were Lord Chelmsford and Sir Bartle Frere who both wrote congratulating Wood and MacLeod for their 'temper, judgment and patience' while Dr Colenso, the Bishop of Natal, who knew more about what went on in Zululand than most white men, confided that Cetshwayo's tone was altered due to the defection of Hamu. It was even as though the Duke of Cambridge, in far off Horse Guards, had anticipated Wood's success for about that time he wrote to Wood:

> Sir, I have the satisfaction to acquaint to you that Her Majesty the Queen has been pleased to approve of your receiving, from the grant for distinguished or meritorious service, an allowance of £100 per annum, from the 2nd ultimo inclusive.
>
> You will receive a communication from the Secretary of State for War as to the mode in which this allowance is to be paid to you.[34]

Having secured Hamu, Wood determined to further his success by bringing out from under the nose of Cetshwayo's *impis* as many of Hamu's people as wished to join their chief. MacLeod had got Hamu as far as Derby, well on the way to Kambula, before Buller and the Frontier Light Horse had taken him over. What Wood now proposed was far more audacious: he planned to strike deep into Zululand, into the heart of Hamu's fiefdom. But as Wood finalised his plans, the fate of a British convoy on its way to Luneburg would once again about-turn the wheel of fortune.

Chapter 3

Massacre at Meyer's Drift

'British soldiers (officers and men alike) will persist in underrating the enemy, especially if he wears a black skin.'

The Graphic, London, 12 April 1879

⸺⸺⸺

By early March most detachments of the 80th Regiment that had been scattered – much to Lord Chelmsford's displeasure – on garrison duties around the Transvaal, had arrived at Luneburg and were under Wood's command. However, large consignments of the 80th's stores and equipment were still *en route* to Luneburg via Derby, carried by unescorted convoys of civilian wagons. One such convoy had refused – with good reason – to proceed further without protection.[35]

The Derby–Luneburg road had become the most dangerous thoroughfare in South Africa. As the road began its approach to Meyer's Drift on the Ntombe River, five miles short of Luneburg, it entered a wide valley commanded on both sides by rugged hills; to the west were the heights of Manyanyoba's stronghold and to the east Mbelini's flat-topped, fortress-like mountain called the Tafelberg. From these two eminences the wagon road, hundreds of feet below, could be viewed for miles in either direction, giving both Manyanyoba and Mbelini ample time to prepare an ambush for their victims.

For weeks past there had been intermittent skirmishing in much of the area surrounding Luneburg. In retaliation for a raid by Manyanyoba's men on the local black Christian inhabitants when many huts had been destroyed, Lieutenant Schwartzkopf of Schermbrucker's Kaffrarian Rifles had led a rather ineffectual attack against the raiders. Shortly thereafter the ubiquitous Buller, with a combined force of the FLH, the Burger Force and 500 of Wood's Irregulars, also attacked Manyanyoba, killing thirty-four of his followers and capturing a number of cattle. However, this attack was also an inconclusive affair and Manyanyoba remained ensconced in his eyrie above the valley. A few days later Colonel Rowlands and a portion of his column on the way to Utrecht attacked Tolaka Mountain, another robber stronghold along the road.[36] Again this was an unimpressive engagement for which Rowlands was severely criticised in the Natal press by some of his colonial officers:

> The feat [taking the stronghold] could have been easily accomplished and thrice the booty [only 200 head of cattle were captured] obtained, thus giving a thorough check to the Tolaka Zulus; but instead of an attack [a follow-up that Rowlands had promised for the following day] at midday we marched to Luneburg . . . Had the success been followed up, this nest of thieves and murderers would have been cleared out; instead of which the road from Derby to Luneburg has been, and continues to be, impenetrable without a strong military convoy.

It was some distance away from the entrance to this dangerous valley that the civilian convoy carrying the 80th's equipment had prudently halted to await an armed escort. On 1 March, Major Tucker, who had taken over command of the 80th only three weeks earlier, ordered D Company, commanded by Captain William Anderson, to march out of Luneburg and bring the convoy safely to headquarters. It was a disagreeable task, a march of some thirty miles through the rain and drizzle, much hampered by the mud that sucked and dragged at the men's boots with every stride. Also, there would have been no option but a rough bivouac overnight, wet and cold, wherever a halt happened to be called. Captain Anderson, twenty-nine years of age, had been in the army for fifteen years, all the while with the 80th, and had served in India, the Malayan Straits Settlements and China.

D Company struggled for three days to get the wagons, heavily laden with Martini-Henry rifles, 150 boxes containing 90,000 rounds of ammunition, a rocket battery, stores and tinned food, to Meyer's Drift but, by 8 March, only seven of the wagons had reached the north bank of the Ntombe River. The remaining eleven wagons were stuck in a quagmire three miles back, at a most hazardous position, only four miles distant from Mbelini's Tafelberg Mountain. What happened next is quite inexplicable; Captain Anderson and his company marched back to Luneburg and, it could be said, left the convoy to its fate.[37] There are different reasons given for their departure: one version seems to indicate that there was a misunderstanding when Anderson received a message from Tucker that was mistakenly taken for an order to withdraw; another version is that Tucker did, in fact, order D Company back to Luneburg as it was required for 'other duties'. Whatever the reason, no disciplinary action was ever taken against Anderson and immediately Tucker became aware of the convoy's predicament he ordered a company-strength detachment, under the command of Captain David Moriarty, to the rescue.

Moriarty, an experienced Irish officer, had celebrated his forty-second birthday the previous day and had, no doubt, reflected that he had spent previous celebrations in far more convivial surroundings. He was a plumpish man with a prematurely white head of hair and a white moustache. He had seen twenty years of soldiering in several different regiments in many parts of the Empire and beyond, including Gibraltar, Singapore, Corfu and India. It was his second tour of duty in South Africa – he had previously served in the territory with the 6th Regiment in 1863. He had arrived back in 1877 and spent most of his second tour in the Transvaal with Rowlands's column. He was an accomplished linguist, fluent in French, German and Spanish. Moriarty had with him two other officers: twenty-nine-year-old Lieutenant Henry Johnson, who had served in China and Malaya, and Second Lieutenant Alfred Lindop. Lindop had joined the army as a private soldier and had reached the rank of sergeant-major in the 28th Regiment. He was later commissioned and, in February 1878, had transferred to the 80th. He had been actively engaged throughout the Sekhukhune Campaign during which he had been appointed ordnance officer to the Transvaal column.

Tucker, perhaps anticipating that the civilian conductors and drivers might well have sustained some casualties whilst left on their own, ordered civilian surgeon William Cobbin to accompany Moriarty. Cobbin had failed the exam of the Royal College of Surgeons on his first attempt and had only qualified as a medical doctor in 1877. He had made his way to South Africa via the P & O Shipping Company, serving as a ship's doctor.

As Moriarty and his column trudged down to the Ntombe River on 6 March, through the continuous downpour, no doubt the men reflected that, despite all the tales of African sunshine, the weather that day was no different to that of the English Midlands at their bleakest. On arrival at Meyer's Drift, the detachment found the river in spate and over 100 feet wide. The seven wagons that Anderson and his men had manhandled to the drift were out of reach across the river, unguarded on the north bank. The remainder were nowhere in sight. Moriarty set his detachment to work constructing a raft which, amid cheers, was launched later in the day at a point a little upstream where the river bank was less steep. During the afternoon, several members of the local German community called to see the 80th's handiwork offering unsought and heavy-humoured advice. Although the detachment was uncomfortable, wet and cold, there seemed to be no further cause for concern.

The following morning Moriarty's force crossed the Ntombe on the raft. He left Lindop and two sections to improve the crossing while he and the remainder of the detachment marched off to find the abandoned convoy, which they located three miles further on. It was laagered after a fashion and there had been a fight. Josiah Sussens, the civilian conductor leading the convoy with eleven armed white drivers and thirty native assistants, had fought off a Zulu attack. They had fortunately been assisted by the arrival of some of Hamu's warriors hurrying to join their chief at Kambula. No doubt much to the astonishment of Sussens and the attackers alike, instead of Hamu's warriors joining in and assaulting the laager, they set about their kin and, with the besieged wagoners, drove them off – but not before the marauders had looted about a quarter of the convoy's draft oxen.

During the next two days, as the pouring rain continued, the soldiers, the wagoners and the remaining 150 draft oxen struggled, in what had become a marsh, to get the heavily laden wagons the three miles to Meyer's Drift. It is difficult to imagine the conditions in which they struggled but MacLeod gives us an insight into the difficulties that he encountered trying to move three light vehicles along the same track:

> We unfortunately took two ambulances and a Scotch cart, the latter to convey reserve ammunition; these all three stuck in the mud and after beating the oxen we had to unyoke them and man the trek carts with 50 or 60 white men to pull each wagon out. We had to offload each time, take the cart through and carry the ammunition boxes separately. One ambulance was so fast stuck in the mud that we had to abandon it.

Wet through, cold and hungry, with most of the wagons up to their axle-trees in mud, there was nowhere to shelter, yet by 9 March all the wagons had been manhandled to the banks of the river. During Moriarty's absence, Lindop had succeeded in floating two of the seven wagons that had been left at the drift across to the south bank.

Tents and blankets had been sent down from Luneburg and for the next two days, with the river still in spate, the soldiers sheltered in their tents but not before a carelessly constructed laager had been formed on the north bank. Across the river the two wagons that had been got across stood side by side. There was a feeling of accomplishment throughout Moriarty's detachment. They were now well out of the dreaded valley, headquarters and the rest of the regiment were only four and a half miles up the road, and civilians continued to pass by about their daily business. It all added up to a feeling of security that was heightened by a visit the following day, during a break in the rain, by Major Tucker. He viewed the laager and later said he had not been satisfied with what he saw but at the time said nothing. The laager had been formed in the shape of an inverted 'V' with the end of the legs resting in the river – this arrangement would have possibly sufficed had the legs been set sufficiently far out into the river so as to prevent intruders from wading around. However, the weather opened a large chink in the laager's defences. As the rain periodically ceased so the river rapidly fell, leaving the ends of each leg high and dry. But Major Tucker had made no comment and, with the detachment still exhausted, Moriarty was content to leave things as they were and trust that all would be well. Tucker complacently took Lieutenants Johnson and Lindop back with him to Luneburg, leaving as a replacement for both officers, Lieutenant Henry Harward. Harward had served in Jamaica, China and in the Ashanti Campaign. He came from a Kentish military family, his elder brother being a colonel in the Royal Artillery. At the age of thirty-two, Harward was a mature and experienced officer.

As Tucker left, Harward crossed by the raft to the north bank and, after conferring with Moriarty, took a rifle and, as a man might take a gun and his dog and shoot a couple of pheasants, took himself off for a stroll. As an example of the cheapness with which life was held at that time and place, he returned later with some cattle and goats stating casually that whilst securing his booty, he had just shot and killed two 'kaffirs'.[38]

Harward hung around for some time with Moriarty in his tent until, finally, Moriarty sent him back on the raft to take charge of the two wagons on the south bank. There he found his senior NCO, Sergeant Anthony Booth and thirty-four other ranks, getting ready to settle down for the night. Booth was a man of fourteen years' service who, in civilian life, had been a tailor's apprentice. He had enlisted in the 80th at the age of eighteen and, at five foot six inches, was of average height.

Across the river, the flaw in the laager's design now became glaringly apparent: the wagons that formed the base of the inverted 'V' were high and dry providing easy access to the position. However, rather than attempt to move the wagons, which was almost an impossibility in the prevailing conditions, Moriarty judged it better to wait and hope the river would rise again and thus secure the laager once more. No doubt everyone was only too happy to have the prospect of dry clothes and a cooked meal.

The men had pitched their bell tents inside the laager while the wagoners prepared to sleep either inside or underneath their vehicles. The ammunition carts and the draft oxen, about 150 in number, had also been brought into the laager. However, Moriarty, disdaining whatever safety the laager might offer, chose instead the relative quiet to be found outside the defences and had had his tent pitched beyond the apex of the laager at the furthest point from the river. Most, it seemed, slept naked, no doubt in the hope that their wet uniforms might dry off during the night.

In fact Standing Orders required the following action to be taken in such a situation:

1. The camp should be partially entrenched on all sides.
2. The troops will invariably turn out under arms at least two hours before sunrise and silently occupy respective alarm posts. They will similarly again fall in every evening at the first post at tattoo.
3. The alarm post of companies, and etc., will be the most suitable positions around the camp on all sides for defence against a night attack.
4. In the neighbourhood of an enemy, troops in camp will lie down to rest with their rifles by their sides, in all respects ready to turn out at the slightest alarm.
5. When in bivouac they should lie down at the alarm post around the position.

With the exception of two sentries placed by Moriarty twenty yards to the front of his tent, and possibly another close to the wagons on the south side, these orders were not followed.

The diminished height of the river and the lack of discipline were not the only flaws: the disselbooms (harness shafts) of the rear wagons had not been

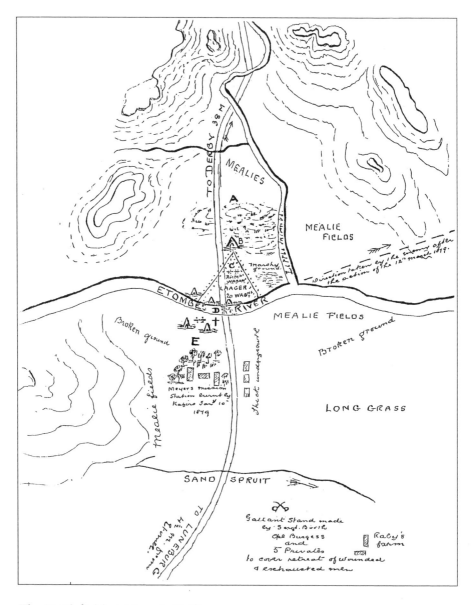

The Battlefield at Meyer's Drift.

A reproduction of a sketch by Major Charles Tucker made shortly after the battle.

Key:

A) Rising ground where the attackers assembled.

B) Captain David Moriarty's tent.

C) Spot where Captain Moriarty was killed.

D) Drift across the Ntombe River, ten feet deep at the time.

E) Camp in the charge of Lieutenant Henry Harward.

Crossed swords symbol: Gallant stand made by Sgt. Anthony Booth.

run under the bottom of the wagons in front which would have butted them together; instead sacks of mealies had been placed in the gaps but only to a height of about two and a half feet. With 150 oxen milling around, with the ammunition carts and the tents all within such a confined space and with the men naked in their blankets, any surprise attack could only result in turmoil and panic – and so it did.

The night passed peacefully enough until 4.30 a.m. However, under the cover of darkness, an immense *impi*, led by Mbelini, the renegade Swazi prince, had by then stealthily surrounded the laager. Except for a select number of warriors who had been designated to fire the first surprise volley into the tents at point-blank range, the rest were naked and armed with either a stabbing assegai or knobkerrie.

Harward on the south bank was the first to wake. He had been startled by shot from across the river. It was the fourth night after a full moon which, at that time in the morning, would have been shining brightly. Even though there was cloud cover, and thick mist along the river, it would not have been completely dark and objects would have been discernable – light enough in fact for Mbelini and his warriors to have travelled and to have deployed. Sergeant Booth's account of what followed would seem to be the most reliable. He, too, had been awakened by the shot. All was quiet on the north bank and, ordered by Harward, Booth shouted across the river to the sentry but received no reply. Eventually the sentry responded whereupon Booth ordered him to inform Captain Moriarty that a shot had been heard and to alarm the camp.[39] A short while later the man called back and told Booth that the men had been ordered to get dressed but would be allowed to remain in their tents. The alarm had not been given.[40]

Booth was uneasy. He got dressed, put on his ammunition belt, and climbed into one of the wagons to smoke his pipe. There he sat until about 5:00 a.m. Then, as it was getting light, the crash of a volley, fired close by, shattered the silence. A glance across the river revealed a nightmare; a massive throng of dark shapes had engulfed the dim outline of the laager. Suddenly from a thousand throats a frenzied yelling momentarily froze and terrified the waking men.

The number of warriors who attacked the laager varies in different accounts from 2,000 to 9,000 but in the dim light the mass seemed limitless. They leapt between the wagons, racing amongst the tents and maddened cattle in wild excitement, eager to find a victim as the men, dazed, naked and terrified, stumbled from their tents. Josiah Sussens, the civilian convoy master, later described the horror as he and his companion, Whittington, scrambled from their wagon:

> He [Whittington] immediately came out and jumped down, but was caught almost as soon as soon as he got to the ground, he was assegaied on all sides. The poor fellow shrieked out but with no avail . . . I ran down between the oxen and made for the river which was about sixty yards off.

I found Zulus shooting and stabbing the people in all directions. The sight was a most terrifying one and one never to be forgotten. As soon as I got to the river I jumped and made a dive, as swimming was too dangerous, the Zulus standing on the bank, and at the edge of the river, as thick as thieves, throwing assegais and aiming their guns wherever they saw a head.[41]

Moriarty was one of the first to fall. Naked, he rushed from his tent with a swarm of warriors upon him, with time only for one last roaring oath: 'Fire away, boys, death or glory!' But there was no attempt to rally. The suddenness of the attack, with the laager utterly unprepared and facing overwhelming numbers, ensured a total Zulu victory within minutes. Some, like Sussens, managed to reach the river, plunge in and hide amongst the reeds. But many of the warriors followed them in and assegaied them in the water. A few survived and, hidden and half-drowned, they listened to the Zulus calling them to come out in the pretence that they were their black allies.

On the south bank, as soon as Harward and Booth saw the start of the awful slaughter, their men were rallied and volley after volley was fired across the river. As the warriors returned fire in kind, the redcoats took shelter beneath the wagons, directing their aim in any direction that might assist the flight of their comrades on the opposite bank. But it soon became apparent that the enemy were crossing the river at some point higher up and would soon encircle their position. And at this point Harward's nerve broke. He saddled a horse, most likely one belonging to the wagons, and galloped off to Luneburg leaving his men to their fate. Harward's report told a different story:

> For fear, therefore, of my men being stabbed under the wagons, and to enable them to retire before their ammunition should be exhausted, I ordered them to retire steadily, and only just in time to avoid a rush of Zulus to a late position. The Zulus came on in dense masses and fell upon our men, who being already broken, gave way, and a hand-to-hand fight ensued. I endeavoured to rally my men, but they were too much scattered, and finding reformation impossible, I mounted my horse and galloped to Luneburg at utmost speed and reported all that had taken place.[42]

Harward wrote his report later that day when wise in the knowledge that Booth and others had survived – the opposite to what he had presumed when he had burst in upon Major Tucker at 6.00 a.m. that morning. In a long and descriptive letter to his father, Tucker wrote:

> On the morning of the 12th about 06:30h, I was woken by a fearful voice saying 'Major! Major!' I was up in an instant, and there at my tent door on his knees, the picture of death, was Harward. He gasped out 'The camp is in the hands of the enemy; they are all slaughtered, and I have galloped in for my life.' He then fell on to my bed in a faint.[43]

Tucker later tried to protect Harward from what was clearly an act of cowardice and desertion, stating:

> On the morning of the 12th, at about 6.30 a.m., Lieutenant Harward arrived at Luneburg from the Ntombi River reporting that the camp and wagons were in the possession of the enemy. I enclose a report [Harward's report above] from this officer . . .[44]

Meanwhile, at the Ntombe, Sergeant Booth, supported by Corporal Burgess, had resolutely taken command of the south bank and had managed to gather to him a few survivors who had crossed the river. But his little group was being hard pressed by more and more Zulus who were fording the rapidly receding Ntombe. With the survivors huddled behind a thin line of riflemen, Booth started a calm and methodical withdrawal towards Luneburg, all the while keeping the enemy at bay with well-timed volley fire. In a letter to his wife, written two days later, he told her:

> When I saw all our men across, about fifteen in number all as naked as when they were born, I sent them on in front and we retired firing. There was hundreds of the kaffirs crossing the river to try and cut us off but we made good our escape to a mission station.[45]

Booth had mistaken a deserted farm for a mission station where, for a while, he made a stand. Several of those in his group, anxious to reach the safety of Luneburg, decided, during a lull in the action, to take to their heels but were later found, having being overtaken and killed. Booth rallied his men once more and continued his masterful fighting withdrawal. The party finally reached safety after skirmishing for almost two hours. On receiving Harward's appalling news Tucker had raised every available horseman at Luneburg and set out at a gallop for Meyer's Drift, meeting up with the admirable Booth and the remaining survivors *en route*. Following in Tucker's wake, at the double, were 150 infantrymen of the 80th.

Tucker and his men were too late. On arrival at the Ntombe, they came upon a scene of carnage and destruction. Dead bodies and equipment cluttered the north bank. Tucker was only in time to witness the Zulus departing with their loot and the 150 draft oxen. Some days later the *Transvaal Argus* reported:

> On inspection of the camp being made it was found that the whole of the ammunition had been carried away, also blankets, rifles, etc. What was left was taken from off the wagons and was strewn all over the place . . . The rockets and rocket apparatus were taken out of the boxes but received no serious damage.

Forty men of the 80th, including Moriarty, were found dead with a further twenty missing, presumed drowned. Surgeon Cobbin was amongst the slain as were seventeen of the wagoners. Twenty-five Zulu dead were counted. It was another British catastrophe that could partly be blamed on the effects of cold and exhaustion coupled with inexcusable indifference and complacency. It was the second severe lesson of the war that the enemy must not be under-estimated, for it had been a daring and brilliant Zulu attack.

Moriarty and Cobbin were buried in the nearby Luneburg churchyard. The rest of the dead were interred in a mass grave that the 80th spent the next three days digging on the south bank.[46] But the dead were not left to rest in peace. Booth confided in a letter to his wife:

> A party went out to bury them [to dig the mass grave] the same day but they have been and took them up again, I mean the kaffirs, and skinned them – so we are ordered out again to go and bury them.[47]

The press were quick to offer opinion and advice:

> The success obtained by the Zulus on this occasion is, broadly speaking, due to the same cause that produced the slaughter at Isandlwana. British soldiers (officers and men alike) will persist in underrating the enemy, especially if he wears a black skin. It is plain by this time that in courage, activity and several other important military qualifications, the Zulus are on a par with some of the best troops in Europe.

The *Transvaal Argus* got closer to the point:

> Why were the whole of the mounted men removed from Luneburg to Colonel Wood's column; surely 50 of Raaff's Rangers or Weatherley's Horse could have been left. It is a well-acknowledged fact that infantry soldiers are unsuited for the performance of escort duties.

A tight-lipped and furious Lord Chelmsford would soon be receiving a reproachful letter from the Duke of Cambridge.[48] There was much to be answered for. Lieutenant Harward, in due time would, quite rightly, face a court martial.

For months no charge was laid against him. It was not until almost a year later, in February 1880, that he was arrested on two charges:

> (1) Having misbehaved before the enemy, in shamefully abandoning a party of the Regiment under his command when attacked by the enemy, and in riding off at speed from his men.
> (2) Conduct to the prejudice of good order and military discipline in having at the time and place mentioned in the first charge, neglected to take proper precautions for the safety of a party of a Regiment under his command when attacked.

His main defence was that he stayed with his men until they scattered and only then, and because he had the only horse, did he gallop away to seek help. Surprisingly, he was acquitted of all charges and returned to duty. Sir Garnet Wolseley emphatically disagreed with the verdict. Although powerless to interfere with the findings of the court, he refused to confirm them and declared:

... that a Regimental officer who is the only officer present with a party of men actually and seriously engaged with the enemy can, under any pretext whatever, be justified in deserting them, and by so doing, abandoning them to their fate. The more helpless a position in which an officer finds his men, the more it is his bounden duty to stay and share their fortune, whether for good or ill.

The Duke of Cambridge agreed and gave orders that Wolseley's comments be read at the head of every regiment. Not guilty or otherwise, Harward's career was finished and he shortly resigned his commission.

Tucker, for a while at least, would be sidelined from promotion and reward. The following year Tucker was moved to put his case to Horse Guards for the attention, no less, of the Duke of Cambridge himself:

> While I desire, both for myself and for the Regiment which I have the honour to command, to thank unreservedly his Royal Highness and you for the brevet just bestowed upon a most deserving officer ... I would however venture, with His Royal Highness's gracious permission, to most respectfully solicit a reconsideration of the decision limiting to one C.B. [Commander of the Bath] and one brevet majority the rewards granted to me and the 80th – a limitation confined solely to us out of all the corps forming Sir E Wood's Flying Column or those who actually served in the African War as long as we did.

The bitterness and resentment that Tucker – and most probably the regiment as a whole – felt echoes down the years:

> If his Royal Highness did not think my services in the latter capacity [Tucker's command of Sir Garnet Wolseley's Headquarters Column amounting to more than 1,000 men] deserving of the recognition granted to officers who held similar positions during the War, I can only respectfully bow to his Royal Highness's decision ...

But HRH remained mute; the stigma of the Meyer's Drift massacre was a millstone that Tucker would have to carry for some time to come.

Booth, the hero of Meyer's Drift, was eventually recommended for a well-earned Victoria Cross. But what seemed to have been overlooked by all was Wood's place in the chain of command, Chelmsford having given the 80th to Wood weeks previously. On 16 February Chelmsford had assured Wood that: 'Rowlands being wanted in Pretoria will leave you all his troops absolutely at your disposal.'

On hearing of the disaster Wood, while in the midst of furthering his political schemes by rescuing the remainder of Hamu's people, had only this to say:

> I went over at daylight to the scene – some 14 miles distant – to enquire into the disaster, and to ensure a system for security being adopted for the future, returning in the afternoon to camp, as I had arranged a long ride for the next day.[49]

A week later, Buller, accompanied by Major Hamilton of the 90th and Major Moysey of the Royal Engineers, arrived at Luneburg to 'inquire into the misfortune'. They stayed the night but seem to have drawn no conclusions.[50] The confident assurance that Wood had given Schermbrucker a few days earlier that he need not fear whilst he, Wood, was in command of the area, was not mentioned.

Chapter 4

The Battle of Hlobane[51]

'Don't delay Colonel Weatherley, the mountain is surrounded.'

Captain R. Barton, Frontier Light Horse

'There was a row of white men thrown over the krantzes, their ammunition was done, they did not fire, and we killed them without their killing any of our men.'

Mehlokazulu, induna of the Nkobamakosi Regiment

Hamu's first request on arriving at Kambula (Khambula) was to ask Wood to rescue his numerous wives. On enquiring how many there were, Hamu vaguely replied 'about 200' whereupon Wood tactfully observed that he would not like the responsibility of rescuing so many ladies unless Hamu accompanied him; after a moment's consideration Hamu replied that, if that were the case, he would do without them.

Wood had been heartily congratulated by Sir Bartle Frere on his political coup, which no doubt prompted him to cap his accomplishment by endeavouring to rescue all those of Hamu's clan who wished to join their prince in exile. However, it would be no easy task. Hamu had fled in secret but now Cetshwayo's warriors would be out in force to prevent any further desertions; to catch them off guard would be difficult. Wood had also contemplated a retaliatory attack on the abaQulusi for some time. Indeed such action was, perhaps, necessary in order to silence the abaQulusi prior to the final advance on Ulundi. In addition reports that up to 7,000 head of cattle grazed the upper slopes of Hlobane were a further incentive.

Hamu's great *umuzi* at kwaMfemfe, was about forty-five miles east of Kambula, situated in fine cattle country between the Black Umfolozi and Mkuzi Rivers and only forty miles from the Zulu capital of oNdini. It would be a hazardous undertaking to penetrate so deep into Zululand and attempt to bring out a column made up mainly of women and children. Wood, against the advice of his officers, decided to accompany the rescue raid that was to be led by Buller at the head of 360 mounted men accompanied by 200 of Hamu's warriors. It was decided that the warriors should take a short cut, over and down Zunguin Mountain, so as to get ahead and have the clan ready for departure as soon as Buller arrived. Against even more strongly worded advice from his officers, Wood made up his mind to accompany the warriors and take the rugged short cut. They set out on 14 March 1879. As Wood and his men descended Zunguin and approached the slopes of Hlobane, the aggressive abaQulusi hurried to meet them and opened fire at long range. It was yet another example that the abaQulusi would not hesitate to fire upon any enemy who passed by.

Once down Zunguin, Wood and his staff waited for Buller and the main column to catch up while Hamu's warriors jogged ahead. It was a long and tiring day, the whole force taking three hours to cover the last seven miles, by when darkness had long since set in. The rendezvous point was teeming with women, children and a number of old men, elders of the clan. Nevertheless, there were still a number of refugees several miles away who were too scared to leave the caves in which they hid. Eventually scouts were despatched and, miraculously, with the help of a three-quarter moon, most of the refugees had arrived by daybreak. During the night Wood had been conscious of Buller's sleepless vigil and his continual pacing. Buller was extremely concerned about their precarious position deep within enemy territory and was well aware that their progress had been followed all day by Zulu scouts.

At daylight, the first of the women and children were led off in the direction of Kambula, escorted by men of the FLH. Amongst them was Mrs Rorke and her small family.[52] Within an hour a thousand refugees were on the move. Wood and Buller remained until after 10.00 a.m. and even then stragglers were still making an appearance. There were many more who would follow and become victims of the fighting yet to come. Even so, many of the defectors had been snatched from under the enemy's nose. The rescue could be compared with a modern day special forces operation, successfully carried out behind enemy lines.

Yet Wood had been extremely lucky. Not one casualty had been incurred, either amongst the troops or the refugees, even though on their way back from Hamu's territory the column was once again fired upon from the slopes of Hlobane. But the outcome could have been vastly different. Some time during the previous day, shortly after the rescue mission had passed the slopes of Hlobane, a large Zulu *impi* had crossed its tracks, heading in the direction of the mountain.[53] It seems that the abaQulusi had been reinforced with a regiment from Ulundi. It says little for the scouting efficiency of either the Zulus or Wood's column that neither detected the presence of the other. (It was Wood's particular boast that, since the previous December, he had native scouts twenty miles to the front of his column and mounted patrols six miles out an hour before daylight.)[54] Nevertheless, Rathbone of the *Natal Witness*, described by one soldier as 'an old salt who can tell a good yarn', reported the raid as 'dashingly performed'.[55]

As the refugees neared Kambula, Wood sent ahead for all available mule carts to assist the flagging women and children. Even the stern and truculent Buller gave a helping hand by placing toddlers fore and aft on his horse.

Once Hamu's people had reached the camp, they were searched, an exercise that revealed a number of firearms and some ammunition. While the warriors remained at Kambula, the rest were transported to Utrecht pending a move to a temporary new home in the Drakensberg. There was more good news that day. Rathbone recorded that:

> Colonel Wood has placed his share [to date] of the prize money amounting to £51 [from the sale of cattle] in the hands of the paymaster for the benefit of any who may suffer through the war, combatant or non-combatant. The first shares of prize money amount to £2 5/- [£2.25] each man, nearly 3,000 shares, white and black sharing alike.

It was little wonder that the other columns of Chelmsford's army envied the cattle-lifting ability of Wood's colonials.[56]

Having successfully accomplished the defection of Hamu and many of his people, Wood considered his next move. He was not fettered by any restraining orders from Lord Chelmsford, who had made it clear that Wood was entirely free to use his initiative and to wage war on the Zulus as he saw best. Hlobane Mountain would be his next objective.

Upward of 600 horsemen were now under Wood's command. In addition to those units already described: the Frontier Light Horse, Raaff's Rangers, Baker's Horse, the Natal Native Horse and Schermbrucker's Kaffrarian Rifles, two additional units had arrived to swell the mounted ranks: No. 1 Squadron, Mounted Infantry (MI) had been on active service for the last eighteen months and had ridden thousands of miles over southern Africa. The men had been recruited from every British infantry regiment throughout the territory. Any man who could ride could volunteer for the Mounted Infantry, and many did believing that life would be easier sitting on the back of a horse. There they had been mistaken, for the MI had seen more action, marched further and lived rougher than any other imperial unit engaged in southern Africa – and, furthermore, they looked as if they had. One colonial officer described the troopers: '. . . their uniform was a red coat, more or less tattered, trousers and leggings ditto, with a battered helmet.'

Most were dissatisfied and wished to return to their parent regiments. For much of the unit's existence, it had been commanded by Lieutenant Edward Stevenson Browne of the 1st/24th, but more recently Brevet Lieutenant-Colonel Cecil Russell, a special service officer from the 12th Lancers, had taken charge, not a popular change as far as the men were concerned. Russell had been a favourite of Chelmsford's and had, like Chelmsford, been an equerry to the royal family. He had also served in the Ashanti Campaign as ADC to Major-General Sir Archibald Alison, who was now Deputy Quartermaster-General, Intelligence Department, the head of Army intelligence, at Horse Guards. Most of No. 1 Squadron, MI, had been out with Chelmsford's column during the Battle of Isandlwana and on return to camp that night had seen the human debris that had once been their comrades. Since that night the Mounted Infantry under Russell's command seemed to have lost heart. Chelmsford had decided to transfer the unit to Wood's column and ordered it to march to Kambula. Russell took the long way around via Newcastle, well away from any likely contact with the enemy, causing Chelmsford to confide to Wood:

> It will be some time before you get any mounted men from Helpmekaar. Between ourselves, Russell appears to have lost heart and allows the men to get out of hand.[57]

Even before Isandlwana, discipline had been poor. Wood had inspected the unit in December 1878 after it had left Rowlands's column and had recorded:

> A more ragged crew was perhaps never got together except professional beggars on a stage. I was much dissatisfied, for the first horse I looked at was about to get a sore back . . . Many of the men had only ten rounds of ammunition.

Weatherley's Border Horse (WBH), sometimes called Weatherley's Border Lancers, was the other recent addition having also served with Rowlands's column. Their commander, Colonel Frederick Augustus Weatherley, was an experienced cavalryman. He had learnt his trade at an Austrian military academy where he had studied for four years, later receiving a commission in a crack continental cavalry regiment. On his return to Britain he served with the 4th Light Dragoons in the Crimea and with the 6th Inniskilling Dragoon Guards during the Indian Mutiny, seeing much action in both campaigns. He had retired to Brighton after fourteen years' service and was given command of a militia unit, the Sussex Artillery Volunteers, and was in fact still its colonel when he arrived in South Africa in 1876. Weatherley established himself and his family in the Transvaal and was deeply involved in the Eersteling Gold Mining Company. Unfortunately, he and his wife had also become involved with a unsavoury character calling himself The Gunn of Gunn, supposedly the holder of an ancient Scottish title. Playing up to Weatherley's vanity, Gunn proposed that Weatherley should oust Sir Theophilus Shepstone as Administrator of the Transvaal. To this end Gunn set about drawing up a petition that finally bore close on 4,000 names. It was triumphantly presented to the government. Shame quickly followed when it was discovered that Gunn had forged all the signatures save a few hundred. Weatherley retired ignominiously from Transvaal politics only to find that Gunn was not only a cad but a charmer and had eloped with his wife. On top of his domestic problems, things were not going well with the gold mining company. No doubt, all these setbacks prompted Weatherley to raise his regiment and ride off to war. He also took with him Rupert, his youngest son, only fifteen years old and disabled (described as 'a cripple' by Dennison) but nonetheless commissioned as lieutenant. The men, totalling seventy-one rank and file, were a mixed bunch representing many nationalities but were organised on regular cavalry lines with NCOs appointed and farrier, veterinary and trumpeter sergeants chosen.

Wood had contemplated an attack on Hlobane as early as 3 March when he suggested the idea to Chelmsford.

> I've converted Buller to my opinion. He wanted to 'try' the Hlobane before raiding past it. 'Tis a double mountain joined by a narrow neck, and has precipitous sides on all but in two or three spots. I am all against 'trying', or fiddling at a place. If we try I say we must go up and if it cost half a battalion and I think we can't spare half a battalion at present . . . I should like to clear it before we go forward, but I don't think we ought to attempt it just now.

A few days later he thought the prospects of a successful attack had improved and wrote again to Chelmsford that, if circumstances in Natal necessitated some kind of engagement, he would attack Hlobane despite the knowledge that the mountain had been reinforced by a Zulu regiment from Ulundi. Having given the matter further thought, Wood contemplated forming a separate column at Zunguin and attacking the mountain from there.[58] By the middle of the month Wood's intentions had become common knowledge with Rathbone reporting:

> It is Colonel Wood's belief that the defection of Hamu has influenced Cetshwayo in trying to make terms with the General. Colonel Wood's operations have greatly embarrassed Cetshwayo. Hamu's warriors will assist in the attack on Hlobane and when this obstruction is removed, the rest of their tribe will come on and join this column.[59]

It would also seem from this report that other members of Hamu's clan were either sitting on the fence or were too apprehensive to follow their chief for the time being.

No doubt the final incentive to attack was Chelmsford's request for a diversion a day or so before he launched his bid to relieve Eshowe, which was scheduled for 28 March. On the 26th, Wood finally made up this mind to attack the hostile stronghold. Not only was Hlobane the main rallying centre of Zulu opposition in the area and the grazing land of many cattle, it was another of Mbelini's hideouts. It was established that not only did Mbelini have a homestead high on the southern slopes but that he had recently moved there from his other eyrie on the Tafelberg. There were scores to settle with the renegade royal Swazi, who for months had terrified the people, both black and white. Mbelini who had masterminded the destruction of Moriarty's laager at Meyer's Drift; Mbelini who as a boy, had been forced to witness the skinning alive of a wild dog and the stitching of its dripping pelt upon his own head in the belief, held by the tribal *izinyanga* (witch doctors), that the nature of the savage beast would be transferred into his soul. Mbelini has been described as an intelligent man, of small stature and dark complexion and a contemporary of the Nkobamakosi Regiment, thus being about twenty-eight years of age.[60] He was also credited by his followers with supernatural powers over the elements including rain and sun. Schermbrucker, being aware of this reputation, had impetuously written to Wood the day after Isandlwana – but with no knowledge of the calamitous battle that had taken place – inadvertently supporting Mbelini's magical claims:

> Yesterday's partial eclipse of the sun (between 3 and 4 p.m.) is looked upon by the natives as a sign of Mbelini's power, who is reported to have particular power over that luminary. If he should have happened to get a thorough good thrashing on that day (which he most certainly did get if it be true that he was engaged with you), it will have had a most demoralising affect upon the Zulu warriors who looked to Umbelini's [*sic*] victory as certain whenever he should meet our forces.[61]

As we have seen, Wood had been engaged with Mbelini's warriors on that day and had broken off the fight on receipt of Gardner's catastrophic news on Isandlwana. Thus, in the eyes of the abaQulusi, Mbelini's power had been responsible not only for Wood's retreat but, in part at least, for the British defeat at Isandlwana.

There were three reasons for Wood to attack Hlobane: to cause the diversion that Chelmsford had requested; to capture cattle and destroy enemy food supplies; and to harass and disperse the enemy prior to the general advance on Ulundi. Nevertheless, even a combination of all three objectives could not possibly justify the risk. Hlobane rose 1,500 feet above the surrounding plain, was four miles long running east to west, two and a half miles wide at its broadest point, and was more or less flat on top. The top was a rock-strewn plateau varying little in height over the first three miles of its length from the east. At the western end it narrowed like the spout of a funnel, plunging down a precipitous scramble of boulders to a narrow hogsback ridge. Further on, the ridge broadened out and was known as the Ntendeka or lower plateau, its all but sheer sides affording in places a hazardous descent to the plain below. The way to the top at the eastern end of the mountain was uncharted and the dangers of the precipitous funnel-like descent (soon to become known as the infamous Devil's Pass), that separated the two plateaus were yet to be revealed. Hlobane, in fact, looked impregnable, as indeed it was apart from one or two alpine-like cattle tracks, for at the edge of the upper plateau there was a collar of perpendicular rock, 300 feet in height, that would have required all the skill of a roped mountaineer to conquer. Around the base of this sheer wall, as far as the eye could see, there was a continuous jumble of massive boulders that had fallen during the millennia to form caverns and labyrinths. And it would have been rash to believe that once the summit had been achieved, the going would be easy. The surface of the upper plateau was a floor of uneven slabs of rock, broken, deformed and hazardous, the worst sort of footing for mounted men. No one inhabited the top of this high place for it was subject to violent storms, lightning strikes, cold and mist – although on a fine summer day there could hardly be a more exhilarating place in Africa – and it was only occupied by the abaQulusi cattle when danger threatened. Otherwise there was a feeling of desolation, even of foreboding, about the place. Many had sensed it and many still do. Bertram Mitford who visited Hlobane in 1882 described how he felt: 'Something of the indescribable desolation seem to haunt the place, as though one were standing alone outside the world.'[62]

As far as is known, none of Wood's colonial aides, scouts or spies, had ever visited the top plateau, with the possible exception of Charlie Potter, a newly appointed officer of Wood's Irregulars. Potter's father, an old time resident of Natal, owned a trading store close to Kambula on the Pemvane River. The Potters had bartered with the Zulus for miles around and had in the past taken their wagons and goods as far as Hamu's homestead. They would certainly have traded with the abaQulusi on the southern slopes of the mountain and it may have been that the young Charlie Potter had once climbed the summit. As an officer in Rowlands's column, Potter had been one of the colonials who had written the complaint to the local press about Rowlands's lack of initiative in not following up the attack on the Tolaka Zulus. Raised in Natal, he spoke Zulu fluently.

Buller and Knox Leet had once climbed the northern face of the lower plateau with a force of seventy men and had found it deserted. On another occasion in February, under cover of thick mist, Buller, Piet Uys and a strong patrol had likewise climbed to the lower plateau and had captured 400 head of cattle, only to abandon them and beat a hasty retreat to the plain below, when 'thousands of Zulus' gathered to cut off their retreat.[63]

Yet, despite the fact that the terrain of the upper plateau and the pathways to its summit were virtually unknown; that except for distant viewings there had been no reconnaissance; that two months earlier Wood and his officers had witnessed 4,000 warriors at drill nearby; that at least one Ulundi regiment had recently reinforced the abaQulusi; that all the mounted men, with the exception of fifty left behind at camp, would be committed; and that the objective was beyond the reach of reinforcements, Wood recklessly pursued his ill-starred plan and, to use his own words when writing to Lord Chelmsford on the 27th, the day before the attack:

> I am not very sanguine of success. We do not know how steep the eastern
> end may be, but I think we ought to make a stir here to divert attention
> from you, although as you can see by our last reports, it is asserted that
> you have only Coast Tribes [generally thought to be less warlike] against
> you, and that all Cetshwayo's people are coming here.[64]

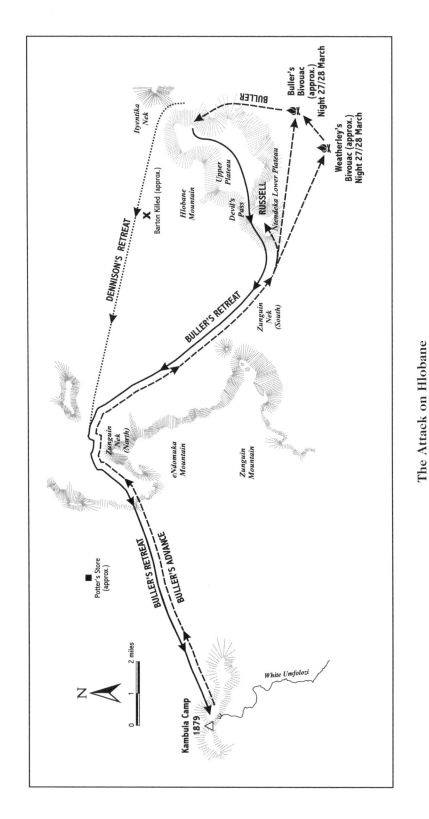

The Attack on Hlobane

The general movements of No. 4 Column during its attack on Hlobane Mountain and its subsequent retreat, 28 March, 1879.

Not only was a Zulu army coming but, unbeknown to Wood, it was already on its way having left Ulundi on the 25th, 23,000 strong, heading to Kambula. Piet Uys also had deep misgivings and a strong sense of foreboding, asking Wood to enter into a pact that, in the event of either of them being killed, the other would take care of the casualty's children.

Wood's plan of attack was simple. He would take the mountain with two columns, one from either end, with the objective of trapping the abaQulusi and their herds in between. Then, having dealt with the warriors, the columns would drive the booty west and down the end of the lower plateau, and so back to Kambula. The columns were to be commanded by Lieutenant-Colonels Redvers Buller and Cecil Russell. Buller's column would consist of: Piet Uys and his small band of burgers; 158 men of the FLH commanded by Captain Robert Barton, a special service officer seconded from the Coldstream Guards; 54 of Weatherley's Border Horse commanded by their colonel; 70 Transvaal Rangers led by Commandant Raaff; 80 men of Baker's Horse commanded by Lieutenant W. D. Wilson; eight men of the Royal Artillery with rocket troughs, carried on pack mules, led by Major Edmund Tremlett; and two companies of Wood's Irregulars commanded by Major William Knox Leet. Buller's column, all ranks, totalled 408 mounted white men and 208 native irregulars.

Buller's principal staff officer was now Captain Alan Gardner, he who had brought the disastrous news of Isandlwana two months earlier. There had been rumours that, in acknowledgement of Gardner's lone and dangerous ride, he was to be recommended for the Victoria Cross – later the award was stated as fact in the *Illustrated London News* of 5 May. The rumour was received amongst some of Gardner's fellow officers on Chelmsford's staff with jealousy and envy, prompting someone to compose a spiteful and malicious ditty, each verse ending:

> I very much fear
> That the Zulus are near
> So, hang it, I'm off to Dundee.

Gardner never got his VC, but the fact that Buller had taken him as his second-in-command was in itself equivalent to a badge of courage.

Cecil Russell's column comprised: 82 men of the Mounted Infantry, commanded once more by Lieutenant Edward Browne; 41 of the Kaffrarian Rifles, who had recently been mounted, led by Commandant Schermbrucker; 71 men of the Natal Native Horse under the command of Lieutenant W. F. D. Cochrane, who had been with the unit at Isandlwana; eleven men of the Royal Artillery, with mule-borne rocket tubes, under the command of Lieutenant Arthur Bigge; 240 men of Wood's Irregulars led by Commandant Lorraine White; and close on 200 of Hamu's warriors led by Lieutenant Cecil Williams, a special service officer from the 58th Regiment. The total force amounted to 205 black and white mounted men and 440 native irregulars on foot.

Buller's column, chosen to attack the eastern end of the mountain, and with the furthest to go, was the first to leave early on the morning of 27 March. Wood's Irregulars – abhorred by most for their cruelty but described as having 'experienced harder work, less comfort and harder knocks' than any other unit – had spent the night with Hamu's warriors.[65] They had been based at Potter's Store – or what was left of it, it having been visited by four Zulu horsemen a few days earlier who had set fire to the stables and dwelling house before retreating to Hlobane – and marched from there at 8.00 a.m., meeting up with Buller's horsemen shortly thereafter. Having crossed Zunguin Nek, half of Wood's Irregulars and all of Hamu's warriors, halted to await the arrival of Russell's column while the remainder of Wood's Irregulars stepped off behind Buller and his men.[66] Their route took them over familiar ground that had been travelled many times previously during Buller's raids into Zululand and more recently on the expedition to bring out Hamu's people: east around the towering shoulder of eNdomuka that rose 1,500 feet above the surrounding country, on through the Zunguin Nek to the open plain beyond, with the great bulk of Hlobane, low on the horizon, and the drop of Devil's Pass just discernable nine miles away. Between the termination of the Zunguin range and the slopes of Hlobane's western end there is an expanse of rising ground about a mile wide. It was here that Wood, standing on the heights of Zunguin, had watched the 4,000 abaQulusi warriors at drill two months earlier. This gap between the two mountains could be taken as a nek or valley; indeed like the gap in the mountains closer to Kambula, it was sometimes mistakenly called Zunguin Nek. This muddle would have tragic consequences and to avoid confusion arising in this narrative, the authors have named the respective neks Zunguin north and Zunguin south and will refer to them as such throughout.

Having skirted the slopes of the lower plateau, Buller and his men pressed on east, riding more or less parallel with the length of Hlobane, but gradually pulling away to the south, in a feint aimed at convincing the abaQulusi that the column was intent on further marauding towards Hamu's domain. At midday Buller called a halt and the mounted units made their way to individual areas close to each other but where the horses could graze. The men off-saddled and brewed coffee.

Weatherley's Border Horse had been the last to leave Kambula and as they arrived Buller called to Weatherley that he had best bear away to the right where he would be free from the crowd and have room to graze. As Weatherley and his men moved off Buller again called, shouting that he would send word when it was time to saddle up and move.[67] Weatherley's Border Horse had their coffee and then in the warm afternoon, stretched out and dozed. Time passed and Captain C. G. Dennison, a frontiersman of considerable experience and Weatherley's second-in-command, grew uneasy.

At about 4.00 p.m., on Buller's orders, a trumpeter sounded 'Fall In' and the various units began to move. However, as Weatherley had not received word from Buller, he was disinclined to budge. It soon became obvious to Dennison and to the men that they had been left behind but Weatherley inexplicably still refused to move, perhaps expecting Buller to present him with a personal order out of deference to his rank and experience. His vanity affronted, he seemed determined to stay. Eventually, Dennison told him plainly that, if he did not give the order to move, the men would saddle up and leave without them. Reluctantly Weatherley gave in but, as the Border Horse rode into the gathering dusk, a light misty rain set in so that the tracks of those ahead could no longer be discerned.[68]

Russell's column with ten miles less to travel, left Kambula at noon, arrived at the base of the lower plateau during the late afternoon and also prepared to bivouac. Wood and his staff accompanied it.

It was intended that both columns, having, it was hoped, deceived the dwellers of Hlobane, would break camp at 3.00 a.m., make their way silently up the mountain at each end and simultaneously fall upon the slumbering abaQulusi. But Mbelini and his followers had not been deceived. Such a massive force of horsemen and black enemies, camped at either end of their fortress, could only mean one thing: they were about to be attacked.

The Battle of Hlobane Mountain has received little attention from historians and military analysts. Perhaps because it was such a disaster it was thought at the time that the less said about it the better – especially so as it was followed the next day by a resounding British victory – and it has thus passed into history almost unnoticed. For instance, for every word written about the Battle of Hlobane most likely 1,000 words have been written about the Battle of Rorke's Drift. But the abaQulusi deserve credit for their victory, as does their commander, Mbelini wa Mswati, and the narrative that follows, based on primary source evidence and on the balance of probability, is most likely what occurred.

Having inadvertently left Weatherley and the Border Horse behind, Buller and the rest of the column continued to ride south-east away from Hlobane. Shortly before darkness fell, a halt was called and, about six miles south of the mountain, the men prepared to bivouac. Wishing to deceive the abaQulusi into believing that they were bedding down, the column demolished some huts at a nearby kraal and used the frames to stoke their camp fires. Then, having off-saddled, the men brewed coffee and cooked green mealies. The usual precaution of posting guards was taken and, aware that their progress had been monitored and the position of their bivouac observed by several 'spies' who had dogged their footsteps, they piled the fires with timber thus giving every impression of being about to settle for the night. But, as the moon set, the column stealthily saddled up and rode into the night, led by Piet Uys. They were guided by the glow of distant lightning that flickered intermittently on the cloud base that had settled on Hlobane, together with the occasional glimmer of a fire – the abaQulusi had lit three beacons on the mountain. Thus the column made its way north.[69]

At about 9.00 p.m. and close to their destination, they halted in a valley. Dismounting in silence and leaving the horses saddled and bridled, the troopers lay down and attempted to rest, each man with the reins of his horse wrapped around his wrist. But there was little sleep to be had. Not long after midnight it rained heavily and continued to do so until two hours before daylight when the troopers, cold and sodden, were given the order to mount. With the exception of a handful of imperial officers, the men were all colonials who had earlier been described, perhaps with undue exaggeration of their shortcomings, as:

> . . . rough, undisciplined and disrespectful to their officers, fiercely slovenly and the veriest of drunkards . . . but looking what they were, just the rough and hardy men to wage a partisan warfare against an active enemy . . . The steeds they bestrewed were as hardy as themselves.[70]

The luck that had ridden with Buller for so many months was shortly to forsake him but for a while yet would hold good. Although completely unaware of the fact, the column had just enjoyed two fortuitous escapes: it had almost bivouacked on top of the Zulu army for, far from being at least a day's march away as was believed, the 23,000-strong juggernaut had been slumbering just beyond Nyembe Hill only two miles from the column's last camp. Again Wood's claim that his troops continuously scouted twenty miles ahead must be regarded with scepticism, though Lieutenant Tomasson of Baker's Horse, a great admirer of Buller, later wrote: 'History says, some mistake as to the placing of the vedettes took place, but not by anyone under Colonel Buller's orders.'[71] Yet, clearly as column commander, the placing of scouts was ultimately Buller's responsibility.

The column's second stroke of good fortune was a missed encounter at dawn with an *impi* led by Mbelini. Believing – or perhaps hoping – that Buller's column had bedded down for the night as their campfires had indicated, the 'spies' that had followed the column for most of the day had sent word to Mbelini who, still flushed with his triumphant victory over Moriarty's convoy only sixteen days earlier, decided to deal with Buller in similar fashion. He despatched half his force, an *impi* 3,000 strong, to overwhelm the slumbering bivouac at daybreak.[72] However, in the rain and darkness, the rival forces had passed each other, missing contact. Had they met, only flight could have saved Buller and his men. Now, the unknown dangers past, the horsemen were well advanced, climbing the eastern slope of Hlobane while Mbelini, at last realising that he had been deceived, hurried in their footsteps.

———※◦◦———

Weatherley, having finally been persuaded to move, had got lost. For a while distant campfires could be seen but, as mist and drizzle set in, the surrounding country became completely obscured. Nevertheless, Weatherley's men kept forging on until, after about two hours, they topped a rise and the weather appeared to have improved for up ahead the night suddenly seemed full of stars. However, this illusion did not last long for almost immediately Dennison realised that they were looking at the distant campfires of a vast *impi*. Fortunately they had found the Zulu army rather than it finding them. Yet, it was difficult to comprehend how such an immense array could be there, just ahead, without it having been detected by the column's scouts. Weatherley, perhaps still sceptical, gave the order to halt and reconnoitre ahead. Dennison immediately volunteered to lead a scouting party and, calling for two troopers to accompany him, men he knew and could trust, the three of them, leaving their horses behind, made their way forward and down a steep incline until they 'neared a ledge, behind which, in the valley below, the light of many fires lit up the sky while coming up from the valley was the hum of many voices.'[73]

Dennison ordered the two troopers to remain quiet and still whilst he crawled forward until, lying flat on his stomach, he could look directly below him. No further away than 'the length of a rifle', a group of head-ringed (and therefore married) warriors sat in conversation. Holding his breath, and with the greatest caution, Dennison withdrew and, with the two troopers, finally arrived back at camp.[74] There the rest of the unit lay in the drizzle, each man holding the reins of his mount while Weatherley and his son Rupert huddled in their cloaks, the boy asleep. It being too dangerous to move in the dark, it was decided to remain where they were until daybreak when, they hoped, they would get their direction again. It was correctly assumed that the Zulu army would not move until after sunrise. At about 3.00 a.m., the mist and drizzle having suddenly cleared, Dennison was able to see the abaQulusi alarm beacons flickering on top of Hlobane. The men were immediately aroused and, as silently as possible, they mounted and advanced towards the mountain, the light from the flickering beacons intensifying all the while and the dark silhouette of their objective gradually looming ahead against the lightening sky. Soon they were able to hear the continuous rattle of rifle fire.

Buller and the rest of the column, with the horsemen to the fore and Wood's Irregulars bringing up the rear, had already began to ascend the mountain, trying to keep some semblance of formation as the men stumbled and the horses backed and plunged amongst the rocks. But their advance had not gone unseen as flashes of lightning had illuminated the struggling column. Two-thirds of the way up, some of the abaQulusi waited and, as Buller's vanguard advanced upon a horseshoe shaped feature resembling a rocky amphitheatre, they were fired upon from caves and rocks on both flanks. Caught in the open, men and horses soon began to fall. The fleet-footed and agile irregulars leapt to the challenge and were soon amongst the rocks 'with praiseworthy courage and rapidity'.[75] Lieutenant Williams and his dismounted troop of the Frontier Light Horse also rushed forward but, as they did so, Williams was shot through the head and killed instantly. In the confusion Gardner, like many others, tried to get to the forefront of the fighting, and at that moment was greeted with enthusiasm by another officer of the FLH, Baron Otto von Stietencron, an Austrian soldier of fortune, who had mistakenly taken Gardner for his brother whom the baron had known at Cambridge. As they paused to converse, the baron was shot with a bullet through the brain, ending a story-book life of adventure that moved the correspondent of *The Scotsman* to record: 'I could a tale of sentiment unfold that no morbid modern woman novelist could surpass.'[76]

The abaQulusi fire did not persist and, with relatively few casualties, the column moved on in open order, each man picking his way amongst the scattered rocks, and eventually reached the summit. There they were ordered to their respective tasks, it never occurring to them that their easy ascent might have been planned in order to draw them onto the mountain where they might be trapped. The abaQulusi needed time for Mbelini's raiders to return from their aborted ambush and for the Zulu army to arrive.[77]

A Troop of the FLH was appointed to guard the approach by which they had ascended – possibly the only line of retreat – and ordered to hold it at all costs while the remainder of the column set about rounding up cattle. As the horsemen moved about their task of gathering bovine booty, they drew further away leaving A Troop seemingly isolated. Before long the troopers became aware of stealthy movements as shadowy figures began to slip between the boulders, ever drawing closer.[78]

Wood's Irregulars soon began herding the plundered beasts, taking them west along the plateau towards the pass, encountering little or no opposition. Troopers riding hither and thither stood guard over these activities, taking the occasional pot-shot at any abaQulusi who had the pluck to attempt resistance. Unlike A Troop at their lonely vigil, the rest of the horsemen were enjoying what had turned out to be a fine sunny day, as a man by the name of Kritzinger, one of Uys's Burger Force, remembered:

> There was a lot of kraals of cattle at the slopes of the mountain and we started shooting Zulus [abaQulusi] to drive them away whilst our loyal natives, Oham's [Hamu's] Zulus, were trying to drive the cattle away which was the object of us attacking Hlobane.[79]

Buller and his staff, in anticipation of meeting up with Russell's column, had ridden west and Knox Leet had already arrived at the cliff-like descent of Devil's Pass. With several other officers he had contemplated sending a number of spare horses back to Kambula by way of the pass but it was unanimously decided that, no matter how carefully the horses might be led, there would be no hope of reaching the bottom without numerous mishaps.

At the western end of the mountain, Russell's column had made the ascent to the lower plateau without incident. The climb in itself was a remarkable achievement for nature had never intended that a horse be capable of ascending a cliff of rocks as steep as a ladder. Having crossed the lower plateau to Devil's Pass, Russell came to the same conclusion as Knox Leet.[80] From where Russell gazed upwards, taking in the boulder-strewn near-vertical ascent, he could see some of Buller's men, already in possession of the upper plateau, moving around and silhouetted against the skyline.

'Large quantities of cattle' were at graze on both sides of the lower plateau and all within easy reach. Russell ordered Commandant Lorraine White to direct Wood's Irregulars to the south, and Hamu's warriors to the north side of the mountain, where they eagerly began to round up every beast within sight, taking their haul straight down the side of the mountain to the plain below, ready to be driven to Kambula. All appeared to be going according to plan with virtually no opposition.

To establish contact with Buller, Russell sent Lieutenant Browne of the Mounted Infantry to climb the pass and find out if assistance was required on top. But Buller in turn had gone looking for Wood who, after spending the night with Russell, had left several hours earlier on his way to join Buller. However, Browne eventually returned after having conferred with Major Tremlett and Knox Leet and was able to report that Buller had also had a successful morning, as was borne out by the large number of cattle that were now being herded down Devil's Pass which, though too steep to risk a horse in ordinary circumstances, was passable for expendable cattle. As Russell later reported, at that moment 'everything appeared to be nearly quiet and the whole object of the reconnaissance to have been gained.'

It would seem, as far as Russell was aware, that the sole purpose of the expedition had been to loot cattle. No attempt had been made to destroy enemy homesteads or barracks and, other than taking pot-shots at abaQulusi who attempted to prevent their cattle from being stolen, there had been no move to pursue the enemy and few of them had been accounted for. As for creating the diversion that Chelmsford had requested, the close presence of the Zulu army had achieved that end. Had Wood's scouts been as efficient as he had boasted them to be, and had he known the whereabouts of the Zulu army the previous day, he could have used his mounted men to far greater profit and with minimal risk, by harassing the enemy's flanks as they marched.

Browne also mentioned to Russell that Buller had examined the pass and, having decided it was impractical for horses, would lead his column back the way they had come.

———»·•·«———

Wood had left Russell's column at daybreak and rode east rather like an umpire on a peace-time army manoeuvre to see how Buller was progressing. It was a fine morning and his young staff officers, and his escort of eight mounted privates of the 90th, chattered unconcerned, enjoying the sunshine and scenery. The Honourable Captain Ronald Campbell, at thirty-one, was the most mature, but had only been in the country for three months. Twenty-year-old Lieutenant Henry Lysons, Wood's orderly officer, known as 'Boy', was the youngest and had only recently arrived, straight from England, to his first posting with the 90th. Llewellyn Lloyd, Wood's political officer, was by far the most experienced man. He had fought in the Langalibalele campaign of 1873–4, taking part in arduous marches through the Drakensberg Mountains and experiencing bitter cold and near starvation. During the Sekhukhune campaign he had been twice severely wounded. Wood was also accompanied by seven native horsemen led by Prince Mthonga kaMpande, a refugee Zulu who was no less than half-brother to King Cetshwayo. During the years prior to Cetshwayo's succession, Mthonga, a remote but possible candidate for the throne, had fled Zululand in fear of his life and had taken refuge among the whites of the Utrecht district.

As they rode following Buller's trail, Lysons and Lloyd were chatting so loudly that Wood feared the abaQulusi would hear them on top of the mountain. Wood's thoughts were morbid ones, wondering whether or not one of the young men would that night be penning a letter to his wife informing her that he, Wood, was dead.[81]

As they climbed higher they came across dead horses and equipment strewn about, evidence of Buller's earlier encounter with the abaQulusi defenders. Wood and his small cavalcade could now clearly hear the rattle of gunfire and see the tail end of Buller's men cresting the summit. But the marksmen who had earlier killed Williams and von Stietencron were still at their post and opened fire.

Here we must pause and explain that there are two versions of what happened next. The first account is that of Wood, published in his autobiography *Midshipman to Field Marshal* in October 1906. The book must have been a bestseller as it was reprinted twice in the first month. His account is the best known and most quoted. Until recently it was assumed that there was no other account, despite Captain Dennison having his autobiography *A Fight to the Finish* published in London in 1904. It was puzzling indeed to read this book and to find that the day of the Battle of Hlobane, one of the most hazardous and dramatic days of Dennison's long and adventurous life, was hardly mentioned. It was not until a few years ago when a chapter, obviously intended to form part of this narrative but which never did, was discovered in the Transvaal Archives.[82] Because the contents of the missing chapter are uncomplimentary and critical of Wood, and as, at the time of publication, Wood was a field marshal and a national favourite, Dennison's cautious publishers must have advised him to withdraw the chapter – or perhaps had even refused to publish at all if the chapter were retained. In any event, it was omitted and remained unseen for almost a hundred years.

Wood's account shall be outlined first.

As the abaQulusi marksmen sprang their ambush, Wood instinctively veered off the track towards the enemy. Only moments before, he had met up with Weatherley and the Border Horse who, having reached Hlobane at last, were not following after Buller but were headed westwards in the opposite direction. Wood ordered them to about turn and ride towards the gunfire but, before they could spur away, the abaQulusi opened fire. Wood and his escort pushed on towards the marksmen's lair, but not so the Border Horse and by the time Wood had reached a stone cattle kraal, still under fire, the Border Horse were lagging 200 yards behind. Having next dismounted all his men, Wood had their ponies secured in the kraal. He, however, retained his horse saying he would lead it as he was a 'bad walker'.

Half a dozen men of the Border Horse were now on Wood's heels while the rest kept their distance and, with Wood in the lead, pulling his horse along behind him, the party scrambled upwards towards the enemy. Soon, a wildly directed fire, coming from behind high boulders, brought them to a halt while from the rear the remainder of the Border Horse, still 200 yards behind, opened fire at the boulders. Lloyd, close at Wood's elbow said: 'I'm glad of that, for it will make the Zulu shoot badly.' Almost immediately he was hit by a marksman who had suddenly risen from the rocks not fifty yards away. Lloyd was mortally wounded, his back broken. Wood tried to lift him but was unable to do so. However Campbell, rushing forward, picked up the dying man and carried him to where the escort was taking shelter. Wood turned to follow Campbell but his horse was shot and killed instantly, knocking Wood down as it fell. Struggling to his feet he too reached the cattle kraal where he found Lloyd already dead. He then instructed Campbell to order the Border Horse to storm the boulders where the marksmen hid. Campbell's orders were ignored; the Border Horse argued that 'the position was unassailable'. Campbell gave the order three times (it is inferred to Weatherley), and then shouted to Wood: 'Damn him! He is a coward. I'll turn them out'. Not to be left behind Lysons shouted: 'May I go?' 'Yes!, forward the personal escort' .

And with that, four men of Wood's personal escort raced after Lysons and Campbell, who was in the lead. There is no mention of any of the Border Horse going forward. Campbell, revolver in hand, arrived panting at a cave and, as he peered inside, half his head was blown away killing him instantly. Lysons, supported by one of the soldiers, Private Fowler, stepped past Campbell's body and fired into the cave, a six-foot-wide passage in the rocks, clearing it of the enemy.

But there were still other marksmen to contend with. Bullets were striking all around as Wood got hold of his baggage horse and tried to lift Campbell's body aboard but the feat was beyond him. Private Walkinshaw, Wood's bugler, came to his assistance and, while Wood held the restive animal, Walkinshaw heaved the bodies of both Campbell and Lloyd onto its back and secured them.

Dennison's account is different.[83]

He first describes how the Border Horse left their bivouac in mist and drizzle and that the weather had cleared by the time they reached the mountain from whence a continuous fire could be heard. As they drew closer a party of horsemen, with Wood in the lead, was seen a short way ahead, galloping east. The party drew rein and Weatherley hastily explained how they had got separated from Buller on the previous day and then imparted the momentous news of sighting the Zulu army. Wood refused to believe him: 'Nonsense, I have had my men out yesterday, there is no Zulu impi about.'

Hearing Wood's retort, Dennison could not restrain himself and butted in: 'I saw them Sir, I was in fact almost within touching distance of them and judge them to be a strong force.' 'Can't be Dennison, you are mistaken.' Wood then dismissed him and Dennison said no more.

Weatherley then turned to follow Buller's tracks up the mountain and Dennison suggested that, as they would obviously come under enemy fire, they should leave the horses where they were, recovering them once they had cleared the way on foot. Wood, overhearing the conversation, countermanded the suggestion saying that the others had gone up with their horses and the Border Horse must do the same. Dennison believed this to be folly but nevertheless started off, the Border Horse in the lead, with Wood and his men following, straight up the track leading to the summit. A short way on Wood gave the order to bear up, towards a cattle kraal behind which, amongst the rocks, it turned out that the enemy were hidden. Dennison surmised Wood's reason for turning in that direction was to secure the large herd of cattle the kraal contained. As they went they passed two dead men, most likely Williams and von Stietencron, killed earlier in the day. Abruptly the hidden marksmen opened fire and the two men who had accompanied Dennison on his reconnaissance of the Zulu camp the night before were shot dead in their tracks and a sergeant was badly wounded. All took cover and Dennison, followed by others of the Border Horse, started working forward, slipping from rock to rock, towards the snipers. Then Weatherley sent word to Dennison that he and the men must return. So they crept back to where Weatherley and his son sheltered, only to be told that Wood had given the order that the Border Horse must charge the enemy position. Dennison was dumbfounded: '. . . where men could only baboon-fashion make progress.' (If there were reluctance on Weatherley's part to go forward himself, it might well have been in deference to his disabled son.)[84]

As Dennison turned to go Campbell rushed past him to his death, calling: 'Forward Boys!'

A few minutes later Walkinshaw lifted Campbell's body back over the rocks, 'Lysons and Fowler giving assistance'. Dennison then recalled:

> I know that Colonel Wood stated in his report that the Border Horse hesitated, hence the reason Captain Campbell rushed forward. What I have stated is simple truth. The Border Horse never deserved a slur in action. Colonel Wood was mistaken.

The *Cape Argus* (of 10 April 1879), whose correspondent accompanied Wood's column, substantiated Dennison's claim:

> Colonel Wood gave the order to Colonel Weatherley to send men in and clear the rocks. The call for volunteers was promptly met, and Lieutenants Poole and H Parminter,[85] of Weatherley's corps, along with Captain Campbell, rushed forward, leading the men on. Almost touching his head with a rifle, a Zulu blew poor Campbell's brains out.

Dennison went on to record that, as soon as Campbell fell, Wood departed, taking one of the wounded Border Horse troopers, with him. In this Dennison was mistaken. In fact, before Wood left, he set about burying his two staff officers, and had the Border Horse stand guard while he did so.

The discrepancies between these two accounts of the same events will be considered at the conclusion of the chapter. For the moment we shall continue with Wood's account.

Walkinshaw, having secured the dead bodies of Campbell and Lloyd on the packhorse, Wood started to retreat downhill: 'The fire from the rocks on all sides was fairly accurate, killing many of the twenty-one ponies we had with us.'

Suddenly Wood remembered that earlier in the day he had borrowed Campbell's prayer book, a gift from his wife and, as he had a funeral service in mind, he not only required the book but felt obliged to return it to Mrs Campbell. However, it had been left in the saddlebag attached to Wood's horse lying dead back up the hill. So Wood instructed Walkinshaw, 'who was entirely unconcerned with the bullets':

> Climb up the hill and get the prayer-book in my wallets: while I do not want you to get shot for the saddle, you are to take all risks for the sake of the prayer-book.

Wood waited while Walkinshaw made his way up the hill in a leisurely fashion. He soon returned, not only with the prayer book but with the saddle also, carrying it on his head. Both men then made their way 300 yards downhill, taking the loaded packhorse with them, being joined by Wood's escort and the Border Horse as they went. When Wood was satisfied that the ground was sufficiently free of rocks to dig a grave, he gave the task to his native escort while the Border Horse stood guard over the proceedings. The only implements available with which to dig were the native escort's assegais. It was a 'laborious business' and at the approach of '300 Zulus', when the grave was four feet deep, 'the men got flurried' and bundled the bodies in. Wood ordered them out and continued with his pious folly while casualties mounted all around him. Finally he read an abridged version of the burial service but not before the Border Horse had lost six men dead and seven wounded – almost twenty per cent of the unit, a high price to pay for a decent burial.[86] One can only speculate that Wood had

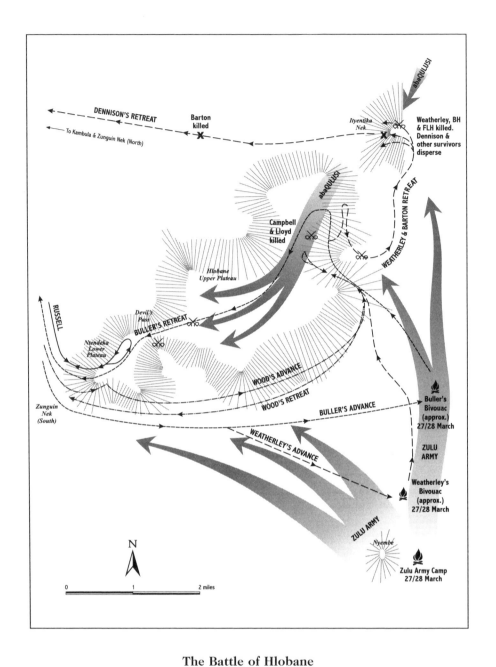

The Battle of Hlobane
A complex engagement and, after Isandlwana, the worst British defeat of the war.

become momentarily unbalanced by the loss of his officers, especially of Campbell of whom he was particularly fond.

On the plateau all firing had ceased and the commotion surrounding Wood's burial service attracted the attention of the FLH. Below them the troopers could now clearly see the abaQulusi trying to surround Wood and the Border Horse. Immediately the FLH opened fire, abruptly dispersing the encroaching warriors. Wood, having been given this respite, ordered Weatherley to follow the track to the summit and join Buller – presumably leaving the dead Border Horse troopers unburied where they had fallen. Wood, however, had decided to retrace his steps and rejoin Russell.[87]

The whole of Buller's column – with the exception of A Troop, FLH, which still stood guard over the way down – had made its way leisurely hither and thither west towards Devil's Pass, gathering cattle as they went. They had been in no hurry; time had flown, however, and the normally aggressive abaQulusi seemed to have been too easily subdued into giving up their cattle. Regimental Sergeant-Major Fred Cheffins of Raaff's Rangers, remembered a feeling of foreboding as the morning wore on:

> While on the mountain many jokes were cracked as everyone thought of the present not of the future. Had we known better the latter provision would have been made for our souls rather than our bodies. At last a sort of reaction set in. Everybody seemed anxious to get down as if a warning voice foretold to them the danger that was at hand.

The Zulu army, that had been observed by Dennison and whose presence had been dismissed by Wood, had long since been aroused and, in three columns, had deviated from its intended course towards Kambula and was now, at a jog, eating up the distance to Hlobane. But, for the moment, it remained unseen in the undulations of the plain. However, Buller and his men were about to confront a more immediate peril.

Mbelini and his warriors had now returned to the mountain, stealthily making their way to the north-east tip of Hlobane where it is joined by the Ityentika Nek. There he rendezvoused with the rest of his forces that had remained on the mountain. The assembly was now 6,000 strong. His plan was simple: he would use the traditional Zulu formation of attack: left and right wings, or horns, moving fast to encircle the enemy and block all escape while the chest moved in to overwhelm. Yet the way that Mbelini planned it, there would be no need for the encircling horns, the mountain itself would serve instead, its sheer rock walls would ensure there was no escape to the north or south. 'Somtseu's impi', as the Zulus called Wood's column, would be crushed in the funnel of Devil's Pass. The few that might escape to the lower plateau, together with those of Russell's column who would also be fleeing from the lower slopes, would be eaten up by the fast approaching regiments of the Zulu king. However, seething with impatience, Mbelini could see that the Zulu army would not be in time to block all escape as already thousands of abaQulusi cattle were being herded away by the hated Swazi mercenaries and Hamu's 'dogs'. It was more than a Qulusi heart could bear, to stand by and watch their beloved beasts being stolen. The abaQulusi would have to manage this battle on their own and hope that Zulu support would arrive in time.

A Troop was the first to see them. Although there had been intermittent sniping back and forth ever since they had been ordered to guard the way down, now, suddenly, the enemy began to mass. One trooper noticed that not only had their number increased considerably, it was also obvious from the colour of their shields, that an entirely new regiment had arrived. Could it have been Mbelini and his followers returning from their unsuccessful attempts to ambush Buller? The terrain to the front of their troop had become 'black with running Zulus', as had the mountainside beyond. The horsemen were in imminent danger of encirclement. Trooper George Mossop, a youngster in his mid-teens, later described his flight as the Zulus came on:

> As one man we rose like a covey of partridges and ran for the horses which were being held sixty yards in our rear . . . I do not remember touching ground even with my toes . . . and we all appeared to reach the horses at the same moment. The plateau just about there was full of scattered Zulus; my pony avoided them instinctively and we passed through safely until I was near the northern cliff.

Others had seen the mass of abaQulusi coming across the Ityentika Nek:

> Strong bodies of Zulus were climbing every available baboon path with the intention of cutting us off from the only two passes by which it was possible to descend. At the same time two larger columns were seen approaching along the top of the mountain to the eastward [from Ityentika Nek].

Buller until now had no idea of the gathering peril and, believing the day's work done, had just given instructions to Captain Barton to return to Kambula with C Troop, FLH, by the way they had come. Barton was to join up with A Troop, relieve them of their lonely vigil, then pick up the bodies of Williams and von Stietencron and take them back to camp. Buller and Barton were unaware that A Troop had already been scattered by the abaQulusi.

Hardly had Barton and his men trotted off when Buller not only saw the massing abaQulusi, but also the fast approaching Zulu army. Realising Barton's danger, Buller sent two troopers after him with a hastily scribbled note: 'Retreat at once to camp by the right side of the mountain.'

This hasty message was to cause their deaths: Buller had assumed Barton would take 'the right side of the mountain' as the northern side but Barton was riding east. When the message was received he thought it was merely a confirmation of his oral orders and he continued to ride on a collision course with the Zulu army.

Buller, now conscious that he had been out-manoeuvred and was trapped with Devil's Pass as his only possible route of survival, 'passed us at a gallop' as one man remembered 'ordering us to ride hard for the krantz at the Nek, the only road open.'[88]

At the other end of Hlobane, on the lower plateau, things had gone well so far. The looted cattle were mostly off the mountain and many, herded by the black auxiliaries, were on their way to Kambula. Russell had cause to be complacent and was about to give the general order for his column to vacate the plateau altogether when a messenger, clearly in a state of alarm, rode up pointing and gesticulating towards the mountains and rolling hills to the south. Russell looked in that direction in some apprehension but for the moment could see nothing to cause anxiety. He noticed what, for an instant, appeared to be shadows moving across the plain below in the direction of Hlobane; then it struck him, there were no clouds to cause them. With fearful realisation he knew he was looking at an immense Zulu army. The time, according to Russell was 9.00 a.m. He immediately scribbled a note to Wood and began to gather his force together. He was already thinking of abandoning the cattle as he believed that now, under threat, he could not possibly protect such a large quantity of beasts. However, once off the mountain, it was his intention to remain near 'Hlobane Hill, and join Colonel Buller if necessary'. With that Russell and his column abandoned its position at the bottom of Devil's Pass, rode back across the nek, led their horses down the western end and with apprehension awaited events.

After having parted company with Weatherley and the Border Horse, Wood and his escort had set off west to join up with Russell once again. Although Wood was shattered at the loss of Campbell and Lloyd together with the rest of the casualties, the operation as a whole appeared to be going well: Buller had taken the upper plateau and the auxiliaries had already been seen driving looted cattle down the slopes. And it was assumed that Russell had experienced little opposition.

Wood and his party had approximately seven miles to ride to meet up with Russell and there seemed to be no need to hurry. The exuberance of the early morning was long since spent and, with the glamour of war now an illusion, Lysons rode in silence while the young solders of Wood's personal escort talked in whispers. Mthonga and his followers scouted ahead and, as they topped a slight rise, Mthonga suddenly saw the rapidly advancing enemy. Wood later reported that, at that moment, he and his escort 'were under the centre of the mountain' so they had about four miles to go to meet up with Russell. Wood immediately scribbled a note:

> Below Inhlobane. 10h:30 am. 28/3/79. There is a large army coming this way from the south. Get into position on Zunguin Nek.[89]

He gave the note to Lysons who spurred away to find Russell while Wood and the remainder of the party, pushing their tired mounts into the best pace possible, fled across the front of the Zulu army. A detachment of the Nkobamakosi regiment attempted to cut them off but without success.

When Lysons arrived at Zunguin Nek (south) Russell had been well aware of the approaching army for almost two hours. He hurriedly read Wood's note and, assuming he had been ordered to take up a position on Zunguin Nek (north), six miles away, he hastened off in that direction having ordered all the cattle to be abandoned. This, in effect, meant abandoning not only the cattle but also the auxiliaries who were herding them. Commandant Lorraine White, commanding Wood's Irregulars, was prepared to stay with his men and sent a staff officer, Lieutenant P. F. D'Arcy, after Russell asking permission to stay and help his men, as D'Arcy later reported:

> I went to Colonel Russell with the above order [Lorraine White's request]. He interrupted me before I could finish speaking and said 'Tell Commandant White to leave the cattle, and push on as fast as he can.[90]

Captain Charlie Potter and Lieutenant Williams, 58th Regiment, both officers of Wood's Irregulars, and Messrs. Calverley and Combrinck attached to Hamu's warriors, all decided to stay with their men and, like many of the men that they chose not to desert, perished with them.

On the upper plateau, the men, still scattered in twos and threes, began to panic as the alarm spread; officers were seen galloping recklessly over the broken terrain while frightened messengers hurried by shouting that the Zulus were close behind. A great scare settled upon the horsemen and many rode this way and that, seeking their officers and comrades only to find suddenly that they were isolated and alone. Then the abaQulusi appeared in their thousands, like magic it seemed, from nowhere. There was only one way to go: follow the rest, follow the retreat that was rapidly becoming a rout, to Devil's Pass. Young William Hussels in a letter to his mother wrote:

> . . . but whilst on top, we were still engaged with some of them, when we saw thousands of others coming in from all directions to reinforce those with whom we were fighting.[91]

Lieutenant William Pickering (who was later to achieve prominence as Cecil Rhodes's right hand man) of Baker's Horse, who only months before had left his job with the Standard Bank to seek adventure, later wrote to his old manager (at the same time expressing the hope that should he survive he would be reinstated in his old job):

> It was then that a regular panic took possession of the men and everyone cantered as hard as possible over the rocky surface of the hill, but when I came to the ridge of the precipice, where 500 horsemen had to go down, I was speechless . . .[92]

George Mossop, separated from his troop, alone and lost in the expanse of the plateau, set off westward:

> Suddenly the ground dipped into a hollow, and scattered about were some 300 to 400 Zulus who, sighting me, began shouting and pointing their spears while they formed a half moon, which covered a considerable distance, cutting me off . . . I think the horse realised the predicament as well as I did, for he was dancing under me with excitement . . . His ears pointed forward and then back and he was pulling hard to get away in the direction of the running Zulus who had almost completed their formation. Cut off on all sides . . . I gave the horse his head . . . He shot off like a rocket down the slope, straight to the centre of the crescent. He again became the wild animal, all his instincts urging him to break away from the enemies who had surrounded him . . . It was a bit too much for me, and taking a firm grip on the reins, I tried to pull him up . . . but made no impression on him . . . When fifteen paces from the enemy, a few on our right rushed in to support those immediately on our front, leaving a narrow gap in their line. Like a hare with a pack of dogs behind it, the horse swerved and darted into the breach . . . Their spears were poised for a thrust, but we had flashed past them before they had made up their minds to strike.

Mossop rode free towards Devil's Pass.

Sergeant-Major Cheffins, who had felt a sense of foreboding earlier in the day when all was quiet, now witnessed the fear and trepidation that followed: 'Everyone seemed struck with panic, and everyone endeavoured to reach the other side of the mountain.'[93]

Captain Barton and C Troop, FLII, on their way to pick up the dead bodies of Williams and von Stietencron before riding back to Kambula, led a charmed life for a while. Somehow they passed the advancing abaQulusi unseen, reached the top of the descent – now deserted by A Troop – and started to go down towards the oncoming tide of Zulu regiments.

Colonel Weatherley and his Border Horse, after their fraught encounter with Wood, had followed Buller's trail and had hardly gained the summit when a hatless youngster rode up and shouted that they were to return to camp at once, as the mountain was about to be surrounded.

The Border Horse carried a wounded man by the name of Sergeant

Hlobane as seen from the Zunguin plateau

Adapted from a drawing by Colonel John North Crealock. Using artistic licence, the distance between the two features has been reduced: the actual distance between the Zunguin plateau and Devil's Pass is over five miles.

Key:

A) The Zulu army approaching from the south, first seen at approximately 9.00 a.m.

B) Buller's column ascended Hlobane in the early hours of 28 March from the east.

C) Devil's Pass.

D) The Ntendeka or lower plateau.

E) (i) Approximate position of Buller's rearguard.

   (ii) abaQulusi reinforcements – possibly Mbelini's returning *impi* – advance across the Ityentika Nek.

F) Ityentika Nek.

G) The direction of Barton's and Dennison's descent.

H) (i) The direction of Russell's ascent in the early morning and subsequent retreat to Zunguin Nek, north.

   (ii) Buller's escape route after descending Devil's Pass.

Fischer and, having reached the lower slopes without incident, halted to make a stretcher for him that could be secured to a pack horse. As they set about this task Barton and his troop overtook them. 'Don't delay Colonel Weatherley', Barton called as he passed, 'the mountain is surrounded.'[94]

Now extremely apprehensive and not wishing to be left behind, they bundled the wounded man onto a horse and roped him in place. Then they spurred after Barton who had got 500 yards ahead and was about to pass between two stone cattle kraals that had the appearance of an ideal ambush site. Barton, sensing the danger, took the FLH through the gap at a gallop but the trap was ready to be sprung and, at point-blank range, the enemy opened fire, emptying a number of saddles and sending terror-stricken horses galloping back into the oncoming riders. Barton, rallying the men as best he could, and with the abaQulusi following, made a hasty retreat, leaving the dead and wounded behind. Then, after combining with the Border Horse, the two units spurred east hoping eventually to find a way off the mountain to the north but they were riding straight towards the Ityentika Nek where Mbelini had marshalled his men, a large number of whom were still there.

With the horses all but done, the pursuing warriors were gaining fast. It was time to try anything to lighten the load, anything that would give their horses a turn of speed. Blankets and saddlebag straps were cut away and the items discarded in their wake. Coffee pots and bandoliers of ammunition followed but the pursuers continued to draw closer. Dennison remembered:

> On behind us came the enemy in swarms faster than we could move. We helped the men on all we could but several were caught and quietly despatched by the enemy. One man, Riley, a trumpeter, we saw dismount from his horse and fire on the advancing foe, then turning the rifle to his head shot himself.

One trooper, a Frenchman by the name of Grandier, was dismounted and caught alive, a prisoner of the abaQulusi; he would have a tale to tell.

Those still mounted pressed on. Barton shouted and suggested they halt and make a stand but Weatherley and Dennison knew that there was too little ammunition to do so; it had either been discarded or whittled away whilst they had stood guard and Wood had conducted his burial service. There was no option but to gallop and hope. Soon they reached Ityentika Nek. It rose before them in a gentle slope to the north but as the lead riders reached the crest they reined to a sudden halt – but only for a moment, just long enough to take in the dizzy descent and to realise there was no escape.

> Then hope gave way, brave men now defenceless became panic-stricken, death pressed on behind and our retreat, to all appearances, cut off in front.[95]

Many scattered believing they would stand a better chance alone – their only chance – but one by one they were caught, and overwhelmed. Some the warriors killed immediately, some lived a few moments longer, long enough to be carried to the edge of the abyss where the warriors swung their victims, as if in play, by their arms and legs, then let them go into the void, seemingly to be suspended for a moment, only to drop and be smashed on the rocks far below. A lucky few managed to evade their pursuers and reached the plain.

Twenty men kept with Weatherley and Dennison and together they veered to the east where the ledge on which they rode ended abruptly with a decline to a small waterfall five feet below.

Dennison pushed through to the front and, trusting his life to his 'noble horse', he spurred forward. The next moment they were sliding, slithering, loose rocks and brambles flying, in a mad descent with those who could follow close behind, while Weatherley, sword in hand, fell with his son under a flurry of assegai thrusts.

But the pursuit was not yet over. Below them a gallery of cliffs still barred their descent. Following the contour of the mountain, Dennison and those who still survived now rode north-east, frantically searching for a gentler slope that would lead them to safety, but all the while encountering more pockets of the enemy. Using their carbines as clubs, swinging them like polo sticks, they battered their way through. Then, a mile or so along the contour, they found a way that bypassed the cliffs enabling them, at last, to reach the plain. Now, with the addition of a few troopers who had made the descent independently, they numbered less than thirty, including Barton and Dennison. But worse was to come. They were being pursued by some mounted warriors of the Zulu army who, having ridden ahead of the main columns, had followed the pursuit and, having being directed to an easier descent by the abaQulusi, were close on the survivors' heels. Barton, who had taken Lieutenant Poole up behind him, had dropped to the rear where shortly, his horse being so exhausted it could hardly stand, both men dismounted. Poole was the first to die and, as Barton faced death, he raised his revolver to shoot the nearest Zulu only to have the weapon misfire. The warrior, now aware that the white man was defenceless and having already killed several that day, decided to take Barton prisoner, following the orders of his king that prisoners should be taken. Barton instinctively realised the warrior's purpose and doffed his hat in submission but, as he did so, another Zulu drew level and shot him. As Barton fell wounded the first warrior, not wishing another to have the credit of killing his prisoner, assegaied and put to death the wounded man.[96]

Dennison and the few that remained continued to ride across the plain towards Potter's Store until finally their pursuers had dwindled to but three. With a few rounds of ammunition remaining, Dennison indicated an ambush site up ahead where the survivors hurriedly dismounted. As their pursuers rode into the trap they were all killed at point-blank range.

On the upper plateau, all who could had fled west where they were not only confronted by the funnel of Devil's Pass but also by a stone wall across much of the approach, narrowing the access to the pass still further. The abaQulusi had originally built the wall to prevent their cattle stumbling down the pass and as a defence against an enemy attempting to take the upper plateau from below. It was never anticipated that it would form so effective a trap for fleeing horsemen. Lieutenant Pickering estimated that the gap was so narrow that no more than four men, leading their horses, could descend together. Cheffins remembered that when he reached the pass:

> A regular confusion took place as everyone wanted to get down first, for it was observed that large numbers of the enemy were making their way to the spot on which we were gathered. It was known by everyone that we were defenceless in hand-to-hand encounters as we had only our rifles which, when once discharged, were comparatively useless at close quarters. And so each one knew as if by instinct that our only hope was our horses. Our prospects were indeed hopeless. The place was most rugged and steep – the most dangerous anyone short of a maniac ever attempted to get over. The greatest difficulty was to get the horses over perpendicular rocks five and six feet high. The horses had to be pushed down, large boulders had to be climbed over. Under any other circumstances no one would ever attempt such a road. To descend such a dangerous mountain with kaffirs on each side armed with guns, assegais and battle-axes is almost too horrid to think about.

In their fear and eagerness to descend the pass some discarded everything that could hinder flight: arms, ammunition and even their horses were abandoned – and without a horse all were dead men. Some did the opposite and, in fear of losing their mounts, hung on to their heads too tightly, preventing free movement, and in consequence man and horse stumbled and fell, bouncing down over the rocks to land injured 160 feet below.

The noise at the crest of Devil's Pass had become demonic. The yells of the ecstatic warriors, the screams of terrified horses, gunfire, curses, and the cries of wounded men and animals merged into a cacophony of dread. An unknown trooper of Raaf's Rangers recorded the terror of the moment as he and a few other brave men attempted to form a skirmishing line to hold their attackers off:

> Leaving our horses with a spare man who took them behind a nearby kranz for cover, we took up positions and started firing at the warriors that were visible, trying to give our rear most men a chance to make good their escape. It was a sad sight we saw as the frightened men and beasts tried to flee these maddened savages who were stabbing and slashing and in some cases pushing men and horses over the plateau's edge. We kept this position for about twenty or so minutes, thus ensuring the escape of at

least some of our comrades . . . I commenced my firing again until I felt a tap on my shoulder. I turned around to find Sergeant Chinn standing above me. He leaned toward me so as to be heard above the noise, and told me to follow him, which I did along with perhaps seven others, from various units, including one man from Baker's Horse.

We scrambled back over the rocky ground towards the spot where our horses were, only to find on reaching there that both they and the horse holders were gone.

By now the pass which led to the lower plateau was choked with men and animals all trying to escape the mountain as much as the enemy. But the Zulus seemed to be everywhere.

As our small band looked down upon this murderous confusion, I truly think I speak for all of us when I say I believed that this would be our last day on Earth – and indeed for some of us it was.

Our trance was broken by a mounted Officer who, as he rode past, shouted 'The game is up Sergeant, give your chaps a chance.' I can only assume that this Officer was in the vanguard of his unit, because before we could move we were being swept down the pass by a wave of men and horses, many of the latter being without riders.

Our group became instantly separated from each other. And although I don't recall many individual instances during the descent, I do recall seeing Sergeant Chinn spin around and fall to one side. I could not get to him for the amount of others between and I felt sure he must be killed or condemned to be so. On this count I am glad to say I was wrong. At this stage I felt very alone, as for the first time during that day I was acting as an individual under no one's direct command. The fear I felt realizing this was most acute. As I reached the Ntendeke I came upon two of my comrades Trooper Banks and 'Jacky' Smith, both of whom I had left on the higher plateau . . .

There his tale ended – the following page of his letter has not survived – and posterity does not even know his name.

When Mossop arrived he found the entrance to the pass 'almost filled with dead horses and dead men both black and white.' He spoke to a man beside him as they both struggled forward: 'Do you think there is any chance of pushing through?' Mossop shouted. The man paused for a moment and replied 'Not a hope', and with that placed the muzzle of his carbine in his mouth and pulled the trigger. 'A lot of his brains and other soft stuff' splashed onto Mossop's neck. Mossop could bear no more and, casting aside the reins of his pony, he madly and blindly bounded down the pass. 'My only thought was to get away from all these horrors.'[97]

But, while most fled, a brave few, Buller, Raaff, Gardner, Knox Leet, D'Arcy, together with a number of courageous NCOs and troopers, rallied and, firing volleys, halted the onrush of warriors. For a moment the rout resolved into a retreat until someone, mistaking advancing abaQulusi for auxiliaries, shouted to cease firing. Obeying that unfortunate command proved calamitous; in moments the warriors were in amongst the rearguard and all organised resistance ceased. On top of Devil's Pass it was now every man for himself.

Kritzinger of the Burger Force reached the pass but found he could not get near the entrance and that the wall built by the abaQulusi blocked further escape. He recalled:

> There were men still hanging on to their horses and trying to drag them along and across the wall and down the slope, and [some] were killed whilst still trying to drag their horses over the wall. I saw all these bunched up in a crowd, and so I worked to the side away from the bunch of struggling men and horses and I backed my horse up to the wall . . . and got him reared up, and tipped him over the wall . . .

As the horse rolled down the slope, sliding on its side, Kritzinger gathered up his gun, which he had propped up against the wall and, jumping over, followed his mount. He found it lying prostate, reluctant to rise. Kritzinger continued:

> I went to my horse and I had one spur left, I stuck this in my horse and he jumped [up] and I had to run down the slope to get clear of him coming down after me . . . I wanted to ride off from the nek right away but one of the Colonial officers said, 'I shall shoot if you ride away, you must stay and fight.' This officer had a revolver and a rifle. I stayed and all the Colonial men, about fifty of them, stayed and shot at the Zulus [abaQulusi] in the krantzes and the Zulus [abaQulusi] climbing up the nek . . . the place seemed to be alive with Zulus [abaQulusi].[98]

Lieutenant Blaine of the FLH, who had stood with the rest firing volleys to the end, now pushed into the crush dragging his horse behind him. He later recalled:

> Then an awful confusion took place – horses fell on top of the rocks and broke their necks and legs – you saw horses on top of men. I was under my horse for about two or three minutes and thought it was all up with me. We shouted to the men not to hurry, but to take it coolly. The kaffirs got in amongst us and assegaied our fellows. We could not hit them even with our carbines for we were too jammed up.[99]

In similar vein D'Arcy wrote:

> I had to think of myself and got half way down when a stone half the size of a piano came bounding down . . . It came right on my horse's leg cutting it right off. I, at the same time, got knocked down the hill by another horse and was nearly squeezed to death . . . I was about to take the saddle when I heard a scream; I looked up and saw the Zulus [abaQulusi] right in amongst the white men stabbing horses and men.[100]

D'Arcy managed to scramble down to the nek below where Buller was holding men in check and where he once again formed a rearguard, most of whom, including Piet Uys and his sons, were among those who had stood firm on top.

———⊶◦⊷———

But where was Russell and his column of 200 horsemen who should have been there at the bottom of Devil's Pass to cover Buller's retreat?

In his report written the following morning Russell stated:

> Shortly before 9.00 a.m. [on the 28th] it was reported to me that a Zulu army was seen on the range of hills to the south of the Hlobana [sic]. At 9.00 a.m. I sent a message addressed to Colonel Wood to that effect, and I collected my force together. I thought that there would be time to get away the cattle. The Zulu army assumed such large proportions and moved with such extreme rapidity that about 10.00 a.m. I thought it necessary to abandon the cattle as I did not see how I was to protect the large number of natives who were driving them. I moved all my force down the hill, I told Commandant White to move his men at once to the Zunguin (as they were in very small numbers and would have only impeded the action of mounted men with whom I intend to remain near the Hlobana Hill, and join Colonel Buller if necessary). At this time I received a memorandum from Colonel Wood, dated 10.30 a.m. desiring me to 'get into position on Zunguin Nek'. I moved to that point, therefore, and remained there till the last of Colonel Buller's force passed towards camp, and I received further orders to move east to cover the natives who were retiring on camp . . .[101]

As we have seen, only Commandant Lorraine White and his officers protested against, what must have been apparent to all, the desertion of Buller's column. Even the fiery Schermbrucker, who had earlier boasted that he would ride alone into the Zulu king's kraal if ordered to do so, failed to object. A closer look at Russell's officers reveals that a number, like Russell himself, had either escaped from Isandlwana or had witnessed the horror of the battlefield that night. The officers of the Natal Native Horse, Lieutenants Cochrane, Raw, Vause, and most likely Henderson, had all fought at Isandlwana, making their escape over Fugitives' Drift; Lieutenant Browne and most of the men of the Mounted Infantry had spent the night in the camp. Had these officers and men not witnessed Isandlwana or its aftermath, they might not have meekly followed Russell's lead.

In defence of Colonel Russell the following appeared in the *Times of Natal* in May:

> We are glad to find the following in a [unsigned] letter from Kambula: 'The censure of Colonel Russell, in covering the retreat of the unfortunate volunteers from the Zlobane [sic] mountain, does not seem to have been well-founded. It was his duty to clear the lower plateau and this he did. He then became aware of the Zulu enemy in the valley below, and then it was his duty to secure the safe retreat of the mounted

infantry and the force entrusted to him – so he proceeded to descend as soon as possible. He got them safely down, and did not even hear the firing on the upper plateau . . .[102]

It cannot be credited that those on the lower plateau did not hear the tumult going on above them and it is at complete odds with Schermbrucker's recollection of events. Schermbrucker even states that the Zulu army was 'unquestionably attracted by the sound of the firing of Colonel Buller's column', whereas Russell's column, close at hand, supposedly heard nothing. Schermbrucker even attempted to justify Russell's departure by suggesting that, having seen the Zulu army, Wood's first concern was for the safety of the Kambula camp. Schermbrucker wrote:

> . . . his [Wood's] resolution was taken promptly and decisively. A messenger was instantly dispatched to Colonel Cecil Russell to appraise him of the approach of an overwhelming Zulu army with instructions to communicate, if possible, with Colonel Buller; both columns, Buller's and Russell's, to retire from the mountain without a moment's delay and hurry via the shortest route and at the highest possible speed to reach the camp.[103]

As we have seen, Wood's message contained nothing of the sort.

By the time the first of the fugitives had run the gauntlet of Devil's Pass and had reached the neck of the lower plateau, Russell's mounted men, having abandoned the cattle and the auxiliaries, were hurrying to Zunguin Nek (north), six miles away.

—※◦❖—

The lower plateau was now a confusion of riderless horses, many broken and wounded, and dismounted men. Mossop arrived at the bottom of the pass, terror-stricken and breathless, and was grabbed in flight by Buller who cuffed him hard and ordered him back to find his pony, for without it he was 'a dead man'. Mossop's fear of Buller, 'that silent saturnine, bloodthirsty man', was as great as his fear of the enemy, and he climbed back, miraculously found his pony and, surviving two awful falls, successfully reached the plain below the plateau.

Buller, again supported by a faithful few, formed a line of defence some way back from the bottom of the pass. The nek between became a no-man's-land into which brave men, miraculously still mounted, rode to take up behind them fleeing comrades, often snatching them within touching distance of the relentless abaQulusi. The list of brave men who saved others from death is long and all fully qualified, but few received that most coveted reward of all, the Victoria Cross.

D'Arcy, on arriving horseless at the bottom of the pass, was rescued on no fewer than three occasions: while running for his life he was picked up by 'a fellow called Francis' riding a saddleless horse and with a riem (length of cowhide) for a bridle, but before they got far D'Arcy gave up his seat to a wounded trooper; again running as fast as he could go and with warriors hot on his heels, D'Arcy was taken up behind Buller himself who undoubtedly saved his life; then, after being dumped by Buller who returned to the fray for others struggling on foot, D'Arcy was given a final lift by Major Tremlett. There seems to have been more to it than that, however, for Buller said of D'Arcy: 'Although dismounted, he rallied the men, saving the lives of many.'[104]

Gardner, who still rankled over the malicious ditty that had accused him of cowardice and therefore, as he confided in his sister, to prove his valour 'went out voluntarily with every charge', also found himself dismounted amongst maddened enemies who were eager to kill him. He was saved by Commandant Brecher, another officer of Wood's Irregulars who had stayed behind when Russell rode away.

Trooper Charley Hewitt who had successfully got down Devil's Pass with his horse intact, rode back across the nek several times to bring in fleeing footmen, one up behind and two hanging on to the stirrup leathers. Hewitt, having been persuaded by an exhausted man to let him ride his horse, dismounted and ran alongside, giving the man his carbine and bandolier to carry in order to lighten the load. Having thus acquired horse and arms, the man spurred off leaving Hewitt to his fate. But other brave men took Hewitt up and finally the cowardly thief was overtaken, relieved of the horse and abandoned.

Corporal Will Vinnicombe of the FLH, an athlete proud of his running prowess, voluntarily dismounted and '. . . gave his horse to two other men saying that the horse could carry two but not three, and that of the three he was best on his legs.'[105] The other unsung heroes were civilian surgeons Connolly and Jolly who not only attended to the wounded throughout the running battle but often, taking their patients' carbines, fired on the enemy.

One of the most notables losses of the day was the death of Piet Uys. Having arrived safely at the nek, Uys glanced back to see one of his sons in difficulty. Forcing his way between fleeing men and horses, Uys reached his boy and they were both struggling to return when a warrior raced up behind and plunged an assegai between the father's shoulders, killing him instantly. Buller was to lament:

> Our loss was very heavy, amongst them Mr Piet Uys, whose death is a misfortune to South Africa. One so courageous and so sagacious I shall never see again, we had better spared one hundred men.[106]

Whilst many fled regardless of others, for some courage and discipline changed the rout once again to the semblance of a retreat. Knox Leet, with his gammy leg (injured a few days earlier in a tug-of-war competition at the camp), also found himself unmounted at the bottom of the pass but managed to catch a pack-horse. He met up with Buller as the remainder of the column was fighting its way towards the far end of the lower plateau and the plain beyond. As they rode, Knox Leet reminded Buller that they had been there during an earlier reconnaissance and that they should go down by the north side as they had done previously. Buller agreed and Knox Leet, assuming that everyone would follow, pressed on to scout the descent accompanied by Lieutenant Dunscombe of Wood's Irregulars, who was mounted, and Lieutenant Metcalfe Smith of the Frontier Light Horse, on foot. It was not long before they realised that the main body had disappeared and that they were being followed by a large number of abaQulusi not far behind. Soon the warriors, shouting loudly to one another, started to close in, shooting as they came. Worse still, Knox Leet had got his direction wrong and the three fugitives were suddenly faced by a precipice. They turned across the face of the enemy and got the direction right, but in doing so came within spear-throwing distance of their foe. Soon a shower of assegais came hurtling towards them and at the same time Dunscombe's horse, completely exhausted, stopped dead. Revolver in hand, Dunscombe dismounted and shot three of his pursuers, one after the other, all within fifteen yards.

Metcalfe Smith, who had followed all the way on foot, was now so fatigued that, unable to go a step further, he just sat down helplessly to await his fate. Knox Leet also stopped in an effort to rally Metcalfe Smith and made him stand and catch hold of the pack-saddle in preparation for a tow. But it was no use and after a few steps Metcalfe Smith was so done-in that he could not go any further. Knox Leet determined to take him up behind but, with no stirrups to the pack-saddle, it was no easy matter. However, Dunscombe provided them with a few precious moments for, having run out of ammunition he had attracted the attention of all the pursuers. While they fell upon him spearing him to death, Metcalfe Smith managed to mount.[107] But he and Knox Leet were all but surrounded. At the same time they could see large numbers of warriors coming along the plain below, attempting to cut them off from Buller and the rest of the column who were now visible descending the mountain to their left. Suddenly, as all seemed lost, the ground became less steep and the valiant pack-horse increased its pace to take them to the comparative safety of Buller's rearguard.

With Metcalfe Smith having dismounted, Knox Leet, with Buller's permission, and still aboard the pack-horse, now forged ahead in an attempt to overtake Russell and order his return. But after two miles even the pack-horse could only muster a walk and Knox Leet stopped and waited for the rest of the column.[108] Finally it caught up and, still keeping a persistent enemy at bay, it eventually made Zunguin Nek (north), encountering Russell on the way. There is no record of what passed between Buller and Russell when the columns met.

In the meantime elements of both the Zulu army and the abaQulusi had overtaken and killed not only many of Wood's Irregulars and of Hamu's warriors, but also a large number of women and children from Hamu's clan who had been making their way to Kambula. The men of Wood's Irregulars who had been deserted by Russell but managed to survive, abandoned the column and were, ironically, later branded as deserters.

➤◦◄

And what had become of Wood and his escort since he had sent Lysons galloping off to Russell at 10.30 a.m.? After he cut across the vanguard of the Zulu army Wood's whereabouts for the remainder of the day are either unknown or confusingly described. One assumes he sent part of his escort off to warn Kambula camp of the approaching enemy and one would also assume that he eventually caught up with either Russell's or Buller's columns during the descent from the lower plateau. However, in his autobiography Wood says nothing of this period and it is not until 7.00 p.m. that he mentions his whereabouts again, stating that he 'remained on the Zunguin Mountain until 7 p.m., hoping to cover the retreat of any more of our men who might come up . . .' Wood also states that he sent a further message to Russell ordering him to cover the retreat of the auxiliaries but, as we have seen, Russell implied in his report that he was ordered to do so by Buller:

> I moved to that point [Zunguin Nek (north)] therefore, and remained there till the last of Colonel Buller's force passed towards the camp, and I received further orders to move east to cover the natives who were retiring on the camp.[109]

Neither Russell nor Buller mentioned having seen Wood and, in fact, Buller was under the impression, until he found him on Zunguin at 7.00 p.m., that Wood had been cut off and killed.[110] However, in a letter written eleven days after the battle, Private Edmund Fowler tells a different story. He describes how, after burying Campbell and Lloyd, they were making their way back to join Russell when they sighted the Zulu army.

> Gallop for your lives men [said Wood], which we did, and a hard run we had of it for twenty-five miles . . . and when we reached camp [Kambula] and told the news it caused a great sensation.[111]

Whatever his whereabouts may have been, Wood seems to have spent the larger part of the day alone, apart from his escort, and had much time for self recrimination and to reflect on his reputation that now lay in tatters. Others would have to be blamed for the tragic outcome of the day. Without admitting that Buller had been duped and had fallen into Mbelini's trap, it could be said that Hlobane had been successfully taken and that Buller and his column would have got off the mountain intact, with 2,000 head of cattle, had Russell remained to cover their retreat. The appearance of the Zulu army could be put down as unfortunate. And Russell, having deserted Buller, would be a self-made scapegoat. To justify and excuse himself for the deaths of his two staff officers, men with influential connections, would be more difficult. But on his eventual return to Kambula that night, when he learned from Dennison of the death not only of Weatherley but of the two officers of the Border Horse, Parminter and Poole, who had led the attack with Campbell against the unseen snipers, he found the opportunity he sought: he would present the cowardice of Weatherley's Border Horse as being the cause of Campbell's reckless courage and death.

The atmosphere at Kambula Camp that evening was heavy with gloom and apprehension as the defeated horsemen shuffled home. Private Banks of the 90th Light Infantry recalled the scene in a letter to his parents:

> I myself saw the men come into camp in twos and threes, without coats, rifles, and ammunition belts, having thrown them away to lighten themselves for running, when their horses were shot or lost. Then there were two on a horse, and perhaps you would see an officer come in mounted behind a trooper, glad to get in anyhow. Now and again, as the men came into camp, you would hear someone ask where was so-and-so?, and the answer would be 'Left behind, he's gone'. Then you could see the face of more than one strong man exhibit that emotion so seldom to be seen except through great trouble.[112]

Another report commented:

> The real truth of this sortie seems to be that while that same evening witnessed the enemy elated at their unexpected and easily won success, it also saw the British force dribbling back to camp in a dejected and disorganised condition.

Sergeant-Major Cheffins diligently wrote up his diary:

> One by one we came, two men on one horse, some men bare-footed, some without hats, coats, guns, ammunition, all these articles were considered by them as lumber and thrown away . . . Those even on horseback cut loose everything in order to pass over the ground with greater speed. When about a mile from the camp we were met by a party with spare horses from the camp from whom I obtained a remount . . . On entering the camp we could read despair on every man's face, not only for our adversaries of the day, but what might be expected from the powerful advance of the Zulu King . . . The disaster which befell us was caused mostly by the careless manner of our commanding officers. Had they forethought when all the cattle were collected, to order the men to an immediate retreat, hardly any lives would have been lost. We would have been able to return to camp loaded with booty . . . In descending the mountain it struck me that some of them were possessed of supernatural power and strength. How we enduring running is surprising (15 miles is a long distance to run and many of them ran the whole way) . . . Our horses must have been inspired as they seem to know as well as the men that danger was near, and that on their speed depended many lives . . . It is interesting to hear the different stories that are now related

respecting our engagement. Men whom I am certain never turned their faces back pretend to give better accounts than those who were defending them.

Dennison and his handful of survivors reached camp long after most had arrived. They had come by way of Potter's Store and heavy rain had drenched them to the skin before they reached the outskirts of Kambula. The campfires gave them direction in the dark and pouring rain. Dennison paused at the officers' mess tent of the Border Horse; it was empty as all except he were dead. Later he encountered Buller who opined that, had he had knowledge of the Zulu army earlier, all the horsemen and auxiliaries who had died might have been saved. Dennison then told him of how he had informed Wood of its proximity but had been curtly contradicted and dismissed. Buller looked Dennison 'square in the eyes and said "I believe you Dennison, what a sad mistake, but say nothing for the present, lay low."'[113]

Two Victoria Crosses were awarded for feats of valour on Hlobane. Wood immediately recommended Buller for the decoration and later also recommended Knox Leet – but only after Knox Leet had found it necessary to do a little lobbying. A week after Hlobane he wrote to a colleague in the United Kingdom:

> Before this reaches you the news of our big fight will have reached you, and the dispatches and newspaper accounts will have furnished you with the particulars . . . I enclose copies of my report. They will, I feel sure interest you, and the General will probably like to look at them. I have, I believe, been fortunate enough to be mentioned in the official dispatches. They all say here that I ought to get the VC for saving young Smith's life at the risk of my own, but Colonel Wood being a VC man himself, it is said, I do not know with what foundation, does not care to increase the number more than he can help. It is also said that there is an objection to recommending Field Officers but that seems absurd. I do not at all know myself whether I deserve it, but if I do it seems very hard that I should not get it. The statement from young Smith was sent in to Colonel Wood. Do you think I deserve it? If so can you assist me in the matter? You have connections with the press, and in that way (of course without compromising me in any way) you might bring public opinion to bear. I think it likely that the 'specials' of *The Times* and *Standard* will report my case, and if so you could easily work it without compromising me. Remember I only ask for you to do this if you think I thoroughly deserve it. Otherwise I would not have it at any price. I feel quite sure I can entirely depend upon you in this matter to act judiciously and energetically – I would of course give my eyes for a VC if outsiders think I deserve it, and it would be a grievous blow to me if I deserve it and do not get it.[114]

At Hlobane there were many as deserving as Buller and Knox Leet and it was not surprising that a correspondent should remark:

> The colonists have done good service in the war and it is to be regretted that they are so generally passed over by the military commanders. There are times, however, when their services have been so signally valuable that it is impossible to ignore them.[115]

Another report was more to the point:

> I am sorry to say that the spirit of confraternity amongst Imperial officers is an affliction of narrow sightedness; and if VCs were given to everyone who assisted to save the lives of his comrades that day, and to none other than the really deserving, the colonials would come in for the greatest share. On that day there were many individual acts of bravery performed by all branches of the service engaged, and there were also some who were panic stricken, and lost all presence of mind, who were not exclusively colonial . . .[116]

Two years later the correspondents would have been even more indignant to learn that, under pressure from 'Boy' Lysons's parents, General Sir Daniel Lysons KCB, who was Quartermaster-General at the War Office, and Lady Lysons in particular, Wood would recommend their son for the Victoria Cross. Not wishing it to appear too great a favour for persons in high places, Private Fowler of the 90th, who accompanied Lysons at the time, was also recommended and both received the award.

Of the 408 horsemen in Buller's column, including eight officers and men of the Royal Artillery, of whom none were injured, ninety-three were killed. All were colonials except for three imperial officers attached to colonial units. A further seven men who were severely wounded made it back to Kambula; the rest of the wounded, those who could not sit a horse, were left to their fate bringing the number of dead closer to 130. As Buller wrote in his official report:

> With so many dismounted men we experienced great difficulty in descending the mountain and, but for the exertions of a few our retreat would have been a rout, as it was we got down with the loss of those men only who were too badly wounded to be kept on horses . . .[117]

Over the coming months several expeditions to bury the dead were reported. On 20 May Wood, with an escort of forty colonials, found a number of skeletons, some recognisable by remnants of kit or clothing. Potter was recognised by his waistcoat and Lieutenant Williams by his boots that had a nametag sewn inside them. The two men were buried together. Wood read the burial service and was the first to throw in the ritual handful of soil. Other expeditions followed but one has the feeling that they were motivated by a desire to see the battle site rather than to find and bury the dead. At the time there was a clamour in the press, both locally and in Britain, for the Isandlwana dead to receive a dignified burial. The public was assured that the bodies of Captain Barton and Colonel Weatherley had been found and decently interred, which was certainly untrue in Barton's case as his body, with his notebook still partly readable, was located – with the assistance of the warrior who had killed him – one year later. Finding specific bodies in the vast area covered by the battle without an army of searchers would have been an impossible task.

However, one British officer who accompanied a patrol to the area several months later wrote a vivid and poignant description of what was found:

> On the crest of the narrow neck [Devil's Pass] we found numerous skeletons, many a good deal broken up, probably by the monkeys [baboons]; on the lower plateau were a few; and at the base of the mountain they lay thickly enough in a broad line, gradually getting thinner, till only detached bones were met, these extending for three miles from the actual mountain . . . the rags hanging here and there about them; some with the hair attached to the scalp.[118]

Today, the only memorials to the dead on either side are the graves of Campbell and Lloyd and a memorial stone, three miles away, where Piet Uys fell; both sites are difficult to find. There are no other memorials or known graves to this forgotten battle in a remote place.

Chapter 5
Kambula

'We were able to see dense masses of the enemy advancing in perfect order in four columns; it seemed their end would never come.'

Cape Argus, 1879

'. . . still they came on with the ferocity of tigers, never halting, never wavering . . . no soldiers in the world could have been more brave than the Zulus that day.'

The Scotsman, May 1879

The gloom and apprehension that had settled over Kambula camp the previous evening, as the defeated and demoralised horsemen reached safety, had largely lifted by morning. With the arrival of Wood's message during the late afternoon of the previous day that a large Zulu army was advancing, the camp had become a hive of earnest activity.

In the absence of Wood, Lieutenant-Colonel P. E. V. Gilbert, 13th LI, was in command and he had immediately set about strengthening the camp's already formidable defences. The dominant feature was the knoll, topping the Kambula ridge, recently fortified by Royal Engineers with sod walls, faced with stone, to about four feet in height. It was a small fort, thirty yards long and ten wide at its broadest point, and completely surrounded by a ditch.

There were 200 heavy wagons attached to the column and of these about 160 had gone to form the main laager, covering five to six acres, in the shape of a lopsided square. The wagons, described by one correspondent as 'these ponderous vehicles', chained together, formed the basis of the fortification in front of which shallow shelter trenches had been dug. The turfs thus removed were placed in front of the trenches to form low parapets, whilst others were piled on the platforms of the wagons to make two-tier firing positions around the circumference of the laager. Buckets of water, positioned behind the trenches, would give relief during the thirsty work that lay ahead. In addition, hundreds of ammunition boxes, each containing 600 rounds of 0.45-inch Martini-Henry cartridges, had been opened and placed conveniently close to the firing line. A smaller laager made up of the

The Battle of Kambula, 29 March 1879

The battle was a resounding British victory. Although it was not the final battle of the war it was undoubtedly the decisive one.

N

0 100 200 300 yards

NKOBAMAKOSI & uVe

Ngobamakhosi & uVe retreat

Nkobamakosi & uVe take shelter

Sortie by horsemen

SITE OF WOOD'S EARLIER CAMP SLIGHTLY FURTHER EAST

ZULU COMMANDERS 1 MILE FROM CAMP

Huts of Black Auxilliaries

ZULU CHEST

uDLOKO, uDUDUDU, mBUBE AND NDLONDLO

Bakery

uNOKHENKE, uTHULWANA AND NODUYENGWE

mCIJO AND uMBONAMBI

FORT KAMBULA

4 mobile guns

1 coy 13th 1 coy 90th

2 Mountain guns

Palisade fence

Cattle Laager

1 coy 13th and oxen

White Umfolozi

90th   90th

500 Horses

13th

13th

Colonials

90th

MAIN LAAGER

Manure heap

remaining wagons, known as the cattle laager, had been constructed fifty yards from the fort on the brink of the steep valley. In reality, instead of cattle the laager would house the 2,500 draft oxen that were as essential to the mobility of the column as motor fuel to a modern-day convoy. The cattle laager was joined to the fort by a wooden palisade, recently put in position at Wood's orders. The palisade was intended to hinder a sudden attack emerging from out of the valley. The cattle laager was similarly fortified with sod walls, shelter trenches and in every way was as prepared as the main laager.

The architect of Kambula's defences had been Major Charles Moysey of 7th Company, Royal Engineers. But Moysey had left Kambula a few days earlier to inspect the defences of Fort Amiel at Newcastle, leaving ten sappers in the charge of a sergeant to complete the work.

Amongst the civilian drivers and leaders, all fully armed, were many men wise in the way of laagering, none wiser than Fred Struben, a noted wagon master from the Transvaal, who, at Lieutenant-Colonel Gilbert's request, strengthened the defences still further by building walls between the wagons, made of biscuit boxes, bags of grain and flour, in fact anything that would stop a bullet or bar entry to an agile enemy. There were other not-so obvious forms of defence: over the past days the engineers had been busy placing range markers in every direction as far out from the camp as cannon and rifle fire would reach. And, around the near approaches, the ground had been sown with any object that would cut or hinder un-shod feet: cast-off horse shoes with protruding nails, broken glass and half buried bits of tin – primitive anti-personnel devices awaiting an unsuspecting enemy.

There were just over 2,200 men to defend the camp, including about 150 black auxiliaries; most of the defenders would occupy the main laager in company with 500 horses and the hospital tent.

The morning had dawned cold and misty. Whilst the senior officers of the previous day's assault on Hlobane set about writing their reports, endeavouring with stilted phrases to present the disaster as an unfortunate affair, patrols, made up of the fugitives of yesterday, rode out to locate the Zulu army. Meanwhile, in the camp, there was an air of calm as the wood-foraging parties that were essential in providing the fuel to cook two meals a day, went about their task as usual. Firewood had initially been plentiful close at hand, but now a trek of five miles with many wagons was necessary in order to bring in sufficient timber. Colonel Wood ensured that the camp had fresh bread daily; the cooks had hollowed out anthills – which made first class ovens that not only baked the bread, but 'furnished forth most appetising breakfasts and dinners'. The main meal was served at midday, 'dinnertime' and was 'eaten in the most primitive fashion, hotly contested all the time by millions of flies, reptiles and other creeping and flying things.'[119]

Unlike the ruthless destruction of all Zulu habitation that would be British policy a few months hence, the nearby homesteads around Kambula had not been molested and, as usual, Zulu women came to the camp bringing for sale milk, pumpkins, melons and other vegetables. These were purchased at a fixed tariff and the market went off in 'a most orderly manner'.

The oxen had long since been herded out to wherever grass could be found and, in addition, there were many captured cattle seeking grazing. Some of these had been looted the day before and driven back to Kambula at great risk by the auxiliaries.

It was a patrol led by the indefatigable Commandant Pieter Raaff which found the Zulu army. Looking down from the southern heights of Zunguin, the patrol could see a black mass, two miles distant, milling around the banks of the White Umfolozi River, probably finishing a lean breakfast. Raaff immediately sent word back to camp while he and the remainder of the patrol stayed to await events. During their wait a lone Zulu, a warrior of Hamu's clan, found them. The previous day, on the retreat from Hlobane, he had been cut off from his comrades and found himself about to be overtaken by pursuing Zulus. Casting off his forehead cloth insignia, he fell in with the enemy, passing himself off as one of them. He spent the night with them, overhearing that it was the Zulu commander's intention to attack Kambula the following day rather than bypass it to fall upon the scattered settlements of Luneburg, Utrecht and Dundee.

Raaff waited until the Zulu army had got into formation and was seen to be on the move. When it became clear that it was heading for Kambula, confirming what Hamu's warrior had overheard, Raaff and his men made haste for the camp and on the way met up with another patrol led by Lieutenant Blaine of the FLH, who had so narrowly escaped death the previous day. Raaff shouted to him to ride for the camp as hard as he could go as the Zulu army was close behind. Blaine, looking back, saw thousands of warriors suddenly top a rise and come on at a jog. The two patrols combined and hastened back to Kambula where Wood had just decided that everyone should have dinner before battle commenced, which meant fetching more firewood to keep the pots and kettles boiling.

Captain John Waddy, 13th LI, was on firewood fatigue that day and had been out since 5.00 a.m. with his company working in the kloofs of the Ngaba ka Hawana range of hills, five miles from the camp. At one point he had imagined he was about to be surrounded and attacked by a Zulu *impi* that suddenly appeared on a nearby hill but closer inspection revealed the *impi* to be some of Hamu's warriors who had 'deserted' the previous day and were now making up their minds whether it was safer inside or outside Kambula camp. No doubt they were well aware of the approaching army.

Waddy shortly had another fright when a mounted infantryman galloped up and informed him that the 'enemy were all around the camp'. Waddy and his men 'abandoned the half-loaded wagon, downed tools and did a sprint of five miles in A-1 time, the mounted infantry sending horsemen to help the lame ducks up the steep hill into camp.'

As the last of the cattle herders and fatigue parties reached the safety of the laager, an awed silence settled over the entire camp; men involuntarily faltered in their stride and for a moment all movement and conversation ceased. The Zulu army had been sighted; the colossus had arrived. So many had heard it described but few had seen it and now there it was. It was viewed with a mixture of dread, fascination and admiration as it began to deploy. Then the spell was broken and 'anxiously every telescope was turned in the direction of the black masses which now covered the hills'. One correspondent was sitting in his tent writing up the events of the previous day 'when a staff officer peeped in and in the most business-like manner informed me that the Zulus were in sight.'

Fifty years later, James Francis, the 'fellow called Francis' who had saved D'Arcy's life the previous day, remembered:

> We saw the great Zulu Army of between twenty and thirty thousand warriors advancing from Zunguin Nek [north] . . . for about four hours they came on slowly, doing manoeuvres in connection with surrounding our camp.[120]

Dennison, the lone occupant of the Border Horse mess tent, lamenting the loss of so many of his comrades at Hlobane, was startled out of his morose reminiscence by a shout of 'Here they come, thick as bees'. Quickly ducking outside he saw, about three miles to the east, a huge column making to pass the camp to the south whilst another, equally strong, was heading, it seemed, straight for Dennison's tent.

The correspondent of the *Cape Argus* reported that:

> We were able to see dense masses of the enemy advancing in perfect order in four columns; their end seemed never to come and no doubt many in the camp were doubtful that they could resist the rush of such masses.

Yet another correspondent – who had just met a companion of the previous day 'whose haggard face betokened how he had been face-to-face with death' – was struck with apprehension at the leisurely and deliberate deployment of the colossus that, it seemed, would inevitably overwhelm the camp. It was an army at the height of its power and accomplishment. It had beaten a British column equipped with the latest weaponry in open battle at Isandlwana; it still held Pearson and his men besieged and humiliated at Eshowe; it had overwhelmed a convoy at the Ntombe River and, the day previously, with the help of the abaQulusi, had slaughtered many horse soldiers previously regarded as invincible. Amongst its regiments it possessed 1,200 Martini-Henry rifles and tens of thousands of rounds of ammunition, all captured from the enemy. Zulu morale and confidence was, at that moment, at its zenith. And, perhaps, no other race on earth could excel its warriors in perfection of human form, fitness and ferocity; they had been described with awe by Sir Bartle Frere as 'celibate man-slaying gladiators'. And, as they would display that day, their valour knew no equal.

Other than their captured British rifles, their firearms covered a range of weapons from modern pieces to Brown Bess muskets that might well have seen service at Waterloo. Most also carried an ox-hide shield, patterned in regimental colours, and at least two spears, one to throw and one to stab, the latter a heavy-bladed weapon called an *iklwa*, an onomatopoeic word from the sucking noise the weapon made when withdrawn from the slain. Today they wore no ornaments, no skins nor feathers to adorn them. They were warriors for the working day. A pouch, a snuff box, perhaps a necklace of spiritual importance, was all they wore except for cartridge and powder bags; one enterprising warrior had skilfully made a cartridge bag from a leather writing case taken from a dead officer at Isandlwana with the officer's initials still visible in gold leaf. Other than such brief items of equipment and apparel they would, as ordered by their king, fight naked.

Overall command of the army, in a political capacity, rested with Mnyamana kaNgqengelele, chief of the Buthelezi clan, commander of the royal and prestigious uThulwana regiment and the most important man in the kingdom next to the monarch himself. At sixty-five years of age, Mnyamana was a man of great wealth and standing, slim, elegant and with a pointed cavalier beard. Moreover he was a father figure to the royal family. However, the battle commander, the fighting general, was Ntshingwayo kaMahole Khoza, he who had commanded the army at Isandlwana with such devastating effect. Although close to his seventieth year he was tough, grizzled, greatly respected throughout the kingdom, and a firm friend of Cetshwayo.

The battle that was about to take place was, in fact, intended to be the 'king's battle' for Cetshwayo had given stringent orders as to how it was to be conducted.[121] Having weighed the cost of attacking a fortified position at Rorke's Drift, the king had ordered that the British should be teased out of their lair by attacking their transport oxen, by making feints, or even limited assaults on farms and settlements. On no account was the army 'to stick its head into the den of the wild beast'.

Most of the warriors were veterans of Isandlwana and each regiment, distinguished from the others by the colour and pattern of its shields, was possessed of pride and rivalry to such a degree that blood would likely be spilt at the slightest suggestion of an affront. Only a year earlier two regiments had clashed and many had been slain over whose honour it was to enter the royal homestead first.

The army had initially been sighted from the camp at around 10.00 a.m. and an hour later had begun methodically to deploy. Then, for a while, all activity ceased; Mnyamana, with the eloquence of the skilled politician, was haranguing the troops, perhaps too skilfully, for it seems his pre-battle speech stirred his warriors to 'burn like a fire', until they became unruly and impetuous.[122] The royal strategy of luring the British from the camp was now forgotten. Furthermore the warriors were hungry, very hungry, and wanted to get on with it. Before them lay another treasure trove of firearms and, in addition, an abundance of food to fill their empty stomachs: they had been on the road for six days, mostly living off the land and their fare had been poor. When the men of one *ibutho* complained of their hunger their commander had pointed towards the camp and said 'There is your dinner.'

The glory and the greatest plunder would go to those first into the camp and the men of the Nkobamakosi regiment, that had taken its place in the forefront of the right horn, were ever watchful of their rivals, the mCijo, which held a similar honour on the opposite flank of the encircling army. Both regiments were manned by young warriors in the prime of life who were reckless of death; they would risk all to be the first amongst the British tents.

In the camp the men's dinners were cooked and dished out earlier than usual. Although all ate eagerly, their food was only glanced at. All eyes were fixed on the silent and now motionless army spread out in line, three miles distant and six miles in extent, over the undulating countryside. Then, at about 12.45 p.m. the *iziNyanga*, (doctors or healers) having completed their pre-battle purification rituals, and Mnyamana's oratory done with, the Zulu Army began to move again.[123]

Standing in the little fort atop Kambula Knoll, watching the never-to-be-forgotten spectacle, Wood at last gave the order and his bugler immediately sounded the alarm, the call that all had been waiting for, its martial notes carrying through the camp and far beyond, like a distant challenge to the warriors of the Zulu army. The 200 bell tents that housed the column, spread in lines here and there about the camp, were immediately dropped by the simple expedient of pulling out the centre pole. Each tent had its 'pole man' who knew the drill and was strong enough to perform the task. It was Wood's boast that every tent could be flat on the ground, giving a clear field of fire, within two minutes of the alarm being sounded. Each man now doubled to his pre-ordained battle position:

To the fort: Two companies, one each of the 13th and 90th Light Infantry, to man the walls under the command of Knox Leet, who was perhaps still contemplating his miraculous escape of the previous day; in addition there was a small detachment of the 80th Foot, manning two 6-pounder Armstrong mountain guns in the charge of Lance-Sergeant Thomas Browne.

To the main laager: Five companies of the 13th, seven companies of the 90th, small detachments of other corps including the Royal Engineers, all the colonial horsemen, some 500 in number, plus the armed civilians, the surgeons and hospital orderlies and, it must be remembered, all the horses.

To the cattle laager: One company only of the 13th commanded by Captain Cox.[124]

Just how many oxen the laager contained is difficult to fathom. It was constructed of about forty wagons and had an internal area of some one and a half acres. As the column had in excess of 2,000 draft animals, one assumes that as many beasts as possible were jam packed inside and the rest turned loose. The infantry manned the shelter trenches and firing platforms – there would be little room for them inside the laager itself. It was the least defensible position and, situated immediately above the steep valley where an enemy could mass unseen, it was the Achilles heel of Kambula Camp.

Outside the fortifications, completely exposed, were the four 7-pounder guns, of No. 11 Battery, 7th Brigade RA, in two sections: one commanded by Lieutenant Frederick Slade and the other by Lieutenant Arthur Bigge, both under the overall command of Major Tremlett, all three officers having survived the attack of the previous day on the mountain.

As the troops stood silently watching the distant army moving closer, Wood in his command post noticed Rathbone, the fiery old correspondent of the *Natal Witness*, standing close by and, no doubt apprehensive of what Rathbone might write of the previous day's debacle, Wood asked his opinion of the attack on Hlobane. Not mincing his words Rathbone replied that depending on the outcome of the day's work ahead, Wood would either be recalled or get a 'cocked hat' (the distinguishing headgear of a general officer).[125]

At 1.30 p.m. the colossus was now less than two miles away and began to move faster. The irresolution of the Zulu army vanished. Suddenly the right horn could be seen rapidly advancing across the north face of the camp. What prompted its sudden breakaway will never be known for certain. Possibly the young warriors lost patience with their elderly commanders; possibly the commanders themselves could not agree either to attack or bypass the camp; possibly the warriors of the Nkobamakosi, no longer able to see their rivals, believed them to be already attacking the camp and decided to pitch in forthwith; whatever the reason, it was apparent that the right horn, approximately 6,000 strong, was either intent on a head-on attack or was racing to join up with the left horn and encircle the camp.

What could be better for the British than an impetuous and uncoordinated attack? If that was not the intention of the right horn, however, Wood immediately grasped the opportunity to provoke it into just such a blunder. Buller was ordered to saddle up and, with about a hundred horsemen, incite the Zulus to attack. A wagon in the main laager was unchained, moved aside and out went the men, mainly from the Frontier Light Horse and Natal Native Horse, with a few Mounted Infantry and Kaffrarian Rifles. What their feelings were, having survived the horrors of Devil's Pass only twenty-hour hours earlier and now about to face a similar ordeal, can only be imagined.

Young Trooper Mossop was among them. His Basuto pony, though badly wounded, had carried him back to camp, but alas the pony was to die later of its injuries, its head cradled in the boy's arms. But this was no time for sentiment. Mossop had been allocated another horse: 'a large brute – a mountain of bones, a coffin-shaped head and a Roman nose'. Mossop asked how he, being so small, was to mount such a large animal. 'Climb up its tail, kid, he's tame enough', was the unencouraging reply. Now, with his toes only just reaching the stirrup irons, Mossop trotted out of the laager with the rest.

Buller shouted: 'Extended order' and, in one single line, riding abreast, they trotted out one and a half miles to within 150 yards of the massive column as, unheedful of the horsemen, it passed across their front. The horsemen had already been told what they must do. On the order they were to dismount, pause, and fire a volley into the passing throng, then remount and gallop for the camp.

With their left arms through the reins, the horsemen brought their carbines up and took aim at the moving black mass of men, dust and shields. The crash of the volley seemed to signal an eruption of violence. The Zulus swerved from their course and with wild yells and hammering of shields turned upon the horsemen who now found it almost impossible to mount. The horses, turned frantic by the oncoming torrent of yelling warriors, struggled to bolt from the restraining hands that held them as the terrified troopers fought to find the saddle.

Mossop, knowing he would never get astride the plunging back of his giant mount, grasped the double bridle and let the horse take flight whilst he, half suspended and half running, kept his distance from the maddened warriors. There were many such instances all along the line, perhaps none more perilous than that of Lieutenant-Colonel Russell who, no doubt anxious to redeem his reputation, had joined Buller in leading out the foray. But Russell was now unable to mount. Sergeant-Major Learda, of the NNH, on seeing him in imminent danger of being overwhelmed, rode back and, with the assistance of several other black troopers, kept the enemy at bay for precious moments. Lieutenant Browne glanced back and also returned to help his unpopular commander. Whilst Learda and his troopers continued to keep the Zulus busy, Browne grasped the bridle of Russell's demented horse allowing Russell to scramble up.[126] Yet, worse was to come. Having seated himself, Russell failed to gather the reins or to get his feet in the stirrups and, with no control, the horse took him careering straight along the line of the enemy. With the warriors only yards away, Browne spurred after Russell once again, managed to grasp hold of Russell's bridle and pull the horse around. Together, with Russell holding on for dear life, they made the safety of the laager.

Mossop also needed help. Despite flying along with the horse in a hop, skip and jump fashion, his weight on the bit had dragged the animal's head around to such a degree that it was looking in the opposite direction – and the Zulus were close behind. Out of the corner of his eye, Mossop saw two men, their horses hindered by marshland, being overtaken and killed. He sensed that his fate would shortly be the same; but help was at hand;Captain Oldham of the Frontier Light Horse came to the rescue and in an instant Mossop vaulted into the saddle, just in time to leave his pursuers behind and reach the safety of the laager. A black trooper of the Natal Native Horse, seeing a Kaffrarian rifleman unhorsed, galloped back and took the fugitive up behind, thus saving him from certain death. Commandant Scherm-brucker was so delighted that he later presented the trooper with £5.

The Nkobamakosi, now followed by the uVe, had taken Buller's bait and were about to be gaffed by the big guns and the infantry. As the warriors surged forward, one man of the Nkobamakosi fleetingly glanced at the white painted rocks and wondered at their meaning. They were, of course, the range markers for the artillery and infantry, their location carefully surveyed and the distances prominently marked by the Royal Engineers. The young Zulus were charging into a carefully designed killing field.

The big guns did not wait for the horsemen to reach the laager but fired over their heads, terrifying the retreating men as much as the Zulus who pursued them.

At 1,500 yards the first shell exploded above the racing warriors, the shrapnel creating appalling carnage as bodies erupted in bloody plumes. But, reckless of death, they came on with the taunting cry: 'We are the boys from Isandlwana!'[127] It was not their intent to kill the whites with the beautiful guns they had captured, their intent was to take the *iklwa* into the British camp and there wash its heavy blade in blood. This they intended to do without any covering fire – for that was unknown – by crossing 900 yards of open ground swept by common shell, shrapnel, case shot, rockets and the volley fire of two crack infantry regiments.

One correspondent described their charge:

> But still they came on with the ferocity of tigers, never halting, never wavering, never flinching or hesitating for a moment.[128]

But of course they could not do it. Their bravery knew no bounds but the task was impossible. They covered 900 yards of death and got within thirty of the main laager but in the end the crushing volleys of the infantry broke them. The Nkobamakosi and the uVe, now decimated, turned their backs on the British camp and took cover amongst an outcrop of rocks, not far from the camp.

Mehlokazulu, a junior officer of the Nkobamakosi, remembered:

> So many were killed that the few who were not killed were lying between dead bodies so thick were the dead . . . Our regiment was so anxious to distinguish itself that we disobeyed the King's orders . . . Had we waited properly for supports we should have attacked the camp on three sides at once, and we should have taken it.

But the battle was far from over. The left horn, made up of the mCijo, the bitter rivals of the Nkobamakosi, supported by the uMbonambi, the Ndluyengwe, uThulwana and uNokhenke regiments, their advance having been hindered by marshy ground, now made all haste, believing the sound of firing betokened the right horn's entry into the camp. However, it was not until 2.15 p.m. that the foremost warriors, glancing up, saw the wagons and sod parapets of the cattle laager a short distance above them. With thousands of warriors almost filling the valley behind them, all eager to push forward and get to grips with the soldiers, the vanguard did not hesitate. Ignoring the volley fire that crashed out as they left the concealment of the rocks, and ignoring dead and wounded comrades who fell on all sides, the Zulus reached the laager, grasping and pulling at the defenders' rifles, climbing the wagons, hammering and pushing at the walls of biscuit boxes, the defenders and attackers each firing point-blank at the other. The noise and turmoil was deafening as men fought hand-to-hand amongst the bellowing oxen. The *amabutho* had found Wood's Achilles heel. They pushed the wagons aside and the oxen that had not been killed in the fighting streamed out of the laager, bucking and snorting.

Just one company could not hold the warriors back and Captain Cox, badly wounded, ordered his men to retire on the fort.[129] Covered by the infantry above, they scrambled up the slope leaving a number dead, including Private Grosvenor who had been assegaied attempting to save the life of a wounded comrade. Trooper Charles Hewitt remembered:

> The Zulus swarmed up those krantzes and after a struggle during which most or all the cattle were wiped out they, the Zulus, got possession of the laager.

With the capture of the laager and the cover it provided, the warriors were now beginning to mass in comparative safety only a hundred yards from the knoll. Thousands more could be seen, a mile or so away to the south-east, descending into the valley that would give them protection all the way to the cattle laager and the doorstep to the fort. Under the direction of Lieutenant Nicholson the mountain guns opened fire to the south-east, their target easy to discern as the Zulus, before descending into the valley, were congregating around the abandoned fortification of Wood's earlier camp.

Mnyamana, Ntshingwayo and other Zulu commanders, positioned beyond the abandoned fort and about one mile from the camp, watched the deployment of their army developing into a successful attack with every prospect of victory. They now committed the 'chest', the uDloko, uDududu, mBube, uThulwana, Ndlondlo and the late arrivals from Hlobane, the abaQulusi, all impatient to repeat the glorious triumph of Isandlwana.

With the cattle laager taken and turned into an assembly area by the Zulus, the spectre of another catastrophic defeat for the British loomed. From the protection of the valley, groups of Zulu skirmishers, picked men with captured Martini-Henry rifles, began to occupy the crest line with its rocks and reverse slope protecting them from British fire. From there the Zulu snipers began to take toll of the infantry and gunners, their marksmanship no longer mocked by the white men. The Zulus' main objective was to silence the guns that still dispensed death and destruction with impunity. Behind any sort of cover the snipers settled to their task.

A dedicated few who had anticipated insufficient natural shelter were seen each one advancing at a jog with a bag of cartridges slung across his shoulder, a rifle in one hand, and the other steadying a rock, carried on his head. Once dumped the rock would give immediate concealment.

The two sections, each of two 7-pounder guns, out in the open, being moved here and there as the ebb and flow of the battle dictated, became prime targets. Within the next hour, Lieutenant Nicholson was mortally wounded, Lance-Sergeant Browne of the 80th, in charge of the mountain guns, was hit by a bullet in the head and both Lieutenants Slade and Bigge had their horses shot from under them.

The warriors at the south-west end of the valley crest line, opposite and only 120 yards from the front of the main laager, also began to be noticed. A sizeable group had taken cover behind the camp manure dump, which over the weeks had produced a fine crop of mealies giving additional concealment. From this position their marksmanship began to take a further toll of the gunners and those in the fort.

To counter a full frontal attack emerging out of the captured laager, Wood ordered out two companies of the 90th from the main laager. Commanded by Major Robert Hackett, pipe in mouth, who had been briefed by Wood, and with bayonets fixed, the sortie doubled smartly to the crest line. With Captain Woodgate leading sword aloft, they swung out, lined the ridge and delivered volley after volley. They were followed by several bugle boys carrying buckets of ammunition who, having delivered their loads, beat a hasty retreat.[130]

Kneeling, but without any cover, the 90th began to take casualties and several men were seen to waver, as if to bolt, until Lieutenant Strong, with sword in hand, strolled in front of his men and restored morale. But their exposed position could not be maintained. The Zulu marksmen in the manure dump and those to the east end of the fort, had the sortie in a cross-fire and casualties began to mount at an unacceptable rate. Thus, having averted an immediate assault, the sortie was ordered to retire. But, as they rose, they received the full force of the snipers' fire. Hackett fell with an appalling wound, a bullet carrying away both eyes and the bridge of his nose; Lieutenant Bright, shot through both legs, would die later that night. The sortie had cost twenty-four casualties.[131]

As the triumphant Zulus followed the sortie up the slope they were met by Tremlett and his guns firing case shot, in effect giant shotgun cartridges, each containing dozens of heavy lead balls. One round could cut a swathe yards wide through an advancing enemy. It would be the guns that would save the day for the British.

Yet the danger was not yet over. The warriors were reforming for another assault and already ambitious regimental groups, still eager to be first into the main laager, were assembling to attack the west wall, which was mainly manned by the colonials.

Mossop, having earlier made the comparative safety of the laager, had found a comfortable position in one of the Boer wagons and had cut a hole through its canvas hood to serve as a loophole. Through this aperture he now watched as:

> . . . a line of Zulus swept around the corner wagon at full speed and raced along our line, seeking an opportunity to enter. As they passed each wagon a sheet of flame and smoke from the Martini rifles welcomed them. They tumbled and fell, but it made not the slightest difference; they did not shear away from the wagons or abate their speed, and they still came on – an endless stream. In a few minutes the whole west wing was engaged, and it being a calm day, the smoke from the rifle fire began to bother us; we could barely distinguish the Zulus only a few feet away. Finding no opening, the Zulus turned and charged the whole line. Crash! – as the shields struck the wagons, and the whole line shook.

The immediate thought was that the Zulus were in, but Mossop, thrusting his head right through his loophole, was able to see a struggling black mass yet to breach the defences, fighting to wrench a wagon out of the line and gain entry. But the wagons were well-secured and before the warriors could succeed, a company of the 13th, from the other side of the laager, arrived at the double and drove the warriors away. Dennison also recorded the incident:

> Loud and continuous was the din of battle interluded with a deep bass and weird battle cry added to the rattling of many thousands of shields by the Zulus as they made successive charges on one or other side of the camp. A sudden cry attracted the attention of an officer of the 90th and myself to the left, and as we looked we saw some soldiers leap down from the wagons on to the ground. Then the shields and heads of Zulus appeared climbing up. The soldiers stood with bayonets fixed and pointed at an angle to meet the foe should they ever get over.

The Nkobamakosi and the uVe, ravaged by the British fire that they had earlier endured, now charged forth again but were immediately engaged by the NNH who had not re-entered the main laager with the rest of the horsemen, having chosen instead to remain outside and harass the enemy. Now, as the warriors emerged from the protection of their rocky ledge, the black horsemen surged forward. Dennison recalled the engagement:

> Their [Zulu] attempts from the north were soon given up for our mounted Basutos [NNH] who had refused to come into the camp, constantly harassed them from the rear as they stormed us from that side which was open country. Splendid service was done by the Basutos which perhaps was never properly appreciated.

On the southern side the Zulus massed and once again almost reached the main laager:

> An induna, riddled with bullets came on, growing weaker as he came, to fall with his face to his foes within twenty-five paces from our wagons.

The guns from the fort and rocket tubes did terrible execution among the enemy . . . fierce but in vain was the onslaught of the brave Zulus who dauntlessly rushed our camp to fall dead or wounded . . . The hospital tents . . . were ere long after the attack commenced in full use.

At the height of the battle one old sweat emerged from the hospital, having had his leg amputated, praising his good fortune and advising his mate that he had lost a leg but would gain a pension for life: ' . . . that's better than any leg – or two for that matter', he shouted.

Now it was the turn of the 13th to sally forth and attempt to retake the cattle laager. But before they did Buller, pacing back and forth, had observed the location of the snipers in the dung heap. He called on some colonials to shoot the daylights out of the marksmen, but he was told that it was difficult as they seldom presented a target. Buller scoffed at the notion and told the men that a Martini-Henry bullet would carry right through the manure and kill anything beyond. No target was required; they could simply pump bullets into the dung heap. This they did and the following day sixty-two dead bodies were found there smattered with manure.[132]

The dung heap having been silenced, the men of the 13th were ready for the sortie. But in the meantime the guns had not paused since the moment the battle started. They had bombarded the distant entrance to the valley and, with musketry support, had kept clear with shrapnel and case the area between the cattle laager and the fort, but still the Zulu warriors continued to assemble and charge. And the British troops were awed by their bravery. It would be they, the British, who would write the epitaph to Zulu valour: 'No soldiers in the world could have been more daring than the Zulus that day.'

Captains Waddy and Thurlow and two companies of the 13th doubled out and lined the valley crest that had been swept clear by the artillery moments before. Firing, and with bayonets fixed, they advanced down the rocky slope pushing the warriors back. The guns followed, manhandled all the way, and firing case shot and shrapnel. In addition the artillery pursued the retreat with rockets that, unlike at Isandlwana, proved a formidable weapon. One warrior remembered: 'The soldiers killed the Zulus with paraffin. I saw the flames, it actually burnt us. Men died of these flames thrown by bullets.'[133]

The colonials, not to be outdone, were led out of the main laager by Commandant Raaff and finally overwhelmed any opposition that remained behind the dung heap. And, from the fort, Captain Laye's company of the 90th doubled out to storm the eastern side of the cattle laager.

It was now close to 5.30 p.m. and the battle had raged for four hours without pause.[134] Over 1,200 Zulus had already lost their lives and suddenly they seemed to know that it was not possible to carry their spears into the British camp against the big guns and the fortifications. They wavered. It was time to go. There would be no repeat of Isandlwana today. The Zulu army turned its back on Kambula and then at a slow jog began to head back the way it had come, back towards Zunguin.

A cheer went up throughout the British camp. Hats were tossed in the air and, as last shots were exchanged with a few warriors who were reluctant to admit defeat, the British cheered again and again. One of those shots hit Alan Gardner, whose assailant was killed in turn by Slade. Gardner was badly wounded and would be out of action for the rest of the war of which he had seen so much. But the day was not over. Although the British admired the Zulus for their courage, there were scores to settle; Isandlwana and Hlobane must be revenged.

The horsemen were once again ordered to mount up. 'The broken relics of the Irregular Horse now sallied out in pursuit', as one observer put it. As they trotted from the laager the infantry cheered again; the tiredness fell away and adrenaline, stimulated by the thought of what they were about to do, filled the horsemen with new energy. Commandant Schermbrucker described the chase:

> We raced helter skelter after the flying Zulus. I took the extreme right, Colonel Buller led the centre, and Colonel Russell, with mounted infantry, took the left. For fully seven miles I chased two columns of the enemy, who tried to escape over the Umfolozi . . . but I was after them like the whirlwind, and shooting incessantly into the thick column, which could not have been less than 5,000 strong. They became exhausted, and shooting them down would have taken too much time; so we took the assegais from the dead men, and rushed amongst the living ones, stabbing them right and left with fearful revenge for the misfortunes of the twenty-eighth instant [Hlobane]. No quarter was given. Unfortunately for our greater success, but fortunately for the Zulus, it became quite dark about half past six o' clock, there being a heavy mist; nevertheless the slaughter continued as long as we could discern any human form before our eyes. . . . So that from the moment we followed them up to the end of the fearful work of bloodshed, there must have been killed not less than a thousand Zulus.[135]

Buller, perhaps rather fancifully, was described as like 'a tiger drunk with blood' with the reins of his horse held in his teeth, wielding a knobkerrie in either hand.

The horsemen were not the only ones to seek revenge. Dennison, who had not joined in the chase, recalled:

> On one side of the camp the men leapt down over the barriers [off the wagons] and I say it now with a feeling of shame, despatched the wounded lying around ere it could be stopped. To try and stop the men from leaving their positions appeared useless as far as the irregulars were concerned. Tommy [nickname for a British soldier] impatiently waited the order which at last came, when all, officers and men, left the laager. Enemy dead and wounded lay thick around. With two other officers

I walked to the edge of the steep decline bordering the Umfolozi, down the side of which our men were advancing, firing on the retreating Zulus who had hung back no doubt for the purpose of aiding wounded friends. One, who apparently hid in the river growth, sprung up with an assegai and shield and rushed a soldier who with his bayonet parried the thrust (his rifle evidently not being loaded). For some minutes the hand-to-hand combat lasted while ever our men stood near watching until it became clear that the active Zulu was more than a match for Tommy, when one of the onlookers shot the noble Zulu. It seemed cruel and we felt so, but such things do happen in most civilized warfare.

In sombre tones, Schermbrucker described the burial, over the next three days, of the Zulu dead:

It was a ghastly ditch, 200 feet long, some 20 feet broad and 10 feet deep which received wagon load after wagon load of the dead bodies of the bravest warriors of a brave people. Full military honours were accorded them, as batch after batch, closely packed, they were deposited in a soldiers' grave. 970 dead bodies were picked up around the camp and fort, of which no less than 350 had fallen close to the fort and in the trenches . . . several hundred corpses were lying about, within a radius of one mile from the camp, and the track of the flying enemy, for several miles, was literally strewn with the bodies of those killed in pursuit.

The losses on the side of the defenders were nineteen killed and fifty-eight wounded, some of whom were so seriously hurt that they died within a few days.

The Hlobane Cover-up

Wood had scored a great victory. Less than twelve hours earlier he had faced the prospect of ruin and recall. Now, as the Zulu army retreated and the horsemen pursued, Rathbone, who could no longer contain his elation, summed up Wood's new situation by shouting at the top of his voice that Wood had 'won his cocked hat!' and if he had anything to do with it, he would see that he got it.[136] Now Wood's dilemma was how best to cover up the debacle of Hlobane. It must not mar the glory of the victory that would propel him to the forefront of current military fame.

On 30 March, the day following the battle of Kambula, he wrote two separate reports to the Deputy Adjutant-General, one for Hlobane and the other for Kambula. His first report commenced: 'I have the honour to report that the Inhlobana [Hlobane] Mountain was successfully assaulted and its summit cleared at daylight on the 28th.'[137]

Although it was true that the summit was cleared Wood does not go on to admit that it was as a result of an enemy strategy to lure his force into a trap. Wood went on to describe events as they happened until the moment he met up with Weatherley and the Border Horse. He makes no mention of

Dennison's reported discovery of the Zulu army, merely stating: 'Colonel Weatherley met me coming westwards having lost his way the previous night and I advised him to move to the sound of the firing . . .'[138]

He then went on to describe how he and his escort overtook the Border Horse and came under fire with Lloyd being killed:

> I directed Colonel Weatherley to dislodge one or two Zulus who were causing us most of the loss, but as his men did not advance rapidly, Captain Campbell and Lieutenant Lysons and three men of the 90th, jumping over a low wall ran forward and charged into a cave when Captain Campbell, leading in the most gallant manner, was shot dead. Lieutenant Lysons and Private Fowler followed closely on his footsteps and one of them, for each fired, killed one Zulu and dislodged another who crawled away . . .[139]

In a few words Wood implies that the Border Horse were cowards and that this cowardice provoked Campbell's rash attack. But, as we have seen, Wood would later elaborate his account of the incident and in particular Weatherley's alleged cowardice.

Wood went on to say that the Border Horse followed Buller's tracks, by now having lost three men dead and seven wounded – but how these casualties came about if they were supposedly cringing behind the cattle kraal he does not say. He only mentions the burial of Campbell and Lloyd as having taken place after the Border Horse had left. He later describes seeing the Zulu army, writing his note to Russell and Russell's mistaken location of the Zunguin Nek and his abandonment of the black auxiliaries. And again there is the inference of cowardice, this time, of course, aimed at Russell:

> Colonel Russell reports that he moved from the Inhlobana [Hlobane] to Zunguin's Nek, but this is incorrect. On the contrary, he went away six miles to the west end of the range misapprehending the position of the Nek, which is at the eastern corner of the range . . . Colonel Russell ordered all the cattle to be abandoned and moved off very rapidly under the western end of the range. He thus uncovered the retreat of Oham's [Hamu's] people about eighty of whom were killed by the Zulus running down from the Inhlobana, they being greatly encouraged by the sight of the large army now moving directly on the western end of that mountain.[140]

Whilst there can be no excuse for Russell's action, especially in failing to support Buller's retreat, in fairness it was Russell who had the correct location for Zunguin Nek. There are several independent statements corroborating Russell's location to be the correct one.

Wood then describes how he sent an order recalling Russell, which Russell obeyed, but too late to save the cattle and the auxiliaries. He concludes by stating that he, Wood, arrived back at Kambula at 7.00 p.m. There is no mention of his being found on Zunguin by Buller after he had been waiting there to cover the retreat of survivors as he would later claim. Wood also infers that the attack itself was a success, which later went wrong due to the cowardice of the Border Horse and Russell, compounded by the unexpected arrival of the Zulu army. It was a day that Wood desired to hide away in the broom cupboard of history.

Buller, writing the same day, stoutly admitted blame for the death of Barton and the Border Horse:

> By right I meant the north side of the mountain but Captain Barton must have misunderstood me to mean the south side, and to my careless expression must I fear be attributed the greater part of our heavy loss on this day.[141]

But Wood crossed out the paragraph, writing: 'Omit this from the Gazette [the *London Gazette*].'

It was four days before the public had an inkling that the battles of Hlobane and Kambula had taken place. On 1 April the *Natal Mercury* reported:

> The following telegram has just reached us from our Maritzburg correspondent. Reference was made to the same matter in the morning's issue; but since then no official information has been received upon the subject. News received from Colonel Buller's column that the Zlobane Mountain was attacked on the 28th, and taken, but 20,000 Zulus surrounded it and recaptured the cattle, after great loss on our side.
>
> Zulus attacked Wood's column on the 29th, and fought four hours, when they were driven off. The loss on our side was seventy men and seven officers. Among the killed were Captains Campbell, Llewellyn Lloyd and Piet Uys.

This was all very vague. The press and public were eager to know more but Wood would ensure that both battles would be presented as one engagement ending in victory.

Six days after the battle the *Natal Mercury* reported:

> Yesterday was a period of intense and continuous excitement in Durban. At an early hour in the morning the skeleton facts declared in Colonel Bellairs' second official report were posted, and soon after published, and it came to be seen that the 'disaster' which had been announced by a local newspaper on the day preceding had been 'wiped out' by a repulse of the most brilliant and successful character – one that will reflect historical renown upon the reputation of the British Army. We need not recapitulate the particulars which are given in copious detail in Colonel Wood's official report . . .

It was not until a day or two later that a report from 'our own correspondent' was published dated 'Kambula April 1st', giving a reasonable, though jingoistic account of both engagements but offering no opinion regarding the cause of the Hlobane debacle other than the surprise appearance of the Zulu army. Later a full list of the Hlobane casualties was published without further comment. There was no outcry. No British or Natal regiments had been involved. Apart from two or three imperial officers the casualties had all been rovers and adventurers – mercenaries. The public would rather dwell on Wood's glorious victory. In fact, within a year or so, it began to be believed that Wood had deliberately planned the events on Hlobane in order to draw the Zulus on to Kambula. A report on troop movements in *The Times* of February 1880 commented:

> Last March, in the operations on Hlobana Mountain – which General Wood knew how to conduct so as to lead up to the glorious victory of Kambula . . .

However, a court of inquiry was duly held 'with regard to the losses of horses and equipment at Slobane [Hlobane], and arrived at the conclusion that no blame attaches to the officer in command',[142] an astounding assumption one would think but quite predictable in the knowledge that the inquiry was conducted solely by Wood's own officers, two captains of the 13th and one of the 90th. Wood never received the sort of grilling that Chelmsford had been subjected to by the Duke of Cambridge after the defeat at Isandlwana.[143] One of the questions that had been asked of Chelmsford was:

> As your Lordship had a considerable number of mounted men . . . it should be stated what steps were taken . . . to reconnoitre and thoroughly search the country on your flanks – it seems difficult to understand how a large Zulu army could have massed itself . . . within attacking distance of your camp without some evidence of its proximity having been afforded?

A similar question could have been posed to Wood and Buller regarding their failure to discover the location of the Zulu army on 27 March. And, no doubt, they would have found it as difficult to explain as had Chelmsford.

Apart from the awards of the Victoria Cross in respect of Hlobane, one further award was approved for Kambula. Lieutenant Edward Browne was awarded the decoration for rescuing Lieutenant-Colonel Russell. Sergeant-Major Learda was awarded the Distinguished Conduct Medal for his part in the rescue. However, a few days after the battle and before Browne's recommendation, Browne approached Wood with a 'straightforward letter, offering to resign rather than serve under Russell again'.

On 10 April Wood forwarded Browne's letter to Lord Chelmsford and commented:

> I forward herewith a letter which must cause you pain. Colonel Buller said to me on the afternoon of the 28th March, when I rode from where Colonel Russell should have ascended, to where he came up, to order him back – 'I'll be D. . .d' Sir, if I serve again in a joint operation with Russell.' I took no notice of this at the time, and should not have

mentioned the circumstances had not Captain [*sic*] Browne told Buller he must see me or resign – the straightforward letter I forward is the result of our interview. As I have already written to you there is no want of personal courage on Colonel Russell's part, but I firmly believe his presence here in command is detrimental to the public service. I am forming a remount depot. I suggest you may consider this communication as confidential and appoint Lieutenant-Colonel Russell to superintend all purchases of horses north of Ladysmith.

Russell duly took command of the remount depot. However, although it is difficult not to believe that he deliberately misinterpreted Wood's orders at Hlobane and decided to lead his column away and leave Buller and the rest to their fate, it is possible that Russell himself could have been a candidate for a Kambula Victoria Cross. Three weeks after the battle, this obsequious letter signed 'J. W. P.' was published in the *Natal Mercury*:

> Colonel Russell,
>   Dear Sir, Allow me to express my humblefulness of heartfelt gratitude, for your noble and gallant conduct in the preservation of my life at the sad risk of your own noble self, from the hands of black savages and unmerciful foes. Dear Sir, I only wish I had it in my power to show you the feelings of my grateful heart, all that I can offer you, noble sir, is my prayer. May God protect you and shield you in all the dangers of war, and may He watch over you and prosper you in all undertakings, may God in His gracious power prosper you in health and wealth in this world, and at last take you to a heaven of everlasting rest, where there are no troubles of war or sorrow, is the prayer of your humble and grateful servant.

Can such a letter be believed? It seems so. The correspondent of *The Times Weekly* reported (on 23 May 1879) that when visiting the hospital during the evening after the battle:

> I saw a man lying with a broken leg; on questioning him, he told me that he was shot during the cavalry engagement of the morning, and assured me that had not Colonel Russell, 12th Lancers, ridden back and lifted him onto his horse, he must have fallen into the hands of the enemy, who were close upon him.

Russell also had friends in high places, in particular the Prince of Wales. He did not linger long at the remount depot, being soon transferred to Major-General Newdigate's division. He was later mentioned in dispatches and, much to Wood's vexation, was promoted without Wood's recommendation prompting Wood to write to Major-General Sir Alfred Horsford, a senior officer at Horse Guards:

> I do feel warmly at the promotion of two men against my wishes – Major Russell and Captain Irvin – when I could obtain no recognition of Captain Woodgate's services. He did everything for me in Ashanti, Russell did nothing but build good latrines for Sir Garnet Wolseley . . .[144]

Later, the war over, Wood was received by Queen Victoria at Balmoral and Sir Henry Ponsonby, the Queen's private secretary, subsequently wrote to Wood:

> The Queen was much pained at what you told her about Russell and at the moment thought you should repeat all you said to her to the Prince of Wales. But upon reflection Her Majesty has come to the conclusion that it might be better for many reasons not to enter into the details of the subject with His Royal Highness . . .

On 30 December Sir Henry wrote again:

> The Queen thought you had mentioned the subject of Cecil Russell to the Prince of Wales – but was not surprised (no more was I) that you had not.
> The Prince of Wales wants Her Majesty to invite Russell to Court as a Zulu Hero. The Queen will not. When I approached the subject at Marlborough House I found they were strong on Russell – but thought he had not been well-treated in Zululand. . . . The Queen says if the subject is dropped, she wishes nothing better. It will be better for Russell and everyone else. But if the Prince of Wales insists on having Russell's services publicly recognised then she must appeal to you as to whether you were satisfied with his conduct at Hlobane . . .

It seems that there was a compromise. In Zululand Russell's local rank had been lieutenant-colonel whereas his substantive rank was only that of captain. Russell was not received as a 'Zululand hero' but was promoted to brevet lieutenant-colonel and was later given the command of his regiment – much, no doubt, to Wood's annoyance.

Chapter 6

The Battle of Gingindlovu

'Take my advice, Mr Dunn, and cross over to this side of the river with all your people, and bring as many more with you as you can. We will give you room to locate them, and will feed them free of expense to you; and after the war is over I promise to see you reinstated in your possessions.'

Lord Chelmsford to John Dunn, December 1878.

———

There can be no doubt that news of the defeat at Kambula travelled to Ulundi with the normal miraculous speed of Zulu communications. Thus the army about to face Lord Chelmsford, as he prepared to fight his way to besieged Eshowe, would have been a demoralised one, giving Chelmsford a greater advantage than the mere diversion that he had hoped Wood would provide.

Chelmsford anticipated giving battle before he could reach kwaMondi, the mission station that had served Colonel Pearson and his men as a fortress for the last two months. The Zulus named the station after Ommund Ofterbro, the serving Norwegian missionary, 'kwa' meaning 'the place of' and 'Mondi' a derivation of his Christian name 'Ommund.' It was located on the outskirts of the Eshowe area.

By late March it was imperative that Pearson be relieved. With his supplies diminished and with starvation hovering only days away, the collapse of the garrison was a real possibility that, should it come about, would be more humiliating in the eyes of the Empire than any of the disasters already suffered by the invading British Army. However, Chelmsford now had might on his side. The army he had assembled, with units newly arrived from England and other parts of the Empire, was more than ten times the size of the one that had faced the Zulus at Isandlwana. The order of battle of the force under the direct command of Lord Chelmsford would be:

1st Infantry Brigade	*Lt-Col F. T. A. Law, RA*
57th (West Middlesex) Regiment	*Col C. M. Clarke*
(7 companies, 640 men)	
2nd Bn, 3rd Regiment (The Buffs)	*Capts W. H. Wyld and H. W. Maclear*
(2 companies, 140 men)	
99th (Duke of Edinburgh's Own) Regt	*Lt-Col W. H. D. R. Welman*
(5 companies, 430 men)	
2nd Infantry Brigade	*Lt-Col W. L. Pemberton, 60th Rifles*
3rd Bn, 60th Rifles	*Lt-Col F. V. Northey*
(6 companies, 540 men)	
91st Highlanders	*Lt-Col A. C. Bruce*
(10 companies, 840 men)	
Divisional Cavalry	
No. 1 Squadron, Mounted Infantry	*Capt P. H. S. Barrow, 19th Hussars*
(70 all ranks)	
Colonial volunteers	
(2 troops – 130 black mounted irregulars and 150 foot scouts)	

The Buffs were well acclimatised, six of their companies having been stationed in Pietermaritzburg in the summer of 1878. The remaining two companies had joined the battalion from Mauritius the previous November, bringing its strength to over 800 men. The Buffs were now split with the two companies in Lowe's brigade about to embark on the relief of Eshowe, where the remaining six companies of the regiment were under siege with Pearson.

Prior to the Battle of Nyezane in January, it had been the Buffs who had burnt and destroyed King Cetshwayo's original military *ikhanda* at Gingindlovu built by him in remembrance of his victory over his brother Mbuyazi at the bloody Battle of Ndondakusuku in 1856. Mbuyazi had a growth of hair in the small of his back, thus being known by the praise name 'Elephant with a tuft of hair'. In his moment of triumph, Cetshwayo named his *ikhanda* Gingindlovu or 'he who swallowed the elephant'. Tommy Atkins, no doubt unable to twist his tongue around the name, and with a soldier's sense of fun, called it, ' Gin Gin I Love You.'

Not all Chelmsford's troops were old sweats. The men of the 3rd/60th, who had recently arrived in Cape Town aboard the *Dublin Castle*, were described by Lieutenant-Colonel John North Crealock, Chelmsford's military secretary, as: 'The youth of the soldiers sent out (except the 57th Regiment) is deplorable and to it alone is to be attributed the behaviour of the 3rd Battalion 60th Regiment.'[145] A little later Crealock would again comment: 'The fact being that the 3rd Battalion 60th Regiment are boys and are suffering naturally enough from diarrhoea from exposure.'[146] Notwithstanding their youth they did at least look smart in their green cloth tunics with scarlet facings – and the officers looked even smarter distinguished as they were by helmets covered in black cloth. On arrival at Durban the battalion paraded before a large crowd:

The Colonel stated that the band would assemble as a band for the last time before going to the front, this morning, after which they would join the ranks, and receive their arms, an announcement which the musicians did not in any way seem to regret.[147]

Other distinguished regiments had also arrived in Durban, a rapidly growing city that was on a war footing:

The main streets were packed with carts and wagons loading and unloading stores, whilst horsemen and pedestrians weaved their way through the maze. Tons of supplies and goods destined for the front clogged the ports. The harbour contained up to thirty vessels with a number waiting at the outer anchorage.[148]

However, social life was evident with hunts, cricket matches, fancy dress balls and concerts.

This was the scene that met the 91st Highlanders when the regiment disembarked from the steamship *Pretoria* on 19 March. Led by Lieutenant-Colonel Bruce, the 91st had left Durban to join Chelmsford at the Tugela River with its pipers playing a lively tune as they marched out of town.

Both brigades were strengthened with a composite force from elements of the Naval Brigade, men from HMS *Shah*, *Tenedos* and *Boadicea*. This last, launched at Portsmouth as recently as 1875, carried sixteen guns and a crew of 426 men. Sub-Lieutenant Arthur Smith-Dorrien, brother of Horace Smith-Dorrien, who was one of the five imperial officers to escape from Isandlwana, was present. The sailors, with their jerseys and open-neck collars and wide-brimmed hats, presented a marked contrast to the red tunics of most of the regular troops, whom the sailors disparagingly called 'lobsters'. The Royal Marine Light Infantry element was commanded by Major J. Phillips and the artillery, with two 9-pounders and four 24-pounder rocket tubes, was under the command of Captain A. L. S. Burrows.

The cavalry included two native units: Jantze's Horse, under Captain Hay, a former Natal Native Contingent officer, and Jantze himself, distinguished by the sword he wore. The other troop had been recruited from the Mafunzi clan and was commanded by Captain Maclean, also a former NNC officer. Both troops had been trained and were equipped with breech-loading carbines. In addition they were smartly dressed in a tan coloured cord uniform, with leggings and a wide-brimmed felt hat.

Two battalions of the NNC, which had yet to earn a reputation for fighting prowess, completed Chelmsford's relief column. These battalions were the 4th Battalion, 7th Regiment, under Captain Geoffry Barton, attached to the 1st Brigade; and the 5th Battalion, 7th Regiment, under Commandant W. J. Nettleton, attached to the 2nd Brigade. These two battalions were formed and renumbered from the old 2nd Regiment NNC which was disbanded on 16 March. Geoffry Barton had previously served with the late Colonel Durnford's invasion column. Prior to crossing the Tugela, every man in both battalions (unlike their kin at Isandlwana) was armed with a Martini-Henry, together with a full field allowance of ammunition.

The relief column, including all units, totalled approximately 3,000 white troops and 2,500 black troops.

Chelmsford arrived in Durban early in March and the relief force assembled at Fort Pearson on the south bank of the Tugela River. It is interesting to note that Law, commanding 1st Brigade, was one of three officers who had conducted the court of inquiry into the disaster at Isandlwana on 29 January at Helpmekaar. Prior to hostilities Chelmsford described Law unfavourably, stating: 'He is not over-fond of work and his present life style suits him down to the ground.'[149] Now, under Chelmsford's direct command, Law's life of idleness would no doubt cease.

John Dunn, with his 150 scouts, was also present. Dunn, a fluent Zulu linguist, trader and sportsman of renown, was one of Natal's most picturesque characters. He had lived for many years in Natal and had been a confidant of Cetshwayo. At one time he was employed by the Natal Government, at the princely salary of £300 per annum, to supervise the import of Tongan labourers. However, Dunn had used his official activities to mask the fact that he was importing guns for the Zulu nation. His salary was stopped but his activities continued. The *Illustrated London News* described him as follows:

He is, nevertheless, reputed to be a wealthy man, keeping up a large domestic establishment in the Zulu style; but when he visits the neighbouring colony [Natal], he appears in the ordinary fashion of an Englishman. In Zululand, he holds the rank of Induna, or state councillor and General, and his diplomatic services may yet be rendered.[150]

Captain William Molyneux, Chelmsford's ADC, described him thus:

John Dunn was a handsome powerful man of about forty years of age, a perfect rider and rifle shot – had the best of saddlery, breeches, boots, and other clothes (which he always got from England, though he had never been there) and but for his large wide-awake hat and tanned face might have been taken for an English gentleman.[151]

Dunn had earlier survived the wrath of Cetshwayo during King Mpande's reign, when, in a dispute over who would succeed their father, Dunn had supported Cetshwayo's younger brother. In due course Cetshwayo was to forgive Dunn and granted him the right to reside in Zululand, together with the allotment of considerable portions of land. Dunn became a close confidant of Cetshwayo in the period up to the outbreak of war in 1879 when he was faced with the dilemma of remaining loyal to Cetshwayo or siding with the British.

In December 1878 Dunn had requested an interview with Lord Chelmsford, during which he was asked his intentions. Dunn responded that he had neutrality in mind, to which Chelmsford replied:

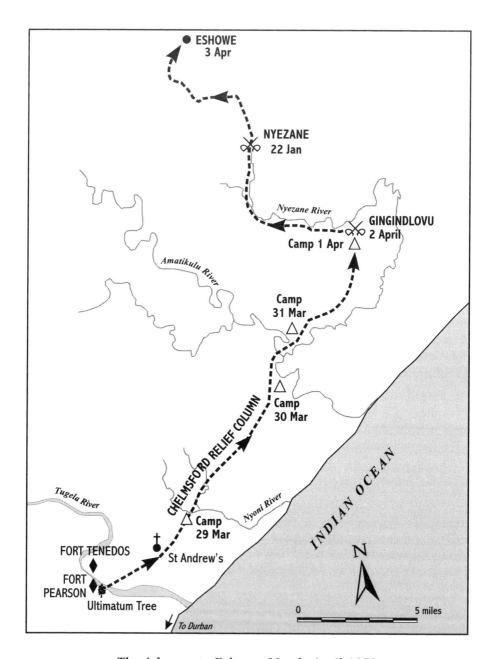

The Advance to Eshowe, March–April 1879
Lord Chelmsford's advance across the Tugela River into Zululand
to relieve Eshowe.

I cannot allow you to do that. You must either take one side or the other, join us, or take the consequences – take my advice Mr Dunn, and cross over to this side of the river with all your people, and bring as many more with you as you can. We will give you room to locate them, and will feed them free of expense to you; and after the war is over I promise to see you reinstated in your possessions.[152]

With such pressure Dunn threw in his lot with the British, formed a corps named 'Dunn's Scouts' and, for the second time, betrayed Cetshwayo's trust. However, the promise Chelmsford had made was, according to Dunn, broken: 'Lord Chelmsford broke his promise as to feeding my people and I had to do so myself at a very heavy expense.[153]

Dunn's personal role in Chelmsford's advance was one of intelligence gathering and advising Chelmsford directly on all matters concerning the Zulu, both military and political.

The outbreak of war had seen a selection of civilian adventurers and gentlemen from well-connected families offering their services. Guy Dawnay, an aristocratic civilian with no military experience and brother of Hugh Dawnay, the 8th Viscount Downe, had already visited South Africa in 1870. Being a keen sportsman and in search of adventure, he linked up with John Dunn on hunting trips, one of which resulted in a lion being killed and eaten. Dunn recorded:

He [the lion] was very fat, and Dawnay and his friend also tried some of the meat, which they said was not bad. I hope my readers will not go away with the idea that the lion was eaten raw, for a large fire was made, and all was well roasted first.[154]

Dawnay heard the news of the British defeat at Isandlwana whilst in Yorkshire and immediately returned to London, and then travelled from the family's Belgrave Square home to board the *Pretoria* for South Africa. He arrived in Durban on 25 March and, through his connections, was invited by Commandant Nettleton to serve temporarily with his 5th/7th NNC. No doubt he was delighted to find John Dunn and his scouts at Chelmsford's side and to renew tales of the past. He described Dunn as 'the general's right hand man'.[155]

The juggernaut was now ready to march to the relief of the beleaguered Pearson.

In January, prior to the invasion, Lieutenant T. R. Main, RE, assisted by sailors from HMS *Active* and a company of Natal Native Pioneers, had installed a pre-fabricated pont or ferry capable of ferrying a company of infantry or a wagon across the Tugela. Following a reconnaissance carried out back in August 1878, Lieutenant-Colonel Durnford had set out plans to propel a pont across the river by using pulleys attached to the main cable, to angle it like a sail against the fast flowing current – a so called 'flying' ferry. When the ferry was actually built, its main steel cable was secured to a tree on the south bank of the river and to an anchor provided by HMS

Active on the opposite shore. In practice, however, it was found easier and faster to draw the pont across the river by means of haul ropes, using manpower and draught animals. From shore to shore, the distance was a staggering 280 yards.

In these operations the Tugela claimed one of the first casualties of the war when a sailor named Martin from HMS *Active* fell off the pont in midstream, to be taken by a crocodile. Main, meanwhile, continued to develop the ferry and a contemporary engraving of the Tugela, published in late 1879, shows a pontoon bridge straddling the river bank to bank, with timber landing piers in position as a further development of the crossing designed to speed up loading and offloading.

At 6.00 a.m. on 29 March the invasion force crossed the Tugela in adverse weather conditions. Normally late March in this region heralds the end of the rainy season and provides the first glimpse of autumn. However, there had been a particularly wet summer in 1878/79. Further heavy rains had fallen prior to the crossing and progress was bogged down by muddy conditions with the river in full spate.

The line of march stretched out over several miles and was vulnerable to Zulu attack. The 1st Brigade took the lead followed by over 120 wagons escorted by the NNC. Each wagon, with its team of oxen, measured over forty yards in length. The 2nd Brigade brought up the rear. A typical day's march would start with reveille at 4.00 a.m. followed by 'stand-to' and breakfast. The column would move off after sunrise shortly after 6.00 a.m.

Lieutenant E. O. H. Wilkinson, adjutant of the 3rd/60th Rifles, described a typical day's march:

> Our order of march in this country is always double fours, whether we are protecting a convoy or not, so that when we halt and front we face outwards, thus preventing these active opponents of ours taking us in front, flank, and rear, as they have done on former occasions, such as Rorke's Drift, Isandhlwana [*sic*] etc.[156]

The average distance planned for each day's travel was in the region of ten miles. The column would then close up and laager. An average wagon was eighteen feet long and five feet high to the base of the canopy. Inside the laager oxen were herded together with the horses, hospital and administrative elements. Outside the laager the infantry would throw up a line of hastily dug shallow firing trenches. Picquets would be advanced some 500 yards to the front and flanks of the camp and mounted patrols thrown out far in advance in search of the elusive Zulu. It was a routine that was physically demanding but accepted by the hardy British soldier, no doubt with a fair amount of grumbling.

The first night was spent in poor weather on the banks of the Nyoni River, with a respectable seven miles having been covered. The oxen were out-spanned to feed before being brought back inside the laager before dusk. Chelmsford, ever mindful of his mistakes at Isandlwana, entrenched the camp and had the wagons drawn up in a square. Again, remembering the lessons of Isandlwana, there was no requirement to erect tents as Chelmsford had ordered that none were to be taken with the relief column. Tents encumbered the quick and immediate deployment of troops into battle positions. Not only would the infantry sleep more or less in their designated position in the square, but there would be no potential obstruction to fields of fire. The infantry spent that night in the space between the wagons and trenches. Under such conditions and with continuous rain, it seems doubtful if many got much sleep.

The following day, the 30th, the column advanced about nine miles and laagered on the banks of the Amatikulu River. This advance was achieved under difficult circumstances:

> Wagon after wagon plunged into the slough, and stopped dead. Extra spans were harnessed on, and after a prolonged scene of confusion, during which the sun rose high in the heavens, the spruit or watercourse was at length overcome. Owing to this delay the advance guard did not arrive within a mile of the Amatikulu River until 2.00 p.m.[157]

On 31 March the whole day was occupied in crossing the river, forty yards from bank to bank and running like a millstream. The infantry struggled across the swollen waters: 'Wading up to their armpits, rifles and pouches on their heads.'[158] The wagons proved an even greater challenge, taking a great deal of time to cross with conductors and voorloopers shouting, cajoling and cracking whips to persuade the terrified oxen to enter the fast-flowing river. Sixteen and in some instances twenty-four oxen were spanned to a wagon. The wet and miserable force managed a march of only two miles that day.

On 1 April the column changed direction and continued northwards towards Eshowe, this time with the 2nd Brigade in the lead. A distance of five miles was achieved before a halt was called. John Dunn now felt uneasy and helped Captain William Molyneux, who had been appointed laager-master for that day, to select a suitable camp-site. Dunn recorded:

> I selected a good position for Gingindlovu camp, as I felt sure there was a strong force of Zulus in the neighbourhood, and I did not like the idea of being caught on the line of march with men of whom I knew nothing.[159]

Within sight of the laager, 1,500 yards away on an elevation to the east, lay the destroyed *ikhanda* of Gingindlovu. The ground on which the square was formed sloped gently from north to south, with Signal Hill, a high crested plateau above Eshowe and bearing a strange similarity in shape to Hlobane, clearly visible in the distance some ten miles to the north-west.

Dunn was right to be concerned that a Zulu attack on the column whilst it was on the march might well prove dangerous. Zulu tactics, however, lacked both boldness and flexibility. No attempt was made to attack at night, thus demonstrating this inflexibility. Opportunities were also lost by their failure to attack lines of communication. In some instances wagons were stretched over miles of territory, with the accompanying troops thinly spread and extremely vulnerable to any form of attack.

Molyneux later recorded that John Dunn asked him, after having laagered on the afternoon of 1 April, to accompany him on a reconnaissance to the valley of the Nyezane River to the north. Prior to setting out Dunn enlightened Molyneux on the finer points of scouting ethics in Africa:

> 'Now you know we are in for a dangerous job, and as I have never been out with English officers before, I should like to be certain, before I start across, that our ideas are the same. In Africa a white man must stand by a fellow while there is life in him; if his friend is dead, then he may save himself. Do you agree?' I managed to satisfy my companion on this score . . .
>
> After a couple of miles Dunn turned off into the bush, pushed through it to the Inyezane, and stopped to listen . . . beckoning me to hold his horse, he stripped, tied his clothes up in a bundle which he gave to me, took his rifle, swung himself into the torrent and, holding onto the branches of a tree that had fallen across it, landed on the other bank and disappeared . . . it was rather uncomfortable work as dusk began to fall, and I was not sorry to see my naked friend wriggling through the grass on the farther bank. I don't know how he managed to get back, for the river had risen ten feet in the hour, and the trunk of the tree was submerged; but he swung himself across somehow, landing blue with cold . . . as we rode he told me that he had seen an impi and a lot of bivouac-fires, that he had nearly been discovered by one of their scouts who, when a clattering crane rose, had advanced to within a few yards of where he lay, that he had been obliged to lie low till the fellow was satisfied and went back, and that he wanted a gallop now to warm himself.[160]

Visible from the camp, the Nyezane River flowed from the north, running across the front of the laager in a south-easterly direction at a distance of approximately one mile from the camp. Smoke was spotted beyond the Wombane Spur three miles north of the laager. This spur formed part of a range of hills in the shape of a crescent, running west to east beyond the Nyezane River. Dunn felt uneasy; he was wary of the column being caught in the open the following day and suggested to Chelmsford that, before breaking camp the following morning, Barrow's mounted men be ordered to scour the area.

Dawnay recorded that a heavy thunderstorm accompanied by two inches of rain broke that afternoon reducing the camp to a quagmire and leaving the men wet and miserable. Late in the afternoon, shots were heard from the outlying picquets. The bugle sounded the 'alarm' and companies rushed to their pre-determined positions. Apart from elements of the Naval Brigade loosing off a few rounds, nothing transpired and it was realised that a false alarm had occurred. If nothing else, the incident had provided an opportunity for a full-scale dress rehearsal for the troops to deploy for battle. As dusk fell, soldiers and officers alike sought out the best positions, as Dunn recorded:

> Tents there were none, so we had to pick out the driest spots under the wagons, the General doing the same as the others. There was no distinction, and no grumbling, and we were all most thankful for something to eat.[161]

Reveille was sounded just after 4.00 a.m. Sunrise was at 6.13 a.m., but Barrow's mounted men had already threaded their way in darkness an hour earlier down to the Nyezane and, at 5.45 a.m., reported Zulus crossing the river. Simultaneously, picquets of the 99th Regiment flung out 500 yards to the north of the square, together with Captain A. H. Bircham's picquet of the 3rd/60th to the north-east, hurriedly returned to report a full-scale attack under way. The Zulus were crossing the Nyezane in force near the old mission station. Then, shortly after sunrise, the initial thick mist cleared and, for the first time in days, the sun made a welcome appearance.

Chelmsford now had little doubt that he was in for a scrap, taking comfort that his column was entrenched and not on the march. The alarm sounded to alert picquets and patrols but every man in the square was already in position. Barrow's cavalry cantered back, entered the square and dismounted, the men holding their bridles tightly to steady their horses and to await the oncoming battle. Both battalions of the NNC were also drawn within to the south side of the laager, the men squatting silently, bunched together, no doubt reflecting on their fate should the Zulu attack break the square. In order to ensure that any firearm discharged accidentally would not cause casualties within the square, the NNC men were ordered to place the butts of their rifles on the ground and muzzles to the sky. The cattle had not been let out to graze that morning and shifted nervously about on the south side of the square.

Chelmsford, mindful of his previous shortcomings, had already issued written instructions:

> Each wagon and cart with the convoys must have some ammunition boxes placed on it in such a position as to be easily got at. The regimental reserve boxes must have the screw of the lid taken out, and each wagon or cart will have a screw driver attached to one of the boxes so that it may be ready for opening those in which the screw has not been taken out.[162]

Clearly this was an admission of the difficulty experienced in the supply of ammunition at Isandlwana. If the boxes could have been opened easily with a heavy blow or kick, as is sometimes suggested in modern accounts, it would not have been necessary to issue explicit instructions for the screws to be removed. The lack of ammunition suffered by the infantry firing line at Isandlwana was not to be repeated in any future battle of the war. A salutary lesson had been learnt at great cost and now, at Gingindlovu, not only had boxes been opened on each ammunition wagon, but also, over and above the issued scale per man, an additional box was opened and placed immediately behind the troops at a scale of one per section of roughly twenty-five men.

In addition cognisance had been taken of paragraph 37 of the *Regulations Field Forces South Africa*, issued by Chelmsford in November 1878, which stated:

> Whenever, therefore, there appears any likelihood of troops' being hotly engaged, thirty extra rounds had better be carried by the soldier.

It is therefore reasonable to assume that all ranks carried the standard seventy rounds plus an additional thirty, totalling 100 rounds in all. Whatever course the battle was to take, there would be no shortage of ammunition.

The square that was formed to meet the attack was about 130 yards per side. Chelmsford's staff had made this calculation: '. . . as giving plenty of room for 2,000 cattle etc. and two men to each square yard, the natives being placed in position behind them, and between the wagons and trenches.'[163]

Eight companies of the 91st manned the west or rear side of the square. Lieutenant-Colonel Bruce's men looked across at level ground that extended for about 400 yards before falling away into a depression, dead ground in which any attacker was hidden from sight. The high grass and bushes in and before the depression and to both sides had been cleared by the mass of wagons, oxen and men of the column, as they had trampled their way on the line of advance towards the laager the previous day. The 91st could clearly see the uMisi Ridge to their front, surrounded by bush and scrub, some 2,000 yards away.

Five companies of the 99th Regiment and two companies of the Buffs occupied the north or left face of the square. All seven companies enjoyed an excellent field of fire, though with observation marred by high grass, shoulder to head height, that afforded the only cover the Zulu had on that approach. It would not stop the murderous volleys of the Martini-Henry. However the contours of the ground were such that the 99th and Buffs could not see the men manning the opposite side of the square.

This south or right face of the square was manned by seven companies of the 57th. The field of fire enjoyed by Colonel Clarke's men was again excellent. The only cover available to the Zulu was the shallow valley of the Gingindlovu Stream, 500 yards from Clarke's position. To mount an assault on the 57th the Zulus would face a daunting uphill sprint, exposed to fire without cover. Beyond and to the east of the Gingindlovu stream the ground rose to a high hill and on its summit, at a distance of 1,500 yards from the square, lay the ruins of Cetshwayo's original Gingindlovu *ikhanda*.

The east face of the square, was problematic from Chelmsford's viewpoint. The six inexperienced companies of the 3rd/60th were positioned there, to face a possible initial direct Zulu assault. The ground to

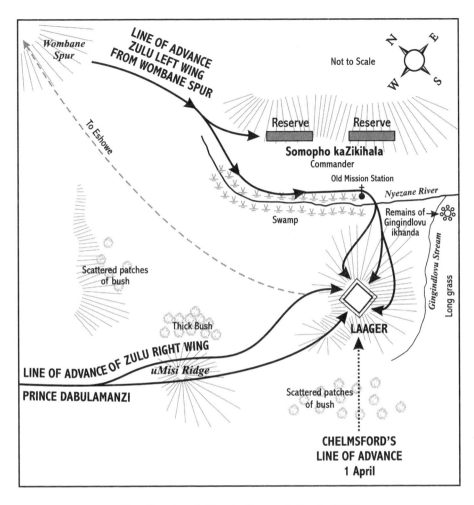

The Battle of Gingindlovu, 2 April 1879

their left sloped down for 1,500 yards to the Nyezane River. On the north bank of the river, and in sight, were the remains of an old mission station. However, 400 yards to their front, covered by thick scrub, lay undulating ground strewn with rocks which would afford the Zulu both shelter and respite from their initial tiring advance. Captain Edward Hutton, commanding K Company, made mention of this ground:

> And from our face the ground sloped towards the stream, but on the extreme right a small donga, flanked in places by patches of bush and occasional rocks, led from the angle of the Gatling gun towards the Nyezane. This species of hollow was dead to us.[164]

Lieutenant-Colonel Northey's men, in view of their youth and inexperience, showed understandable signs of apprehension and officers spoke quietly to calm nerves.

The Naval Brigade, with its artillery, formed the anchor of each corner of the square. On the north/east corner, Senior Lieutenant (Gunnery) F. R. Carr of the *Boadicea* positioned his two rockets from the Rocket Battery. The 60th and the Buffs were on either flank. On the south/east corner, Major J. Phillips of the Royal Marine Light Infantry, in command of a company of Marines, carefully moved a ten-barrelled hand-cranked Gatling into position. The second Gatling was positioned, together with Naval Headquarters, on the south/west corner. Commander J. Brackenbury was in overall command of both Gatlings. Finally, Senior Lieutenant A. Kingscote, a gunnery officer from the *Tenedos*, completed the square on the north/west corner with two 9-pounders. Beyond the wagons on all sides, a shallow shelter trench, eighteen inches in depth and with a parapet thirty inches in height, had been thrown up the previous afternoon. It was sufficient to provide a degree of cover against Zulu fire and to anchor the line.

Lord Chelmsford wisely decided not to ride, but rather to control the battle by moving about on foot from any potential crisis area to the next. To the undoubted amusement of the troops, he wore his red nightcap throughout the engagement. Unwisely, neither his assistant military secretary, Lieutenant-Colonel John North Crealock, nor his ADC, Captain William Molyneux, followed his example, both being mounted throughout the battle.

Regimental commanders gave the nod to their adjutants and the command went out to fix bayonets. Steel crashed into steel in a resounding, morale-boosting, chilling sound, as bayonets were locked. Then came the sharp order: 'No independent firing – volleys by companies when they are within 300 yards.'[165] The square now prepared itself for the battle in the full knowledge that defeat would result in death.

In early March the call had gone out for the *amabutho* to reassemble at the principal military *ikhanda* of oNdini. Although his army had been victorious at Isandlwana, the severe casualties suffered, both killed and wounded, were uppermost in Cetshwayo's mind. Clearly attacking any entrenched British position represented an unacceptable risk.

The Zulus in any case had difficulty in comprehending the British way of fighting. To hide behind dug-in positions and use rifles instead of engaging in hand-to-hand combat was foreign to the Zulu perception of war. To their mind it was nothing less than cowardice. Cornelius Vijn, author of *Cetshwayo's Dutchman*, wrote in 1880:

> The general remark of the Zulus was, 'Why could not the whites fight with us in the open? But, if they are too much afraid to do this, we have never fought men who were so much afraid of death as these. They are continually making holes in the ground and mounds left open with little holes to shoot through. The English burrow in the ground like wild pigs.'

Cetshwayo was convinced that success would be his if, and only if, the British were attacked in the open, when they were undefended by earthworks and the like. His strategy was, unfortunately from a Zulu perspective, never extrapolated into the concept of attacking the lines of communication. Such a strategy could have extended the war by a considerable period by inflicting a series of embarrassing defeats on the invading force. Time was not on the side of Cetshwayo. He could not keep his army in the field indefinitely, nor, unlike for the British, were endless reinforcements available. The realisation that his kingdom was being invaded on two fronts had resulted in a strategy of splitting his *amabutho* into two separate commands, with Wood's column perceived as the greater threat. No fewer than 20,000 warriors were allocated to the north; the warriors sent south to face Eshowe were numerically far inferior to the northern force.

Overall command of the southern force was given to Somopho kaZikihala who was chief of a section of the Thembu people and part of Cetshwayo's inner circle. He controlled an area just north of Eshowe from his *ikhanda*, emaNgweni. Also under his command was none other than Prince Dabulamanzi, who controlled the immediate surrounds of Eshowe and had led the attack on Rorke's Drift. His name was derived from the verb *ukudabula* that means 'to tear or split' and *amanzi* or 'waters'. It is said that his father, King Mpande, was crossing the Blood River when his wife gave birth. On 24 May, in celebration of the Queen's birthday, all the British troops would be issued with a tot of rum and the navy their grog. The men jocularly referred to the issue as a 'Dabulamanzi' or 'twice watered.'[166]

Companies of the Nkobamakosi *ibutho*, under the fearless Sigcwelegecwele kaMhlekehleke of the Ngadi lineage who had led his regiment at Isandlwana, formed the 'chest' or main strike force for the Gingindlovu battle. Sigcwelegecwele's prowess in battle, together with his outstanding physique, described by Bertram Mitford following their meeting in 1882, set him apart:

> A fine looking man, in the prime of his life, tall and broad-shouldered, and carried his shaven head as erect as if it ought to wear a crown instead of a shiny ring of mimosa gum . . . and I thought that if the Ngobamakosi could show many men like its chief, small wonder at it being the crack corps.

Elements of the uNokhenke, uMbonambi and the Hlalangwezwa regiments were all present, as was chief Mavumengwana kaNdlela Ntuli, second-in-command at Isandlwana. The Hlalangwezwa regiment was commanded by Phalane kaMdinwa who had previously been appointed to high office by King Mpande. Somopho's army was estimated to be in the region of 10,000–12,000 men.

Aware that a strong enemy force had crossed into Zululand on 29 March, Somopho hastened to assemble his *amabutho* in order to attack the relief column before it could reach Eshowe. First, however, Prince Dabulamanzi, one of the few mounted Zulu commanders, persuaded Somopho to allow the *amabutho* to rest after the strenuous exertions of hastening to the assembly point near Eshowe.

There can be little doubt that a detailed reconnaissance of the laager had been made, either by scouts or by local *izinduna*. Based on this intelligence, Somopho split his force into three elements. The first, positioned behind uMisi Hill, would launch its attack from the west. Its objective was to encircle the western and northern sides of the square; command of this force was given to Prince Dabulamanzi.

The second element, under the command of Sigcwelegcwele, was to move from the valley behind Wombane Spur, where it had spent the night of the 1st, advance three miles along the far bank of the Nyezane River and then cross the river near the old mission station. It would then split into two columns and advance to encircle the east and south sides of the square. The third force was to be held in reserve on the hills to the north-east of the Nyezane.

Although no primary source evidence exists, it is probable that Somopho attempted to direct the battle from these hills. Shortly before the first streaks of dawn at 6.13 a.m., the warriors of Somopho crossed the Nyezane, clad only in loin skins and armed with old weapons supplied in the past by John Dunn, together with a sprinkling of Martini-Henry rifles captured at Isandlwana. They advanced then fanned out into two columns, taking advantage of the long grass to mask their movements, determined to dig the 'wild pigs' out of their burrows.

They moved swiftly to their objective, which was the eastern face held by the 3rd/60th. The second column veered to its left, taking advantage of the cover afforded from the shallow valley of the Gingindlovu Stream. It then swung round to attack the 57th. Both these columns had a shorter distance to cover than Prince Dabulamanzi's force advancing from behind uMisi Hill to the west; hence the timing of the overall attack lacked a degree of co-ordination. Somopho, unable to exert any direct control due his distant position, could only watch.

Dunn recorded that the cry went up: 'There they are.'

The Zulus advancing on the 60th, led by Sigcwelegcwele, broke into a fast walk. To the west, Dabulamanzi's warriors emerged slowly from the bushes and scrub behind uMisi Hill to form the delayed Zulu right horn. Apart from the odd shot fired by retiring picquets and Barrow's mounted men, the square was silent. Captain William Molyneux recorded that the officer in charge of the Gatlings pleaded with the nearby Chelmsford, who was observing the Zulu advance, to allow his crew to test the range on the Zulus. Chelmsford, although keen to maintain strict fire control, relented, and Molyneux went on to record:

> The Chief [Chelmsford] who was close by did not object to the range being tested, providing he stopped at once. A final sight, and, I am sure, quite two turns of the handle was the response, and there was a clear lane cut quite through the body of men . . . the Captain of this gun was a veteran, and afterwards during the fight his exhortation to his crew would have made, when carefully expurgated, an admirable essay on behaviour under fire.

Still the warriors closed the gap and still the troops sweated waiting for the order, then suddenly, all hell let loose as Chelmsford nodded and the order rang out, 'FIRE.' Dawnay recorded: 'I never imagined even such a crash as the whole thing.'

Captain E. T. H. Hutton of the 3rd/60th recorded:

> The Zulus broke into three lines, in knots and groups of from five to ten men, and advanced towards us . . . The Zulus continued to advance, still at a run, when they began to open fire. In spite of the excitement of the moment, we could not but admire the perfect manner in which these Zulus skirmished A small knot of five to six would rise and dart through the long grass, dodging from side to side with heads down, rifles and shields kept low and out of our sight. They would then suddenly sink into the long grass and nothing but puffs of curling smoke would show their whereabouts. Then they advanced again, and their bullets soon began to whistle merrily over our heads or strike the little parapet in front. We had been ordered to reserve our fire, and then fire by volleys at 400 yards distance. The Gatling had begun, however, and it was with difficulty that I could make the order to fire be heard by my company. Not ten minutes had elapsed from the time that the first moving mass of the enemy was seen among the trees on the Inyezane to the moment we began to return their fire; so rapid had been this perfect advance on the part of our savage enemy.

From this description it is clear that the Zulu commanders who had been present at Isandlwana had learnt an important lesson. Frontal advance in mass extended line was now replaced with smaller groups or knots of men moving under cover and returning fire as and when the opportunity occurred. Notwithstanding this highly sensible change in tactics, the overwhelming firepower of the massed square was to prove too much for the gallant Zulu.

A few days before, on 25 March, Chelmsford had elevated Dunn to the position of personal advisor:

> Dear Mr Dunn,
> I am much obliged to you for your suggestions regarding the employment of your men as scouts, which will be carried out. I think it will be very advantageous if you yourself were to accompany me as far as the Inyenzani [*sic*] River. I would not ask you to go further. Your presence with me would ensure the efficient scouting of your men, and I feel sure that I should derive much assistance from your experience of Zulu warfare and from your knowledge of the country passed through . . .
> I should not of course ask you to do any work with the scouts, but simply to accompany me as advisor.[167]

Now, throughout the battle, Dunn seemed to enjoy his elevated status. Being an accomplished hunter and exceptional shot, he soon entered the fray. Climbing atop an ammunition wagon, he waited for the Zulus to get within 300 yards before engaging his enemy, claiming that he 'fired over thirty shots, and missed very few'. Molyneux, watching Dunn, observed that he 'picked out an Induna or two'.

Dunn noted that the volleys fired by the companies were striking well above their mark:

> I called to Lord Chelmsford, asking him to give orders for lowering the sights. This was done, and the soldiers began to drop the enemy faster and, consequently, check the advance, but again, when I had my sight down to one hundred yards as the Zulus came nearer, I noticed that the soldiers had up the three hundred yard sights . . . I was much disappointed at the shooting of the soldiers. Their sole object seemed to be to get rid of ammunition or firing so many rounds per minute at anything . . . it didn't matter what.

This seems rather a harsh judgement in view of the controlled volley fire that was being delivered, but then Dunn, being an experienced hunter, would perhaps expect his high standards to be the norm for ordinary soldiers.

The battle began to increase in intensity with the rockets hissing their way skywards. Dawnay, however, was critical of the gunners' efforts:

> The rockets and shells were tried at them; I can't say, though, I was impressed by the accuracy of either. One rocket struck the ground not a quarter of a mile away and came straight back over the camp! The big bodies of Zulus broke up in skirmishing order before crossing the ridge, and the way they came on was magnificent.

As the initial attack gained momentum within the first ten minutes, so did the intensity of fire put down by the warriors and British casualties soon began to occur. Brevet Lieutenant-Colonel Francis Vernon Northey, commanding the 3rd/60th Rifles and standing near the Gatling on the southeast corner of the square, was struck by a bullet just below the right shoulder. He was helped to the ambulance wagon, where it was initially thought that the wound was not serious, but the bullet, instead of exiting, had worked its way to lodge itself against his spine. He succumbed to his wound four days later.

Lieutenant-Colonel Crealock received a slight wound when a bullet grazed his upper right arm and Captain Molyneux had his horse shot from under him. Captain Barrow sustained a slight wound to the right thigh from one of the bullets thudding into the square. In the first few minutes of the action the 3rd/60th took five casualties, including Colour-Sergeant Dallard, who was shot in the head but survived. With these casualties and with the knowledge that their colonel was struck down, morale began to sag. Company commander Edward Hutton later wrote:

> A few men showed signs of firing wildly, but a smart rap with my stick soon helped a man to recover his self-possession ... the firing now became pretty hot, and the whistling of bullets continuous. In spite of our steady fire the Zulus continued their advance nothing daunted, the force attacking our front utilising cover. The donga to the right of my company appeared to be full of Zulus, who by groups of ten or fifteen began to make rushes for a clump of palm bush ten yards from us.[168]

The young soldiers of the 3rd/60th now started to waver, as one of their officers recorded:

> Our men were awfully frightened and nervous at first, could not even speak and shivered from funk, so we the officers had enough to do to keep the men cool.[169]

However, the crisis passed, as the Zulus were unable to concentrate sufficient men to organise a determined rush at the square, the Gatling being decisive in spewing its hail of death. The Zulu momentum faded away and the warriors pulled back looking desperately for cover. The time was approximately 6.40 a.m., and Chelmsford, perceiving a general retreat, sent Barrow's MI prematurely out of the square to follow up the supposed victory. The Zulus had by no means given up and rallied to drive Barrow's 150 mounted men back, as Molyneux recorded: 'The Chief, fearing Barrow may be cut off, ordered me to recall him. It was done only just in time, for we had to fight our way back.'

Meanwhile Colonel Clarke's 57th on the south face were far steadier and more experienced than their counterparts. The Zulu left horn, now in dead ground some 500 yards distant from the 57th, made a concerted uphill rush to close with the square, only to be met by controlled volley fire. Captain

Hinxman, commanding one of the companies, received a gunshot wound to the right leg and three other soldiers were slightly wounded, but the Zulu attack was repulsed with ease.

Elements of the Zulu column that had pushed Barrow back, now veered off to the long grass facing the 99th and the Buffs, to be joined by men from Prince Dabulamanzi's force, who had entered the fray and were moving rapidly to encircle the west and northern faces of the square. Volley after volley crashed out, bringing the attack to a halt. The long grass may have hidden the Zulu attackers from sight but it was no protection from the bullets that saturated the area.

Twenty-nine-year-old Lieutenant George Johnson was the 99th's musketry instructor, having graduated with a first-class certificate from the School of Musketry at Hythe. He had positioned himself on the right flank of the regiment where it linked with the Buffs. His youthful looks had previously drawn the attention of Chelmsford, who politely inquired as to his length of service, no doubt registering surprise at the answer. Anxious to join the fray, Johnson now grabbed a Martini-Henry from one of his men and began firing at a Zulu sniper, then suddenly placed his hand to his breast and exclaimed, 'I am shot.' Within minutes he lay dead on the field. The 99th was also to lose Privates Smith and Lawrence killed in the battle and four other soldiers wounded.

At approximately 7.00 a.m. Lieutenant-Colonel Bruce's 91st at last came into action as Dabulamanzi's right horn started to envelop the rear face of the laager. During the fire-fight that ensued, the 91st lost one man killed and four wounded.

The brave and suicidal assault of the Zulus on all fronts had now lost momentum and there was a lull in the firing. The bugle sounded 'cease firing' and Chelmsford ordered Barrow out again, this time accompanied by Jantze's Horse. The time was now approximately 7.15 a.m. and the battle had lasted just over an hour. Both battalions of the NNC were now also ordered out of the square in pursuit. Having suffered a few casualties whilst within the square, they needed little encouragement. With memories of the fate of their comrades at Isandlwana, they had many a score to settle, as Molyneux remembered:

> One of our native battalions had come across a crowd of wounded Zulus in a patch of bush, and with the chivalry peculiar to the nature of the semi-civilised, were killing them in cold blood and celebrating the heroic deed by a war song.[170]

The infantry manning the square were not allowed to pursue as Chelmsford had little wish to break the laager formation in case of a Zulu counter-attack. In any event, without mounts the infantry were relatively immobile. Captain Hutton's repeated request to be allowed to move forward and fire on the retreating Zulu was met with an emphatic 'no one must leave the laager'.

This was too much for Commodore Richards, commander of the Naval Brigade. Disregarding Chelmsford's orders, he advanced along with his flag-lieutenant to the cheers of the bluejackets.

> 'Go to it, Admiral!' they would shout. 'Now you've got 'em! Look out Sir, there's one to the right in the grass!' till everyone was roaring with laughter.[171]

Barrow's men, armed with sabres, now commenced the dreadful execution of the defeated Zulu, as Chelmsford was to record:

> Led by Captain Barrow's horsemen, the pursuit was carried on several miles. This officer reports the sabres of the Mounted Infantry to have proved of the greatest service, some fifty or sixty men having been sabred . . . from the chance wounded men we have found five miles away, and the execution done at long range by the artillery, I have no hesitation in estimating the enemy's loss at 1,000 men.[172]

Somopho himself, being located with the reserves on the hills to the north, took no part in the battle and quietly retreated. It is doubtful in any event that he would have been in a position to exercise any influence on the outcome of the battle in view of the distances involved. As at Isandlwana, the reserve remained intact and uncommitted, seemingly to enjoy the spoils of victory, but seldom it seemed to influence the course of a battle.

The chase continued for two or three miles with no quarter asked or given. Those found wounded were shot, sabred or speared to death. Driven against the banks of the Nyezane, many Zulus were drowned in their efforts to escape. An old Zulu enjoyed better luck as he zigzagged his way past some of the NNC with bullets snapping at his heels. The officers greeted the poor marksmanship with a degree of sympathetic satisfaction, as the Zulu finally disappeared beyond range and made his escape.

Very few prisoners were taken. Several Zulus were found wearing 24th Regiment belts and pouches taken at Isandlwana, 'while one gentleman went so far as to embellish his person with an officer's sword', reportedly that of Lieutenant Porteous of the 1st/24th, killed at Isandlwana.

Some 600 Zulus were buried in communal graves within a 1,000-yard radius of the camp. The soldiers buried 473 and the Marines 127. Bodies too numerous to locate, many of the wounded having crawled to die some distance from the field of battle, were left as carrion, to remain untouched as skeletons for years to come. The average rate of ammunition expenditure of the infantry manning the square was calculated at about six rounds per man. Add to that a similar average for the cooks, bottle-washers, administrative elements and others, all armed with Martini-Henry rifles and who used the wagons as firing platforms, plus the ten rounds average fired by the irregulars, and the ammunition expenditure comes to a total of approximately 40,000 rounds. In addition the Gatlings, extremely effective, fired 1,200 rounds and the 9-pounders some forty rounds of shrapnel and shell. Overall, the ratio of rifle ammunition expenditure to Zulu casualties would seem to reflect the poor marksmanship highlighted by Dunn. There are two possible reasons for this. The first was that smoke generated from rapid fire within a relatively tight square formation tended to obscure the target. This occurred when individuals, against orders, fired at will as opposed to in controlled volleys. Thus the adjutant of the inexperienced 3rd/60th, Lieutenant Wilkinson, recorded:

> One lesson we learnt in our fight was, that with the Martini-Henry men MUST fire by word of command either by individuals, or at most by sections: independent firing means in twenty seconds firing at nothing, and only helped our daring opponents to get close up under cover of our smoke . . . and I feel sure that for the future we at least shall check our fire in drilling the men, and practice only volley by sections.[173]

Guy Dawnay with the NNC recorded: 'Of course, the general fire of the men did little except make a smoke and spoil our shots.'

The second possible reason was that, when controlled volley fire was being used, the individual soldier was obliged to fire on command, irrespective of whether or not he had a target in his sights. This represented a possible waste of both effort and ammunition. However, volley fire by company sections allowed smoke to clear, thus enabling the adjacent section to then fire a volley on command at identified targets.

The number of Zulus killed in action or who later died of wounds was estimated at 1,000–1,200 out of a total force of 12,000, of which a considerable body was never committed to the attack. Placing a reasonable estimate of Somopho's reserve to be in the region of 4,000 men, or one-third of his total force, this would mean that a maximum of 8,000 men actually mounted the attack. Extrapolated, this would then place a high figure of fifteen per cent of the attacking Zulu force being killed in action or dying of wounds, a proportion that was, from a Zulu viewpoint, unsustainable.

Total British Army and white colonial casualties resulting from the action were two officers and four other ranks killed, with three officers and twenty-three other ranks wounded. The Naval Contingent suffered one officer and six ratings wounded and the NNC lost seven killed and fifteen wounded.

Two months later the war correspondent for the *Illustrated London News* visited the battlefield and recorded:

> A sharp canter of ten minutes brought us up to the Laager, which is still covered with debris. A great many Zulu shields are scattered about the field; any heap which gives the slightest covering is a sure find. The tombstones of Lieutenant Johnstone [*sic* Johnson] and some men of the 99th and that of Colonel Northey, which lies close to them, were rapidly sketched. These were in a good state of preservation; the wooden fencing around Colonel Northey's tomb has a rustic aspect, and the gravestone looks solemn and impressive alone in the centre of this dreary plain.

Epsom was in fact to be Northey's final resting place after the steamship *Tom Norton* had brought his body back to England in mid-December 1879.

If Kambula was the decisive battle of the war, Gingindlovu was to provide another nail in the coffin. The defeat was enough to convince Cetshwayo that a negotiated peace settlement was the best option open to him, but this was an option that Chelmsford would not under any circumstances entertain. There was the small matter of Isandlwana to be avenged and that required a decisive and final military solution.

Chapter 7

The Relief of Eshowe

'Consider all my instructions as cancelled, and act in whatever manner you think most desirable in the interest of the column under your command. Should you consider the garrison of Eshowe as too far advanced to be fed with safety, you can withdraw it.'

Letter from Lord Chelmsford received by Colonel Pearson at Eshowe on 28 January.

———•◦•———

Communication, other than by messenger, existed between the relief column and Pearson at Eshowe by means of the heliograph. This device was invented by Henry Mance in 1869 and first came into use in India in 1873. By the time of the Zulu War it had already seen service in the Afghanistan campaign. The equipment consisted of a mirror mounted on a stand, and used the sun's rays to flash a Morse-code signal at the rate of fifteen to twenty words a minute to a receiving position which could be more than thirty miles away, subject to the local geography and prevailing weather conditions.

The heliograph put into use at Eshowe was improvised and constructed from a mirror found there by Colonel Frederick Forestier Walker, Pearson's Principal Staff Officer. It measured 18 inches by 12 inches and was mounted on a high point of the fort known as Stony Hill and operated by men of the Royal Engineers. The Naval Brigade had established an improvised heliograph station at St Andrew's mission station, two miles north of the Tugela River, on 4 February and it was from there that communication was initially established with Eshowe. Frustrations caused by cloud conditions were frequent, with one amusing incident being recorded:

> When Col. Pearson asked as to the health of his pregnant wife, the signal reported Mrs Pearson is . . . and cut off. Several anxious hours later, the heliograph opened up again with: . . . well, and delivered of a baby daughter.[174]

The Gingindlovu battle, witnessed from Eshowe at a distance of ten miles as the crow flies, was immediately acknowledged and congratulations proffered, as Chelmsford recorded:

> At 8.00 a.m. Colonel Pearson, who, through a glass, had witnessed the fight from Eshowe telegraphed his congratulations to us.[175]

At daybreak the following day, Chelmsford marched out of Gingindlovu, accompanied by the 57th, 3rd/60th and 91st Regiments, together with John Dunn's Scouts and fifty-eight wagons containing stores for Eshowe. He left the 99th Regiment, the two companies of the Buffs, the Naval Brigade and the NNC to defend the camp. The distance by road to Eshowe was fifteen miles and the column, led by the 3rd/60th with Chelmsford in the van, stretched over four or five miles during the advance.

Lieutenant Main, RE, now holed up in the fort, recorded the event:

> On the afternoon of the 3rd April we moved out along the new road some 500 strong to meet the head of the relieving force. The scene 'beggars description' some of our men were so weak and delirious with joy that they actually cried. One of the relieving force, mistaking me, I suppose for a pal, in the dusk, said 'However did you find this b . . . y place?' Melton Prior the artist was one of the first to arrive at a canter and called out 'First in Eshowe,' to which one of our Tommies feebly replied 'You're three months late.'[176]

As the main force approached Eshowe:

> All at once Lord Chelmsford called out, 'Here's Pearson', as that gallant officer on a grey horse, and looking very jolly, as well he might, dashed round the corner of a hill four and a half miles from the camp, and hastened up to the General. 'How are you?' said his Lordship, as he grasped the hand of the Colonel, and hurried on with him to the scene of his long imprisonment.[177]

Chelmsford himself reached Eshowe at 5.30 p.m. The 3rd/60th was at least an hour behind and the 91st, bringing up the rear, only arrived at midnight. Nevertheless, 'As the 91st Highlanders marched up the valley, their pipers struck up "The Campbells are coming".'[178] Chelmsford was greeted with cheers and showered with congratulations.

The ten-week siege had taken its toll, with the death of four officers and twenty-five men. Many of the garrison were sick with fever and diarrhoea, whilst scarce items of food were bid for at a premium. A tin of sardines fetched eleven shillings (£0.55) and a pound of tobacco the exorbitant price of £1. The relief column had arrived just in time as only five days' rations remained.

The architect of Pearson's fort was thirty-six-year-old Captain Warren Richard Colvin Wynne, in command of 2nd Company, Royal Engineers. The full establishment for such a command was six officers and 200 other ranks but Wynne's command was seriously under-manned, comprising four officers and 120 other ranks, not all of whom were in Eshowe. The officers serving under Wynne were the bespectacled Captain D. C. Courtney and Lieutenant H. B. Willock, with Lieutenant Main (of 7th Company, RE) attached.

The news of the defeat suffered at Isandlwana had been received four days after the event, the news being conveyed by runner. The Sappers had then redoubled their efforts to fortify the station, as Wynne, who kept a diary, recorded:

> Commenced revetting the south face with hurdle revetment. Commenced excavating north face . . . RE employed profiling, felling timber, tracing and superintending.

The church was converted to a hospital and catered for up to 120 patients a day. When they completed the fort, the Engineers were tasked to build a new road because the existing road was poor and ran through dense bush. Wynne's dirt road is still in use today and runs east of the military cemetery near the ruins of the old fort.

To relieve the boredom troops enjoyed daily band concerts, attended church parades, Bible classes and even played cricket. However, life was tough as the food was monotonous, with weevils finding a home in the biscuits. The lack of medical supplies resulted in deaths that might otherwise have been avoided. The rainy season that continued through the summer months added to their misery. When the siege was finally lifted, over 200 troops were evacuated by transport, as they were too weak to march.

The waspish Lieutenant Main, subsequently mentioned in dispatches, was particularly critical of his commander:

> I soon saw that Colonel Pearson was of the safety first type and that he did not grasp the fact that our role was one of active and not passive defence, if we were going to help Natal. To sit tight till we were relieved by someone was an easy task, as long as the food lasted, but not a very useful one. We could easily have lured the Zulus into the open to their certain defeat, as our men were still boasting of their easy victory at the Inyezane, but as soon as we sallied out in force the retire was sounded by Pearson from the fort and we were drawn in again . . . but it was easier to sit tight and to gain the name of 'The Bulldog of Ekowe,' as Pearson did later on in England.

At one stage of the siege, Pearson debated with his officers the merits of abandoning Eshowe altogether and Main recorded:

> But, eventually, owing to the powerful argument of Capt. Wynne, who pointed out that if we retired the Zulus would certainly follow and ravage Natal, it was decided to remain, sending back all the mounted men with a convoy of empty wagons and 1 Co. 99th. The credit for this action was entirely due to Wynne as all the others wobbled till he spoke.

On 9 April, his birthday, Wynne died at Fort Pearson, racked with fever exacerbated by diarrhoea. He was buried at the Euphorbia Hill cemetery near Fort Pearson. He was extremely popular, as Corporal Garner of his company recorded in a letter to his own wife:

> Every man in the company regrets his death. I can safely say there is not a man but would do anything for him, he was so respected by them. It was a sad sight to see our men standing over his grave with tears in their eyes. Captain Courtney was the only officer present, the others being up country, but he was so deeply cut up he could hardly read the Burial Service.[179]

Fever and diarrhoea also accounted for twenty-two-year-old 2nd Lieutenant Arthur Clynton Baskerville Mynors of the 3rd/60th. Deeply religious, the popular old Etonian died seventeen days after Wynne, also at Fort Pearson. His final moments were poignantly described by fellow officer, Lieutenant Edward Hutton:

> His servant, Starman, got up and was about to smooth his pillow for him, when the boy, with a smile that I will never forget, turned and whispered, 'Hush, don't touch me, I am going to heaven,' and so fell asleep.[180]

On 4 April, the day after the siege was lifted; Barrow and his mounted men were ordered out of the fort to burn Prince Dabulamanzi's *ikhanda*. Chelmsford and his staff decided to witness the event and reached their destination after a brisk six-mile ride. The *ikhanda* was duly torched, but not without resistance, purportedly from Dabulamanzi himself, who opened fire from high ground at a distance in excess of 1,000 yards. Dunn then fired three rounds in reply before Dabulamanzi retreated and the duel was abandoned. Strangely Dunn never recorded the incident in his memoirs. Three Zulus were captured in the engagement and two were subsequently killed.

The evacuation of the fort at kwaMondi mission station commenced on 4 April. Chelmsford's relieving column left on 5 April, whereupon the Zulus immediately torched the fort. The mission station was never rebuilt and to this day the earthworks and remains are clearly visible. That night Chelmsford camped near the banks of the Nyezane River and, as usual, sentries and picquets were thrown out in advance of the laager. Standing orders were that if shots were fired at night, the picquets and sentries were to withdraw inside the laager.

At 3.15 a.m. a shot rang out, fired by a 91st sentry. Dunn's Scouts immediately evacuated their picquet positions and began to fall back to the laager. The men of the 3rd/60th picquet thought they were under a Zulu night attack, with consequences that Dawnay recorded:

> Their appearance [Dunn's Scouts] created a panic among the 60th picket, who bolted, leaving their officers, and I believe their arms and helmets, on the ground. Their comrades in the trenches, seeing a lot of men coming at a run to them, fired and killed or wounded five of their own men, and eleven of Dunn's. It has thrown a deep gloom on the camp.

Dunn also recorded the incident with anger:

> I seized my rifle and jumped up, but what was my horror when I recognised the voices of some of my unfortunate native scouts calling out 'Friend! Friend!' which they had been taught to respond to the challenge of the sentries. I called out, 'Good God! They are shooting my men down!' and ran out, calling on the soldiers to stop firing. On passing the line of fire I came upon one of my men lying dead in the trench, with a bayonet wound in his chest. On examining the lot I found ten more wounded, two of whom died the next day. To account for this mishap, I must describe the mode that has been adopted as regards the placing of the night picquets that were stationed all round the encampment. My men were stationed outside as fielders to the soldiers' picquets with orders that, on the alarm being given, they were to retire in order on the soldiers, and each lot to retreat to the enclosure. Well, it appears that an alarm had been given for no cause whatsoever, and my men had retired and were coming on with the soldiers, when, although it was known that there was a picquet in that direction, they were taken to be Zulus. The picquet, being of the 60th Rifles, wore dark uniforms. The white picquet took the brunt of the firing off my men, five of them being hit, and in trying to rush the enclosure eleven of my men were bayoneted, three of whom died.

Chelmsford, speechless with rage convened a general court martial:

> I can offer no excuse or explanation of what occurred, beyond the youth of the men of the 60th, for it was perfectly well known to officers and men that these scouts were in front.[181]

A sergeant on picquet duty from the 3rd/60th was reduced to the ranks and sentenced to five years penal servitude but the sentence was later quashed.

Having served under Chelmsford's direct command and been in close proximity to him at all times, Dunn's opinion of Chelmsford was perspicacious:

> During the short time I was with Lord Chelmsford, the opinion that I formed of him was that he was a thorough gentleman and a good and brave soldier, but no General. Should this ever meet his eye, I hope he will forgive me, but my reason for forming this opinion was that I could see that his personal pluck led him to have no regard for the safety of his men. He would select any spot for a night encampment without studying the surroundings. Another of my reasons for my opinion was that he did not keep his men sufficiently together on the line of march, so much so that if the Zulus had been properly led they would have given us much trouble, and cut the column up.

Chelmsford crossed the Tugela back into Natal on 7 April, buoyed not only by relieving Eshowe, but also by the crushing defeat inflicted on the southern Zulu *impi*. There was further good news for reinforcements were pouring into the colony. In total 418 officers, 10,000 other ranks and 1,900 horses had embarked for South Africa to add to the force already under Chelmsford's command.

Chapter 8

The Four Generals

'I fear that the spirits and courage of our army are flagging, they seem to be beginning to fear the Zulu.'

Letter written on 22 June by Frances Colenso, daughter of Bishop Colenso

—»·•·«—

After the news of Isandlwana reached Horse Guards, The Commander-in-Chief of the British Army, the Duke of Cambridge, wasted little time in dispatching reinforcements. Sir Charles Ellice, the Adjutant-General, recorded in a private memorandum:

> As soon as the news of the Isandlwana disaster arrived, HRH selected for service at, and dispatched to the Cape, not one, but three General Officers (Major-Generals Crealock, Marshall and Newdigate) and to these he shortly after added a fourth: H Clifford – all these were mentioned in both regimental and staff service and of proven ability – one of these, Major General Clifford, had moreover great experience in Kaffir warfare, knew the Zulu country and was peculiarly fitted to assume command in case Lord Chelmsford should resign.[182]

Horse Guards' choice would shortly come under extreme criticism, as none of the selected four, and particularly not Crealock, excelled themselves, and it was Sir Garnet Wolseley, not Clifford, who was eventually selected to supersede Chelmsford.

In the meantime, however, Wood's victory at Kambula, together with Chelmsford's own victory at Gingindlovu, had re-energised the campaign. Most of the promised reinforcements had already arrived and, having shaken off their sea legs, were ready to move. Key to Chelmsford's strategy was an effective deployment of his resources. For the first time regular cavalry units with British-procured mounts had arrived in Durban and were ready for action. The infantry and artillery reinforcements allowed Chelmsford the luxury of creating two divisions, together with properly organised lines of communications. Also at his disposal were Wood's and Pearson's existing columns, both of which could be incorporated more flexibly into his tactical thinking.

His original axes of advance in January had been threefold: the coastal route; the central route through Rorke's Drift; and the western route via

160

Utrecht. As a result of the demise of the old central column at Isandlwana, Chelmsford was reluctant to mount the second invasion through Helpmekaar and Rorke's Drift. The reasons he gave were:

> Rorke's Drift was abandoned by me as a line of advance on account of the Greytown–Helpmekaar road, after Isandhlwana, being considered dangerous by the native wagon drivers and leaders who, when the news of the disaster reached the Colony, abandoned their wagons and ran away. It had also the disadvantage of being exposed from the Indeni [Quedini] Forest direction which it was impossible to watch properly.[183]

This decision denied Chelmsford the use of the shorter, inland route to Ulundi. His reasons were not altogether convincing, as the Quedini Forest stretched below the Mangeni Falls area some miles south of any proposed advance route. The most probable reason was the psychological aspect of exposing the advancing troops to the scene at the Isandlwana battlefield where the dead still lay unburied. However, this too could have been avoided had he moved onto the Nqutu Heights north-east of Isandlwana, thence east to Isipezi Hill and onto the Babanango–Ulundi track.

Chelmsford instead chose to use the inland route via the Dundee and Utrecht area, probably influenced by Wood's victory at Kambula and the fact that Wood was familiar with the topography. The delay in moving his troops to an assembly point so far north in all probability cost Chelmsford his position. Certainly, he was criticised from within his command.

Following Gingindlovu, Guy Dawnay left Nettleton's NNC and was appointed to the Intelligence Department in General Newdigate's column, attached to Major-General Marshall's staff. He recorded criticism of Chelmsford:

> All this makes one still more mad at finding oneself here . . . I hope that the General will now close this road, and Conference Hill, Kopje Allein, and Landsman's Drift, open up the Rorke's Drift road, which is 90 miles shorter from Maritzburg, and with different companies, remove from this line, establish two ports between Rorke's Drift and Habanango [*sic* Babanango], and then hurry up to the front himself.[184]

The third alternative open to Chelmsford was the coastal route across the Tugela, thence to Eshowe and on to St Paul's. The Ulundi plain lay to the north-west of St Paul's and this was by far the quickest invasion route. Chelmsford never considered concentrating his entire army to use the coastal route in the belief that the country south of the Mhlatuze River was too difficult to traverse. In fact, had he advanced along the coastline towards Port Durnford before striking north-west to Ulundi, it would, in all probability, have resulted in an early end to the war. The threat of a Zulu invasion into Natal had receded with the defeats suffered at Kambula and Gingindlovu, thus obviating the necessity to guard, in strength, the entire Natal border. On the coast route he could have been supplied from the sea and his commissariat problems would have diminished considerably. The delays he experienced were, to a large degree, due to the scarcity of both wagons and oxen together with so many men being tied up in escort duties. On the route he chose the speed of his advance was the speed of his supply train.

Chelmsford was familiar with logistical problems as his experience, prior to his arrival in South Africa, had been his service with the commissariat in the Crimean and Abyssinian campaigns. Commissary-General Edward Strickland had been appointed by Chelmsford to solve his logistical problems during the first invasion. With a crisis apparent, due largely to the non co-operation of Sir Henry Bulwer, the Lieutenant-Governor of Natal, who showed little enthusiasm for the invasion plan or for the use of Natal levies across the border, Chelmsford requested the implementation of martial law. Bulwer opposed this request and the matter was dropped.

—————•◦•◦•—————

The arrival of reinforcements for the second invasion, although welcome, greatly exacerbated Chelmsford's logistical problems. The wagons and oxen needed to sustain such a force on two fronts were simply not available. Consequently, on 14 May, Chelmsford wrote to the Duke of Cambridge, admitting that his transport system had broken down.

However, the towns on the invasion route were experiencing a boom. Hotels had sprung up every few miles and provided luxuries at a price. Trade boomed at Ladysmith where William Clarke, the owner of the Royal Hotel, experienced full occupancy:

> The two stores either side of the hotel, Randles' and Arbuckles' were doing a roaring trade. Mr Spettigue the Chemist, had established himself directly opposite the Royal, a very strategic setting in view of his love of the bottle and the frequent murderous brawls that took place in the bar. He was doing a brisk trade with his well-known 'Horse specific.' Charles Duff Fyfie, the superintendent of roads, was under immense pressure. Hundreds of heavily laden wagons were on the move, breaking down the approaches to the fords, chewing the level roads into a morass, scarring the veldt for hundreds of yards on either side of the track and scouring out deep runnels on the hills.[185]

Upon Fyfie and his small native band depended the movement of the army; indeed he and his cohorts were the unsung heroes of the bedevilled commissariat.

During his Ashanti campaign, Sir Garnet Wolseley had made use of native labour instead of animal-drawn wagons to carry field supplies. Before he reached South Africa to supersede Chelmsford, his plan to overcome the logistical problem was the mass use of native porters:

> If I could now only form a great base on the sea near Crealock's present position & land at least a month's supply for everyone there, and unite

the two columns, get rid of the wagons & substitute about 10,000 carriers instead, I think I could see my way to a speedy termination of this war.[186]

This alternative was open to Chelmsford but never seriously considered due to Bulwer's opposition. Had Chelmsford insisted on the imposition of martial law (following which wagons and supply services could have been requisitioned at fixed prices rather than procured at inflated market prices), he may well have considered alternate plans for the second invasion. Instead Chelmsford made the mistaken decision to open two fronts.

The first force would invade along the coastal route and cross the Tugela near Fort Pearson, whilst the second and larger force would advance initially to Dundee and then establish a supply depot at Landman's Drift, the designated assembly area for the launch into Zululand.

On 22 April, Newdigate visited Wood at Kambula. The following day they made a reconnaissance south-east, to the neighbourhood of Inhlazatye Mountain, a prominent feature 6,000 feet above sea level. To its east lay Ulundi. This route was then accepted by Chelmsford as the main invasion path and a new supply depot to service this route established at Conference Hill, north of Landman's Drift. However, having established this depot, Chelmsford then changed his mind. In a letter to Wood, he wrote:

> If we advance from the Utrecht base by road south of Inhlazatye, we are at once on the line of retreat of any force raiding across the Tugela, and can really give Natal very effective assistance. If however we take the northern road (via Inhlazatye Mountain) and a raid be made into Natal I feel sure that I should be blamed for my strategy and very properly so.[187]

This decision resulted in the depot at Conference Hill being moved south to Koppie Allein. Chelmsford's reasoning ignored the fact that the defeats suffered by the Zulus at Kambula and Gingindlovu had affected their offensive capability. A raid in any strength in sustained depth and duration into Natal was highly improbable.

A new invasion route was now selected along the Babanango track to Ulundi, though it had some drawbacks as Chelmsford recorded:

> I am willing to admit that the Babanango road is the worst of the two, but I am certain that I am right in determining that our main line of advance shall be made upon it.[188]

Major Clery spelled out the confusion that existed in April due to Chelmsford's vacillation, when writing to Sir Archibald Alison of Army intelligence:

> The first orders, when they came, were to fill up Helpmekaar and Rorke's Drift for a fresh advance, with a considerable fort to be built at the latter point. When this was nearly completed and 1,000 tons of stores accumulated at Helpmekaar an order was issued that the Rorke's Drift line would be abandoned, and that by Landman's Drift and Conference

Hill substituted, and that all these supplies were to be removed to Dundee, a fort built there and fresh stores erected. The advance depot (1st) was to be at Conference Hill and iron stores have just been erected there. Within the last few days this, it appears, is to again be altered and the line of advance to be by Koppie Allein and over by the Nhlabamkhosi . . . I do not doubt it will all come right in the end, but this delay is very wearing and unsatisfactory.[189]

Sir Garnet Wolseley viewed this as: 'A direct violation of all strategical theories, and carried out in defiance of every tactical principle'; adding that he believed it was: '. . . conceived in ignorance of war's science & carried out in violation of all the principles of its art.'[190]

On 23 May Sir Garnet had an interview the Duke of Cambridge:

He [the Duke] asked me if I could explain the reasons that must have influenced him [Chelmsford] in making such a faulty plan of campaign: I said I could not beyond supposing he had done so with a view to convenience of supply and the idea that by operation in four columns he would best protect Natal from invasion The subject was a delicate one as I knew H.R.H. had defended Chelmsford and it was not my business to find fault with the strategy of a commander who had been selected by the C. in C.[191]

Is such a serious charge warranted? Two of the accepted principles of war are worthy of close examination in the context to Wolseley's charge of 'ignorance of war's science'.

<hr>

Selection and maintenance of aim. The aim should be single, clear-cut and unambiguous. Unfortunately, in Chelmsford's case, short of enforcing the ultimatum issued to Cetshwayo, there seemed no clear-cut aim. On the one hand Chelmsford recorded: 'I was requested to place the troops at my disposal in such positions as would best defend the colony',[192] but on the other: '. . . troops were to move across the lower Tugela and Blood Rivers, there to remain halted with the object of showing that the government had every intention of enforcing terms.'[193]

Clearly the aim of defending the colony was linked to an alternative aim of offensive action to enforce the terms of the ultimatum. The situation was further clouded by Sir Henry Bulwer's assumption that the quarrel was with King Cetshwayo and not the Zulu people, a totally misplaced viewpoint. The Zulu people deeply resented the invasion and, with the exception of Hamu and his followers, rallied to their king.

There is other evidence for what Chelmsford planned. Major Gerald French, in his biography of Chelmsford written with access to Chelmsford's papers, suggested: 'Lord Chelmsford's force entered Zululand in three columns . . . right, centre, and left . . . with the object of converging on Ulundi, the King's Kraal.'

Major Cornelius Francis Clery, Colonel Glyn's principal staff officer, was critical, stating that the aim, if any, was nebulous. In a letter to Sir Archibald Alison, dated 18 March, he said:

> Practically therefore the plan of campaign was this: each column was to start from its own point for the King's kraal, Ulundi, and get there as best it could or near it.[194]

On 21 April, prior to the second invasion, Chelmsford redefined his aim in a letter to Sir Bartle Frere:

> My own view is that we should keep the Zulus collected together, and to prevent them as much as possible settling down in their own kraals, where they would be able to reap their own crops and where they would not feel the inconvenience of a state of war. This can be done by threatening the country in as many directions as possible.[195]

Finally, Clery, in a letter to Alison in late April, was adamant that no specific objective existed:

> At this very moment I regret to say that I don't believe the general has any plan, or knows what he is going to do. I do not say this lightly, but unfortunately from conviction.[196]

Strategic military objectives are seldom achieved without a clear unambiguous aim. In military teachings the selection of aim is always in the singular. A clear unambiguous aim and directive to Chelmsford should perhaps have been something akin to: 'To defeat the military power of the Zulu nation as expeditiously as possible.' This would be in support of the political aims of Sir Bartle Frere to subjugate Zululand.

Concentration of Force. With the invasion force divided into separate columns, out of direct communication with each other and unable to provide mutual support, this principle was ignored. The initial result was the Isandlwana defeat. During the second invasion, the formation of two divisions, neither able to offer mutual support to the other, was in flagrant opposition to this principle of war.

Whether or not Chelmsford's initial arrogance regarding the Zulu fighting capacity was the primary cause of the disregard of these two principles, Sir Garnet's assessment of Chelmsford was both conclusive and damning.

The 1st Division, South African Field Force, was commanded by Major-General Henry Hope Crealock, older brother of Colonel John North Crealock, Chelmsford's Assistant Military Secretary. Crealock senior had been commissioned into the 90th Light Infantry in 1848. He saw active service in the Crimea and the Indian Mutiny and, prior to his South African appointment, was the Deputy Quartermaster-General in Ireland. Like his younger brother he was a talented artist, his best known work being *Deer Stalking in the Highlands of Scotland*.

The 1st Division's initial area of operations was the coastal region, previously under the command of the newly promoted Brigadier-General Pearson. Its task was to advance from Fort Pearson and, in accordance with Chelmsford's orders:

> Form an entrenched position on the Nyezane river and throw into it two months supply for your whole force; then from there move along the coast road across the Umhlotosi River and attack and burn the Mangweni kraal which is near the Empangeni Mission station. Then if possible move against the Undine kraal and burn that. From that point you will be able to judge whether you can again cross the Umhlotosi River and reach St. Paul's on the main Ulundi road . . . the Umhlotosi is very difficult for ox-wagons to cross and the bush in it very thick.

Chelmsford then went on to add that Crealock would have to make his own decisions:

> I always considered that this force [Chelmsford's own northern force] must trust entirely to its own resources, and not rely upon any help from the coast column, which was virtually an independent force.[197]

Crealock's orders were vague to say the least. Tasked to burn 'two kraals', he was then to attempt to reach St Paul's and thereafter to act on his own initiative. No clear instruction was given to link up with the northern column, or firm orders to advance on Ulundi with the aim of bringing the Zulu to battle. Nor did he achieve any success in containing Zulu forces in the coastal area and, when the call to arms was issued by Cetshwayo to his *amabutho* in June, Crealock failed to pin down or contain any of the Eshowe area *amabutho*. The final battle of Ulundi would be fought with all available Zulu regiments. None would be left to engage the 1st Division.

A man of the calibre of Wood might well have relished the directive Chelmsford issued to Crealock. It was tantamount to a licence to act with total independence, unencumbered by further directives or controls from higher command. However, Crealock sadly lacked both drive and initiative. Notwithstanding his commissariat problems, his activities elicited little in the way of praise from either his peers or the rank and file.

Sir Garnet Wolseley's views on Crealock were less than flattering:

> We reached Crealock's Column before dark – He came out to meet us. Just the same vain swaggering snob he has always been. I believe his manner to his Staff & all about him is most disagreeable & his manner to the men, as it always was in the 90th, is offensive. I hate hearing him speak to soldiers as he addresses them as if they were dogs and not men – most of them are more men than he is a man.[198]

Nonetheless, Crealock had under his command a considerable force:

Order of Battle: 1st Division

1st Brigade

2nd Bn, 3rd Regiment (The Buffs)
(8 companies)

88th Regiment (Connaught Rangers)
(6 companies)

99th (Duke of Edinburgh's) Regiment
(8 companies)

2nd Brigade

57th (West Middlesex) Regiment
(8 companies)

3rd Bn, 60th Rifles
(7 companies)

91st Highlanders
(8 companies)

Maj-Gen H. H. Crealock

Brig-Gen C. N. Pearson
Lt-Col H. Parnell

Lt-Col W. Lambert

Lt-Col W. H. D. R. Welman

Col C. M. Clarke
Major J. R. K. Tredennick

Major A. Tufnell

Lt-Col A. C. Bruce

Crealock's command therefore comprised no fewer than forty-five imperial infantry companies. The artillery included ten 7-pounder guns with Lieutenant-Colonel F. T. H. Law in command.

Captain Bindon Blood commanded 30th Company RE, complete with a full complement of wagons, draught animals and a half pontoon section of the Bridging Battalion, Royal Engineers. The pontoon was known as the Blood Pontoon after its commander. Blood came from an old Irish family. An ancestor, Thomas Blood, had stolen the Crown Jewels, but was later pardoned by Charles II, and another ancestor, Colonel Holcroft Blood, though an engineer, had commanded the guns at the Battle of Blenheim.

The division also had under its command, the 4th and 5th Battalions, 7th Regiment Natal Native Contingent, commanded by Captain Geoffry Barton and Commandant W. J. Nettleton respectively. Both had fought at Gingindlovu.

John Dunn's Scouts completed the division.

High incidence of sickness was to add to Crealock's problems. The Natal winter was notorious for ills, as the *Illustrated London News* reported:

> There are eight hundred men hors de combat from the 1st Division. This is a big number out of a force of less than six thousand. If the present rate of sickness continues there will be no field officers left at the disposal of the General. Brigadier [*sic*] Clarke is now laid up with fever. Yellow jaundice has recently appeared among the troops. A great deal of sickness may be ascribed to the effluvia which arises from the carcasses of oxen in different stages of decomposition. These lie in the road where the troopers have to escort the convoys, and at every hundred yards this horrible atmosphere has to be breathed.[199]

Crealock, perhaps due in part to the general state of health in his division, was to earn an unenviable reputation as a laggard, his command being universally branded as 'Crealock's Crawlers.'

Whatever his failings, he disapproved of Chelmsford's campaign plan. In a letter of 1 May, written to Sir Archibald Alison, Crealock said:

> Had Chelmsford thought proper to have concentrated his column of advance and held onto his wings, concentrated, I think we should have been able to pull through, as we need not have had double lines of command as at present.[200]

This was valid criticism indeed, for a single swift thrust might well have ended the war and obviated the necessity for Horse Guards to replace Chelmsford.

The continued dissatisfaction with the progress of Crealock's command was reflected in a letter of 26 June written by Colonel Arthur Harness to his family:

> We are all very angry at Crealock not coming on. He should be up with us now . . . He was ordered to move on 1 June but I believe he says he won't move till he has three month's supplies.[201]

After the Battle of Ulundi, Crealock was the butt of numerous jokes in the army and South African society. On 29 July at a dinner party hosted by Sir Henry Bulwer, a guest remarked: 'Have you heard the news? They've found Crealock.' This brought the house down in a roar of laughter, for in one of Chelmsford's telegrams that had been published he concluded by asking plaintively, 'Where is Crealock?'[202]

John Dunn, who spent most of the second invasion by Crealock's side as advisor on Zulu matters, related an incident that caused much amusement in the division:

> We were riding in the direction of Guzana's kraals, when we espied a cow running towards us, the General called out, 'the first man that reaches her can claim her.' I was in advance, and was reigning in my horse to give the General the lead, which, fortunately for me, he took. As soon as he got up to the cow she charged him, and before he had time to get out of her way, she struck his horse with her horn between his hind legs, ripping out his entrails. I then shot the cow; but the General lost a good horse, as it died shortly afterwards.

The Natal press published a report on this unusual happening as: 'During a reconnaissance a cow charged General Crealock and gored his horse, which died almost immediately.'[203] Clery then mocked the incident in a poem that he sent to Alison, titled, *Sic itur ad Astra* ('Such is the way to the stars').

Dunn noted his personal views on the general in his memoirs published in 1886:

> The opinion that I formed of this General was that he was a good commanding officer, looking well after his commissariat, and sick in the Hospital, but if ever he should read this, he must excuse me saying that

if fighting had occurred he would not have shone as a General. But I might be wrong.

Thus the 1st Division was, due to the limitations of its commander, to play a minor role in the second invasion.

———※◦◦◦———

Order of Battle: 2nd Division	*Maj-Gen E. Newdigate*
1st Brigade	*Col R. Glyn, 24th Regiment*
2nd Bn, 21st Royal Scots Fusiliers (6 companies)	*Major A. G. Hazlerigg*
58th (Rutlandshire) Regiment (6 companies)	*Col R. C. Whitehead*
2nd Brigade	*Col W. P. Collingwood, 2nd/21st*
1st Bn, 24th Regiment (7 companies)	*Major W. M. Dunbar*
94th Regiment (6 companies)	*Lt-Col S. Malthus*
Artillery	
N Battery, 5th Brigade (6 x 7-pounders)	*Lt-Col A. Harness*
N Battery, 6th Brigade (6 x 9-pounders)	*Major F. T. Le Grice*
Engineers	
5th Company, Royal Engineers	*Captain W. P. Jones*

Major-General Edward Newdigate was born in 1825. He was educated at Sandhurst and commissioned into the Rifle Brigade. He served in the Crimean War and in the Red River expedition in Canada. After his return to England he was appointed to command the Chatham District, then a substantial fortress on the approaches to London. From there Horse Guards selected him as one of the four major-generals to serve under Chelmsford and, on arrival in South Africa, he was appointed to command the 2nd Division in its advance to Ulundi. Newdigate was small in stature, with a round face, short light hair and whiskers. Lieutenant W. E. Montague, who served in his division, described him as:

> Pleasant to talk to, rather fond of laying down the law, and always dressed in the neatest of uniforms. His buff leather straps over both shoulders were spotless, and his gold-banded hat shone throughout the campaign with untarnished lustre. We liked him, men and officers, and were only sorry that Lord Chelmsford's presence with the Division allowed him no opportunity of proving his soldier-like abilities.[204]

Newdigate's command comprised no fewer than twenty-five imperial companies including those of the 1st/24th whose ranks had been decimated at Isandlwana and had since been made up to strength by large drafts.

It has long been assumed that the troops who reinforced the depleted 1st/24th were raw young men. In fact they were soldiers who volunteered for transfer from fifteen different regiments, a total of 525 all ranks under the initial command of Colonel H. F. Davies, Grenadier Guards. However, amongst them were many young and inexperienced soldiers who had just completed their training. Mindful of the fate of their battalion at Isandlwana, their fear of the Zulu was very much in evidence and further misfortune was to dog them.

They embarked at Woolwich aboard the SS *Clyde*, destination Cape Town. The *Clyde* ran onto a reef in the early hours of 2 April 1879 just off Cape Town. Davies, with luck on his side, organised the evacuation of all ranks, together with the full horse complement. No lives were lost and the men were transferred from the slowly sinking *Clyde* onto the *Tamar* and taken to Simons Bay. However, arms and ammunition, including Gatlings, sank with the *Clyde*.

The men arrived in Port Natal on 11 May and formed part of the 2nd Division. Certainly Chelmsford saw to it that neither Glyn nor the regiment would take part in the final Battle of Ulundi, thereby avoiding the risk of further casualties. This, however, was in direct contradiction to the Duke of Cambridge's wishes. In a letter dated 6 March to Sir Bartle Frere, the Duke stated: 'I have strongly urged the general to keep the battalion of the 24th Regiment thus reorganised on the front and give it a chance of obtaining fresh laurels.'[205] This was advice Chelmsford was to ignore.

The 2nd Battalion, 21st Royal Scots Fusiliers, also had a troubled journey. This battalion's transport, the *City of Paris*, ran onto rocks in attempting to enter Simons Bay. The captain managed to save the ship by reversing engines, but not before sending signals of distress and preparing the lifeboats for use. The battalion eventually reached Durban aboard the *Tamar* on 31 March. From there it marched to Klip River *en route* to Utrecht. The entire local school played truant to watch the extraordinary sight of the men wade through waist-deep water, then saw them: '. . . step briskly in dripping kilts behind the skirling pipes. The African women were horrified by these bearded females.'[206] On 30 April the Fusiliers reached Dundee, described by an eyewitness thus: 'It looked very soldier-like as the column came swinging over the ridge, with its kilted pipers playing a pibroch at its head.'[207]

The 58th Regiment embarked at Plymouth in the hired vessel *Russia*. Prior to embarkation they were inspected by no less a luminary than the Duke of Cambridge. They disembarked at Durban on 4 April and marched straight to Pietermaritzburg.

The 94th Regiment was hastily brought up to strength in Aldershot with a draft of 350 men. Its arrival in South Africa was fraught with danger as the *China* ran into a gale force wind that necessitated sailing some distance off course before finally arriving in Durban on 2 April.

Lieutenant-Colonel Arthur Harness, who had lost two of his 7-pounders at Isandlwana, commanded the artillery. Not only was his depleted N Battery, 5th Brigade, brought up to strength, but it was reinforced by N Battery, 6th Brigade, commanded by Major F. T. Le Grice and equipped with the more effective 9-pounders, which would play a significant part in the Battle of Ulundi.

The 2nd Division was tasked to move north. Wood and Newdigate were to operate in tandem, thereby creating a dilemma for Chelmsford. Wood held the rank of colonel and logically, being junior, would come under Newdigate's command. However, Wood's reputation, despite his setback at Hlobane, was largely unsullied and indeed much enhanced following his success at Kambula. Chelmsford had no wish to subordinate him to Newdigate and accordingly wrote to Wood on 17 March: 'I apply today to High Commissioner for your being given local rank of Brigadier General.'[208]

Approval was granted, effective 10 April 1879, and Wood was accordingly given an independent command known as 'Wood's Flying Column'. The Zulus invariably have a nickname for people and Wood was known as *Lukuni*, from *ukuni*, a log of wood, applied to one of a seemingly hard, unyielding nature. Certainly Newdigate was no match for Wood but resented the fact that Wood was not answerable to him.

The third of the major-generals was Frederick Marshall. Educated at Eton, he had gained his commission in the Life Guards in 1849 and served in the Crimean War as ADC to Sir James Scarlett. Chelmsford appointed him to command the Cavalry Brigade, which comprised the 17th Lancers and 1st King's Dragoon Guards.

Sir Garnet Wolseley was scathing in his opinion of Marshall:

> [I know] how weak we are in General Officers fit for command, but H.R.H. prefers idiots like Marshall whom he has sent out to be made a K.C.B [Knight Commander of the Bath], to really good first rate men like Colley [Wolseley's Chief of Staff]. He knows he can never have anything to fear from a man of Marshall's calibre.[209]

The 17th Lancers were commanded by Colonel D. C. Drury-Lowe who was somewhat fortunate in that the regiment's previous commander, Lieutenant-Colonel Thomas Gonne, had made himself *hors de combat* as a result of an accidental gunshot wound prior to embarkation. Lowe was hastily summoned as replacement. The 17th Lancers were best known for their proud battle honours gained during the Crimean War that included their famous charge at the Battle of Balaclava, immortalised in the poem *The Charge Of The Light Brigade*. They accordingly disembarked from the *England* at Durban to much fanfare.

The 'Death or Glory Boys', as the 17th Lancers who wear the grim skull and cross bones on their sleeves are called, have their whole heart in this expedition. This regiment contributed most numerously to the Light Brigade, whose charge at Balaclava lives forever in the poetry of war . . . the soldiers are men of fine appearance, and in their blue uniforms and white facings, as they led their horses away from the wharves, they looked the very picture of what cavalrymen should be. They are young, lithe, tall, well set, and of excellent physique . . . the horses had been stabled on the upper and main decks, where, housed in with little pent roofs, were horse boxes each filled with a charger – outside, the slinging was very successfully carried on, and the horses were landed at the railway wharf with equal smartness.[210]

When the brigade reached Dundee in early May, the locals were enthralled.

The glamorous Lancers in their snowy plastrons and white-seamed jackets, and the 1st King's Dragoon Guards, with booted overalls and gold lace all complete; looking, as an officer confided to Bindon Blood, 'like a lot of damned tenors at an opera.' There was plenty of dashing sword play to watch.[211]

The work-load of a horse in the Cavalry Brigade was demanding. In action, or on patrol, the horse carried:

Sword, carbine, 100 rounds of ammunition, blankets, picket pegs with valise and cloak, in addition to the trooper, made up a weight most distressing and inconvenient.[212]

The 1st King's Dragoon Guards were commanded by Colonel H. Alexander, and came down from Manchester to embark on the *Egypt*, which left Southampton on 26 February. On arrival, they immediately linked up with the Lancers at a camp established at the foot of the Berea in Durban, and were described by the local press as follows: 'The uniform of the Dragoons is scarlet, and the facings blue, the trousers bearing yellow stripes.'[213]

Within weeks, the trying conditions would reduce the splendid appearance of the men of both Lancers and Dragoons to that of a rag-tag force, whilst officers of all units dressed as they pleased.

Lord Chelmsford as often as not wore 'mufti' – uniform was not easy to replace at the front – a light grey suit, with grey-canvas tops to his riding boots, always kept beautifully clean; and a revolver slung over the shoulder, with sometimes, though rarely, a sword below.

Buller was likewise dressed in 'mufti', rather seedy, with a grey wide-awake hat, tied round with a bit of red cloth, the badge of the volunteers.

Lord William Beresford . . . in a most correct suit of 'mufti' – and was easily known among the rest by his Elwood helmet and grey silk puggaree, used by the staff in India.[214]

Chelmsford expressed his initial delight at the condition of all the cavalry horses on arrival:

> The following day I inspected the 17th Lancers at their camp about four miles from here . . . I was delighted with the appearances of the men and horses. The latter have been landed in the most perfect condition, and altho' not quite fit as yet for any very hard work, so far as appearance and condition are concerned they left little to be desired.[215]

It was an opinion that would change within weeks. The horses would fast lose their splendid condition in trying conditions, coupled with fodder rationing. In late June, Chelmsford recorded:

> I agree with Colonel Lowe that the poor condition of the horses is due to want of a proper quantity of fodder . . . the oats served out have been of very inferior quality, but 8 lbs. is the largest quantity that can be issued, having regard to the amount of transport available.[216]

Captain W. E. Montague confirmed the poor condition of the mounts:

> One of the saddest sights amongst us was the condition of many of the horses of the Lancers; too many, indeed, now but the framework of the animals which landed in such excellent condition at Durban two months previously . . . and rations of these were cut down as we advanced. I remember a trooper passing the troops drawn up for the church service one Sunday morning riding his own and leading a second horse to water. Fifty yards beyond the square, the latter tucked his legs under him and lay down, dying where he lay, too weak to struggle.

Any shortfall of mounts was procured locally, though not always with success. Hope Crealock wrote to his brother in April:

> Healy [Assistant Commissary-General] arrived today . . . His account of Drury L and the remount depot at P.Maritzburg was very amusing, how he walked into the stable, and without examining a single horse condemned the lot en gros, with that magnificent superiority of intellect belonging to the British Dragoon who knows no horse flesh but English. I will venture to bet there were some good ones amongst them, and brutes well adapted for our work here.[217]

The respective merits of the English cavalry horse and the local Basuto pony were well debated. The former usually stood some sixteen hands and was not acclimatised to South African conditions, whilst the latter were stockier and averaged some fourteen hands. Certainly W. Tomasson, who served with Whalley's Irregulars, a unit of Wood's colonial cavalry, felt that the local horses fared better:

> In the Zulu War and at a later date, when alongside the K.D.G.'s and 17th Lancers, we congratulated ourselves on not being mounted on English horses, the majority of whom gave way under the hardships of the campaign.

The Cavalry Brigade's area of operations was contiguous to that of the 2nd Division and Marshall came under Newdigate's command as part of his division.

In a letter to the Duke of Cambridge, dated 14 May, Chelmsford wrote:

> I trust however that with the reinforcements now in the field, we shall be able to finish the Zulu War before the dry season deprives us of the necessary grass. The troops are ready, but the supplies and transport for Genl. Newdigate's force are not yet at the front in sufficient quantities . . . I am afraid Strickland [chief commissariat and transport officer] has been badly served by many of his subordinates who have deceived him as to the amount of supplies sent forward.

He went on to relate the difficulty experienced with oxen, the backbone of the supply system:

> Oxen bought in one part, die if worked in another. They thrive on grass in one district and fall sick if kept long on different grass. They require to be very carefully worked and driven, or they are certain to die or become inefficient, and, if exposed in winter to the cold S.E. wind, even in the day time, great loss of life is certain to ensue.[218]

Transport demands were continually being made. On 19 May Wood wrote to Chelmsford: 'General Newdigate wants 348 wagons to enable him to advance. I cannot get enough from Pretoria whence mine are drawn.'[219] Finally Crealock added to Chelmsford's problems by writing to him on 28 May: 'I require 500 oxen to complete wagon transport. Commissariat inform me they cannot complete me.'[220]

Major-General the Honourable Sir Henry Clifford was appointed Inspector-General of the Lines of Communication and Base up to the Zululand border. Once into Zululand, Major-General Marshall assumed responsibility, much to Clifford's disgust. Clifford's headquarters was initially established at Durban and he had the unenviable responsibility of attending to all transport and supply problems.

Clifford had been gazetted into the Rifle Brigade in 1846. He had already spent time in Southern Africa fighting against Sandile in 1847 and, as a twenty-eight-year-old captain, had served in the Eighth Frontier War in 1852–4. He was to distinguish himself by winning the Victoria Cross in the Battle of Inkerman during the Crimean War. He then went on to assume an appointment as an Assistant Adjutant-General and acted as ADC to the Duke of Cambridge. His selection by Horse Guards was aimed at relieving Chelmsford of the commissariat problems bedevilling the campaign. However, friction arose, due no doubt to Clifford's confrontational attitude. In many instances Clifford's tone and manner were superior, which failed to go unnoticed by many of the high command. Hope Crealock wrote to his brother in April, knowing that the contents would probably reach the ears of Chelmsford:

> I don't know, because I have not been told, what relation I am to Clifford, but he is assuming a tone of dictation in his communications which I do not propose to pay any attention to.[221]

Clifford's dictatorial manner knew no bounds. On 28 April, for example, he sent a brusque telegram to his superior Lord Chelmsford: 'Harrison and Heimage's reports on roads should be sent on to me. Their reports must not be acted on without my order or that of my officer or confusion will be the result.'[222]

Clifford and Commissary-General Strickland, who came under Clifford's command, differed on policy. Clifford wished to establish a central board that would operate according to the principle of 'willing-seller – willing-buyer' so that, once fair prices for transport were established, wagons and oxen would become available for purchase. Strickland, on the other hand, despite Bulwer's views, wanted martial law in order to requisition both men and transport. Clifford in due course came to the conclusion that Strickland was inefficient and a difficult relationship ensued. Eventually Clifford's 'board system' prevailed and the supply of transport improved, but not significantly enough to help the second invasion.

On the advance to Landman's Drift in May, Dundee became a ghost town as units of the 2nd Division moved out.

Horse, foot, guns and thousands of rattling ox-carts were on the move. An immense serpent of russet dust crawled across the green land to the Blood River. While General Newdigate established his H.Q. at Landsman's Drift, the traffic hacked the veldt and every hillside was scarred with wagon parks. Axes sounded constantly as the Army, voracious for fuel, slashed at every patch of bush, and the Doornberg became a target for foraging parties. A week or two, and the camps moved forward again until the final week of June saw them over the border into Zululand.[223]

Wood's Flying Column had meanwhile been patrolling aggressively into Zululand, reconnoitring the Babanango track to establish its suitability for use as an axis of the advance to Ulundi. On 5 May, the long held position at Kambula was abandoned and on 12 May a position established at Wolf Hill, south of Kambula.

At the end of May, the whole of the 2nd Division, Lord Chelmsford and his staff were ready to cross the Blood River into Zululand, whilst the Flying Column had moved from Wolf's Hill south to Munhla Hill, approximately eighteen miles east of Chelmsford's position. After two months of tactical manoeuvring, positioning and re-positioning, the advance to Ulundi commenced.

Little did Lord Chelmsford realise that he had lost the confidence of both

Horse Guards and the government. On 23 May, with the approval of Prime Minister Disraeli, Sir Garnet Wolseley was informed that he was to be Chelmsford's replacement and would leave Dartmouth for Cape Town aboard the SS *Edinburgh Castle* on 30 May.

The memorial on the banks of the Ntombe River to the men of the 80th Regiment. In 1879, the road to Derby continued on up the valley to the left. The high ground to the far right is the Tafelberg, Mbelini's stronghold. *(Ron Lock Collection)*

Meyer's Drift. The cutting for the old wagon road to Derby is still clearly visible. At the time Mbelini launched his attack, the river was in spate and overflowing its banks. *(Arthur Konigkramer Collection)*

It was from this jumble of rocks on Hlobane that the abaQulusi snipers shot Campbell and Lloyd. The cattle kraal where the ponies were sheltered is just below the rocks. *(Ron Lock Collection)*

The southern side of Hlobane looking west. The stone cattle kraal where Wood and his staff sheltered is indicated by an arrow. *(Jack Crutchley)*

The stone wall that the abaQulusi built at the top of Devil's Pass to prevent cattle straying, and which later obstructed the routed colonial horsemen, is still there. *(Ron Lock Collection)*

The entrance to Devil's Pass. The huge boulders in the foreground are replicated all the way down the pass to the nek below. *(Ron Lock Collection)*

The Ityentika Nek and hill beyond where the Border Horse and elements of the FLH were surrounded. Many were killed including Colonel Weatherley and his son. *(Ron Lock Collection)*

The vandalised memorial to Piet Uys on the Ntendeka Nek with Devil's Pass in the background. It is believed locally that graves and memorials contain treasure, hence the excavation. *(From the Hackett Collection)*

The British cemetery at Kambula. The main laager was just beyond the present-day grove of wattle trees on the right. The redoubt and guns were on the mound in the centre of the picture. The Nkobamakosi and uVe regiments were decimated as they charged the defences across the open ground. *(Arthur Konigkramer Collection)*

Kambula. The shallow valley, looking west, from just below the position where the cattle kraal was located. The Zulu left horn advanced along the valley from the east and from its concealment repeatedly attacked the British defences.
(Arthur Konigkramer Collection)

The memorial to the Prince Imperial and the graves of the colonial troopers situated above the donga where they met their deaths. *(Ron Lock Collection)*

Itelezi Hill from the north, a landmark for the British during the second invasion.
(David Rattray Collection)

The British cemetery at Gingindlovu is on the south-eastern edge of the position
of the British square. In the far distance to the right, the Eshowe escarpment.
(Ron Lock Collection)

The war memorial at Ulundi, situated on the ground occupied by the British square, is dedicated to both the Zulu and British dead. *(Ron Lock Collection)*

The graves of unknown British dead situated just below the remains of Fort Nolela. *(Ron Lock Collection)*

Cetshwayo kaMpande,
king of the Zulu nation.
(Local History Museum, Durban)

Colonel Evelyn Wood who commanded
British forces at the battles of Hlobane
and Kambula. *(John Young Collection)*

Lieutenant-Colonel Redvers Buller,
the dashing commander of colonial
cavalry. *(John Young Collection)*

Colonel Hugh Rowlands's ill-fated No. 5 Column marching on Sekhukhune's Transvaal stronghold. *(The Graphic)*

Captain Norman MacLeod, who negotiated the defection of Prince Hamu kaMpande, and later inherited the ancient Scottish title of MacLeod of MacLeod. *(By kind permission of Chief John MacLeod, MacLeod of MacLeod)*

Prince Hamu kaMpande arriving at Kambula Camp. British propaganda cast Hamu as a drunkard, hence the bottle of gin that he holds. *(The Graphic)*

A Zulu warrior with a headdress of sakabuli bird feathers and a bravery claw-necklace award. *(Denis Montgomery)*

A senior Zulu commander, possibly of the 2,500-strong mCijo Regiment. *(Local History Museum, Durban)*

A dramatic contemporary illustration from *The Pictorial World* depicts a Buller-led cattle raid. However, the majority of the raiders would have been armed with carbines rather than swords. *(Collection of the late S. B. Bourquin)*

The slightly built Mbelini *(right)* rests on the boom of a transport wagon. He led the dawn attack on Captain Moriarty's convoy camped on the banks of the Ntombe River. *(Collection of the late S. B. Bourquin)*

Lieutenant and Quartermaster John Newman, 90th Light Infantry *(centre, front row)* and his staff. Note the rum barrel on the left. *(Museum Africa, Johannesburg)*

The warrior clans of Mbelini and Manyanyoba fall upon the convoy of the 80th Regiment in a dawn attack.

A fine study of a Zulu chief, councillors and guards. *(Local History Museum, Durban)*

Captain Ronald Campbell, who lost
his life on Hlobane Mountain.
(KwaZulu-Natal Archives)

Commandant Friedrich
Schermbrucker, commander of the
Kaffrarian Rifles. *(Ron Lock Collection)*

Commandant Pieter Raaff of Raaff's Transvaal Rangers, one of the most experienced frontiersmen in southern Africa. *(Museum Africa, Johannesburg)*

Major William Knox Leet of the 13th Light Infantry commanded Wood's Irregulars and was awarded the Victoria Cross for his gallantry during the retreat from Hlobane. *(Royal Archives, Windsor)*

Captain Robert Barton, had just assumed command of the Frontier Light Horse when he was killed on Hlobane. *(KwaZulu-Natal Archives)*

Colonel Frederick Augustus Weatherley had seen much service in many parts of the Empire before settling in the Transvaal and later raising Weatherley's Border Horse. *(Ron Lock Collection)*

Above: Warriors, possibly of the Umlanga regiment judging by their age and shield colours, stand guard beside their chief, possibly Ntshingwayo kaMahole, the Zulu general who commanded at both Isandlwana and Kambula. *(KwaZulu-Natal Archives)*

Left: The warrior carries a shield in the colours of the uNokhenke, one of the last regiments to be raised by King Mpande. Such men as these were described by Sir Bartle Frere's daughter as being 'reckless of death'. *(Local History Museum, Durban)*

Commandant Pieter Raaff *(seated centre right)* and his officers of the
Transvaal Rangers. *(Museum Africa, Johannesburg)*

Skirmishes between mounted colonials and abaQulusi warriors occurred frequently
prior to the Battle of Hlobane. *(John Young Collection)*

Captain J. Waddy, 13th Light Infantry, was in the thick of the fighting at Kambula. (*Somerset Light Infantry Museum*)

Lieutenant-Colonel J. C. Russell, 12th Lancers, led the western assault on Hlobane, but was then sent to command a remount depot. (*12th Lancers Museum, Derby City Museum and Art Gallery*)

Lieutenant Edward Browne won the only VC awarded at Kambula. (*Royal Regiment of Wales Museum*)

Commandant Charles Dennison, second-in-command of Weatherley's Border Horse, 1879, seen here seated left, *circa* 1900, when he raised and commanded Dennison's Scouts. He was later described as having seen more active service in South Africa than any other living man. (*Ron Lock Collection*)

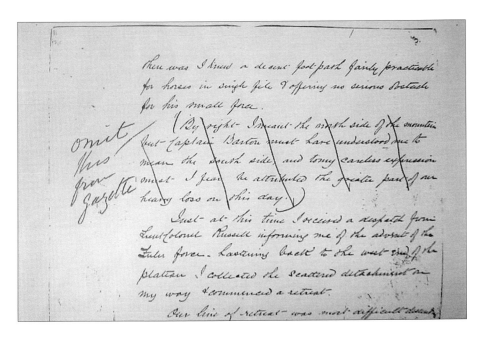

Redvers Buller's report on the Battle of Hlobane with the paragraph confessing to his error crossed out by the hand of Evelyn Wood. *(Local History Museum, Durban)*

A contemporary lantern slide, although inaccurate in much of its detail, nevertheless conveys the confusion and terror of the fighting at Devil's Pass. *(John Young Collection)*

Left: An artist's impression of the last moments of Colonel Weatherley and his son. *(Rai England Collection)*

Below: Colonel Wood reads the burial service for Campbell and Lloyd while men of the Border Horse, to their cost, stand guard. *(By courtesy of the artist, A. A. Race)*

Commandant Piet Uys *(centre)* who was killed on Hlobane while saving the life of one of his sons. *(Collection of the late S. B. Bourquin)*

The field bakery of No. 4 Column, with a pile of freshly cooked loaves, gives an idea of the roughness of conditions while on campaign. *(Museum Africa, Johannesburg)*

Lieutenant Arthur Bright, age 21, was mortally wounded during the bayonet charge of the 90th at the Battle of Kambula. *(John Young Collection)*

Mr J. M. Rathbone, noted war correspondent of the *Natal Witness*. *(Ron Lock Collection)*

Lieutenant Frederick Nicholson, RA, who was mortally wounded at Kambula while directing the fire of his guns. *(Royal Archives, Windsor)*

Major R. H. Hackett, 90th Light Infantry, was severely wounded at Kambula, losing the sight of both eyes. *(Royal Archives, Windsor)*

This sketch of the Battle of Kambula by war artist Melton Prior, who was not present during the engagement nor ever visited the site, is highly inaccurate: the redoubt is too large; the shallow valley which sheltered the Zulu left horn is shown as a cliff-sided chasm; and the onslaught of a thousand warriors against the cattle kraal is depicted as a minor skirmish. *(Illustrated London News)*

Lieutenant-Colonel Redvers Buller winning his Victoria Cross for the rescue at Devil's Pass of Captain Cecil D'Arcy. *(John Young Collection)*

Above: The probable escape route of Dennison and Barton off the Ityentika Nek. The route follows a present-day path that has most likely existed for centuries. There are still mealie fields, as mentioned by Dennison, at the bottom of the descent. *(Jack Crutchley Collection)*

Above left: Fort Pearson seen from the west, with the Indian Ocean in the far distance. The Ultimatum Tree by the Tugela River is hidden from view. *(Museum Africa, Johannesburg)*

Left: The field hospital adjacent to Fort Pearson. *(Local History Museum, Durban)*

Officers and men of the Natal Native Contingent adorned with headgear and uniforms as varied as their weapons. *(Local History Museum, Durban)*

John Dunn and his headmen. *(Collection of the late Colonel S. B. Bourquin)*

Replacement trestle and pontoon bridge over the Tugela River.
(Illustrated London News)

The death of Lieutenant Frederick John Cokayne Frith, 17th Lancers.
(Illustrated London News)

The march to Eshowe. This contemporary illustration gives some idea of the enormity of Lord Chelmsford's transport problem. *(Illustrated London News)*

Inside the British laager at Gingindlovu. The Natal Native Contingent, out of the line of enemy fire, wait in anticipation of pursuit. *(Illustrated London News)*

The Zulu attack having failed, mounted infantry and colonial horsemen pursue the beaten enemy. *(Illustrated London News)*

The ill-fated patrol of the Prince Imperial pauses to brew coffee. Moments later the Zulu attack was sprung and the prince killed. *(Ron Lock Collection)*

Chief Sabuza, headman of the village where the Prince Imperial met his death. Note the temporary nature of his hut, his village having been burnt in retaliation. *(KwaZulu-Natal Archives)*

Louis, the Prince Imperial of France, killed whilst accompanying – or some believe leading – a British patrol. *(KwaZulu-Natal Archives)*

British infantry take their toll as brave Zulu warriors charge the square at Gingindlovu. *(John Young Collection)*

A contemporary photograph of the British cavalry horses being taken to water at
the Umfolozi River, opposite the Nqunqa Bluff, the scene of fierce fighting.
(Local History Museum, Durban)

A fanciful illustration of
Lord Beresford winning
the Victoria Cross by
rescuing Sergeant
Fitzmaurice. *(John Young
Collection)*

Lt Alfred Henderson commanded No 4 Troop, NNH, at Isandlwana and served under Capt 'Offy' Shepstone during the second invasion. Photo, *c.* 1880. *(By kind permission of Gaz Griffin of the Henderson family)*

A fine old Zulu warrior. Sigananda Shezi was born about 1800 and was present at the death of Piet Retief, the Boer leader killed by King Dingaan, in 1838; at the Battle of Ndondakusuka in 1856; the battles of Isandlwana and Ulundi in 1879, and in 1883 he saved King Cetshwayo's life during the Zulu civil war. During the early stirrings of what became known as the Bambata Rebellion, he was arrested by the colonial authorities and died in prison, aged 100, in 1903. *(By kind permission of Mr Arthur Konigkramer)*

Lord William de la Poer Beresford who was awarded the Victoria Cross for gallantry during Buller's reconnaissance towards Ulundi on 3 July 1879. *(John Young Collection)*

Zibhebhu kaMaphitha and his wife. Zibhebhu was an outstanding leader, who played a major role at Isandlwana, Kambula and Ulundi. *(KwaZulu-Natal Archives)*

Colonel Richard Harrison, RE, Quartermaster-General to Lord Chelmsford's invasion columns. *(John Young Collection)*

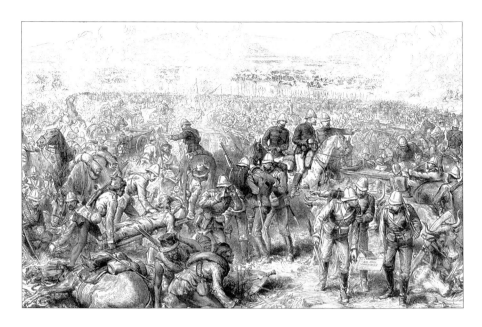

Inside the British square at the height of the Battle of Ulundi. In the centre, mounted, Lord Chelmsford confers with his staff. *(Illustrated London News)*

The final act. The burning of oNdini. *(Illustrated London News)*

Chapter 9

The Death of the Prince Imperial

'What can excuse the pusillanimous eagerness to escape which led Lt. Carey to gallop five hundred yards before he turned his head?'

United Services Gazette, 28 June 1879

Among the many new arrivals who had disembarked at Durban none caused a greater sensation than Louis, Prince Imperial of France, son of the deposed Emperor Napoleon III and great-nephew of the mighty Napoleon Bonaparte. It was a strange place, it might seem, for such a prestigious foreign personage.

In 1870 France had fought a disastrous war with Prussia resulting in the exile of the emperor. He and his family fled to England and lived under the protection of Queen Victoria. The glorious military future that the emperor and his wife Eugenie had visualised for their son seemed gone forever. However, the boy held the hope that one day he would return to France and take his rightful place as emperor – a hope that was not without a chance of fulfilment.

Napoleon III died when Louis was seventeen years old and the prince persuaded his mother to let him enter the Royal Military Academy at Woolwich, there to be trained as an artillery officer. He insisted that he be treated as an ordinary British cadet without favour or privilege. His exuberant nature and charm – despite a tendency to show off – endeared him to his fellow cadets and he finally graduated seventh out of a class of twenty-four. However, it was deemed to be politically incorrect to commission Louis as a British officer. So, when the rest of his class went to their various postings as Royal Artillery subalterns, Louis had to be content with the status of 'honorary officer', his uniform devoid of any badges of rank. In this capacity he joined No. 11 Battery, 7th Brigade RA, at Aldershot. There he revelled in a soldier's life and formed strong friendships with his brother officers, two of whom were Lieutenants Bigge and Slade. It was not long before the battery was sent off to the war in South Africa but Louis, fretting for action and bereft of comradeship, was left behind.

Eventually, with many political hurdles conquered and with the reluctant consent of the Empress Eugenie, Prime Minister Disraeli and Queen Victoria, it was agreed that Louis could proceed to Natal and there join Lord Chelmsford's staff as an observer in a non-combatant capacity. Louis had other ideas. Writing to Bigge, shortly after gaining permission to proceed, he concluded: 'I hope soon to be with you, we will fight side by side.'[224]

Louis's arrival in Cape Town caused a sensation. With the lack of popstars, footballers and the like to idolise, ordinary people saw their heroes in royalty and members of the armed forces:

> All the ships in the roads had been dressed and the arrival of the 'Danube' [the vessel by which the Prince had travelled] had been for the whole town a day of entertainment and public festivity. A grand evening party took place at Government House and all the public and private persons of note of the Colony were invited.[225]

The prince moved on to Durban, with less acclaim it seems, a few days after the Battle of Kambula had taken place. Fired by the news of Wood's success, he longed to become part of the action. With all his other concerns, however, the last thing that Lord Chelmsford required was the added responsibility of safeguarding a headstrong and fearless prince. However, he had orders from the Duke of Cambridge to: 'Kindly tender him a position to see as much as he can of the columns in the field.'[226]

Louis, having equipped himself for the campaign, was taken in tow by Chelmsford and together they travelled up-country, eventually visiting Wood who had remained camped at Kambula where the lingering sights and smells of battle were still discernable. The prince was enthralled and a few days later was gratified to come under distant enemy rifle fire. When eventually he met up with his old comrades of 11 Battery, Bigge admonished him to take care and later wrote:

> . . . knowing his temperament I implored him not to do anything rash and to avoid running unnecessary risks. I reminded him of the Empress at home and his political party in France.[227]

Chelmsford, having put his mind to finding a safe billet for his charge, allocated him to Brevet Colonel Richard Harrison, RE, who had been ordered to reconnoitre and map the route for the coming re-invasion of Zululand. Chelmsford had made it clear to Harrison that the prince should always be well protected by a strong escort.

In camp, Louis became admired for his kindness and martial talents:

> The intrepidity of the Prince is subject to all the conversations in the camp – his dexterity in all the physical exercises is admired by his companions in arms. His zeal to learn about everything touches and stuns everybody. When he rides, men come from everywhere to see the lightness and skill with which the Prince jumps in the saddle without the use of stirrups.[228]

So wrote a French correspondent, Paul Deléage of the newspaper *Le Figaro*, who was accompanying Wood's Flying Column.

Within a few days of having arrived at Chelmsford's advance camp, Louis was permitted to accompany Harrison on a four-day patrol into Zululand. They were accompanied by one of Harrison's staff officers, Lieutenant Jahleel Carey, who not only spoke French fluently, but, as a schoolboy in Paris, had heard the 101-gun salute that proclaimed Louis's birth.[229]

Their 200-strong escort, drawn from the FLH, Baker's Horse and the NNH, was led by Buller himself. On the second day of the patrol, a number of Zulus suddenly appeared on a nearby hill. Buller sent the NNH in pursuit and to his consternation and rage suddenly saw Louis spurring after them, waving his sword. But Buller's consternation quickly turned to dread as over 200 warriors rose from the long grass ready to engulf both Louis and the NNH. Baker's Horse went to the rescue and fortunately extracted the prince without injury. On his return to camp Buller refused to accept any further responsibility for Prince Louis.

On 18 May the prince persuaded Harrison to let him accompany a reconnaissance that Harrison was about to lead. The objective was to scout and map a route 'along the Ingutu [Nqutu] into the Nondwini valley' in the direction of the Zulu capital. They were to be escorted by Captain Claude Bettington of No. 3 Troop, Natal Horse (Bettington's Horse). Bettington had spent much of his early life in New Zealand following a colourful career driving cattle and running livery stables. Later he arrived in the Eastern Cape, where he took part in the Frontier War of 1877–8. Then, having received news of Isandlwana, he hurried to Natal where he formed the troop of mounted colonials that subsequently bore his name. The prince had taken a liking to Bettington who showed qualities of aggressive leadership, coupled with a disregard for his personal safety – qualities that the prince could readily identify with, as the Empress Eugenie wrote some months later:

> . . . Major [*sic*] Bettington, an officer legendary for his knowledge and cunning in local warfare. There was no ruse or trick in which he could not forestall the native Zulus, and the Prince felt the greatest respect for this tough and experienced officer.[230]

During the reconnaissance the prince kept copious notes, and on return to camp wrote a detailed nine-page report that revealed an aptitude for clarity, and detail that included correct use of compass bearings together with the accurate recording of distances. Throughout the reconnaissance Bettington had kept strict discipline. At night, the troopers forming the guard were positioned around the camp in a wide circle, yet, if Bettington perceived danger, he had no hesitation in immediately striking camp and, in darkness, moving to a more secure site. The only complaint of significance recorded by Bettington was targeted against an officer whose name would, within a few days, hit the headlines: 'So the night passed, troubled only by false alarms given by Lieutenant Carey.'

The prince concluded his report by recommending a line of advance not only suitable for wagons but with crucial access to firewood and water. What Louis omitted from his report was the part he had played in a contact with Zulus who had been stalking the patrol. Some sixty warriors had been seen on the high point of a nearby ridge, patiently observing the progress of the reconnaissance force and blocking its path to a large *umuzi* that lay ahead. Eventually the Zulus, wishing to protect their village, opened fire. Bettington, followed by the prince sword in hand, immediately charged and killed two warriors. The *umuzi* was then taken and, to the surprise of the attackers, they found a saddle, the property of Major Wilsone Black, that had been looted at Isandlwana. Harrison, present throughout the engagement and responsible for the prince's safety, made no effort to restrain the prince, who was clearly a fearless and high-spirited young man, ambitious to prove his valour. Perhaps Harrison, in the days to follow, would regret allowing the prince the excessive degree of freedom that would soon lead to tragedy.

On 28 May, Chelmsford ordered a reconnaissance to be made to the north of Itelezi Hill. Harrison, who had numerous other duties to attend to in addition to reconnoitring the road, gave the job to Carey, with the prince as his assistant, an assignment that required them to ride ten miles out from the camp over ground not entirely unknown, other patrols having travelled in that direction during the preceding weeks.

The next day, Chelmsford decided to survey the route himself and communicated by heliograph to arrange a rendezvous with Wood and Buller so that they could all inspect the track together. Wood and Buller failed to arrive at the appointed spot and Chelmsford, along with Carey, proceeded with a reduced escort of eighty mounted men. The official War Office *Narrative of Field Operations* confirmed that the reconnaissance penetrated deep into Zululand as far as the junction of the Tombokala and the Ityotyosi Rivers and noted that 'the Prince Imperial, who had been attached to this branch of the staff, had taken part in several of the reconnaissances.'

Chelmsford's second invasion of Zululand was set in motion on Sunday 1 June, with his invasion force marching to the area of the Itelezi Hill. Beyond Itelezi, designated as the divisional campsite for the night, the road ahead had yet to be clearly defined. Carey wished to reconnoitre once again the area surrounding the junction of the Tombokala and the Ityotyosi Rivers. Louis's task that day was merely to ride in advance of the army and mark the campsite at Itelezi. The two missions were not linked.

There are conflicting reports as to the sequence of events that followed. According to Deléage, who was present, Carey finally persuaded Harrison to let him accompany the prince. Deléage had accompanied Carey on the previous reconnaissance and had ridden with several other patrols into Zululand. An escort was now essential, but in Deléage's experience escorts were difficult to obtain as the officers of the cavalry brigade not only resented the headquarters' staff but were, in addition, most uncooperative when it came to allocating men.[231] Deléage had in fact recorded a problem of this sort which occurred a week earlier:

> I left Landman's Drift with Lieutenant Carey. Our escort was made up of three Lancers, three Dragoons, two kaffirs on horses and a member of the Commissariat in charge of a mule loaded with supplies for the men and the horses. Our expedition was due to last two days . . . As we set out from the camp, Lieutenant Carey told me all the troubles of every kind he had had at the Cavalry Headquarters to obtain his escort and in spite of the express written orders from Lord Chelmsford that he had with him. It seemed, from what the lieutenant told me, that the Cavalry Headquarters vigorously resented providing escorts for officers from General Headquarters.[232]

Deléage went on to relate that Carey was first denied an escort of regulars, the cavalry officer informing him that he would not have Carey giving orders to his men and that he had better go and find some colonials. This Carey tried to do only to find that all the colonial horses were in poor condition due to excessive patrolling. Returning to the cavalry headquarters and waving Chelmsford's written order, Carey finally managed to extract a meagre escort of three lancers and three dragoons.

It may have been similar bloody-mindedness that resulted in the escort that had been ordered on 1 June failing to arrive. And it was not until well into the morning that the prince and Carey moved off with only six men from Bettington's Horse, accompanied by one Zulu scout who was mounted on Louis's spare horse.

Originally it had been intended that Bettington himself would lead the patrol, but he had been ordered elsewhere. Sergeant Robert Willis had turned up in his place, supported by Corporal Jim Grubb, a man of many years' experience in Africa and who could speak Zulu fluently. However, since Grubb was only a corporal, it was unlikely that his advice would be sought or heeded by either Carey or the Prince.[233]

The patrol had not gone far before they encountered Harrison and another officer, Major Francis Grenfell, who all rode together for a while. A little later, when the prince had cantered ahead, Harrison asked Carey what had happened to the NNH escort that was supposed to accompany them, along with Bettington's men. Carey replied that he would collect six troopers from a group that he could see scouting ahead in the distance. He then tried to call the prince back, but Harrison indicated that he should not be interfered with and waved him on. Shortly, the group split up, with Harrison and Grenfell heading directly to the new camp site. Harrison's lack of concern over the prince's meagre escort may well have been due to his assumption that the prince would join his group at Itelezi and, having marked the camp-site, would go no further. Later in the day Harrison met up with Lord Chelmsford but made no mention of Louis's whereabouts.

Meanwhile Louis, having completed his task at Itelezi, rode on with Carey and the escort towards the junction of the Tombokala and Ityotyosi Rivers. Looking about him, Carey realised that the NNH patrol they had observed earlier was no longer in sight, but nevertheless proceeded without its support. Thus, Carey and the prince, each with less than a month's experience on the frontier and with an utterly inadequate escort, rode deeper into Zululand. Carey also deferred to Louis's royal rank, or perhaps believed that, if the prince wanted to take command, Harrison would not want Carey to interfere. Whatever the reason, from then on it was the prince who gave the orders.

Some time during the afternoon the patrol looked down on the valley of the Ityotyosi River and began descending towards what appeared to be a deserted *umuzi*, unaware that their movements had been under observation for some time from nearby Mhlungwane Hill. The patrol now approached the homestead of Sobhuza, the local chief. Waist-high tamboekie grass grew almost to the threshold of the huts, as did a few patches of mealies. A hundred yards to the north, a deep donga cut across the landscape. Louis ordered the troopers to dismount, knee-halter their mounts and collect fuel to brew coffee. A pet terrier belonging to Bettington's Horse had accompanied the patrol and it soon attracted the interest of some native dogs, a sure sign of recent human occupation. Someone also spotted freshly chewed sugar cane by one of the huts. These signs should have provoked the utmost alarm followed by immediate withdrawal, but instead the coffee was put on the boil and the men lounged around smoking while the horses wandered into the long grass. No look-out was posted and no search made of the vicinity. A further discovery of warm ashes in front of one of the huts seemed to cause no concern.

Meanwhile the Zulus on Mhlungwane Hill, approximately forty members of the Nkobamakosi and uMbonambi *amabutho* who were on a scouting mission, realised their numerical advantage and quietly moved to surround their unsuspecting target. Meanwhile, Corporal Grubb, feeling uneasy, suggested that the party should move off, but his warning went unheeded. The Zulu guide that accompanied the patrol then spotted a couple of advancing warriors and gave the alarm.

The prince immediately gave the order to 'stand to your horses' followed by the commands 'prepare to mount' and 'mount'. Carey was already on his horse when Louis gave his order 'prepare to mount', but before the rest of the men could get astride their saddles a volley of rifle fire erupted from the tall grass.[234]

Immediately following the volley, the warriors, mostly armed with assegais, charged forward, yelling cries of 'uSuthu' and the patrol dissolved into a mêlée of bolting, terrified horses with equally terrified men trying to hang on to their mounts for dear life. Carey was the first away, followed by Trooper Cochrane, both riding with their heads down as they crossed the donga and galloped off between two fields of mealies. Corporal Grubb, also astride his horse, headed for the donga, but not as quickly as Trooper Abel, who, as he passed Grubb, was shot in the back and, together with his mount, crashed to the ground.

Trooper Rogers had just caught his horse when the Zulus fired and, before he could grab a stirrup, the animal bolted, leaving him stranded. Likewise, the friendly Zulu who had been riding the prince's spare horse made no attempt to mount but took to his heels instead, heading for the donga. Sergeant Willis sank into his saddle at the very moment the volley rang out, while Trooper Letocq, half-way onto his horse, dropped his carbine as he scrambled for the reins. It seems his fear of the consequences of the gun's loss outweighed his fear of the enemy and he dismounted in an instant, grabbed the fallen carbine and vaulted back into the saddle as his horse sprang away. He galloped after Corporal Grubb, to whom he shouted: 'Stick firm to your horse, boy, and put in the spurs; the Prince is down!'

Louis's frightened horse desperately attempted to bolt after the others. With his mount already at a gallop, Louis grasped the leather wallets strapped to the front of his saddle and, lifting himself off the ground, swung his legs upwards in an attempt to vault into the saddle, a feat he normally accomplished with ease. But with the force of the sudden strain the straps broke and Louis fell under the hooves of his flying horse. Trampled and dazed, his right arm injured, he got to his feet, reached for the heirloom sword of his great-uncle, Napoleon, to find the weapon gone, lost in the grass. Now afoot, and with warriors fast approaching, Louis discarded his empty scabbard and headed for the donga.

Trooper Rogers, horseless and alone, watched the stampede of his comrades. He must have known he was done for; nevertheless he rammed a bullet into his carbine and, instinctively seeking shelter, turned towards the huts. A dozen warriors rushed towards him as he fired a single shot that missed. He was overwhelmed in an instant.

Trooper Abel had come down with his horse just above the donga. Both were badly injured and unable to rise. Umtunzi, the first warrior on the scene, paused and threw an assegai into the struggling trooper. A moment later he was joined by Inyadana, and together they stabbed both man and horse. Umtunzi, with his claim to first blood, began to strip the dead man, so Inyadana, leaving him to his grisly task, ran towards the donga that Louis, revolver in hand, had just entered. At that moment Zabanga, a warrior of the uMbonambi regiment, came out of the long grass bordering the donga and threw an assegai at Louis that sank deep into his thigh. The prince was about to die. All his military accomplishments had been to no avail, but the knightly attribute of courage did not fail him. With his right hand he pulled the assegai from his thigh and, holding it as a sword, rushed at Zabanga, who, fearing death by his own bloodied blade, ran for a short distance, then halted. Louis, with his revolver in his left hand, fired two shots, both missing their mark. Zabanga then crouched and flung another assegai, hitting Louis high up in the chest as he tried to transfer his pistol to his right hand. Prince Louis staggered back as other warriors sent their spears thudding into his body. He collapsed to a sitting position, his weapons dropping to the ground. For a moment he sat thus, and then they were upon him, seven warriors in all.

With a fatal thrust of an assegai that penetrated his right eye, the Zulus killed a great prize that they could have delivered to their king.[235] Had they made Louis captive, King Cetshwayo could have tried to dictate his own peace terms to Sir Bartle Frere and Lord Chelmsford and, in turn, they would most likely have been obliged to comply.

Had Louis lived, there existed the possibility that one day, he might become Emperor of France – a development that would undoubtedly have changed the history of Europe. It is interesting to contemplate also that Louis, the great-nephew of Napoleon, was slain by the warriors of Cetshwayo, the nephew of King Shaka, sometimes called the Black Napoleon of Africa.

Meanwhile Carey, having galloped three frantic miles from the scene of the ambush, came across a group of mounted men on reconnaissance. The time was 4.00 p.m. and Carey had the misfortune to bump into none other than Wood and Buller. The conversation is reported to have been on the following lines:

Buller asked Carey: 'Whatever is the matter with you?', to which Carey responded: 'The Prince Imperial is killed.' After further dialogue Buller, white with rage, snapped: 'You deserve to be shot, and I hope you will be. I could shoot you myself.' Wood apparently then joined the conversation, asking Carey to confirm the Prince Imperial's death and, on Carey nodding, Wood snapped: 'Then, Sir, what are you doing here?'

At first light on 2 June, as patrols set out to search for the Prince Imperial's body, Chelmsford penned a telegram to Colonel Stanley, the Secretary of State for War, outlining the circumstances:

> Prince Imperial acting under orders of the a.q.m. General [Colonel Harrison] reconnoitred on first June road to camping ground of June second accompanied by Lieutenant Carey ninety eighth . . . and six white men and friendly Zulu . . . troopers are reported missing by Lieutenant Carey who escaped and reached this camp after dark and from the evidence taken there can be little doubt of the prince being killed . . . I myself was not aware that the prince had been detailed for this duty.

Two issues arise, the first that Chelmsford made clear, correctly, that the responsibility for the reconnaissance leading to the Prince Imperial's death was not his. Second, and of more significance, was that the Prince Imperial's mission, as outlined by Harrison, was to find a suitable camp site to which the invasion force would advance the following day.

Carey was debriefed immediately on return to camp and dined that evening with Harrison, Grenfell and other staff officers in Harrison's tent. Years later in his biography, *Recollections*, Harrison recalled that when

Carey broke the news to him, he responded: 'You don't mean to say you have left the Prince?' To which Carey responded: 'It was no use stopping, he was shot at the first volley.'

That night, Carey penned a letter to his wife:

> I am a ruined man I fear, though from my letter which will be in the papers you will see I could do nothing else . . . I have been so laughed at for taking a squadron with me that I had grown reckless and would have gone with two men . . . the men all bolted and I now fear the Prince was shot on the spot as his saddle is torn as if he tried to get up. No doubt they will say I should have remained by him, but I had no idea he was wounded and thought he was after me . . . as regards the Prince, I am innocent, as I did not know he was wounded . . . I have been a very, very wicked man, and may God forgive me! . . . of course, all sorts of yarns will get into the papers, and without hearing my tale, I shall be blamed, but honestly, between you and me, *I can only be blamed for the camp* [authors' emphasis]. I tried to rally the men in retreat and had no idea the poor Prince was behind . . . if the body is found at any distance from the kraal tomorrow, my statement will appear correct. If he is in the kraal, why then he must have been shot dead, as I heard no cry.[236]

A pall of gloom and depression extended throughout both the 2nd Division and the Flying Column. The prince, acknowledged universally as brave bordering on reckless, was immensely popular. For the next week Carey continued with his staff duties, though most officers considered that a signal disgrace had fallen on British arms, with Major Grenfell confirming the prevailing sentiment:

> It was a sad sight, as we, his English brother officers, stood over the dead body of the hope of the Imperialists of France, the Prince's two servants weeping bitterly, and we all felt the great disaster and the deep disgrace which had fallen on the British army.[237]

Lieutenant Frederick Slade, RA, was more forthright in his views:

> Neither Carey nor his men made the slightest attempt to stand, and in plain words they ran away . . . I cannot tell you what we all think of Carey's behaviour.[238]

A court of inquiry, presided over by Major-General Marshall, recommended Carey be tried by general court martial. For the first time, Carey stated to Marshall's inquiry that it was the prince, not he, who exercised command over the escort party. Major Anstruther, 94th Regiment, was appointed officiating judge-advocate and was instrumental in framing the charge:

> For having misbehaved before the enemy on June 1st, when in command of an escort in attendance on His Imperial Highness Prince Napoleon, who was making a reconnaissance in Zululand; in having, when the said

Prince and escort were attacked by the enemy, galloped away, and in not having attempted to rally the said escort or in other ways defend the Prince.[239]

The charge was a euphemism for cowardice, although the word itself was not in use at that time when framing charges. Under military law, if Carey were found guilty, the court had the power to impose the death penalty, subject to confirmation and appeal.

The court assembled at Camp Upoko on 12 June, with Colonel Richard Glyn presiding and Captain W. M. Brander, 2nd/24th Regiment, prosecuting. Carey chose to defend himself. The first and critical mistake made by Glyn was a technical one of not recording in the proceedings that the members of the court were duly sworn.

Evidence led by the prosecution showed that Carey, in accordance with Queen's Regulations, was in command of the party by virtue of being the senior combatant officer present. The Prince Imperial, attached to the staff, did not hold a commission and as such, when on active duty, came under the command of the senior officer present.

This was technically correct. However, a subaltern of Carey's rank and modest social status could hardly be expected to counter every suggestion and command made by a person of the prince's standing. Evidence showed that it was the prince who gave instructions throughout the reconnaissance and who had ordered the descent into the valley: 'The Prince said, "we will go down to the huts by the river, where the men can get wood and water and cook something."'

Carey's defence rested on his maintaining that, first, he was not in *de facto* command of the reconnaissance and second, that he was under the firm impression that the prince had initially escaped. It was only during the brief rally that took place well clear of the donga that Carey realised the prince was missing. By then it was too late to return. Carey referred to the small escort by confirming that Colonel Harrison had given permission for the patrol to start without the appearance of the additional six Basuto horsemen. This permission was as a result of pressure applied by the prince, impatient to proceed.

Survivors were cross-examined and it remained clear that all had fled on the basis of *sauve qui peut*, or 'every man for himself', and that no real attempt was made to rally the patrol at any stage. It became equally clear that it was the prince who had issued all commands and effectively controlled the reconnaissance.

Nevertheless it was, in the court's eyes, unacceptable to abandon the prince without an effort being made to rally. Lieutenant Carey was found guilty of the charge and sentenced to be cashiered, although Lieutenant Main, originally selected as a member of the court, only to be replaced at the last moment by a fellow Royal Engineer, Captain Courtney, heard otherwise. He recorded from memory in the 1920s: 'The sentence of the Court was never divulged, but I gather from Courtney (who was much upset) that it was "death."'[240]

The findings, being subject to confirmation in England, were never published in South Africa. Carey remained under arrest, relieved of all staff duties and, as was military custom, not allowed to wear his sword. In disgrace and escorted by Captain E. B. Evans, RA, he embarked on the troopship *Jumna* for England.

When news reached Europe, the feeling in France was one of anger. There was speculation that the prince's death had been contrived by the British. Rumours circulated that Carey had been given orders to slash the saddle girth; that the Freemasons were responsible; that Bismarck planned the event; or that socialists engineered the prince's death. The Bonapartists blamed, with some justification, England, the queen and her government, for allowing the prince to embark on such a venture. As for the British Army, it was ridiculed and shamed.

On 25 June, Queen Victoria wrote to Prime Minister Disraeli: 'The accounts from the Cape fill one with redoubled anxiety, for if so precious a life was not more cared for, how much less will others be!' The Empress Eugenie was inconsolable: 'But her heart is broken and her health seems sadly shaken. She can eat nothing and hardly sleeps. But how could it be otherwise.'[241]

It was not until August that the Judge Advocate-General, J. C. O'Dowd, presented his report to the queen. 'The Judge Advocate-General humbly submitted to Her Majesty not to confirm the findings and sentence of the Court.'[242] The possibility that the court had not been sworn, which precluded it from acting as a properly constituted court of law, was an underlying reason. However, O'Dowd accepted that the evidence submitted in the findings did indeed prove that Carey 'did not attempt to rally the escort or otherwise defend the prince.' But did this constitute 'misbehaviour?' Not in the judge advocate's opinion: 'Lieutenant Carey's conduct in precipitately retreating was free from the taint of military misbehaviour as charged.'

In other words, the principle of *sauve qui peut*, although having no formal application in British Army field practice, was upheld. The evidence also showed that the prosecution had failed to prove that Carey 'was in command in the sense that would throw this responsibility upon him'. Accordingly, Carey was exonerated, restored to his newly promoted rank of captain that had been gazetted in England a few days after his arrest, and freed to return to regimental duties. The press in England was divided, with a great deal of sympathy shown towards Carey. Queen Victoria privately thought otherwise:

> This evidence is terrible. Indeed every word seems to me most unfavourable in every way towards all those who deserted the poor young Prince. All seem to have been indifferent to his fate.[243]

However, Paul Deléage published his account of these events in Paris in 1879 under the title *Trois Mois chez les Zoulous et les Derniers Jours du Prince Impérial* ('Three months with the Zulus and the last days of the Prince Imperial'). This showed that Carey had other motives for persuading Harrison to allow him to accompany the prince on the reconnaissance. Harrison's culpability was also questioned. It will be recalled that Deléage was the war correspondent for *Le Figaro* and in close contact with the prince throughout his stay in Zululand.

Rumours were already circulating in camp on the evening of 1 June that the prince had been killed. Deléage, on hearing of such rumours, made an approach to Lord Chelmsford, who in turn directed him to Colonel Harrison's tent. Lieutenant Carey was dining with Harrison and, according to Deléage, was not at all keen to be disturbed. Deléage, not to be denied, persisted:

> I was not a news correspondent looking for details but, before all, a Frenchman eager to know what happened and mainly if the news about the Prince's death was genuine.

Carey reluctantly agreed to leave the dinner table to relate the day's events:

> As far as the Prince was concerned, Lieutenant Carey pretended to know nothing of the Prince's fate until, having crossed the donga two or three hundred yards from the kraal, he looked behind for the first time to see the Prince's horse riderless.

This was tantamount to an admission that Carey had left the prince to his fate and, furious, Deléage withdrew from the tent without further conversation, leaving Carey to digest his dinner.

Deléage then related that, on the morning of that fateful day and prior to departure from Koppie Allein, Prince Louis had asked Harrison's permission to select the next camp-site. Such a reconnaissance would involve covering ground that had been well traversed and was not considered dangerous, extending as far as Itelezi Hill only. Deléage stated that both the prince and Carey asserted that their patrol was to go to the Itelezi area only and: 'for all of us on the General's staff, the prince was not going as far as the Ityotozi valley'. This also explained the modest original escort of twelve men allocated for the duty: 'The whole thing was thought to be so innocuous that neither the Prince nor Colonel Harrison had given orders to prepare an escort.'

Carey, on the other hand, had a different agenda. His task of mapping roads and selecting a possible route of advance had already taken him to the Ityotyosi Valley through which he had recommended a line of advance for the column. His recommendation had been met with hilarity, as several deep dongas *en route* were deemed impassable. Deléage reported a conversation he had with Carey on 31 May, where Carey stated:

Lord Chelmsford laughed at me, telling me there was a donga thirty feet wide, and asked me how the column would cross. I answered that in my opinion he was mistaken but his Lordship's views troubled me.

From Carey's viewpoint a second reconnaissance was imperative to justify his recommendation and, accordingly, Carey asked Harrison if he could accompany the prince on his mission to locate a suitable camp site. Harrison initially refused, but then relented, this being confirmed in Harrison's cross-examination at the court martial:

> The prisoner and the Prince were doing different work on the same road, prisoner verifying work already done, and the Prince making a more detailed report of the road for the march of the troops. The Prince had orders to choose a camp.

What Harrison omitted to mention was that the task allocated to the prince was but seven miles from Koppie Allein, while Carey's objective was eight miles further on, and in considerably more dangerous territory. Deléage argued that, had Harrison refused permission for Carey to join the patrol, the tragedy would not have occurred. However, having reached Itelezi Hill, it was an easy matter for Carey to persuade the ever-eager prince into undertaking an extended reconnaissance: 'They know the Prince will not refuse any danger.'

Carey defended his decision not to wait for the remaining six Basutos by remarking to Deléage on 2 June, when on the way to recover the body:

> Look, I know that if I insisted on waiting for the Basutos, I would not be held to blame – but the Prince was eager to leave and I did not believe it right to use my authority.

Harrison, aware of Carey's purpose, should have given the prince a firm instruction not to proceed beyond Itelezi Hill, his original mission. Harrison, having been entrusted by Chelmsford with looking after the day-to-day security of the prince, and in full knowledge of the 'gung-ho' and exuberant nature of his ward, failed to exercise due caution. The Adjutant-General, C. H. Ellice, voiced the views of the Duke of Cambridge:

> If Lieutenant-Colonel Harrison had displayed more firmness in his instructions to Lieutenant Carey and to the Prince, His Royal Highness cannot but think that the train of events would have been averted.[244]

In short, the blame for the tragedy rested largely on the shoulders of Harrison for failing to ensure clear concise orders were issued to restrict the movements of the prince. Ultimately, unrestrained, Louis paid the price for his own folly. However, as a result of the court martial, the full weight of popular blame for the debacle now fell on the shoulders of Carey.

Finally, the question arose whether the behaviour of Lieutenant Jahleel Carey, notwithstanding the judge advocate's legal opinion, was in accordance with the unwritten law of 'comradeship'.

The Gurkhas of Nepal, have a motto cast in stone, *kaphar hunu bhanda marnu ramro* ('it is better to die than be a coward'). However, in circumstances when all is lost, can the principle of *sauve qui peut* apply? Was Carey justified in leaving the scene in the belief that all was lost and that, had he returned, he too would have lost his life to no avail?

Courage, leadership by example and fearlessness in action, are all noble attributes. However, the true colours of an individual, whatever pre-battle training and conditioning may have been done, are only revealed in action. When the fire-fight increases in intensity, when the battle swings in an unexpected fashion, when men about you, your comrades, are falling, when a withdrawal threatens to turn to a rout, then, and only then, can judgement be fashioned. Colonel Russell, for example, was found wanting in courage in the days after Isandlwana and, as seen, at Hlobane.

The issue of whether Carey or the prince effectively commanded the fatal patrol in no way controlled Carey's subsequent behaviour. His letter to his wife, before discovering the body the following day, indicated that he had seen the prince's horse without a rider and thus knew that the prince was down. His failure to attempt to assess the situation on crossing the donga, indeed, by leading the escape by example instead of stopping to ascertain the predicament of the prince, who at that stage was still alive, placed a severe question mark against his courage. It was not sufficient for Carey to assume all was lost without making an effort to rally. Had he done so at the donga, a mere 200 yards away, he might well have seen the prince being pursued. Had he returned immediately, was there not a chance, however slim, of mounting the prince behind him? Carey faced the ultimate test in courage, a test he sadly failed.

Did Captain Edward Browne and Troop Sergeant Major Learda decide that it was every man for himself at Kambula? Did Private Wassall in the Buffalo River near Isandlwana? In these instances these brave men gave no thought to saving their own skins. The ultimate hallmark of bravery, for which British arms have never been found wanting, is disregard for one's own life in order to save the life of a comrade.

Very likely, had the escort been commanded by the likes of Bettington, an officer of this calibre would have sacrificed his life in order to save that of a comrade, irrespective of rank. Bettington, a great admirer of the prince, wrote to the Duke of Bassano in words that ring true:

> I trust that Her Majesty [the Empress Eugenie] knows that had it been fated that I should have been in Carey's place I should have taken the same care of His Highness as I did on former occasions, and that if I could not have saved him I would have remained with him.[245]

Lieutenant Carey was directly responsible for the reconnaissance finding itself well beyond the geographical bounds of the prince's original mandate. Notwithstanding the Prince Imperial's standing, Carey failed to exercise due military caution in that he remained in an untenable position where the ambush took place. He failed to ascertain the whereabouts of the prince when he saw his riderless horse near the donga and finally failed to mount any effort to rescue the prince.

Many sympathised with Carey's predicament, including Chelmsford who, in mitigation of Carey's sentence, wrote: 'I have no reason to believe, however, that Lieutenant Carey is wanting in personal courage, but think he lost his head.'[246] Many disagreed with Chelmsford and found Carey's conduct wanting and unbecoming of an officer. Sir Garnet Wolseley was one, and his condemnation was damning:

> I cannot see how any officer can ever again associate with Carey who has been convicted of cowardice by his own profession. Technically in the eyes of quibbling lawyers the proceedings may not have been strictly regular, but the fact that he was tried by a court of officers & found guilty of cowardice remains . . . I would not shake hands nor associate with such a man and I think that in saying this I merely echo the sentiments of the army.[247]

The words of John Dunn spoken to Captain Molyneux prior to the battle of Gingindlovu (excepting the racial connotations) ring as true today as they did over a century ago: 'In Africa a white man must stand by a fellow while there is life in him; if his friend is dead, then he may save himself.'

Clearly, the rules under which *sauve qui peut* could be exercised were well known, rules that Carey could and should have instinctively obeyed but lacked the courage to do so.

Chapter 10

Advance to Contact

'The maps of Zululand are almost useless for military purposes as the country has never been surveyed with any pretension to accuracy.'

Lord Chelmsford to the Secretary of State for War, Colonel Stanley, 10 June 1879[248]

—————•◦•—————

With the death of Ronald Campbell at Hlobane, Wood faced a severe staff problem. Major Cornelius Francis Clery, Wood's previous principal staff officer had been transferred to Glyn's column prior to the first invasion. Campbell had been promoted by Wood to assume Clery's duties and Wood now requested that Clery be posted back to him. In a letter to Chelmsford, dated 1 April, Wood commented:

> To suit me, I shall never adequately replace Campbell. He was strong where I am weak. Careful, methodical, a rapid writer, most fascinating manners, he was beloved by all. I can, however, get on well with Clery, and it will be a great advantage to have a Major as Chief Staff Officer.[249]

In a letter of 13 April to Sir Archibald Alison, Clery wrote:

> Ronald Campbell, Coldstream Guards, who succeeded me when I left Wood, was killed in their last business, and Wood very kindly wrote to the general at once to ask that I should go back to him. I have not heard the result yet. Wood has been doing very well ... he is certainly the only column commander out here who has shown a particle of ability, and the work so essentially that of details, exactly suits his remarkable capacity for taking trouble ... I shall be much disgusted if I am not allowed to go back to him.[250]

Chelmsford agreed to Wood's request and Clery joined the Flying Column in May, filling a key position.

The objective, Ulundi, lay approximately 100 miles' travel east of the supply depot at Landman's Drift. As the advance progressed, supply depots had to be established on the line of advance. Each depot required fortification and protection.

—————•◦•—————

The first was named after Major-General Newdigate and was built on the banks of the Nondweni Stream and located some thirty miles into Zululand, due east of Koppie Allein. Two companies of the 2nd/21st Regiment, together with two Gatlings and a company of the NNC, were detailed for permanent garrison duties. A squadron of the King's Dragoon Guards was also stationed at Fort Newdigate with a roving task of ensuring that the lines of communication remained open.

Fort Marshall was established on 18 June ten miles south of Fort Newdigate and close to Isipezi Hill on the track to Ulundi. The Zulu army, on its way to mount the attack on Isandlwana, had camped close by, the old camping site being clearly visible. Larger than the other forts, it was strategically placed to command the Babanango range of hills to the east. A further two companies of the 2nd/21st Regiment, together with a squadron of the 17th Lancers and two 7-pounders of Harness's N Battery, 5th Brigade RA, were left as permanent garrison. Colonel Collingwood, his brigade now diluted, and no doubt much to his disgust, was appointed to command both Forts Newdigate and Marshall.

The third depot, built on 23 June, was named Fort Evelyn after the Flying Column commander. It was positioned twenty-five miles east of Fort Marshall among the headwaters of the Mpembeni River. The garrison comprised two companies of the 58th Regiment commanded by Brevet Major E. Foster with a further two 7-pounders of Harness's battery under Lieutenant William James Fowler. A forty-eight-strong troop of the Natal Light Horse completed the garrison.

Communications were established by means of heliograph and, weather conditions permitting, all forts, together with Koppie Allein and Landman's Drift were now in contact with each other. The final objective, Ulundi, lay a tantalisingly close thirty-five miles east-northeast.

The architects of the forts were undoubtedly the Royal Engineers and their Assistant Engineers, some of whom were special service officers. Together these officers not only supervised the construction and layout of each fort, but were responsible, with the pioneers under their command, for ensuring that streams, rivers and the numerous dongas that criss-crossed the advance route were made passable. The senior Royal Engineer in Wood's column was Major C. J. Moysey, whilst Captain Walter 'Pompey' Jones, so nicknamed after his service in Portsmouth, commanded 5th Company, RE. Under his command was Captain D. C. Courtney together with fifty-five all ranks.

In addition to the forts the advancing columns were to form laagers each night. However, Newdigate's views on how this should be done differed from those of Chelmsford. The former had originally constructed three separate laagers placed in echelon. Numbers one and three contained the hospital tents, ammunition wagons, horses and mules, while the centre laager contained the cattle. Tents were pitched around the faces fifteen yards from the wagons. Chelmsford, however, disapproved of three interlocking laagers and ordered Newdigate to form a large, single laager. Whatever the merits of either design, this was yet another example of column commanders, such as Newdigate and Glynn, having to obey Chelmsford's directions on matters that should have been left to them.

Wood, however, would brook no interference. The Flying Column formed no fewer than four laagers with troops entrenched front and rear. At night groups of six men, each group including two men of the NNC, were advanced a hundred yards in front of the entrenchment. In addition, Wood formed a corps of native scouts who were pushed out a mile in advance of the laager. This tactic was used throughout his advance.

However, guard duties around the camp were not always straightforward. The first 'friendly fire' mishap during the advance into Zululand occurred on 6 June, as Fort Newdigate was nearing completion. The phenomenon now termed 'battle fatigue', coupled with the reputation the Zulus had earned at Isandlwana, placed the wearied 2nd Division's inexperienced infantrymen at breaking point.

At 9.00 p.m. that evening three shots rang out, the signal warning of a Zulu attack. The bugle call 'assembly' was sounded and, needing little encouragement, men rushed into their laager positions, frantically loading weapons. Shots were then fired, causing panic amongst the oxen and horses and soon a crescendo of volleys from the picquets posted 500 yards in advance of the camp rang out, to be joined by two rounds of case fired from the 9-pounders. Dawnay recorded the events:

> We all ran out buckling on swords, and filling our pockets with cartridges . . . a regular blaze of rifles now going on round the laager, and men firing wildly, under, and on the wagons.

Amid the hubbub the NNC sat huddled in the middle of the laager shifting nervously, whist officers rushed out of their tents, many still wearing red nightcaps. Twenty minutes later a bugle sounded 'cease fire' and Newdigate and his staff took stock. Seven men were wounded, (including five Royal Engineers from 5th Company) four horses killed, in excess of 1,200 Martini-Henry rounds expended and two rounds of artillery fired at imaginary targets. Tents were riddled with bullet holes and there were near-misses, as Harness recorded: 'My helmet has a bullet clean through it.'

Newdigate angrily gave the assembled men a severe tongue-lashing:

> Then our General followed, and gave his censure pretty freely on the wretched scare; and shame sat on many a face at its recollection. Not a Zulu had been seen . . . the picket who commenced firing at what it thought was some 'blacks', but might have been a cloud.[251]

The artillery officer who had opened fire was Major Le Grice, N Battery, 6th Brigade, who, when asked for an explanation, blithely responded '. . . that he wished to show the enemy they had big guns and deter them from coming on.'[252] Major Clery summarised the affair by saying:

'It was a very bad business in scares, but privately the fact is that the young soldiers who have come out are in mortal funk of the Zulus.[253]

Wood's seasoned troops of the Flying Column contemptuously renamed the depot 'Fort Funk'.

A contributory factor to the behaviour of the garrison may have been news that had reached the camp the previous day of the death of Lieutenant Frederick Frith, adjutant of the 17th Lancers. The twenty-one-year-old, ex-Haileybury College subaltern had been gazetted into the 17th Lancers at the relatively young age of eighteen and, within a short period of two years, was appointed adjutant, a position normally reserved for a regiment's most outstanding and competent young officer.

General Marshall, with a composite force of the 17th Lancers and King's Dragoon Guards, had moved out in the early hours of 5 June to reconnoitre east as far as the Upoko River valley. Buller and his irregulars, including Shepstone's Edendale troop of the Natal Native Horse, had already set off independently and had become involved in a skirmish with a large force of Zulus which was pushed back across a stream and on to the slopes of the Zungeni Hills. Here the Zulus found protection in a rocky ravine, thick with chest-high grass and thorn bush. Buller crossed the stream, ordered his troops to dismount and, standing on an ant heap, directed fire whilst quietly observing the results through his field glasses. The Zulus by this time had been reinforced and next started to outflank Buller, who ordered his men to retire back across the stream. The Zulu fire from the protection of the cover now intensified, resulting in casualties.

> The scene was pretty in the extreme, to see the whole face of the hill dotted with little puffs of white smoke. We had eight or ten men hit – none mortally, and fifteen horses, killed or wounded.[254]

At this stage Major-General Marshall arrived on the scene, anxious not to miss the fun. To Buller's astonishment, Marshall ordered Colonel Drury-Lowe's three troops of lancers to advance across the stream and into the ground, strewn with boulders, from where Buller's men had just retired. Drury-Lowe could hardly succeed where Buller had failed and this error of judgement was to cost the life of the 17th's adjutant.

Drury-Lowe formed his men into line. In front of him was a mealie field planted close to the water. Beyond lay the upper slopes of the Zungeni Hills where, protected by boulders, high grass and thorn-bush, the Zulus waited. Despatching one troop to his left, Drury-Lowe ordered his trumpeter to sound the 'gallop'. Lances lowered, the remaining two troops of lancers cut a swathe through the mealie field, watched by the astonished Buller. As throughout the campaign, Zulu bullets missed their mark wide and high. Better marksmen could well have decimated Drury-Lowe's lancers.

Since it was soon apparent that the attack could not reach the Zulus, the order was given to fall back across the stream and, whilst Frith was conferring with Drury-Lowe, both made conspicuous by their cream Cape horses, a bullet hit Frith in the chest. 'The fatal shot seemed to come from nowhere.'[255] As he slumped forward, Trumpet-Major Dunn, riding by Drury-Lowe's side, dismounted and lifted Lieutenant Frith's body off his saddle, only to find that he had been killed instantly. His lifeless body was placed back across the saddle and the Lancers slowly withdrew. Marshall covered the retreat by placing a troop of King's Dragoon Guards along the bed of the stream, the other flank being covered by Captain Theophilus 'Offy' Shepstone's Edendale Troop of the Natal Native Horse. The jubilant Zulus taunted the withdrawal, hooting loudly and casting aspersions on the bravery of British. Without infantry support, there remained little alternative other than to beat an ignominious retreat from an attack that should never have been ordered. It was: 'A place where no horse could go, the last which cavalry should attack.'[256]

Frith was a popular officer and his death was perceived by his peers to be the result of foolhardy tactics. His body was placed in an ambulance and, escorted silently back to the base by his regiment. That evening, a burial service took place near a stream below the camp. Lord Chelmsford was present and, as the body was lowered into the grave, a guard of honour of Frith's much loved regiment stood dismounted on either side of the grave with lances held in the right hand, shaft hilts resting on the ground. On the command 'salute' the left hands of the honour guard moved smartly across their chests to touch the lances. No doubt many a tear was shed.

> Here, as elsewhere, were no volleys fired. In the dim light the uniforms were blended into one grey mass, hardly to be distinguished one from another. 'Our Father' repeated reverently by the little group of soldiers, sounded strangely solemn and peaceful after the bustle of camp.[257]

——◆——

The fragmentation of the Cavalry Brigade between Forts Newdigate, Marshall and Evelyn resulted in Marshall being appointed 'in charge of the line of communications from the frontier up to the army,' a task that Major-General Clifford viewed as his territory, causing further friction.

It was now essential that sufficient logistical supplies be accumulated at the forts to sustain an advance on Ulundi. Chelmsford placed such importance on the mission that he instructed Wood to command the operation.

The Flying Column, less Buller's cavalry, returned from Koppie Allein with 620 fully laden wagons and without incident. Wood, with a justified air of superiority, marched triumphantly past Newdigate's division, bands playing a lively tune. However, Newdigate's men were not silent, with Dawnay voicing the 2nd Division's opinion:

> Wood gets everything; he is to go in front, and advance at once; he has got all our provisions, forage, and all the Gatlings are to be sent to him; that is, he will have six, while we will have none. He has a separate command

entirely, which is what neither Marshall nor Newdigate have now; it naturally gives rise to a deal of jealousy.[258]

Despite the fiasco of Hlobane, such was the confidence placed in Wood that it soon became apparent to all that the battle-proven Flying Column would lead the advance to contact.

Each ensuing day heralded hard physical work for the infantry. Fortified by an issue of coffee before marching, the troops helped voorloopers cajole the oxen and push wagons over drifts, make camp, prepare laagers, dig entrenchments, cut wood and throw out picquets. This had all to be done whilst the column was strung out on the extended line of march, with the men in constant fear of a Zulu ambush. At night rifles were secured to the central pole of each tent, within easy grasp should the alarm be raised.

Animals suffered greatly, with oxen dying by the score and horses being reduced to skin and bone. The commissariat staff, however, took advantage of the dead oxen to supplement ration supplies. Attempts to make the oxen more palatable failed miserably. Neither roasting, boiling nor stewing could improve the hard, tasteless meat served week after week.

The winter days, by comparison to England, were warm, with cloudless skies drying up streams and leaving the once mud-caked dongas brick hard. Sunset was around 5.15 p.m. and night brought a sharp plunge in the temperatures, causing troops to shiver under their single issue blankets. With their tunics in tatters and boots greased in an effort to preserve and waterproof them, the men seldom enjoyed an opportunity to wash or bathe and personal hygiene suffered. Chelmsford's army was a far cry from the spick-and-span regiments which marched off the docks at Durban in April. Men seldom shaved and beards were the fashion, with Wood setting the style, his beard cut to a point and copied adoringly by many of his column.

The cavalry, in spite of the condition of their mounts, enjoyed a better lifestyle. Marshall's lancers were flung out wide and tasked to undertake detailed reconnaissance.

Buller's irregulars coped better with the local conditions, than their imperial counterparts. Buller himself, a man of few words, commanded enormous respect and, when he did speak, he was instantly obeyed. His independent band of irregular ruffian mercenaries and mounted infantry roved far and wide, implementing Chelmsford's scorched earth policy. Valleys were searched, homesteads torched, mealie fields destroyed, grain pits looted, cattle rounded up and life made intolerable for innocent Zulu elders, women and children whose men-folk had departed to rally to their king. Day after day the telltale smoke rising into cloudless winter skies indicated yet another group of deserted *imizi* in flames, the direct result of intelligence reports brought back by the column's natives who were used for reconnaissance. The method of destruction was always the same:

> A number of dogs, homeless and hungry, peer in at the unwonted intruders, and howl their disappointment at finding them white. Then a

match is applied to the weather side of the hut, and the dry mats crackle and blaze up high and fierce; the smoke rises in dense columns from each hut fired in succession, and in a few minutes the kraal is but so many glowing cones of red-hot fire . . . the work of destruction is complete, and the party rides away towards the next valley.[259]

Chelmsford was relentless and uncompromising in following his aim to bring the Zulu kingdom to its knees. His next major objective was the Mthonjaneni Heights, twenty miles north-east of Fort Evelyn. The heights made up a massive feature that dominated the area. The name was derived from the Zulu 'at the spring' and this was the spot used by King Dingane to obtain water for his exclusive use.

Fifteen miles to the north-east lay the final objective of Ulundi. It took Wood ten days from the time he occupied the heights of Babanango to make his way to the western end of the Mthonjaneni Heights. The track leading to the top of the heights, known as 'Jackal Ridge', was difficult to navigate being criss-crossed by near vertical slopes, making the progress of wagons near impossible. Oxen were released from their harnesses and troops put to the difficult task of pushing and pulling the wagons along. The ground fell away into the precipitous eMakhosini Valley in which numerous homesteads were located. Animals suffered through lack of both fodder and water with the commissariat staff being the only beneficiaries as they continued to invent ways to cook an ox.

The ridge finally gave way to a plateau, off which, to the east, a track led to St Paul's. Crealock's 1st Division was expected to advance to St Paul's and from there, establish communication with Chelmsford. 'Nothing is to be seen of General Crealock's column, although we have a commanding view of the range that he must travel for 20 miles.'[260]

Once again the question was asked, 'Where is Crealock?' 'Jokers say he awaits the arrival of a bag of pepper; others say that he is waiting the staff officer's stock of cigars.'[261] Crealock would remain the butt of unpleasant, yet justified humour throughout the campaign.

A wag on Wood's staff took the opportunity to amuse the officers' mess by producing a sketch showing three horses in a race for Ulundi, named 'Chelmsford', 'Wait-a-While', and 'Invincible'. 'Chelmsford', ridden by Wood, reached the water jump [Umfolozi] and refused. 'Wait-a While', ridden by Crealock, was a mile behind and reduced to a walk, whilst 'Invincible', ridden by Sir Garnet, was closing fast.

Newdigate's and Wood's commands now laagered at the northern end of the heights accompanied by 500 wagons and 8,000 miserable, bellowing oxen. The camp was named Fort Victoria and, coincidentally, was located on the same ground on which the Voortrekker leader Andries Pretorious had formed his laager during his pursuit of King Dingaan.

The ground was marked by scrub, thorn bush, long grass and masses of aloes interspersed with various species of the mimosa tree. Nevertheless, it

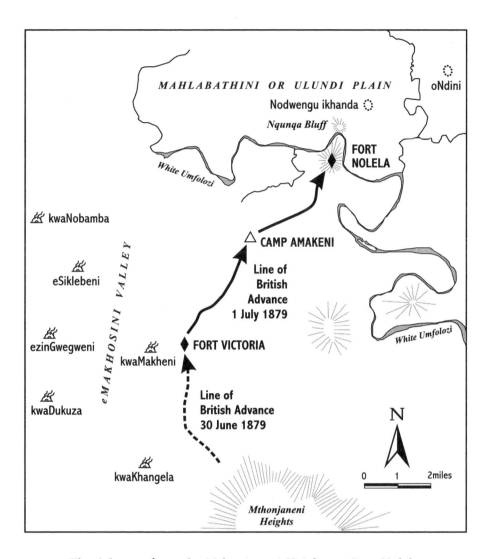

The Advance from the Mthonjaneni Heights to Fort Nolela

was bleak and exposed to high winds with visibility on occasions being severely restricted by heavy mist. The only water supply was from 'Dingane's Stream' 500 yards to the east of the plateau. This supply was supplemented by a trickle of water oozing out of a rock formation to the west. Thirteen miles to the north-east lay the Umfolozi River.

Buller's immediate priority was to torch the *amakhanda* in the eMakhosini valley. His irregulars now continued their grim work of destroying the infrastructure of Zululand. Numerous small *imizi*, together with three large *amakhanda* were burnt, and their grain pits destroyed.

On the afternoon of 28 June, Captain Herbert Stewart, brigade major of the Cavalry Brigade, and his mounted escort spurred their sweating English mounts up Jackal Ridge and onto the Mthonjaneni Heights to report to Chelmsford. They had ridden hard from Landman's Drift, carrying a message from Sir Garnet Wolseley demanding an immediate situation report, together with details of any proposed future movements. Chelmsford sat down at his field desk the same afternoon and penned a detailed response, indicating that he was within striking distance of Ulundi and intended to advance without tents but with ten days' provisions to the Umfolozi; he went on to add:

> As regards my future operations, after Ulundi and the surrounding military kraals have been destroyed, it is difficult to write confidently. I very much question being able to hold on to the Ulundi Valley even if it were advisable, which I doubt.[262]

On 30 June, leaving behind B and F Companies of the 1st/24th Regiment under the command of Major Upcher as garrison on the Mthonjaneni Heights, Chelmsford, with the Flying Column in the van, advanced down towards the Umfolozi. The troops, lightly equipped, were accompanied by 200 ox-wagons loaded with ammunition and rations. Buller's cavalry surged ahead to clear the way and report any Zulu movement. They made a halt short of the river and commenced making camp. Ahead and seven miles to the north, lay their objective.

At 3.00 p.m. the same afternoon Lieutenant James Henry Scott Douglas, 21st Royal Scots Fusiliers, left Fort Evelyn escorted by Corporal Cotter, 17th Lancers, on the twenty-mile return journey to the Mthonjaneni Heights. The twenty-six-year-old subaltern was chief of the signalling staff of the 2nd Division. On the morning of the 30th the weather had been overcast, thus preventing any communication with Fort Evelyn's heliograph. Chelmsford's response to Sir Garnet was of sufficient importance for Scott Douglas to be ordered to deliver the message personally to Fort Evelyn for onward transmission. He was anxious to return that evening as he suspected that a major action was imminent, an action he had no intention of missing. In spite of the garrison's efforts to persuade him to return in daylight the following morning, he left on the return journey with Cotter two hours before nightfall. By 5.00 p.m. a thick fog had shrouded the heights, causing Scott Douglas and Cotter to take the wrong track. They found themselves approaching the deserted mission station of KwaMagwaza where they rode straight into the arms of a powerful Zulu *impi* on its way to join the main army. While attempting to withdraw, they were pursued and cornered. Scott Douglas managed to fire five rounds from his revolver but was killed together with Cotter in a flurry of stabbing blows.

Their non-arrival back at Newdigate's camp caused concern and, on 3 July, a search party led by Lieutenant Warren of Buller's Irregulars set out on an extensive search that was unsuccessful. A week later, however, Commandant Lorraine White's irregulars located the bodies and Wood came to inspect the scene:

> I found the body of Corporal William Cotter, 17th Lancers, as pointed out by a private of Wood's Irregulars, and about a hundred yards on the Kwamagwasa side of it the body of Lieutenant Scott Douglas. Both soldiers had been killed by assegai wounds, I imagine four or five days ago. Neither body had been mutilated ... I sent back to camp for entrenching tools and a clergyman, when the Revs. Coar and Baudrey attended, and buried the bodies in the presence of the Lieutenant-General Commanding.[263]

Their graves, on high ground in a remote part of Zululand, were marked by: '. . . two trees, quaintly-shaped aloes, the only trees in that direction for many miles. Not a sound disturbs their rest.'[264] Cotter's corporal's stripes, together with his good conduct badge and lance pennant were sent to his mother, accompanied by a personal letter of sympathy from Wood. Scott Douglas's revolver was recovered, but his sword was missing, presumed taken by the Zulus.

The incident had a curious postscript, however. Many years after the war, a sword was recovered from a Zulu homestead and positively identified. It had Scott Douglas's name and regiment engraved on the blade. Its whereabouts then became a mystery until 1972, nearly a century after the Anglo-Zulu War, when an advertisement appeared in the *Houston [Texas] Post* that read:

The Wilkinson Sword Carried by a Zulu General
In 1879, Lt Scott-Douglas [*sic*] of the 21st Royal Scot's [*sic*] Fusiliers was proceeding across Africa to join in the last battle of the First Zulu Campaign. En route he met 500 Zulu warriors. They gave his captured sword to their general. His story is in the book 'The Washing of the Spears.' His sword is at the Gallerie d'Afrique.[265]

The late Donald Morris, author of *Washing of the Spears*, had his attention drawn to the advertisement and visited the gallery. He subsequently confirmed that the sword had been acquired from a collector in Dallas. How it had ended up in Texas is unknown. The sharkskin grip remained intact and the steel blade, though pitted, was still sharp. The sword was on exhibition and not for sale, indeed it had an honoured place in the gallery.

On 1 July, at 7.30 a.m., Chelmsford resumed the advance through difficult country covered in scrub, rocks and long grass. The track was narrow and the heat, despite it being winter, was oppressive. Once the troops were off the heights, water was only obtainable by digging diligently in dry sluits. Two hours before sunset, Wood halted and laagered with Newdigate's division forming its camp half a mile to the rear and in open ground. Chelmsford correctly judged this arrangement to be unsatisfactory and, with Zulus showing themselves in force on the northern banks of the river, Chelmsford ordered Newdigate to close the gap and form a single fortification, known as Fort Nolela.

The litany of false alarms and accidental discharge of firearms was to continue. Tension among the young soldiers, aware that a battle was impending, made the night picquets nervous and jumpy. The remaining five companies of the 1st/24th Regiment were on duty that night at Fort Nolela. The NNC provided the advanced picquets, with the companies of the 1st/24th on duty in front of the shelter trenches. At midnight an officer of the NNC moved out to inspect his picquets. One of the NNC men, seeing a shadow approaching, promptly fired a shot.

Immediately the entire NNC picquet bolted back towards the laager. In doing so, they penetrated the inner line of the 1st/24th who assumed that a Zulu attack was under way. They, in turn, after firing at the NNC, retired smartly back inside the laager causing great panic. Drury-Lowe was amongst those injured in the confusion, as was Newdigate himself.

Viscount St Vincent, attached to the 17th Lancers, recorded the scene:

> The natives jumping over the shelter trench among our men (24th Regiment) are taken for Zulus. A most discreditable scare is the result Our men leave their arms in the trenches and bolt . . . not a man is left to defend the laager . . . in the scramble to get into the laager our Colonel [Drury-Lowe] has his head cut open, and everyone is more or less knocked about. However, the men come to their senses and are much ashamed of themselves.[266]

Drury-Lowe was not the only sufferer, as Lieutenant Main noted:

> The panic mongers however did not get off altogether, as in their hasty retreat they knocked over Evelyn Wood's tent and he was furious. He managed to catch nine or ten of them and at daybreak held a court martial & inflicted a summary punishment of fifteen lashes on each offender.[267]

Under the circumstances, it is hard to pass judgement on the behaviour of untested young 24th Regiment infantrymen, particularly in light of the established reputation of the Zulu to show no quarter, demonstrated clearly at Isandlwana. Clery felt that, as a result of their actions, the entire regiment was further disciplined: 'In punishment the battalion was left behind to garrison the laager when the force marched out for the action at Ulundi.'[268]

Just before sunset the following day, to Chelmsford's astonishment, another message arrived from Sir Garnet, this time curt to the point of rudeness. The messenger was Guy Dawnay who had left Landman's Drift on the night of the 1st, riding non-stop except to change horses. Chelmsford opened the envelope and read:

> Concentrate your force immediately and keep it concentrated. Undertake no serious operations with detached bodies of troops. Acknowledge receipt of this message at once and flash back your latest moves. I am astonished at not hearing from you.[269]

It was apparent that Chelmsford's original response, sent off at first light on 29 July, had not reached Sir Garnet, who was by now anxious to halt operations, combine Crealock's 1st Division with Chelmsford's command and make the final attack on Ulundi himself. Chelmsford conferred immediately with Newdigate, Wood, Buller and his own staff. All no doubt concurred that the advance should continue, despite the latest dispatch, as Molyneux remarked: 'The order to fall back on General Crealock, I am afraid, made us all laugh.'

Chelmsford had endured far too much criticism to allow Sir Garnet the glory of final victory. Only by ignoring Sir Garnet's orders could he hope to salvage a degree of honour and partially restore his damaged reputation. Captain Montague voiced the opinion of the majority:

> Under our chief we had waited, worked, and fought; and it was hard on him as on us to see another come, hot-haste at the eleventh hour, to snatch victory all ready prepared to hand.[270]

Brevet Major Matthew Gossett, ADC to Chelmsford, made an annotation on Wolseley's telegram: 'Lord Chelmsford was, when this telegram was received, about to march to the Umvolisi [Umfolozi] and would not suspend operations.'[271] Thus the die was cast; there would be a deliberate but justified disregard of orders which, in the event of any setback, would have resulted in disgrace for Chelmsford.

Below, and in view of Fort Nolela, stretched the meandering White Umfolozi River, so named from the Zulu word *mfulawosi* that refers to a fibrous bush found growing on the banks of the river. On the opposite bank of the Umfolozi and commanding the drift below Fort Nolela at a distance of 400 yards from the river, was a high rock-covered bluff, named Nqunqa, which was occupied by Zulu marksmen who dominated the crossing area. It was impracticable to occupy the bluff at night, as lack of support from the fire-base at Fort Nolela, together with the fact that the Umfolozi separated the fort from Nqunqa, made such an operation hazardous. Thus the tasks of water collecting, washing and bathing were approached with the utmost caution and invariably resulted in sniper fire and casualties.

Beyond the river on the northern bank, lay the Mhlabathini plain, on which all the great *amakhanda* stood, including oNdini, the royal homestead of King Cetshwayo kaMpande. Nearby, in the sacred eMakhosini Valley, lay the grave of the founder of the Zulu nation, Zulu Nkosinkulu, as well as the graves of past Zulu kings, including Phunga, Mageba, Ndaba, Jama and Senzangakhona (who was Shaka's father). In times of stress, famine or war, the Zulu nation would gather here in multitudes to pay homage to their departed leaders.

The final objective was at last within sight and Chelmsford anxiously contemplated his plan of action. Would the Zulus have the temerity to launch a direct assault on Nolela? In view of its fortification Chelmsford thought not; alternatively would the Zulu attack him in the open if he were to cross the Umfolozi and advance onto the Mhlabathini Plain?

In his dispatch to Sir Garnet dated 28 June he had written: 'I am, however, hopeful the enemy will stand, and give the troops under my command the opportunity they are longing for.'[272] His worst fear, as he peered across the river from under his characteristically positioned low white helmet, was that the Zulus would melt into the hills and not give battle. With an extended supply problem and Sir Garnet breathing down his neck, it was not a situation he relished facing. During the evening of 2 July, Chelmsford therefore conferred with his divisional commanders to decide on a means of precipitating a battle.

Chapter 11

The Dilemma of the Zulu Monarch

'Since quite enough men, white as well as black, had
fallen in the war, and it was time now to make peace.'

'King Cetshwayo kaMpande', Journal of Cornelius Vijn

<hr>

As early as April, Cetshwayo had found himself on the horns of a dilemma.
The euphoria of the victory at Isandlwana, albeit tempered by the heavy
casualties sustained, had been dulled by the defeats suffered at Nyezane,
Rorke's Drift, Kambula and Gingindlovu. Would the king's regiments
respond to a fresh call to arms? Their mobility hinged on their living off the
land and a major reason for their inability to remain in the field following a
battle was the lack of adequate food supplies, as mentioned by many Zulus
in later years as 'the suffering of the starving troops'. This, coupled with the
compulsory rituals carried out after a battle, resulted in the immediate
dispersal of warriors back to their respective *amakhanda* spread throughout
Zululand. Thus strategic planning was impossible for Cetshwayo, who
commanded a citizen force that responded to his call in times of need,
rather than a standing army under his immediate control.

At the outbreak of the conflict at most perhaps 40,000 warriors were
deployed. The army, more especially the regiments made up of young
warriors, was confident of its martial superiority over any opposition. This
ardour had been subsequently reduced by the number of those killed and
the sight of the wounded who managed either to crawl back or be carried
back to their villages. Consequently, both Cetshwayo's offensive and
defensive capabilities were severely diminished. Perhaps as much as twenty
per cent of his army was *hors de combat*. The shock of the extent of these
casualties reverberated around the kingdom, as exemplified by what
happened when an *umuzi* received the news of their *induna*'s death at
Isandlwana.

> They kept wailing in front of the kraals, rolling themselves on the ground
> and never quieting down; nay, in the night they wailed so as to cut
> through the heart of anyone. And this wailing went on, night and day, for
> a fortnight.[273]

This scene was repeated throughout Zululand. While British reinforcements poured into the colony, the Zulus were unable to replace their losses owing to their limited population. As Cetshwayo glanced across his royal *ikhanda* that dominated the plain, he may well have reflected on the grave of his father, King Mpande, that lay a mile or so to the north-east. Little did he dream that this sacred Zulu shrine was soon to be desecrated.[274]

Realising the hopelessness of the situation, Cetshwayo now actively sought an honourable peace. As the invading force advanced, each day brought news of the mass destruction of homesteads eventually totalling many thousands of individual huts. To this misery would be added the threat of starvation, directly attributable to Chelmsford's scorched-earth policy with its ruthless destruction of grain pits and mealie fields and the confiscation of all cattle.

Six major *amakhanda* situated on the Mhlabathini Plain constituted the heart of Zululand and all were now under direct threat. Nearest to Fort Nolela, close to the northern bank of the Umfolozi River and situated west of the track leading to oNdini, lay Bulawayo. At a distance of two miles north-east of Bulawayo, was Nodwengu. Between Bulawayo and Nodwengu and a mile to the north, lay the Indabakawombe *ikhanda*, all three military homesteads forming a loose triangle. The largest and most prominent *ikhanda* was that built by Cetshwayo, the royal homestead of oNdini, Zulu for 'the heights', indicating its impregnability. It was located a mile north-east of Nodwengu and above the Mbilane stream. Its massive size may be judged by its diameter of 750 yards, whilst its outer circumference measured almost one and a half miles. The King's *isabaye* or cattle kraal was ninety acres in extent and over a thousand huts were constructed between the outer and inner fences. Cetshwayo, influenced by John Dunn, had constructed a European-style house for his own use named *indlu mnyama*, or 'black house', made from materials supplied by the missionary, Ommund Ofterbro. The *ikhanda* of Gqikazi was located a mile to the north-west of oNdini. To Gqikazi's east, lay the last of the six *ikhanda*, that of eMlambongwenya, built for King Mpande's mother, Songiya. It was here that Shepstone had conducted Cetshwayo's colonial coronation service six years earlier.

When news was brought in June that the British had crossed into Zululand, Cetshwayo implemented a two-pronged strategy, namely to put out peace overtures and, in the event of such overtures failing, to prepare for battle.

The cry *'aye hlome'* rang out throughout Zululand – 'take up arms'. This time the call was not answered with the alacrity that had greeted the cry earlier in January, but nevertheless the *amabutho* obeyed the king's order and slowly converged on Ulundi. Those from afar were directed to ravines and valleys to bivouac. It was the duty of the king to provide cattle for slaughter to ensure the men were well fed. The Zulu army that finally assembled from all four corners of the kingdom during the second half of June included all the regiments that had fought in the major battles of the war.

On arrival, each regiment reported to the royal *ikhanda* where initial doctoring took place. This would probably have been undertaken in mid-June and would have included the killing and skinning of a bull. Long strips of meat duly roasted and smeared with *insinzi* (powdered medicine) were thrown into the air to the men who formed a large semi-circle. Mpatshana kaSodondo of the uVe regiment described the proceedings:

> The piece bitten off is chewed and then spat out on the ground whilst the juice is swallowed . . . Should the strip of meat fall to the ground at any moment, it may not be picked up. It is then supposed to have lost all value for the purpose in hand . . . Two [bulls] are never killed. Every atom of the bull remaining over is then burnt to cinders. The doctors even collect all the ashes and pitch them into a large and deep pool where they sink, and so prevent anyone getting at and purloining them.[275]

One marvels at the skill of the war doctors to cut sufficient strips thin enough to suffice for all present. Following this initiation, no sexual intercourse was allowed. This rule was rigidly obeyed to the extent that food delivered by the women would be dropped off at a distance. The carriers would then beat a hasty retreat.

In due course and immediately before an impending battle, further indoctrination would take place, following which over 20,000 men would be at their monarch's bidding, ready for the final defence of the old Zulu order.

Palls of smoke drifted across the eMakhosini Valley, visible all across the great plain. Buller and his units had busied themselves burning homesteads that included the *amakhanda* of kwaMakheni, kwaDukuza, kwaKhangela, ezinGwegweni, kwaNobamba and eSiklebeni, all located to the south of the river.

Unwittingly, Buller's men had committed a sacrilege that the Zulu nation would not forget. The sacred *inkatha* 'yezwe yakwaZulu' was kept in the eSiklebeni *ikhanda*. The *inkatha*, eighteen inches in diameter, was similar in shape to that of a car tyre. It contained *nsila* ('body dirt') of the king and his predecessors. It also contained some of the contents of a pit into which warriors were compelled to vomit during certain ceremonies.

Other ingredients included in the *inkatha* included the body dirt and hair of previous monarchs, bits of clothing obtained from rival chiefs and straw from the royal *ikhanda*. On the death of a monarch, a part of his personal *inkatha* was incorporated within the national *inkatha*. The whole was then wrapped into the skin of a python. This was the most sacred heirloom of the Zulu nation and was considered to be possessed of great magical power. The *inkatha* coil represented the unity of the nation. The Zulu nation without its *inkatha* was a nation without its soul. Should the *inkatha* be lost by whatever means, including fire or deliberate destruction, the omens were calamitous; sickness would prevail and the spirits would vent their anger.

It seems that Buller had now reduced the sacred *inkatha* to no more than ashes amongst the smouldering ruins of eSiklebeni. The omens for the Zulu nation in the years ahead were seemingly dark indeed. The James Stuart Archive, however, relates a different version. By this account, on the crowning of Cetshwayo, the *inkatha* was removed from eSiklebeni to oNdini where it was housed in 'the most sacred shelter', eNkhatheni, a hut within the royal *ikhanda*. Accordingly, the *inkatha* was not destroyed before the battle but when oNdini was torched immediately afterwards. Either way, in Zulu eyes, the British were the cause of its destruction.

Cetshwayo now pursued his policy of negotiation with Chelmsford, using Cornelius Vijn, a young Dutch trader who had spent the duration of the war more or less under 'open arrest' in Zululand, working as a go-between and scribe. Although Vijn felt his life threatened as a result of justifiable Zulu anti-white sentiment, Cetshwayo's patronage guaranteed his safety.

On 4 June, on hearing that the invasion into Zululand had commenced, Cetshwayo contacted his old confidant, John Dunn, who was accompanying Crealock's 1st Division, and asked him to intervene:

> He wishes you [John Dunn] to ease his mind by using your influence with the great white Chiefs to get them to cease hostilities until he [the king] can hear the reason for his being destroyed. You are his father, and a child may be beaten, but let it be told why.[276]

Dunn, now totally committed to the British cause, responded that it was too late for him to intervene. Simultaneous to his appeal to Dunn, Cetshwayo sent three trusted messengers, namely Mgcwelo, Mtshibela and Mphokotwayo, to seek out Chelmsford. The three arrived under a flag of truce at Wood's camp and made, on Cetshwayo's behalf, an impassioned plea for peace.

Chelmsford responded in writing, the letter headed, 'Message from Lord Chelmsford to Zulu King.' It was a demand that the 7-pounder guns captured at Isandlwana, together with all arms, ammunition, and animals taken by the Zulu, be immediately returned. In addition, a regiment of the king's army was required to submit itself and lay down its arms. The terms bordered on humiliation. A further condition was that only known messengers of rank were to bring a response, specifically those present when the British ultimatum had been delivered in December of the previous year. If Cetshwayo acquiesced, then final terms would follow.

Cornelius Vijn was not present when the messengers arrived back from Wood's camp, but was immediately summoned. He hurried back from the Black Umfolozi River and translated the note. Then, on or about 12 June, Cetshwayo replied. Frustrated, he asked Chelmsford how peace was possible.

Ask them how I can make peace when the Queen's Army is daily capturing my cattle, burning my kraals, and killing my people. But, if they go on doing what they are now doing, it will not be my fault if a calamity comes; and then they will say, if white-men lose their lives, 'It is all Cetshwayo's doing.'[277]

In the following two weeks no fewer than four messengers arrived at Fort Marshall, forty-five miles west of Ulundi, only to be refused entry by the officer commanding, Colonel Collingwood. The messengers had left Cetshwayo on or about 12 June. Their delay can only be explained by their either having been detained or, alternatively, been too frightened to approach the fortification. What should have been a two-day journey inexplicably took ten days. In due course the messengers reported back to Cetshwayo that they had been unable to deliver his message as, 'If they came back they would be shot.'

Despite messengers being under flags of truce they were not always accorded reasonable treatment. At Eshowe, for example, two *bona fide* messengers were declared to be spies, manacled and imprisoned for six weeks.

Cetshwayo, aware of the progress of Chelmsford's force, desperately sought to avoid a conflict he knew he could not win. Another message was sent, this time accompanied by gifts of two magnificent elephant tusks, 100 oxen and an assurance that the two 7-pounders captured at Isandlwana would shortly be returned. Chelmsford, realising that the military initiative had passed to him, contemptuously rejected the offerings: 'You have not complied with all the conditions I laid down. I shall therefore continue to advance.'[278]

Chelmsford now needed time to fortify and secure his advance from Fort Victoria to Fort Nolela, so he added a rider that he would not cross the Umfolozi until 30 June in order to 'allow' Cetshwayo time to comply with the conditions demanded. This would give him the opportunity he needed to consolidate his position. The tusks were returned but the cattle retained. Yet another tusk offered to General Crealock was accepted by him and sent on to the Secretary of State for the Colonies. Reputed to be the 'finest specimen', it was seven feet in length.

The thousands of warriors assembled on the Mhlabathini Plain could see strange flashes of light from Fort Victoria. The heliograph to Fort Evelyn was active and Cornelius Vijn, aware of an impending battle, feared for his life.

Cetshwayo's last message to Chelmsford was dated 30 June and was delivered by the king's messengers, Mfunzi and nKismane, both senior in rank. The message indicated that the two 7-pounders and more oxen would be delivered to Chelmsford the following day. Mfunzi also carried a prize trophy to be handed to Chelmsford, the sword of the Prince Imperial. Vijn added a pleading addendum to the note: 'If the English army is in want for the country, please do me a favour to call me by bearer, that I might get out of the country.' He then scribbled in pencil on the envelope a useful piece of intelligence. 'Be strong, if the King send in his army, they are about 20,000.'[279]

Chelmsford wrote a final response from 'Camp Amakeni', located midway between Fort Victoria and the Umfolozi River. Buller's men, unaware of its importance, had days previously burnt the *ikhanda* of Makheni. It had originally belonged to Senzangakhona and, on his death, was rebuilt by Mpande. The name Makheni meant 'the perfumery' for it was here that the king was ceremoniously anointed with perfumed herbs and here that Cetshwayo had been crowned King of the Zulu Nation six years earlier. Camp Amakeni was to be Chelmsford's penultimate stop before establishing Fort Nolela. Chelmsford's letter promised '. . . not to burn any kraals until Thursday 3 July provided no opposition is made to my advance', but it never reached the Zulu monarch.

It is speculated that, at this stage, the hopelessness of the Zulu cause as expressed by their commanders (in direct contrast to the aspirations of the young warriors determined to fight) resulted in Mfunzi being denied access to Cetshwayo. The probable reason was linked to Zulu custom that anyone who had 'come from the enemy' might not appear before the king, being 'unclean'. From Chelmsford's viewpoint, a lack of response, probably much to his relief, opened the way for the final advance to contact. From Cetshwayo's viewpoint, he still wished for a settlement and did not give up hope. The young bloods of the many regiments spread across the plain, however, had other ideas.

The Zulu commanders had not been idle. The approaches west of oNdini near the Mbilane Stream were prepared for ambush. The waist-high grass was knotted together close to the ground, thus presenting a trap for the cavalry. Both sides of the ambush area provided cover for the wily Zulu. If the British mounted men could be enticed into the trap it would become a killing zone.

Meanwhile, the active and outstanding Zulu commander Zibhebhu kaMaphitha, a close confidant of Cetshwayo who had been wounded at Isandlwana, now occupied the Nqunqa Bluff, opposite Nolela Camp. From there he and his men brought fire to bear on the British as they went about collecting water and bathing. The sniping began to cause casualties and was to continue until the morning of 4 July.

It was recorded, but probably exaggerated, that the Zulus occupying Nqunqa Bluff were intrigued by the sight of white soldiers leaving camp in droves and squatting in a line, trousers half-mast. Could it be that the British also possessed *izinyanga* and that a strange ritual was doctoring them for battle? In reality they were looking down on the latrines and, if true that large numbers were so occupied, the cause may well have been the commissariat's various ways of cooking oxen.

On 2 July Cetshwayo made a last vain appeal. Three hundred selected white cattle from the prized iNyonikayipumuli royal herd were assembled.

Prior to driving them to the Umfolozi as a peace offering, Cetshwayo gathered his army together in a huge semi-circle and addressed them. Among the throng was Mtshapi kaNoradu of the Khandempemvu regiment who later recalled:

> He then came into the semi-circle of men and said, 'O, Zulu people, I see that the white people have indeed come. I see that though you blunted them at Sandhlwana [*sic*], the next day they came on again [at Rorke's Drift]. Though you blunted them at the stronghold of Rawane [Hlobane], the next day they came on again [Kambula]. Then you came and told me that their army had driven you back and had done you harm. I now say that these oxen must go as a peace offering to the white people.'
>
> Then Matatshile kaMasipula of the Emgazini said, 'No, Nkosi. Is the king beginning to speak thus even though we Khandempemvu are far from finished?'
>
> The King replied, 'Matatshile, what do you mean by far from finished? Where is Zikode kaMasipula? Where is Mhlazana kaNgozaka Ludaba? Where is Mtshodo kaNtshingwayo kaMahole? Where is Mahu? Where is Somcuba kaMapita? So you are far from finished? How is it that you can say that? Where is Gininda kaMasipula? . . . Yeh! Matatshile . . . if the white men keep advancing when so many of them have been killed, what is there to stop them?'[280]

Cetshwayo was making direct reference to prominent Zulu *izinduna*, in some cases the sons of senior commanders, who had been killed in action, including the son of Ntshingwayo, the commander at Isandlwana, and Zikode and Gininda, sons of Masipula, Mpande's chief minister.

Cornelius Vijn confirmed that Cetshwayo addressed his troops, voicing his concern that, in the event of defeat: 'You will all run away, and the whites will follow and capture me only, and afterwards carry me away.' Whereupon his regiments, with one accord spoke: 'Whether the day be won or lost, they would come back to him.'

The assembled army could clearly understand that their king had no wish to fight and feared for his own safety, confirmed by Cetshwayo's orders to his isiGodlo girls to collect all his personal belongings and hide them. His goods were carried far off to the Hlopekhulu Mountain, three miles southeast of the capital and lowered by ropes into deep caves, the operation being supervised by his men-servants. In due course, his personal belongings were to be looted by the very men responsible for their safekeeping.

It was time for Cetshwayo's final effort to avert war. He now ordered his prize cattle to be brought to the Umfolozi River and offered to the British general as a peace offering. In Zulu culture it was a gift of magnanimous proportions. The herd, bellowing as the cattle were driven forward, was stopped well short of the Umfolozi and intercepted, according to some reports, by the young bloods of the Khandempemvu regiment who refused the herd further passage, preferring to fight. This version of events, however, contradicts Cetshwayo's own, as related to R. C. Samuelson, who was Cetshwayo's interpreter while the king was in captivity in Cape Town:

> Chief Sibhebhu intercepted them, led the Ngobamakosi [*sic*] regiment forward, and when these had got as far as the Nolela krantz, overlooking the said White Umfolozi Drift, some of Chief Sibhebhu's men fired at the soldiers, who were having a wash in the river, and precipitated the Ulundi fight.

Whichever version is correct, it was plain that Cetshwayo's authority was severely undermined. There would be no peace offerings. It was time to hold an inner council; time to prepare his army for action; time for the drums of war to roll.

On the evening of 2 July Cetshwayo held his last council. Present were Zibhebhu kaMaphitha, Mnyamana kaNgqengelele, Sihayo kaXongo, Cetuga, Phalane kaMdinwa, and Mavumengwana kaNdlela. Sigananda Shezi, an old ally and confidant of Cetshwayo was also by his side. Now nearly eighty years old, he had witnessed the death of Piet Retief in 1836, had been with Cetshwayo at the Battle of Ndondakusuku in 1856 and had even been present at the Battle of Isandlwana. Although not recorded, in all probability Prince Dabulamanzi kaMpande, Ntshingwayo kaMahole Khoza and Prince Ziwedu kaMpande, younger brother of Cetshwayo, were also present.

No doubt the timing of the final doctoring of his army would have been on the agenda, as would have been a decision whether or not to cross the Umfolozi to attack the now fortified British position. It was apparent to the Zulu commanders that the British would advance on to the plain, precipitating, from a Zulu perspective, a defensive wait-and-see strategy. With the monarch's negative views apparent, the morale of his *amabutho* was probably affected. At a time when strong leadership and clear strategy were called for, Cetshwayo failed.

The order was given for the final doctoring rites. Poison was poured into the waters of the Umfolozi immediately below Nqunqa Bluff in the hope that the white troops would be affected, 'but none of the European troops died as the doctor had declared they would do.'[281] Regiments were ordered to kill and consume cattle at night and the spirits of the ancestors were to be appeased by praises recited by all *izinduna*.

On the night of 3 July, 20,000 warriors, by order of Cetshwayo, began the great chant of Senzangakhona, father of King Shaka. Senzangakhona had elevated the chant to 'the status of the national hymn', to be sung during the 'first fruits' ceremony. Now this melodious chant, for there were no words, echoed across the plain filling the men with pride and courage. 'Their hearts become enraged, and they thirst for battle.'[282] The Zulu women gave full encouragement and the shrill staccato sounds of ululation filled the amphitheatre.

Across the Umfolozi the white men, 'holed up like pigs', would hear the great chant, bass and tenor in perfect harmony, sung as only Zulus can sing, and tremble with fear. The warriors continued their doctoring until the early hours of 4 July, when slowly the war songs and chants abated and the nation waited for sunrise.

———◆———

Chapter 12

The Battle of Ulundi²⁸³

'Destruction on a grand scale followed the events of 1879 and the dignity of our kingdom has not yet been fully restored.'

Prince Mangosuthu Buthelezi, Traditional Prime Minister to the Zulu Nation

———◦◦◦———

The military adage 'time spent on reconnaissance is seldom wasted' might well have been uppermost in Chelmsford's mind as he surveyed his objective, the royal *ikhanda* of oNdini, through his glass. The area between Nodwengu and oNdini was dead ground and it became apparent that a full reconnaissance would be necessary to test Zulu strength and to select a possible site on which to give battle. Chelmsford conferred with Wood and Newdigate and concurred that Buller's irregulars were better suited to the task than Marshall's regular cavalry.

At noon on 3 July Buller, mounted on 'Punch', described by war correspondent Archibald Forbes as 'the very ugliest horse of his day in all South Africa', led his mounted men across the Umfolozi River. Buller was not unduly worried about Punch's looks, however, as the horse had been 'salted' to the third degree and was therefore believed to be immune to the dreaded horse sickness. Over 500 strong, the mounted reconnaissance splashed across the drift. Baker's Horse had been tasked to secure the nearby Nqunqa Bluff opposite the British camp. They crossed immediately below Fort Nolela while the remainder of Buller's force crossed the river a mile downstream.

Buller's staff officer and second-in-command, Captain Lord William Leslie de la Poer Beresford, 9th (Queen's Royal) Lancers, was an Irishman of considerable charm and ability. He had been stationed in India as ADC to Lord Lytton, Viceroy of India, when news of the Isandlwana defeat reached him. He immediately applied for six months' leave and embarked for South Africa, arriving in April. He had hoped to find a position on Major-General Marshall's cavalry staff. Captain Alan Gardner's wounds, received at Kambula, provided an opening for Beresford to be appointed in his place. It was an inspired choice, for Beresford's undoubted skills were used in controlling and exercising discipline over the colonial irregulars, described by Archibald Forbes as follows:

> [They] consisted of broken gentlemen, of renegade sailors, of fugitives from justice, of the scum of the South African towns, of solid Africanders [sic], of Boers whom the Zulu had driven from their farms. Almost every European nationality was represented; and there were men from the United States, a Greaser, a Chilean, several Australians, and a couple of Canadian Voyageurs. One and all were volunteers, recruited for the campaign for five shillings a day.

Captain William Hugh Tomasson, adjutant of Baker's Horse, was equally scathing:

> Discharged soldiers and sailors, cockney and countrymen, cashiered officers of army and navy here rubbed shoulders . . . of these nations, Danes made the best and Americanised Irish the worst soldiers.

The only uniformity about Buller's tough band of mercenary irregulars was a bandolier filled with cartridges slung over the shoulder, together with a broad brimmed 'wide-awake' hat, worn to shield the eyes from the sun. They could be likened in some respects to Boers, who would respond to the call in a loose manner, appearing and disappearing at will, with little respect for punctuality, but who were excellent marksmen and not afraid to fight. Whatever their varied backgrounds and code of conduct, Buller and Beresford, both leading by example, had forged them into an effective fighting force.

These were the men of Baker's Horse, Bettington's Horse, Raaff's Transvaal Rangers, D'Arcy's Frontier Light Horse and Whalley's Natal Light Horse, most of whom, as already mentioned, had fought under Buller. Baker's Horse, known as the 'Canaries', from their yellow uniform facings, also enjoyed a reputation for imbibing, being known as 'Baker's Boozers'. How they obtained their grog was not clear, as Wood enforced a strict policy of flogging all peddlers of liquor. No doubt the continual burning and looting of homesteads provided a local source of native beer (*utshwala*) for consumption, sufficient to earn the Canaries their reputation and circumvent any potential disciplinary proceedings.

Bettington's No. 3 Troop, Natal Horse, was now reduced to fourteen Europeans, all former members of the disbanded 3rd Regiment, NNC, and, because of the size of his command, was incorporated into Shepstone's troop of the Natal Native Horse.

Buller had overall charge of the Natal Native Horse, commanded by Captain Cochrane, including Shepstone's Edendale Troop. Both units had fought at Isandlwana and, as a single entity, at Kambula. Shepstone, originally attached to the 2nd Division, was placed under Buller's command during May. The Native Horse proved invaluable as scouts and cheap at the price of £5 per month, with the added proviso that they supplied their own mounts.

The only regular mounted troops under Buller's command, as mentioned previously, were No. 1 Squadron, Mounted Infantry, commanded by Captain Edward Browne, 1st/24th Regiment.

After crossing the Umfolozi, it looked initially as if Baker intended to bypass the Nqunga Bluff. Then, in a deliberate movement, he swung left and, at the gallop, took the hill from the rear, much to the surprise of the Zulus hidden amongst the rocks. Leaving ten killed in the encounter, the Zulus, not wishing to be cut off, hastily retreated on to the plain. Ordered by Buller to hold the bluff, Baker consolidated his position to cover any possible retreat.

To secure his left flank, Buller ordered the NNH to take up a position on a small koppie. From there, looking through his field glasses, Cochrane could discern the *ikhanda* of Nodwengu, about one mile to the north-east. He also saw a strong force of 8,000 warriors converging on Nodwengu from the direction of the Gqikazi *ikhanda* to the north:

> The Zulus marched in companies, chanting their terrible war song as they went, and very soon reached Nodwengu, into which they filed in splendid order.[284]

After this force had assembled in strength at Nodwengu, an order was then given to the entire Zulu army to withdraw to an *ikhanda* north of Ulundi, possibly eMlambongwenya: 'In half an hour I saw four regiments on the march from various points to a kraal above Ulundi.'[285] Clearly the Zulus intended to lure the mounted irregulars into a pre-conceived ambush.

Beresford, having already lost two horses during the campaign, was now mounted on a frisky chestnut and, cantering in the van of the advance, approached the Nodwengu *ikhanda*. As he drew closer, a small group of Zulus broke and fled at a lope towards oNdini. Bringing up the rear was a Zulu of magnificent proportions, a seasoned ringed warrior who appeared unconcerned by the advancing horsemen. Abreast of Beresford and in the van, rode Piet Raaff and a civilian reporter, McKenzie of *The Standard*. At a gallop all three thundered after the Zulu, who by now had realised his peril. Those in camp stood on wagons and peered eagerly across the Umfolozi to catch the action. Beresford took the lead and closed with his adversary. Turning to face the onslaught, the Zulu pushed his spear upwards only to be thwarted by Beresford who, in a single motion, deflected the spear and pushed his sabre through the defensive cow-hide shield and into the warrior's chest, killing him instantly. The action was made famous in a dramatic sketch later published in the *Illustrated London News*. The warrior's assegai was claimed as a souvenir, taken back to England and stood in 'the corner of Bill's mother's drawing room'.

At a sharp pace the advance continued: D'Arcy's troop on the left flank, Raaff on the right and Buller in the centre. They bypassed Nodwengu to their right and headed for oNdini, some thinking that the capital had been abandoned. The valley of the meandering Mbilane Stream separated Nodwengu from oNdini and it was here that the Zulus attempted to lure Buller into their preconceived trap. A body of warriors was seen retreating down the slope into the valley, herding goats towards the stream. The wily Buller, sensing all was not well, attempted to restrain the charge, as recorded by the correspondent of the *Natal Witness*.

> We had gone 500 yards in this direction when I heard Colonel Buller shout out to his men to halt, and then followed the ominous order to retire. Just then I saw a long line of Zulus rise from the grass but 200 yards ahead, and turned my horse in an instant. No sooner was I turned than I saw a second line of Zulus at right angles to the first, coming up on our right.[286]

Buller yelled, 'Fire without dismounting', as 5,000 Zulus, concealed in the bed of the Mbilane Stream, sped to encircle his force.

Commandant Raaff had already withdrawn to a ridge near Nodwengu and, from this position, gave fire support to Buller's force, which retreated at the gallop. Had Zulu marksmanship been the equal of their guile and bravery, the irregulars would have suffered severely: 'If they had known how to shoot, which happily for us they did not, nearly every saddle ought to have been emptied.'[287]

As it was, Trooper Pearce of the Frontier Light Horse was shot and killed instantly. Trooper Peacock of the Natal Light Horse was hit by a bullet and fell from his horse. Buller, assisted by Captain Prior, lifted Peacock onto Sergeant Kerr's horse, but Peacock was so badly injured that he fell off, to be killed by the advancing Zulus. Trooper J. A. Raubenheim of the Frontier Light Horse was also wounded in the initial volley, whilst Sergeant Fitzmaurice of Browne's Mounted Infantry lay in agony, trapped beneath his dead horse.

The Zulus triumphantly surged forward, but this was no time for *sauve qui peut*. Beresford, with fellow Irishman Sergeant E. O'Toole of the Frontier Light Horse, turned back immediately to release Sergeant Fitzmaurice and, whilst O'Toole kept the threatening Zulus at bay, Beresford managed to help the sergeant onto his mount. It was touch and go, for without O'Toole's help, it is unlikely that either Beresford or Fitzmaurice would have survived. Archibald Forbes recorded that an argument ensued between the two, Fitzmaurice pleading with Beresford to save himself. Forbes went on to record:

> Going into Beresford's tent the same afternoon, I found him fast asleep, and roused him with the information which Colonel Wood had given me, that he was to be recommended for the Victoria Cross. 'Get along with your nonsense, you impostor!' was his yawning retort as he threw a boot at me, and turned over and went to sleep again.[288]

Wood, in his post-battle report, made no specific mention of Beresford's action other than: 'Lord William Beresford and Lieutenant Hayward also brought dismounted men out of action.'[289]

Lieutenant T. R. Main and other officers stood on wagons in the camp to get a clear view of the action, as Main recorded:

> Many acts of gallantry were performed, and several VC's won. Amongst them Ld Wm. Beresford brought back a wounded man on his horse, but as he had taken him off from another man's horse when near the river there was considerable difference of opinion as to whether he deserved the VC which he received.[290]

Main's judgement may not have been a fair one as he would not have been able to see the action near the Mbilane stream where the initial rescue took place, as it was hidden from his view in dead ground. It is also possible that O'Toole and Beresford shared the load on their return to camp. Beresford's bravery in this, and his conduct in the battle to follow, were beyond reproach. He was recommended for the Victoria Cross, but would not accept the award: '. . . unless that recognition were shared by Sergeant O'Toole, who he persisted in maintaining, deserved infinitely greater credit than any that might attach to him.'[291] Sergeant Edmund O'Toole was duly awarded the Victoria Cross.

Whilst Beresford and O'Toole were saving Sergeant Fitzmaurice, Trooper Raubenheim's predicament remained precarious. Captain D'Arcy spurred his horse to where Raubenheim lay. The Zulus were closing fast but D'Arcy dismounted and managed to heave the wounded man onto his saddle. He quickly remounted, holding the dazed Raubenheim steady. With the yells and commotion, together with Zulu bullets flying high, the petrified horse bucked and threw both riders to the ground. Unfortunately D'Arcy fell heavily, landing on his revolver and injuring his back, whilst the shocked Raubenheim ended up dazed and unable to move. D'Arcy, not strong enough to lift Raubenheim's dead weight onto his saddle, decided, justifiably, to save himself. He managed to control his horse and remount, leaving the unfortunate Raubenheim in the hands of the fast closing Zulus. For his bravery, D'Arcy was also awarded the Victoria Cross, but his back injury meant that he was unable to lead the Frontier Light Horse into battle the following day, leaving command of his unit in the hands of Captain Alfred Blaine.

Sergeant-Major Simeon Kambule of the Edendale Troop, NNH, was also conspicuous in acts of outstanding bravery during the reconnaissance. He was awarded the Silver Medal for Distinguished Conduct in the Field. Part of his citation read:

> The reconnaissance towards Ondine the day before the battle of Nodwengu, Simeon Kambule saved the life of an officer of the Frontier Light Horse, by bringing him out of a very heavy fire behind him on his horse.

The Reverend Owen Watkins published a contemporary article on the Edendale Troop in the *Methodist Recorder*:

> Simeon Kambule received the Distinguished Service Medal from the hands of an English General, at a grand parade of the Troops; had he been a white man, he would have received the Victoria Cross.

After the various rescues the triumphant Zulus pursued Buller vigorously until within range of Baker's covering fire from Nqunqa Bluff. This, together with support from Major Le Grice's 9-pounders, which fired a few rounds of shrapnel from Nolela, caused the pursuit to be abandoned. It did not stop the triumphant Zulus from yelling insults and making clear the fate that awaited the invaders on the morrow.

Buller, through exemplary leadership, had not only extricated his command from disaster, but had seen enough of the terrain to enable him to select the exact spot on which to do battle the following day. Chelmsford thought so highly of Buller's reconnaissance and of the conduct of the force under his command, that, in his speech before his departure from Cape Town in August, he said:

> One of the finest episodes during this eventful war was the reconnaissance made by the mounted force of the flying column under Lieutenant-Colonel Buller on the day preceding the battle of Ulundi. Gentlemen, on that day, dash and daring, steadiness and coolness were all conspicuous at the proper moment; and it will be gratifying to you to know that, with the exception of one squadron of British infantry, the force in question was entirely colonial, and two thirds of it was from the Cape Colony.[292]

Not before time, the conduct of the colonials was given full recognition.

On Buller's return, Chelmsford made up his mind to bring the Zulus to battle and instructed Lieutenant-Colonel Crealock, his Assistant Military Secretary, to assemble the senior officers to receive their orders in the late afternoon of 3 July. Present were Newdigate, commanding the 2nd Division, with his staff; Marshall, commanding the Cavalry Brigade; Wood, Buller and the Flying Column's staff; Brown, Commander Royal Artillery and Moysey, Commander Royal Engineers.

No doubt an expectant hush fell on the group as Chelmsford outlined his plan. The Umfolozi was to be crossed in force on 4 July. All troops were to 'stand to' in silence at 03.45 a.m. in order not to alert the Zulus, and reveille was to be sounded at the usual hour of 05.15 a.m. Prior to the troops forming into columns at 05.00 a.m., a breakfast of coffee and biscuits was to be issued; in addition, two days' rations were be carried. Buller's Horse was to lead the advance over the Umfolozi, secure the bluff, fan out and form a protective screen. Wood's column was then to cross followed by Newdigate's infantry. Marshall's cavalry and Shepstone's Horse were to secure the rear. After the bluff was secure and the scrub and bush nearby cleared, the entire force was to form square on the high ground, with ammunition wagons, water carts, Royal Engineers, NNC, and medical personnel all positioned inside the square. The artillery was initially to move parallel to the sides of the square, but all batteries were to be allocated positions within it. The final battle position for the square was to be selected by Buller, using intelligence gained from his reconnaissance. Thereafter the irregular cavalry were to engage the Zulus and draw them on to the square. Finally, in order to ensure co-operation between the Flying Column and the 2nd Division, Wood and Newdigate were to co-ordinate inter-locking unit positions.

Newdigate's division totalled 1,884 white all ranks, 540 black troops and eight guns. Wood's column totalled 2,281 white all ranks, 465 black troops, four guns, two Gatlings and a rocket trough. In total 5,170 all ranks, including parts of six imperial infantry battalions, twelve artillery pieces, 354 regular cavalry and 652 irregular cavalry, were now poised to cross the Umfolozi and give battle.

A, C, D, E and G Companies of the 1st/24th Regiment, commanded by Major W. M. Dunbar were, to their intense disappointment, left to defend Fort Nolela under the overall command of Colonel William Bellairs, DAQMG. This arguably was a poor decision and contrary to the wishes of the Duke of Cambridge. Perhaps Chelmsford had no wish to risk further casualties for a regiment that had already suffered grievously, although uppermost in Chelmsford's mind remained the fear that the Zulus would melt away and not give battle. In all there were 900 white troops, 250 native troops and a single Gatling left behind under Colonel Bellairs's command at Fort Nolela.

At 6.00 p.m. on the 3rd Wood briefed his officers, detailing the order of advance for his battalions. He then addressed his troops and, in ringing tones, told them that the Umfolozi would be crossed the next day:

> The column would go into action tomorrow morning, and he advised us to be very steady, no matter if we were compelled to fight back, but he had not the least doubt that by this time tomorrow evening, Ulundi with its great kraals would be in flames and not a Zulu in sight for miles.[293]

This speech was greeted by cheers.

Simultaneously, Newdigate briefed his division, but his performance was spoiled by the appearance of indecision, as described by Arthur Harness in a letter to his family:

> I can assure you even when he is explaining what he wants there is a hesitation and weakness about it that you feel he may change his mind at any moment . . . Everyone feels the same.[294]

That night, weapons were cleaned; the ammunition issue brought up to the scale of 100 rounds per man and, a lessons learned from Isandlwana, all holding screws on ammunition boxes were loosened.

An air of anticipation filled the men. Sleep was impossible and the entire force waited, fully dressed under a blanket or greatcoat, for the pre-dawn call. At last the long, physically demanding campaign was coming to an end and they knew that their commander, Lord Chelmsford, would fight the final battle, not Sir Garnet Wolseley. Mixed with the anticipation was fear, as all were mindful of the Zulu victory at Isandlwana and the consequences of defeat. That night the sounds of drums, together with the swell of Zulu war chants filled the plain. At midnight, Chelmsford, fearing an attack, ordered all horses picketed outside the Flying Column's camp to be drawn within the laager, a task that took two hours to complete.

During the early hours of the morning, the Edendale Troop quietly gathered in a circle. They were poised for their third major battle and expected a titanic struggle. Led by Sergeant-Major Kambule they answered the Zulu chants by singing Methodist hymns.

Reveille sounded sharp at 5.15 a.m. on 4 July. The troops, however, were already formed up according to plan and waiting to move. An hour earlier the artillery horses had been harnessed to the gun carriages and all cavalry horses saddled and led outside the laager. A white mist covered both banks of the Umfolozi and obscured the view of the plain. The Zulus could neither be seen nor heard.

Promptly at 5.45 a.m. Buller splashed across the lower drift and secured, unopposed, the Nqunqa Bluff. At a fast pace he moved up a narrow path leading from the ford to the main Ulundi track. Vultures gorging on the bodies of men and horses slain during the previous day's action flapped grotesquely aside, making way for the advancing irregulars. Baker was deployed to the left, the Frontier Light Horse in the centre and Whalley's troop to the right. Buller, anxious to maintain complete control, cantered from one flank to another.

Close to Nodwengu, Baker's Horse stumbled across the bodies of Troopers Pearce and Peacock, killed the previous day. They were naked and had been ritually disembowelled. Nearby, the body of Trooper Raubenheim was found tied to a stake. There would have been no point in tying a dead body to a stake and it would be reasonable to conclude that, at the time of capture, Raubenheim was still alive and was subsequently tortured, his body parts used thereafter for doctoring purposes. It was the only recorded incident of torture inflicted by the Zulus on prisoners. Tomasson, Adjutant of Baker's Horse, later wrote:

> . . . worse than all, the body of the poor prisoner, tied to a sort of stake, and tortured and mutilated in a fearful manner. This sight is not one calculated to animate one with a spirit of mercy and threats loud and deep are uttered on the perpetrators.

Buller had now accomplished the first part of his mission. He had secured Nqunqa Bluff, established that there were no Zulu in strength to oppose the crossing and fanned out on the Mhlabathini Plain, well in advance of the infantry to provide a protective umbrella. Wood was later to record in his report: 'Here again Colonel Buller gave us such aid as has seldom been afforded by Light Cavalry to a main body of troops.'

At 6.45 a.m., one and a half hours after Buller had crossed, the 80th Regiment, led by Major Tucker, waded knee-deep across the Umfolozi. The infantry cleared the north bank and were followed by six artillery guns that took the drift at a canter. The remainder of Wood's infantry then crossed, followed by Chelmsford's headquarters, Newdigate's division, and the balance of the artillery. Three squadrons of 17th Lancers, King's Dragoon Guards and Shepstone's Natal Native Horse brought up the rear; the time was 7.30 a.m.

The broken ground on the north bank proved difficult to traverse and the column heaved its way up the slope in double column of fours, men slipping as their drenched boots failed to find a foothold. The plain lay one and a half miles to their front.

At this stage, when Chelmsford was most vulnerable, a determined Zulu attack might have proved decisive, while the formation was extended on the line of march. Each ox wagon alone took forty yards of space, with the mule wagons taking thirty yards. In double column of fours, from van to rear, the length of the column would be approximately 4,000 yards. Had the Zulus been successful in closing with the column, Fort Nolela would not have been in a position to provide fire support, as friend and foe would have been intermingled in close-quarter battle. For the Zulus, this represented a lost opportunity, a result of them never wavering from their predetermined and inflexible plan to lure the British on to the plain and engage them in the open.

At 7.30 a.m. Tucker's 80th squelched their way to open ground. Here they halted whilst Wood's staff issued commands to form square. Five companies of the 80th formed the front. Immediately to their rear, was Walter Jones's 5th Company, RE. The right face was occupied by eight companies of Major E. L. England's 1st/13th Light Infantry, which moved quickly into position hurried by their adjutant, Captain E. J. Gallwey. Major Rogers's 90th Light Infantry, with Adjutant Lomax issuing orders, occupied the left face. Wood's seasoned veterans were now in position.

At this stage, Newdigate's column was in the process of clearing the bank with Lieutenant-Colonel Malthus's 94th Regiment in the van. Malthus immediately moved four of his companies after Roger's 90th, completing the left face. His remaining two companies were allocated to the rear of the square. Behind Malthus, four companies of the 58th Regiment, with their commanding officer Colonel R. C. Whitehead, moved below the 1st/13th to complete the right face. Finally, two companies of the depleted 2nd/21st Regiment under Major A. G. Hazlerigg, joined Malthus's two companies, thus completing the rear of the square. Prior to the rear face closing, Lieutenant-Colonel John Tatton Butler Brown's twelve artillery pieces moved into the square. Finally, forty-eight ammunition, hospital and water

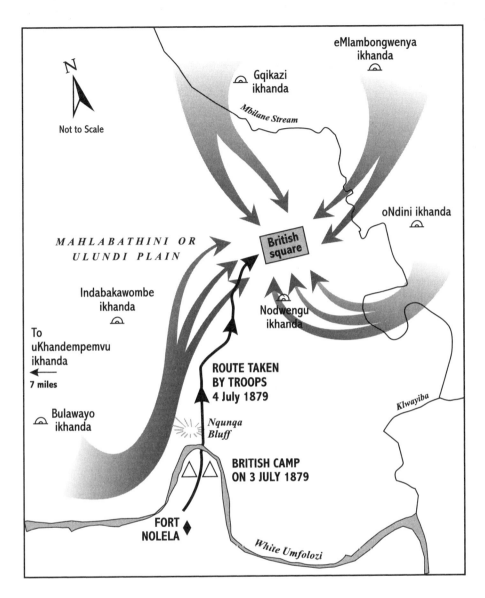

The Advance before the Battle of Ulundi
Lord Chelmsford's advance over the Umfolozi River
to give battle at Ulundi, 4 July 1879.

wagons were manhandled into the square, accompanied by Bengough's NNC battalion.

The sweating troops, despite the morning chill of winter, were now in position on the open plain and the garrison, watching from Fort Nolela, was able to discern the formation fine-tuning its drill. In reality, the 'square' was an oblong, 150 yards by 270 yards and nearly nine acres in area.

The command 'fix bayonets' now rang out. Each man responded to the well-rehearsed order by grasping his bayonet socket in the left hand while simultaneously pushing the muzzle of the Martini-Henry forward with the right hand. The bayonet was then drawn and as soon as the point cleared the scabbard, the socket of the bayonet was connected to the muzzle of the rifle and pressed home by turning the locking ring. As at Gingindlovu, the resounding sound of steel on steel crashed out, filling the men with pride and a sense of invincibility. The four-deep column of infantry then snapped to the order position.

Buller's cavalry still provided a protective screen to the front, whilst Shepstone, on Chelmsford's orders, torched the deserted Indabakawombe *ikhanda* located to their left.

Chelmsford was now ready to move towards oNdini and gave the command for the square to advance. Astonishingly, Wood had ordered the 1st/13th band to take their instruments into battle and now, as the sun rose over the hills, stirring martial music filled the plain as a mass of redcoats, regimental colours unfurled, together with their supporting cavalry and artillery, made their way inexorably towards their objective: 'The Colours were flying and the bands were playing as we advanced, and the sun shone on the glittering bayonets, lance and rifle barrels.'[295] It was the penultimate occasion that British infantry would advance to battle with colours unfurled, the last being the storming of Alexandria by the South Staffordshire Regiment in 1882.

Lord Chelmsford, positioned behind the front face, kept the direction of the advance under control by ordering a wheel to the left or right when needed.

Shepstone, again on orders, started to torch the deserted Nodwengu *ikhanda* to his right. Dense smoke rose and Buller immediately counter-manded the instruction 'for fear that the Zulus might take advantage of the smoke and creep up'. oNdini now lay beyond Nodwengu and, to align the front of the square to face oNdini, Chelmsford gave the command to wheel sharply to the right. The infantry responded with ease but the wagons and guns had to be pushed and pulled to achieve the correct alignment. Chelmsford now shouted to Buller to ask if the square should halt, but Buller responded by continuing the advance until a knoll, located on the previous day's reconnaissance, was reached and only then did Chelmsford give the command to halt.

The time was 8.30 a.m.

Orders now screamed out for regiments to dress on their markers and to

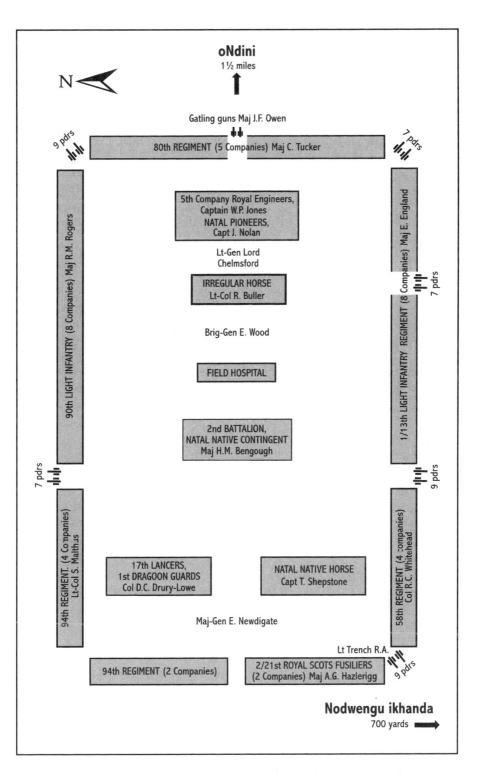

oNdini
1 ½ miles

N

Gatling guns Maj J.F. Owen

9 pdrs

7 pdrs

80th REGIMENT (5 Companies) Maj C. Tucker

5th Company Royal Engineers,
Captain W.P. Jones
NATAL PIONEERS,
Capt J. Nolan

Lt-Gen Lord
Chelmsford

IRREGULAR HORSE
Lt-Col R. Buller

Brig-Gen E. Wood

FIELD HOSPITAL

2nd BATTALION,
NATAL NATIVE CONTINGENT
Maj H.M. Bengough

90th LIGHT INFANTRY (8 Companies) Maj R.M. Rogers

1/13th LIGHT INFANTRY REGIMENT (8 Companies) Maj E. England

7 pdrs

7 pdrs

9 pdrs

94th REGIMENT (4 Companies) Lt-Col S. Malthus

58th REGIMENT (4 companies) Col R.C. Whitehead

17th LANCERS,
1st DRAGOON GUARDS
Col D.C. Drury-Lowe

NATAL NATIVE HORSE
Capt T. Shepstone

Maj-Gen E. Newdigate

Lt Trench R.A.

94th REGIMENT (2 Companies)

2/21st ROYAL SCOTS FUSILIERS
(2 Companies) Maj A.G. Hazlerigg

9 pdrs

Nodwengu ikhanda
700 yards ➡

The British Square at the Battle of Ulundi, 4 July 1879

straighten each line of the square. Ammunition carts were evenly spaced and Wood, in the knowledge that the Engineers were to his immediate rear, asked Chelmsford's permission to entrench. Chelmsford refused, saying: 'No, they will be satisfied if we beat them fairly in the open. We have been called ant-bears long enough.'[296]

Chelmsford's main concern was now to place the guns into their pre-determined positions and ready them for action as quickly as possible. Brown, the overall artillery commander, ordered the guns to be unlimbered and pushed into position. Lieutenant-Colonel Harness, Newdigate's artillery commander, with Major Le Grice's battery under command, also rapped out orders. Lieutenant E. H. Elliot, in charge of two 9-pounders of N Battery, 6th Brigade, initially positioned at the left rear, moved himself to the front left angle of the square, the 80th to his right and the 90th to his left. Captain Crookenden and Lieutenant Wodehouse, from the same brigade, had a shorter distance to manoeuvre their two 9-pounders and moved between the 58th and 1st/13th on the right face. The brigade's remaining two 9-pounders were placed, under Lieutenant Trench, at the angle between the right and rear face.

As the main Zulu attack was expected to come from the direction of oNdini, the two Gatlings of 10th Battery, 7th Brigade, under Major J. F. Owen and Lieutenant H. M. Rundle were rapidly deployed at the centre of the front face and in between the companies of the 80th. Their ammunition limbers were positioned immediately behind them. Harness's remaining two 7-pounders of N Battery, 5th Brigade, under Lieutenant C. S. B. Parsons, were placed on the left face between the 90th and 94th Regiments.

Major Tremlett, commanding 11th Battery, 7th Brigade, completed the deployment of the guns by positioning two of his 7-pounders under Captain H. R. Y. Browne and Lieutenant F. G. Slade between the companies of the 1st/13th on the upper right face. The remaining two 7-pounders, under Lieutenant Davidson, were positioned on the front right face angle. The artillery deployed facing the Zulus totalled six 9-pounders, six 7-pounders, two Gatlings, and a rocket trough carried by Tremlett's batteries; all were now ready for action. The Gatlings, each as heavy as a 12-pounder, were manned by a crew of four; one man to lay, one man to crank, and two more to reload the drums. The ammunition column, commanded by Captain R. Alexander and including sixty-four other ranks, now placed shrapnel, shot and case beside each gun position.

The *Field Service Pocket Book* defines the frontage needed by a square as 'two men per one yard'. The order to implement the square's predetermined battle position was now given, with the two front ranks kneeling and the remainder standing:

> The men in the fourth ranks filling the intervals between the men of the third ranks, 1st and 2nd ranks kneeling, remainder standing, and all with fixed bayonets, glinting in the early morning sun.[297]

As at Gingindlovu, the Natal Native Contingent were huddled at the rear of the square, their rifle butts on the ground, muzzles pointing up at the sky, and the men shivering with apprehension. This time, however, Lord Chelmsford and his staff remained mounted, as did Newdigate and Wood. The square now prepared for the Zulu onslaught, confident that the firepower massed was the greatest that had ever been assembled in Southern Africa.

In the hills surrounding the amphitheatre, the Zulu army slowly stirred, observed the billowing smoke from yet another act of vandalism and wondered if the 'burrowing wild pigs' had at last left their hole and, for the first time, had the courage to do battle in the open. King Cetshwayo, however, not taking a chance, had left oNdini on the evening of 3 July for eMlambongwenya. On the morning of the battle, he moved a further four miles north-east to the uMbonambi *ikhanda* where he posted look-outs to report on the battle. Prior to his departure on 3 July, he addressed his *amabutho* for the last time:

> As the white army was at his home, we could fight. That we were to fight the army in the open; to attack between Nodwengu and Ulundi kraals where we did fight.[298]

The Zulu field commanders surveyed the scene as the mist overhanging the Umfolozi slowly lifted, revealing the disturbing sight of many more mounted men than anticipated flung across the plain. Prince Ziwedu kaMpande, Cetshwayo's brother, was present, as were Prince Dabulamanzi kaMpande, Mavumengwana kaNdlela Ntuli, Sihayo kaXonga and his son Mehlokazulu kaSihayo, together with the Isandlwana and Kambula veteran, Ntshingwayo kaMahole Khoza. It is not certain if all the commanders took part in the battle; some may have held a watching brief. However, it pleased the high command that the white army was moving onto the Mhlabathini plain and moving towards oNdini, exactly what Cetshwayo wanted, a battle in the open.

The moment had arrived to move off the heights and on to the plain. Sigcwelegcwele kaMhlekehleke, commanding the combined Nkobamakosi regiment and uVe corps, moved towards the still smouldering Nodwengu, the result of Shepstone's aborted efforts to torch the *ikhanda*. His objective was the right rear of the square. Conflicting reports place Prince Dabulamanzi 'on a bay horse' with the uMbonambi regiment, whilst Zibhebhu kaMaphitha, also present, was reported to have had overall command of the left horn.

At about 8.30 a.m. the uThulwana regiment, commanded by Mavumengwana kaNdlela, together with the uNodwengu corps commanded by Seketwayo, closed on the right face of the square. The uDloko regiment under Ndungundungu kaNokela moved towards the Mbilane Stream to assault Wood's 80th Regiment that formed the front face of the square. The mCijo corps, based near the Bulawayo *ikhanda*, was tasked to assault the north-west face. It is possible that elements of this corps, together with the Khandempemvu regiment based seven miles north-west of Bulawayo, moved initially to the area of Nqunqa Bluff to block any potential retreat of the British. This move was short lived and described by Major William Dunbar, commanding the five companies of 1st/24th Regiment at Fort Nolela as follows:

> Between the hours of 8 and 9 a.m. on that date [4 July] upward of ten thousand Zulus were in sight and apparently closing in on us with a view to repeat 'Sandwhlana' [*sic*] and it was not until a portion of the enemy's right wing had approached to about 900 yards from the laager, they wheeled round and breaking into a run, closed on the column with you . . . I trust you will credit us with being prepared to repeat Rorke's Drift had the Zulus attacked.[299]

However, Bellairs had strict instructions that on no account was the garrison left under his command to open fire unless first attacked, as Lieutenant Main remembered:

> A large impi, 4 or 5 deep, came close to us, as it felt its way to connect up with the other horn of their army. We could have made great havoc among these men, but our instructions were precise that we were not to fire, unless attacked, so we let them pass unmolested.

Finally, the Zulu right horn, comprising the uMxhapho regiment commanded by mBube, the iQua and uNodwengu corps, commanded by Seketwayo, together with the uDududu regiment, moved against the 90th and 94th Regiments on the left face of the square:

> They advance in beautiful order, covered by skirmishers, apparently in one long continuous line about four deep, with intervals between the regiments . . . it is evidently their object to surround us, with their largest force in the rear to cut off our retreat; it was a grand sight.[300]

The mCijo and Khandempemvu at this stage abandoned their cut-off position at Nqunqa Bluff and moved at a fast walk towards the motionless square, thus completing the encirclement.

Buller's irregulars now went to work. Shepstone's Native Horse and Bettington's men engaged the Zulus near Nodwengu, opening fire at 300 yards, allowing the Zulu to close to within 100 yards before retiring, drawing them on to the square. The Natal Native Horse, having experienced defeat at Isandlwana, were, as at Kambula, reluctant to enter the square, much preferring to take their chances outside. Shepstone reported: 'It was with difficulty I got the men to retire into the square.'

Meanwhile Baker's Horse, the FLH commanded by Blaine, Raaff's Rangers and Whalley's Natal Light Horse were all flung out in a wide circle, tasked to engage and draw the Zulus on to the square. Buller, seeing an opportunity to flush out a body of Zulus, now ordered Baker to send twenty troopers down the slope of the Mbilane stream: 'Draw them on, don't let anyone dismount, and mind that donga to your right', shouted Buller.[301]

Captain Parminter, obeying the command, led his troop at a canter straight into a large body of Zulus who viewed the few mounted men more as an irritation. One trooper, 'a pig-headed German' disregarded orders and dismounted to fire more accurately, only to find himself unable to remount as his terrified horse bucked and plunged. Parminter rode back and, in an action similar to Beresford's the day before, saved the trooper's life.

> Captain Parminter rides up to him with another, and helps the man to mount; now they turn, for there's only just time to get away. As they turn to get go, the Zulus, some of whom had crept down the donga, redouble their exertions to cut them off . . . these last three ride at a furious pace over the ground, knowing that one false step is certain death. The place is pitted with the artificial holes dug and covered by the enemy, and the grass plaited.[302]

This was yet another instance where a possible Victoria Cross award was not considered as both men were colonials.

By 9.00 a.m. the square had made way for the 17th Lancers to enter, with the 2nd/21st Royal Scots also opening a gap in the rear face finally to admit Shepstone's and Bettington's men. Whilst the cavalry were jostling their way into the protection of the square, the artillery, positioned slightly in advance of the square, opened fire at a range of 2,000–3,000 yards. The opening salvo burst amongst the dense mass of advancing Zulu, causing immediate casualties.

Behind Nodwengu, the Zulu left horn, finding shelter in a shallow valley out of sight of the British, started to mass for an attack, protected from view by dense bush and chest-high grass. At a given signal the warriors rushed into sight, bravely charging the right rear of the square occupied by Hazlerigg's 2nd/21st and Whitehead's 58th companies.

Frederick Trench's 9-pounders immediately fired three rounds of case at point-blank range. The two companies of the 21st, not waiting for the 'fire by volley' command, opened fire independently. Zibhebhu had selected the weak point of the square with precision insofar as the shelter from Nodwengu where he had massed, was a relatively short sprint to the square once the warriors had emerged from the dead ground. Encouraged by cries of 'Usuthu', the Zulus charged. The 58th company flanking Trench was not aligned to give fire support and was therefore quickly ordered partially out of the square and wheeled right. 'I ordered No. 4 Section to cease fire and turned No. 3 Section half right and fired volleys in that direction.'[303]

Newdigate, sensing a crisis, ordered all possible reserves, including the men detailed as escort to the 58th's colours, to rush into the space between Trench's two guns and give fire support. This was a desperate measure as the colour party (two colours) seldom consisted of more than two ensigns and four sergeants.

Chelmsford galloped back and, surveying the scene, gave instructions for Walter Jones's 5th Company, Royal Engineers, to double back the 200 yards from the front face and position themselves behind the 2nd/21st as reserve. Such was his anxiety, that he also thundered, 'Men fire faster! Cannot you fire faster?' No doubt the other Engineer officers within the square, Harrison, Moysey, Anstey, Chard, Porter and Commeline, all looked on anxiously.

The battle had reached a critical stage as the Nkobamakosi and uVe surged forward, only to be met by heavy volleys. Nevertheless, the square started to take casualties with Lance-Corporal Tomkinson, 58th, and Private Coates, 94th, being killed by return fire. 'As it was 2 or 3 officers drew their swords or revolvers expecting a hand-to-hand fight of it.'[304] Poor visibility, caused by the lingering clouds of smoke generated by the Martini-Henry volleys, did not deter the Zulus as the attack now developed on all sides of the square.

Owen and Rundle, commanding the Gatlings, watched the uDloko regiment, spurred on by Ndungundungu, cross through the cover of the Mbilane Stream and head straight for them. The Gatling's recommended rate of fire was between 250 and 300 rounds per minute, a rate that was maintained at Gingindlovu. Now, as the gunners cranked the handles, both Gatlings experienced stoppages, which after the battle were blamed on 'bolts' dropping off the guns to the ground. A more likely cause of the stoppages was that the handles were cranked faster than the recommended rate. In all, six stoppages were experienced during the battle; nevertheless, both Gatlings fired 3,000 rounds.

The casualties within the square increased, with both men and horses being hit. Lieutenant Archibald Milne, Chelmsford's naval ADC, who was mounted and riding near Chelmsford, was slightly wounded when a bullet nicked his upper arm. 'I saw his coat torn from the elbow to the shoulder by a bullet.'[305]

Bullets were now flying high over the square as the Zulus had yet to master the art of firing 'low and slow'. Lieutenant Richard Cotton, Scots Guards, acting orderly officer to Major-General Newdigate, received what was initially thought to be a fatal head wound from a spent round, but recovered quickly. The new adjutant of the 17th Lancers, Lieutenant Herbert Charles Jenkins, received a direct shot to the jaw, later classified as 'dangerous'. This did not deter him from binding the wound and readying himself for the charge. His commanding officer, Colonel Drury-Lowe, having been trampled the night before in a friendly fire episode, was now knocked off his horse, this time by another spent bullet. He astonished those nearby, who thought that he had been killed, by promptly remounting. The dressing station established in the middle of the square, and marked with 'the red cross of St George flying overhead', was now busy as casualties poured in, with Surgeon-Majors Anderson and Brown attending to the wounded.

Those killed were instantly buried in a shallow grave, with an army chaplain, the Reverend Coar, presiding over the service as bullets whistled overhead: 'A touching picture enough as the bodies were laid in the hastily made grave.' The long-suffering horses did not escape the carnage: 'The unmistakable thud of bullets as they strike horse or man is often heard. Horses spring up into the air as they are struck, sometimes crying in their agony.'[306]

By about 9.10 a.m. all regiments of the square were engaging the Zulu with controlled volley after volley, halting the charge and decimating the Zulu ranks. No matter how the Zulus varied and shifted the point of attack, they were met by a hail of bullets. The reserves, standing well back but still being shelled by the artillery, remained uncommitted and unwilling to join the fray. Puzzled by their inability to penetrate the square, the Zulus often later called the action the battle of 'ocwencweni', or 'sheet iron', a reference to the impenetrable line of bayonets glinting in the sunlight.

Many British sources indicate that the nearest the Zulus got to the square was thirty yards. However, the war correspondent Melton Prior related: 'I can say that I personally went out and reached the nearest one in nine paces, so their onslaught was pretty determined.'[307] Zulu oral history claims that at least some Zulus reached the square. Matatshile kaMasipula, who had questioned Cetshwayo during the pre-battle briefing, was one:

> Towards the conclusion of the battle, Matatshile charged the square, protected by quickly put-up zinc [bayonets], and as he tried to enter he was bayoneted and killed. The same thing happened to Dumusa kaSidamba kaNtshona.[308]

Both were members of the Khandempemvu regiment.

Zulu morale faltered as the murderous onslaught of artillery and Martini-Henry fire continued to take its dreadful toll. No fewer than 130 rounds were fired by the 7-pounders together with sixty-eight from the 9-pounders. In addition Tremlett's battery fired off three rockets. Whilst the Zulu reserves still watched, the attacking regiments now wavered. The spirit and determined leadership that had been seen at Isandlwana, Hlobane and Kambula were absent, directly attributable to the heavy casualties sustained in these actions.

> At the Ondine battle, the last, we did not fight with the same spirit, because we were then frightened.[309]

> We had not much heart in the fight when we saw how strong the white army was, and we were startled by the number of horsemen.[310]

On 13 July Wood wrote to Horse Guards in a similar vein:

> An Induna who was wounded at Kambula and surrendered yesterday, said 'Our hearts were broken at Kambula. I did not go within shot of you this time.'

Chelmsford now sensed that victory was his and instructed the bugler to sound 'cease fire'. It was time to apply the *coup de grâce*. As the infantry fire died away, Chelmsford ordered: 'Lancers out.' Drury-Lowe immediately responded: 'Stand to your horse . . . prepare to mount . . . mount.' The time was about 9.30 a.m. and the battle had lasted but thirty minutes. By comparison the attack on Gingindlovu had lasted approximately one hour, whilst the determined attack on Kambula had been pressed home for five hours.

The 94th Regiment opened a gap on the rear face of the square and, spurred by Chelmsford's command 'Go at them Lowe', five troops of the 17th Lancers, twenty-four men of the King's Dragoon Guards under Lieutenant R. A. B. French-Brewster, and Browne's Mounted Infantry poured out of the square. The Lancers, pennants furled in battle, were cheered on by the infantry. They then paused, wheeled left and formed line to face Nodwengu.

Wood simultaneously ordered Buller to begin his work of execution. In his post-battle report, Buller stated that he exited the square in the opposite direction to Drury-Lowe, thus indicating the front face of the square, an area where the retreating Zulus were relatively thin on the ground. Clery was critical of Buller's move, pointing out that:

> Buller made a mess of the pursuit having started in the wrong direction, and only employed, at first, a part of his men. But this was only an error of judgement, and the Zulus gave up the fight so much sooner than we anticipated that this probably had something to say to it. But had the pursuit been better directed the Zulu loss would have been much heavier.[311]

Drury-Lowe's trumpet-major now sounded the charge. In a single parade-ground movement, the 'Death or Glory Boys' dropped their lances to the right side of the horses' necks and relentlessly pursued the Zulus into and through Nodwengu. Regrouping, Drury-Lowe then wheeled to his right in an effort to get to close quarters with the fleeing warriors, who, by this time, had been reinforced by reserves on the lower slopes of the hills beyond Nodwengu. A heavy fire was brought to bear on the Lancers and at that moment a troop leader, Captain the Honourable Edmund Wyatt-Edgell, received a direct shot to the throat, killing him instantly. His body was taken to the casualty station within the square and 'our fallen Captain was buried in his cloak on the battlefield'. This galvanised the 17th into further action, no quarter asked or given: 'And if we needed anything to madden us more than we were already maddened we had it in the sight of his emptied saddle.'[312]

Very few prisoners were taken that day, an outcome considered by the British as retribution for Isandlwana. 'Pig-sticking', 'just like tent-pegging at Aldershot', and 'mincemeat' were expressions exchanged.

Even the fleet-footed warriors could not outpace the charge of the Lancers who set about their grim task with relish: 'The Lancers did well.

I know each man I had anything to do with had a lance through him before he could move, whether wounded or not.'[313]

They moved through the thick grass and many a Zulu was flushed out and dispatched. Before long the horses were blown and at 10.00 a.m. Drury-Lowe ordered a withdrawal to the square, his men having, by his count, killed over 150 Zulus. Guy Dawnay, Drury-Lowe's galloper, was sent back to report 'a black swarm of Zulus retreating on the ridge of the far hill', whereupon Trench fired a dozen or so shells from his 9-pounders, some of which were 'going well to the mark'. That night many of the Lancers boasted that they had 'killed four Zulus each'.

Close on the heels of the regular cavalry, Shepstone's Horse and Bettington's fourteen European volunteers worked their way slowly through the scrub and long grass hunting for Zulus. Bettington 'cut down and shot all men who were skulking behind bushes near the square'. In total, Bettington's men claimed to have killed forty-five Zulus, an average of three per member of his troop.

Cochrane's Natal Native Horse, cheered on by the infantry, chased the Zulus through the Mbilane Stream and beyond towards oNdini, using their carbines to devastating effect. The prevailing mood of the day was captured when one of Cochrane's men dismounted besides a Zulu wounded in the leg, politely asked questions of local interest and on completion of the conversation:

> He quietly shot the man, mounted his horse, and joined again in the chase . . . there was much cruelty that day, for every wounded man was killed.[314]

Baker's Horse were also ruthless in their execution, in retaliation for the Zulu tactic of feigning death and then coming to life to take a pot shot. Their regimental mascot, a dog named Lion, was well versed in sniffing out those feigning death, whilst ignoring those actually dead. Running about the field, Lion would first sniff and then bark furiously at a living Zulu, who would then be dispatched.

In some instances Zulus put up a resistance of sorts, an example being recorded when Baker, wishing to collect a souvenir, ordered one of his troopers to pick up two fine specimen spears lying by a Zulu, whereupon the Zulu 'springs up, levels his gun and fires, missing his mark and killing Lieutenant Addie's horse.' The Zulu was immediately shot.

Groups of Zulus hiding in whatever cover they could find were relentlessly hunted and executed. Adjutant Tomasson related an instance of finding a Zulu marksman in a donga, peering in the opposite direction looking for a target:

> Just then an incautious movement on our part makes him look behind: he sees us, not soon enough to turn round and fire though, as a revolver bullet crashes through his back; and he rolls down the bank dead.

Baker's Horse, resting for a moment at the Mbilane Stream to quench their thirst, sighted a Zulu hiding under over-hanging branches near the bank. A closer investigation showed a further five nearby. In a short while the stream continued its gentle flow, the light coloured water changing its colour to deep crimson.

The NNC, remarkably cowed during the initial fire-fight, now exuded confidence and bravado, joining in the slaughter with gusto, showing no mercy in dispatching Zulu wounded. Led by Major Bengough, with his galloper Lieutenant Henry Lukin by his side, the NNC noisily stalked their prey. Hours after the battle, shots resounded as an occasional Zulu was found and killed, ironically with 'several [hiding] in ant-bear holes'.

During the course of the hunt, Lukin sustained a serious wound in his calf. 'Lukin, you're hit,' said Bengough. 'It's nothing, I'm all right, Sir,' answered Lukin, who then promptly lost consciousness and fell from his horse. Recovering his senses he remounted and made his way back for treatment within the square.

In all 35,000 rounds were fired that morning, with the ammunition expenditure being just under seven rounds per rifle. However, the hotly engaged 2nd/21st Regiment, 205 strong, fired a total of 1,739 rounds, averaging nearly eight and a half rounds per rifle.

The cavalry rested awhile before Chelmsford gave the order to destroy all *amakhanda*. The indefatigable Buller shouted: 'Now then, who's first into Ulundi?'

A group of officers that included Buller, Beresford, Milne, Baker, Dawnay, interpreter Drummond, together with civilians Archibald Forbes and Melton Prior, accompanied by numerous troopers, started the mile-long dash for Ulundi. Lord Chelmsford followed with a strong escort. Beresford was credited with being the first to arrive by dint of hurdling the palisade, thereby earning everlasting fame and thereafter being known as 'Ulundi Beresford'.

Baker, however, was the first to reach the private quarters of King Cetshwayo. The hope of finding hidden treasures quickly evaporated when a locker standing in the corner of the room was kicked open to reveal nothing more than an assortment of various newspapers and magazines dating back many years, including copies of the *Illustrated London News*, *The Times*, *The Standard* and *The Graphic*. One presumes the illustrations held a fascination for the monarch, for included were pictures of the marriage of the Prince of Wales.

Buller now ordered Tomasson to torch the royal *ikhanda*. The thatch in winter was bone dry and dense plumes of smoke rose as hut after hut was set ablaze, symbolising the end of the traditional Zulu way of life. The ferocity of the battle, from a British viewpoint, may be seen as retribution for Isandlwana, Rorke's Drift, Hlobane and Meyer's Drift. The fearsome reputation of the Zulu for neither asking for nor giving quarter, together with their custom of ritual mutilation perceived by most as barbaric, became reasons enough to answer in kind. In Victorian times, such response was acceptable; today it is questionable.

Buller and his party made their way back slowly to the Mbilane Stream to find the men enjoying a delayed breakfast. Missing from the party was the Honourable W. Drummond, found later to have been killed by Zulus as he meandered alone through oNdini.

Few Zulus were captured, reports indicate a maximum or four. The army that took the field was estimated at 25,000, of whom only 15,000 were committed to the battle, the balance being held in reserve. The Zulu loss was placed at a minimum of 1,500 killed, representing a casualty rate of ten per cent. A once proud army, together with its commanders, quietly melted away.

Chelmsford's demeanour, once victory was assured, changed markedly. The frown was, for the first time, replaced with a smile. The anxious months had taken their toll and, with Sir Garnet breathing down his neck, he had just, only just, managed to bring the campaign to a successful conclusion and thus salvage a degree of pride. He had not yet finished, though. Whilst mopping-up operations were in progress and the wounded receiving attention, he ordered Shepstone to move seven miles west and torch the major *ikhanda* of Khandempemvu.

Shepstone set off, accompanied by Claude Bettington together with a dozen of Commandant White's irregulars. It was a hazardous operation as militant Zulus were in evidence. Wood had promised Shepstone help that failed to materialise:

> The promised 'supports' never appearing in sight, I had to return to camp
> by a different route through the thorns, to avoid being cut off by a large
> body of the enemy.[315]

On the return journey, Shepstone saw many mutilated bodies, including those of women who had been watching the battle from the surrounding hills and had been caught by the deadly artillery fire.

Chelmsford started his leisurely return to Fort Nolela at 2.00 p.m. only crossing the Umfolozi three hours later, progress being bogged down by the pace of the stretcher bearers carrying the wounded. Troops stopped here and there to collect souvenirs such as shields and spears whilst the band of the 1st/13th Light Infantry lustily played 'Rule Britannia' and 'God Save the Queen'.

The casualty return submitted by the Deputy Assistant Adjutant- and Quartermaster-General, Major F. W. Grenfell, on 4 July, showed two officers killed (Wyatt-Edgell and Drummond), three 'dangerously' wounded, six 'severely' wounded and ten 'slightly' wounded. Of the wounded, Lieutenant Pardoe, 1st/13th, succumbed to his injuries on 14 July. Ten other ranks were killed and sixty-nine wounded. Horses, both English and locally acquired, suffered grievously, with twenty-eight killed and forty-five wounded, from a combination of Zulu rifle fire and close range work of the assegai.

That evening, the Edendale troop again gathered to sing hymns, this time unanswered from across the now silent Mahlabathini Plain.

The 17th Lancers were grief-stricken over the loss of their adjutant. During the night, his body having been exhumed from the battlefield, he was given a second burial, as Lieutenant Main witnessed:

> On the night of the 4th I was dogged tired and was sleeping at 8.00 p.m. on the top of a wagon. Suddenly I woke with a start, and had a vision which made me rub my eyes to be certain I was awake. A circle of officers, holding lanterns around something in a blanket, with one individual apparently in a white shirt. I soon grasped that the burial service was being read, so was informed that the body of Wyatt-Edgell had been brought alongside my wagon for internment [*sic*]. After some time the whole party set to work to collect boulders & stones to build a sort of cairn over the body, & then they left me alone with the corpse in the darkness, rather a gruesome ending to an exciting day. Later on the body was exhumed & forwarded to England for burial. Wyatt-Edgell was, I believe, heir presumptive to the Barony of Braye.

Wyatt-Edgell was indeed subsequently exhumed and finally laid to rest at Stanford Hall, his family home in Leicestershire.

When news of the defeat reached Cetshwayo, he left the uMbonambi *ikhanda* and joined Mnyamana kaNgqengelele Buthelezi, his trusted senior advisor, at the latter's homestead of ekuShumayeleni, three days march from Ulundi.

> All day we kept walking, without sleep . . . I still remember how sore our feet became through walking among the thorns, especially at night when, without even a footpath to guide us, we could not see where we were going . . . no, my friends, we Zulus are really tough people![316]

At Fort Nolela, a ration of rum was issued and all were in high spirits. The news of the victory had to be delivered to Landman's Drift for onward transmission by telegraph and Guy Dawnay was chosen to carry the dispatch. Chelmsford had yet to receive a detailed casualty report, which resulted in Dawnay delaying his departure till 8.00 p.m. 'after dining with Newdigate and helping to drink some Ulundi champagne specially reserved'. Archibald Forbes, who had initially asked Dawnay to carry his press report, now decided time was of the essence and proceeded to beat all to the post by personally conveying the news ahead of Dawnay.

With a four-hour start, Forbes rode at a furious pace to Landman's Drift, commandeering both horse and escort, reportedly waving papers as some sort of authorisation. A frustrated Dawnay followed on behind to find that both remounts and escorts had been requisitioned by the ubiquitous Forbes at Forts Evelyn, Marshall and Newdigate

Dawnay, following Forbes's footsteps and after a twenty-five hour ride, eventually handed Chelmsford's dispatch to General Marshall at Landman's

Drift. From there a cable line had been laid to Ladysmith by C (Telegraph) Troop. RE, under the command of Major Alexander Hamilton. Referred to as the 'air-line', the cable was designed to hang from poles or trees. Communication from Ladysmith through to Durban was via a commercial telegraph line. As the news spread it was greeted with relief throughout the colony.

The forty-one-year-old Forbes was not to be denied in his attempt to be first with the news and his 'ride of death', as it became known, was in due course eulogised, with the *Illustrated London News* printing a picture of him galloping across the veld. Suggestions were made that he be awarded the Victoria Cross, a view not shared by Lord Chelmsford which, in turn, resulted in vitriolic attacks by Forbes on Chelmsford's conduct of the war.

Sir Garnet was reported, according to Fleet Surgeon Norbury serving with Crealock's 1st Division, to have received the news of the battle on the same day:

> News arrived on the 4th that Lord Chelmsford had been victorious in a great battle at Ulundi, and had burnt the royal kraal. Numerous Zulus came in and surrendered, and were permitted to reside, in the bush, between the camp of the Natal native regiment and the sea.

The distance from Ulundi to Port Durnford is eighty miles. The earliest the defeated Zulus would have departed the battlefield would have been approximately 10.00 a.m. and even at a fast jog, those participants in the battle could not have covered the distance during daylight. It is more likely that the Zulus used their method of shouting from hill to hill and that this resulted in the news reaching the coast within hours. L. H. Samuelson recorded this technique shortly after the war:

> Particular arrangements for forwarding news were made by them [Zulus] in times of war . . . and lines of communication were established from hill to hill.

Sir Garnet only received definite news of the battle from Archibald Forbes on 6 July. He immediately penned a letter to Chelmsford: 'I congratulate you most sincerely upon your brilliant success just reported to me by Mr Forbes.'[317] The sincerity of the letter, in view of the disbelief and disappointment voiced by Sir Garnet's staff that greeted the news, was questionable. It remained for Chelmsford to hand in his resignation and leave the political morass, together with the onerous task of capturing King Cetshwayo, in the hands of Sir Garnet Wolseley.

The destruction of the old Zulu order was now complete.

Bertram Mitford, a Cape civil servant and author, visited the Anglo-Zulu War battlefields in 1882 and poignantly described his visit to the site of the battle that vanquished the Zulu nation:

> Skulls and bones bleaching by hundreds in the grassy bottoms, instead of the fierce and dauntless savages who formerly peopled this place and

marched in serried battalions up to the very mouth of the cannon, to be mown down like grass, but to fall as valiant warriors, shouting their battle cry . . . as true patriots defending their homes . . . no one will grudge them due praise for a long and stubborn defence of their country . . . but the blood of thousands of their bravest has been poured out like water . . . truly one feels that the greatness of a nation lies buried here.

Chapter 13

Epilogue

'I am satisfied that the power of the Zulu Nation has been completely broken, and there can now be no necessity for keeping together even such a force as I have lately been commanding.'

Lord Chelmsford to Sir Garnet Wolseley, 5 July[318]

<hr />

Although the Battle of Kambula was a crushing defeat for the Zulus and, in particular, for the abaQulusi in whose territory it was fought, it did not immediately pacify the region. Mbelini returned to his eyrie on the Tafelberg from where he again set about raiding white farms. However, in the meantime he had interrogated the one and only white man to be taken prisoner during the whole course of the war. It will be recalled that a Frenchman, Trooper Ernest Grandier of the Border Horse, a former stonemason of Bordeaux, was captured on Hlobane. The astute Mbelini, assessing that the prisoner could be of more value alive than dead, questioned Grandier for some time but, having learned nothing of any importance, had him stripped naked and sent off to Cetshwayo as a present.[319]

There is no doubt that Grandier suffered a great deal of hardship from exposure, hunger and rough handling. On reaching oNdini he was again interrogated in the presence of the king while a man of mixed blood acted as interpreter. According to Cornelius Vijn, the Dutch trader who spent the whole of the war stranded in the Zulu capital, it had been Cetshwayo's intention to keep Grandier a captive and to release him later, as the king had quickly realised that the Frenchman was of no value as a negotiating tool. However, within days news arrived that Mbelini had been killed, prompting Cetshwayo to change his mind and to return Grandier, under escort, to Mbelini's followers to do with him as they wished. Still naked and half-starved, the Frenchman was led off on the eighty-mile return journey to Hlobane, his escort comprising just two warriors, one armed with an old gun and the other a spear. Somewhere along the way, as his escort took their ease and dozed, Grandier sprung upon the warrior carrying the spear and, grasping the weapon, plunged it deep, killing the man instantly whilst the other warrior fled. That was the basis of Grandier's story when he was found, about twenty-five miles away from Hlobane, nineteen days after he had been taken prisoner. Many disbelieved his story but as Vijn had heard of his presence at oNdini there can be no doubt that Grandier had been taken to the king and had escaped. The press, who were looking for a good story following a quiet spell after the Battle of Kambula, vied with each other in compiling lurid accounts of Grandier's ordeal during captivity. But, apart from being footsore, half-starved and knocked about a bit, the only prisoner of the Zulus who lived to tell the tale recovered and seemed none the worse for his experience.[320]

When the news of Mbelini's death reached Cetshwayo, it was assumed that he had been killed at Kambula but in fact it was a seventeen-year-old white youth, Heinrich Filter, who mortally wounded Mbelini, one of Zululand's greatest generals.[321]

Within days of the Battle of Kambula an *impi* of Mbelini's warriors, 400 strong, attacked the farm of Piet Uys, whose dead body still lay sprawled at the bottom of Devil's Pass, and drove off thirty cattle and 1,500 sheep. The following day, Mbelini himself raided a Luneburg farm driving off a number of horses. But the raiders were spotted by a British patrol led by Captain John Prior, 80th Regiment. The patrol was accompanied by Heinrich Filter, acting as interpreter, Heinrich having himself escaped from Hlobane only a week earlier. Shots were exchanged, killing one of the raiders and wounding another. Heinrich, being locally raised, immediately recognised the leader as Mbelini and set off in pursuit, subsequently inflicting a wound from which Mbelini bled to death. A few days later Heinrich's own family farm was raided and a number of horses driven away. As there was no military presence nearby, Heinrich decided to pursue the raiders himself, aided by a few farm workers. They rode into an ambush and Heinrich was taken prisoner. Such was the propinquity of white and black in the Disputed Territory that Heinrich was known and well-liked by some of his captors. He came close to being released, but his fate was sealed by the arrival of Mbelini's brother who insisted that Heinrich, by wounding Mbelini, had spilled royal blood and that therefore the penalty must be death. Heinrich, sitting on an anthill with his head in his hands, was immediately put to death.[322]

Long after the Battle of Ulundi, Manyanyoba and his warriors who had collaborated with Mbelini in the destruction of Moriarty's convoy at Meyer's Drift, refused to capitulate. It took a specially formed British column to bring about their final surrender and then only after the column had experienced ridicule and humiliation. At first, after spending much time and effort in constructing a road of sorts to the doorstep of Manyanyoba's mountain fastness, the British tried to smoke him out by piling and burning brushwood and trees, gathered at tremendous effort, at the entrance to his caves. But all that emerged were howls of derision as the besieged invited the besiegers to come in and get them.[323]

As the British column withdrew to think again, they were sent on their way with catcalls and the warriors, having surfaced, 'now bounced on the top-most stones of the hill'. The following day the soldiers returned, this time attempting to dynamite the caves. But the two NCOs laying the charges not only blew up the entrance, they blew themselves to smithereens in the process while Manyanyoba and his clan escaped through a concealed exit.[324] Eventually, Manyanyoba surrendered and later, as a fragile peace gradually descended on Zululand and the Disputed Territories, he and his followers were removed to the Nqutu District to be watched over by '. . . our firm friend Hlubi [formally a senior NCO of the Natal Native Horse] to whom this district had been given [by the British]'.[325]

<hr />

Meanwhile, with the Battle of Ulundi over and won, Lord Chelmsford had time to take stock of his position. With Sir Garnet now on the scene, Chelmsford held no formal appointment. He offered his immediate resignation, together with a request that he be allowed to return to England: 'I trust that my request to be relieved of my command may be considered as a reasonable one.'[326] Sir Garnet accepted the offer with alacrity. On 15 July Chelmsford and his staff, together with Wood's Flying Column, met Sir Garnet at St Paul's. The atmosphere was strained, with Wolseley commenting: 'I cannot say my meeting with Chelmsford was a pleasant one.'[327] The following day, at Wood's request, the ragged but proud men of the Flying Column were inspected by their new general officer commanding who seemed well pleased, Wolseley remarking that they 'marched past remarkably well'.[328]

The parade was followed immediately by another of a different nature, this time a flogging parade, a sentence imposed on three of Wood's Irregulars found guilty of murdering Zulu wounded, presumably at Ulundi. If this were the crime being punished, Drury-Lowe's lancers and Buller's troopers were almost certainly guilty of the same offence during the relentless pursuit of the Zulus following their defeat, in which nearly all wounded were dispatched.

Chelmsford, despite his victory, was damning in his condemnation of both Newdigate and Drury-Lowe, with Wolseley noting: 'Chelmsford tells me that Newdigate is no use, and all tell me that Drury-Lowe is useless also – such men has the Duke [of Cambridge] selected for command here.'[329] Lack of confidence in Newdigate's ability would have accounted for Chelmsford heavily favouring the Flying Column in both the advance to contact and the Battle of Ulundi.

Chelmsford left for Cape Town and sailed for England on 27 July, accompanied by both Wood and Buller. Loyalty had seemingly little place in post-war relations, as both these subordinates were open in their criticism of their chief. Despite the favours and opportunities Chelmsford had bestowed on both – and especially on Wood – they slyly confided behind his back that they had no wish to return to England in the same steamer as

Chelmsford, and that 'nothing would ever induce them to serve under him again.'

When they arrived at Plymouth, the euphoric crowds that lined the docks greeted all three as national heroes. Chelmsford, ever a favourite with the royal family, by 'coincidence' found the Prince of Wales, aboard his yacht *Osborne*, there to greet him. As a gesture of his esteem, the prince took Chelmsford aboard and later they both rowed around the harbour.[330] Finally, Chelmsford, triumphant, departed by train to Bath where the Abbey bells were set ringing and the mayor and corporation, in their official robes, were waiting to congratulate him. Wood and Buller, arriving at their destinations, received similar adulation. The horses were unharnessed from their carriages so that the admiring crowds could pull their vehicles the final mile.[331]

Meanwhile, in Zululand, Sir Garnet was unable to impose his post-war political solution whilst King Cetshwayo remained at large. On 10 August Wolseley ironically established his headquarters in the middle of King Cetshwayo's destroyed *ikhanda* of oNdini, to be joined by John Dunn and Cornelius Vijn. Most of the senior Zulu commanders had already submitted or were in the process of submitting, including Dabulamanzi and Ntshingwayo. Chief Zibhebhu expressed a wish to submit, but feared for his life, as he had been directly responsible for British casualties inflicted on 3 July when Zulus, on the Nqunqa Bluff, had fired at British soldiers bathing in the Umfolozi. Zibhebhu eventually surrendered to Sir Garnet on 27 August.

On 20 August, now desperate to apprehend the king, Wolseley ordered the burning of all homesteads and the confiscation of cattle in any area where the local inhabitants were thought to be concealing their monarch's whereabouts. Chief Mbopha kaWolizibi of the Hlabisa clan, a person of high rank in the kingdom, whose father was the brother of King Mpande's mother, was tortured with hot irons in an attempt to elicit information.

Cetshwayo was eventually cornered in the remote *umuzi* of kwaDwasa in the Ngome forest, twenty miles north-west of oNdini, and surrendered on 28 August, together with his entourage of twenty-two Zulu men and women, to Major Richard Marter, 1st King's Dragoon Guards. The following night eleven of the group attempted to escape and, in the ensuing fight, five were shot and killed, whilst the remaining six got away. The party that was eventually escorted into Wolseley's camp on 31 August comprised the monarch, seven men and five women. The same day, without being interviewed by Wolseley, Cetshwayo was placed in an ambulance and sent to Port Durnford where he embarked aboard the steamship *Natal* for Cape Town. On 24 September, the *Natal Mercury* published a description of Cetshwayo:

> Those who have seen the photographs 'from a painting' are made to
> believe he is monstrous in face and form – a huge carcass with fiendish

countenance. He is nothing of the sort – the face is massive, open, and good-natured, and lights up quickly at a pleasant thought or a humorous suggestion – all those who see the king will be astonished that one in such good condition and with so good a face should ever have been the great war spirit of the land.[332]

Mr Longcast, the interpreter who accompanied him to Cape Town, recorded the ruthlessness of Cetshwayo's pursuit. Whilst the British were on the trail of the monarch, no Zulu, despite flogging or threat to life, betrayed him:

> We could get nothing from the Zulus. We were treated the same at every kraal. I had been a long time in Zululand, I knew the people and their habits, and, although I believed that they would be true to their king, I never expected such devotion. Nothing would move them. Neither the loss of cattle, the fear of death, nor the offering of large bribes would make them false to their king.[333]

Perhaps the most extraordinary thing about the entire war, after the British had fought the Zulus in the open and had beaten them at Ulundi, was the warriors' good natured acceptance of their defeat, bearing in mind the ruthless devastation that had accompanied the British advance on the Zulu capital. Within weeks small British patrols (many of them seeking to capture the king), hopelessly outnumbered and days from any possible assistance, were chatting to Zulus with whom they had fought, as the warriors brought in and surrendered their weapons. For many, it would be their first contact with Zulus at close quarters and they were impressed:

> Troops of Zulus now began to arrive in answer to our summons, treading invariably one behind the other in Indian file, often hundreds of yards long, according to the number. . . . the men were naked, all but the 'moucha' [a short skirt, back and front, made from strips of cowhide], walking magnificently, upright and springy, their skins like satin, their faces far above the usual Negro type, and their figures pictures of grace and activity they came on without the slightest show of fear, straight into the camp . . .[334]

Lieutenant Henry Harford of the 99th Regiment, who had earlier lived in Natal and who could speak the Zulu language, found himself accompanying a patrol that had penetrated deep into Zululand in its quest to capture the king. Arriving at the homestead of a powerful clan in the far north of the country, Harford and a fellow officer had to stroll through an assembly of over a 'thousand warriors in full fighting costume' before they reached the presence of the chief. Once the *indaba* concerning the whereabouts of the king was over, a warrior:

> . . . came up and asked if any of us had been at Isandlwana, and on telling him that I was out with the contingent at Isipezi at the time of the fight, he caught hold of both my hands and shook them firmly in a great state

of delight, saying it was a splendid fight. 'You fought well, and we fought well', he exclaimed and then showed me eleven wounds that he had received . . . I now had a look at his wounds. One bullet had gone through his hand, three had gone through his shoulder and had smashed his shoulder blade, two had cut the skin and slightly into the flesh right down the chest and stomach, and one had gone clean though the fleshy part of the thigh. The others were mere scratches in comparison with these, but there he was, after about eight months, as well as ever and ready for another set to. Could anything more clearly show the splendid spirit in which the Zulus fought us? No animosity, no revengeful feeling, but just sheer love of a good fight in which the courage on both sides could be tested and it was evident that the courage of our soldiers was as much appreciated as that of their own.[335]

Within months white traders were again plying their wares in Zululand while adventurers were able to travel for weeks in the territory, from one end to the other, and to report on their encounters, such as those experienced by Bertram Mitford on Hlobane. Mitford had climbed the mountain alone, conscious of all the recent horrors that had taken place there, when he was suddenly startled to see 'two stalwart warriors' calmly watching him from only a few yards away:

I saw that one of them carried an assegai with a blade like a small claymore, and, seeing, coveted and resolved to have it if possible. I climbed to where they stood; the warriors greeted me as usual and of course were anxious to know all about me. The one with the assegai was a fine tall fellow, with a cheery countenance and hearty manner, and we speedily became friends . . . He belonged to the Udhloko Regiment, and had been present at the attack on Rorke's Drift, which battle he proceeded to fight over again for my enlightenment with an effusiveness and pantomimic accompaniment thoroughly Zulu; going into fits of laughter over it, as though one of the toughest struggles on record were the greatest joke in the world.[336]

Mitford tried hard to barter the weapon from his new friend without success: it was the weapon he had carried at Rorke's Drift the warrior said. But nevertheless they continued to chat:

The sun had gone down, the hush of evening had fallen upon the low mountain side and upon the dark forms of the two Zulus where they stood among the grey rocks . . . and we stood there in friendly converse, representative of the two nations, civilised and barbarous, who had fought so fiercely and poured each other's blood like water upon the rugged sides of this very mountain.[337]

With Cetshwayo finally imprisoned at the Cape, Wolseley set about his programme of divide and rule, fragmenting Zululand into thirteen 'chiefdoms'. John Dunn received the biggest chunk with Hamu coming a close second. A strange choice of a chief was Hlubi, an ex-senior NCO of the Natal Native Horse who had fought alongside the British at Isandlwana. He was given the chiefdom of the Nqutu area that included the Isandlwana battlefield. Ntshingwayo kaMahole, the victorious general of Isandlwana, was given an adjacent chiefdom. The remaining territories were allocated to other powerful generals or princes of the royal blood whom Wolseley calculated would no doubt resist any attempt by Cetshwayo to reclaim his kingdom in the unlikely event that he escape from Cape Town. The repercussions of Wolseley's scheme are evident in kwaZulu-Natal to this day.

But Cetshwayo did 'escape'. After languishing in the Cape in an 'open prison', a farm called Oude Molen, it was finally agreed, in 1882, that he could travel to England and present his case. Paradoxically, the British public, who three years earlier had regarded Cetshwayo as a terrifying monster, suddenly found him to be a '. . . far cry from the primitive savage who had been described in official reports before and after the Zulu war. In fact, it was not his savagery but his humanity that made the greatest impression.'[338] He became a sensation and was wildly cheered wherever he went:

> The lively curiosity shown when Cetshwayo arrived at the Plymouth docks was nothing compared with the daily scenes which took place outside his London house. The pavements swarmed with sightseers and the roads were constantly jammed with carriages. The government was obliged to station a posse of policemen outside Cetshwayo's front door. The semi-hysterical crowds made it impossible for any of the Zulus to leave the house.[339]

Perhaps Cetshwayo found his freedom in London more confining than his imprisonment in the Cape. After an audience with Queen Victoria at Osborne House on the Isle of Wight, Cetshwayo also managed to escape from the adoring crowds of London and eventually returned to Zululand. However, his return was conditional: there would be little that he could do without the consent of the British government, represented in Zululand by the British resident. Just a year after his return, he died. Most believed that he had been poisoned either by the British or by a rival faction. Cetshwayo's death and the succession to the monarchy provoked a civil war that caused further death and destruction in Zululand. However, it is interesting to contemplate the effect that Cetshwayo's incarceration in Cape Town Castle had had on his resolve and dignity. When his brother had surrendered to British troops shortly after Ulundi, he had not been intimidated by the victors, treating them, in fact, as inferiors:

> One day came a brother of Cetshwayo's, not unlike him in face and form. He was enormously fat, standing over six feet in stature, perfectly naked, all but for the 'moucha' and came forty miles to surrender to us, on foot. His bodyguard consisted of six rough-looking Zulus, who squatted with

their master opposite the tent door, as though they were equals. But there was no mistaking the chief; his composure was intense, the indifference with which he treated everything about so delightful, and his whole attitude truly royal. An officer wishing to possess something of his as a memento asked him to give him the rough stick he carried. He raised his eyes for a second and replied in his low, soft voice: 'That stick has touched my hand, and there may be some of my own royal sweat upon it. I am a king, and nothing of a king's can touch a stranger and not be defiled.'[340]

Cetshwayo on the other hand, once equally as regal and arrogant, was reputed to have made the following statement shortly after arriving in the Cape:

> My father, the Government, came to chastise me for my wrongdoing. I caught the stick with which he wished to beat me and broke it. I did wrong to fight, and I am punished. I am no longer a king; but the English, I find, are a great people; they do not kill those who have fought with them. I am satisfied to be in their hands . . .[341]

Cetshwayo was finally laid to rest on 23 April 1884 twelve miles south-west of Nkandla near Mome Gorge. Plans to upgrade his burial site are currently under consideration.

Prince Dabulamanzi, that most ubiquitous of Zulu generals, was not offered a chiefdom but continued to prosper until 1886 when he was accused of stealing Boer cattle. Arrested by a field cornet, Dabulamanzi and his son were being escorted to Vryheid when both attempted to escape back into Zululand. However, they were caught again, but outside Boer jurisdiction. After a scuffle Dabulamanzi was shot in cold blood by one of the Boers by the name of van der Berg. Both the Boer and Natal governments issued orders for van der Berg's arrest but he fled to Swaziland and the case was never brought to trial. Dabulamanzi was buried at Nodwengu, a mere eight miles from the memorial that marked the spot where the Prince Imperial fell (not the Nodwengu near the site of the Ulundi battle).

Sigananda Shezi went on to save Cetshwayo's life in 1883, when the latter, during a fight against Zibhebhu, was hiding near the Umfolozi River, incapacitated as a result of a leg wound. He was rescued by Sigananda, who mounted him on a horse and rode him to safety. Arrested by the British prior to the Bambata Rebellion, Sigananda died at the ripe old age of about about a hundred in 1903.

John Dunn, under Sir Garnet's patronage, was virtually king of all he surveyed. His domination of the area between the Tugela and Mhlatuze Rivers was marked by the erection of no less than seven major homesteads and his ownership of thousands of cattle. At an early age, prior to his friendship with Cetshwayo, he had married Catherine Pierce, whose father was English and mother Cape Malay. On his death in 1895 he left forty-eight recorded Zulu wives and well over a hundred children. He was buried two miles from Gingindlovu on the farm Emoyeni. Generations of Dunns still live north of the Tugela and many are currently involved in land claims dating back to the nineteenth century. Today, a bronze bust of John Dunn, presented by his descendants, stands in the old KwaZulu-Natal parliament at Ulundi.

Cetshwayo, however, never forgave Dunn for his treachery:

> Dunn persistently misrepresented me, he took my property, he seized the cattle of the people who pleaded for my return, he is now building and creating his harems through me and my property, he is the cause of the war . . . Who would stay with a rat in his hut that ate his food?[342]

The Empress Eugenie, determined to visit the scene of her beloved son's death, arrived in Cape Town on 16 April 1880, accompanied by Sir Evelyn and Lady Wood, Napoleon de Bassano, Captain Bigge, Lieutenant Slade, Surgeon-Major Scott and Mrs Ronald Campbell. The party lived under canvas for most of the trip and travelled as part of a convoy of twenty mule-wagons. The empress herself travelled with Lady Wood in a 'spider' (a light horse carriage), drawn by four horses and driven by Wood himself. Corporal William Clarke of the Natal Mounted Police, who in later years rose to the rank of colonel and commanded the force, was one of twenty troopers detailed to escort the convoy and kept a diary of events.

On 14 May, the group arrived at Kambula where the empress placed wreaths and planted bulbs on all graves in the cemetery. Four days were spent at Kambula before the party moved to Hlobane where a camp was erected at the base of the mountain. Clarke, and a fatigue party of twenty Zulus, carried a stone cross that Mrs Campbell had brought out from England, up the mountain to Campbell's gravesite and there it remains, battered and overgrown, to this day. The group then moved on to Fort Warwick, near Itelezi Hill, as Clarke recorded:

> Here I was sent with six men to dig up the box containing the entrails of the Prince Imperial, the body having been embalmed by Dr Scott, who removed the heart, which, I believe, was sent to Paris.[343]

On 20 May Clarke, accompanied by the Zulu who had slain Captain Barton, returned to Hlobane to locate Barton's remains. The skeleton was found, together with his cap and pocketbook. His sword was returned by a Zulu and 'we buried the remains and erected a cairn of stones over the spot.'

Finally arriving at the place of the Prince Imperial's death, the empress handed out flower seeds and Clarke 'planted mine in the grave of [the trooper of] Bettington's Horse who was also killed on the 1st of June.' On the anniversary of her son's death, Empress Eugenie spent a solitary vigil by the cross that marked the spot where her son fell. It was a clear windless evening with candles, placed at the base of the cross, glowing softly.

There was no breath of air, but towards morning they suddenly began to flicker by a wind that was not there. 'Is it you beside me?' the over-wrought woman called out. 'Do you want me to go away?'[344]

Empress Eugenie grieved for two more days before leaving for Pieter-maritzburg.

Carey, who was held by many to be responsible for the prince's death, died about four years later at Karachi, India. The medical verdict was a ruptured intestine that led to peritonitis. Prime Minister Disraeli had the final say on Carey's conduct in a letter to Queen Victoria:

> He is a caitiff [a cowardly person], and yet after the court martial had so mismanaged the case it is highly probable that, if their verdict had been sanctioned, this mean wretch might have been transfigured into a hero or martyr.[345]

And what of British notables? Wolseley eventually achieved his ultimate ambition by superseding the Duke of Cambridge as the Commander-in-Chief of the British Army. Chelmsford never received another active command but remained a favourite of the royal family. Wood finally became a field marshal but was never really a distinguished general.

In the eyes of the public, Buller continued as the epitome of the British fighting commander until twenty years later, in 1900, not 120 miles from Ulundi, when he fought a battle against the Boers on a hill called Spioenkop. Several other old Zulu War comrades were present: Woodgate, who led the bayonet charge of the 90th at Kambula, was one and Major Sidney Strong of the Scottish Rifles (the old 90th) was another. Now a major-general, Woodgate led the attack on Spioenkop and was mortally wounded, as was Strong. The battle, like Isandlwana, was a catastrophic defeat for the British and, again like Isandlwana, the British casualties were estimated at 1,700. When one of his generals had suggested to Buller that Spioenkop should be attacked, Buller had replied that he had a dread of mountains – no doubt his thoughts were of Hlobane.

Newdigate, on his return from South Africa, went on to command the South-Eastern District until 1885. In 1887 he altered, by royal licence, his surname to 'Newdegate'. In 1888 he was appointed Governor of Bermuda. He died in 1902.

Colonel Richard Harrison, RE, notwithstanding the Carey debacle, went on to achieve great distinction, high rank and a knighthood. Engineers from 7th Company, RE, made the tin coffin in which the Prince Imperial's body was sent back to England. What is not generally known is that, some sixty years before, the Emperor Napoleon had been buried in a vault on St Helena built by Engineers of the Honourable East India Company. When Napoleon's body was repatriated for burial in Les Invalides in Paris, the vault was opened by men of the Royal Sappers and Miners. The original lead-lined coffin was then put into a wooden coffin, again made by the Engineers, and placed on a cart also built by the Sappers to convey the remains to the French warship *La Belle Poule*. Thus Harrison played his part in the corps' long-standing role as 'undertakers to the Bonapartes'.

Captain Alan Gardner, after being seriously wounded at Kambula, languished in the makeshift hospital at Utrecht for weeks and was eventually invalided back to England. The stigma of the mocking ditty seems to have influenced his thoughts on his future in the army; he left the service and successfully stood for Parliament.

Henry Lukin of Baker's Horse, wounded at Ulundi, enjoyed a distinguished career. Major-General Sir Henry Lukin, KCB, CMG, DSO, Chevalier of the Légion d'Honneur, and Order of the Nile, died at Plumstead, Cape Town, in 1925.

Of the many British officers who took part in the Anglo-Zulu War, few were honoured or remembered by their names being given to towns, mountains or other features in Natal or Zululand. A notable exception was a naval officer, Commodore Richards, who, it will be remembered, left the square at Gingindlovu against Chelmsford's orders to attack the Zulus. On 13 July, just ten days after the Battle of Ulundi, Richards wrote to the Admiralty: 'I enclose herewith a tracing of a survey made by the officers of HMS *Forester* for their Lordships' information.'[346] Richards was referring in part to the naval survey of the Zululand coast and in particular to a natural harbour a hundred miles north of Durban. He had modestly named the harbour after himself, calling it 'Richards Bay', and it is today a large, thriving port.

The imperial and colonial regiments met their various destinies: the 21st, 58th, 80th, 88th, and 94th Regiments all went off with Wolseley to Sekhukhuneland, the 94th to be decimated five months later by the Boers at the Battle of Bronkhorstspruit and their colonel killed. The 13th LI, after twelve years service abroad, returned to Britain as did the 1st/24th and 57th, while the 58th and 60th remained in Natal. Others went to more exotic destinations around the Empire: the 3rd to Singapore; the 4th to Bombay; the 2nd/24th to Gibraltar; the 90th to India; the 91st to Mauritius and the 99th to Bermuda.

Of the colonials, only Raaff's Rangers and the Border Horse remained with Wolseley. Commandant Raaff's services were duly recognised with the award of a CMG. Whalley's Horse was disbanded in August together with most of the other units, only to be raised again from time to time as circumstances dictated. For instance the Natal Native Horse was raised again in 1900 and yet again in 1906; Baker's Horse, disbanded on 2 August, almost immediately after Ulundi, saw service again a year later in Basutoland.

Bengough's Natal Native Contingent, which had fought throughout the war, was disbanded in September. The men of No. 1 Pioneer Company, Natal Native Pioneers, while on the march to be disbanded, expressed the wish not to proceed via Middle Drift as they thought that they would have to repair the road as they went. This was construed as mutiny and two of the ringleaders were flogged, receiving twenty-five lashes each. The men of Shepstone's Horse handed over their rifles at Fort Napier, Pietermaritzburg, and were paid off in September.

The finest regiment of all, the Frontier Light Horse, with five VCs to its credit (including those of Buller and Beresford), was disbanded with unseemly haste. Although colonial in almost every respect, it was, in fact, an imperial unit by virtue of its being financed by the British government rather than the colonial one. However, with Ulundi fought and the war won, the Imperial government disbanded the Frontier Light Horse the very next day. Let young George Mossop, who survived Hlobane, take up the tale:

> Next day Buller left, after wishing us good-bye and thanking us for our services. We then trekked to Landman's Drift, to the south of Utrecht – a disreputable looking lot of men – where we were deprived of our horses by a grateful government, and told to walk to Pietermaritzburg, a distance of some hundred miles, to be disbanded.[347]

However, Mossop pleaded that he had joined at Blood River, near Utrecht, and was discharged there and then, receiving his pay of £80 with which he bought a horse. He arrived at Utrecht at nine o'clock at night in midwinter.

> It was bitterly cold, the blanket I had been using belonged to the government and was handed over, therefore I had only the threadbare, torn clothes I was wearing. Proceeding to the hotel, I was told by the proprietor that he did not cater for my class; he not only refused me accommodation, but would not even sell me a bundle of forage for my horse.[348]

The war was over and, as after other wars before and since, in times of peace soldiers were no longer men of consequence and many, like the Zulu warriors they had fought, found themselves destitute and forgotten.

Notes

1   Laband, *Lord Chelmsford's Zululand Campaign 1878–1879*, p. 71.
2   Draft of a letter for the consideration of HRH the Duke of Cambridge, Commander-in-Chief of the British Army, prepared by General Sir Charles Ellice, Adjutant-General, PRO WO 30/129 56316.
3   Copy of the note scribbled by Gardner held at Killie Campbell Africana Library, Durban, KCM 89/9/27/3.
4   Journal of John Scott, at the time a senior NCO of the 90th Light Infantry. He later became colonel of the Cape Town Highlanders. South Africa Public Library, Cape Town. By courtesy of Colonel J. J. Hulme, late Durban Light Infantry.
5   Wood, *From Midshipman to Field Marshal*, Vol I, p. 295.
6   Royal Windsor Archives, VIC/Add E1/8514.
7   Royal Windsor Archives, VIC/Add E1/8513.
8   Royal Windsor Archives, VIC/0 33/49.
9   Royal Windsor Archives, VIC/Add E1/8525.
10   Vijn, *Cetshwayo's Dutchman*, p. 28.
11   Wood, *From Midshipman to Field Marshal*, Vol I, p. 259.
12   Ibid., p. 293.
13   Account of a meeting held at Utrecht, 5 December 1878. Wood Papers, Killie Campbell Africana Library, Durban.
14   Regulation No. 145, Rules Captured Cattle, *Regulations Field Forces, South Africa 1878*.
15   Account of a meeting held at Utrecht, 5 December 1879. Wood Papers, Killie Campbell Africana Library, Durban.
16   Fenn, *How I Volunteered for the Cape*.
17   Williams, *Rowlands, VC: The Life and Career of General Hugh Rowlands*.
18   Fenn, *How I Volunteered for the Cape*.
19   Williams, *Rowlands, VC*.
20   Ibid.
21   Ibid.
22   Laband, *Lord Chelmsford's Zululand Campaign*, p. 104.
23   Copy of a letter written in pencil, undated, in private collection. By courtesy of Colonel J. J. Hulme.
24   Buller to Wood, August 1880. Killie Campbell Africana Library, Durban. KCM 89/9/34/10.
25   Wood, *From Midshipman to Field Marshal*, Vol II, p. 29.
26   Tomasson, *With the Irregulars in the Transvaal and Zululand*.

27 Document relating to King Cetshwayo's coronation, Local History Museum, Durban.

28 Dunn, *John Dunn, Cetshwayo and the Three Generals*.

29 Lock, *Military Illustrated*, April 2003.

30 Document relating to King Cetshwayo's coronation, Local History Museum, Durban.

31 Laband, *Lord Chelmsford's Zululand Campaign*, p. 32.

32 MacLeod to Wood, 4 February 1879, PRO 179/132.

33 Ibid.

34 Killie Campbell Africana Library, Durban. 89/9/27/6.

35 A contemporary letter, *Army Historical Research Society*, Vol XXII, No. 89.

36 Williams, *Rowlands, VC*.

37 Hope, *The Zulu War and the 80th Regiment of Foot*, p. 69.

38 Emery, *The Red Soldier*, p. 158.

39 Letter of Sgt Booth dated 14 March 1879. Hope, *The Zulu War and the 80th Regiment of Foot*.

40 Ibid.

41 Lock and Quantrill, *The Red Book*, p. 168.

42 Hope, *The Zulu War and the 80th Regiment of Foot*.

43 *Army Historical Research Society*, Vol XXII, No. 89.

44 Hope, *The Zulu War and the 80th Regiment of Foot*.

45 Ibid.

46 Lock and Quantrill, *The Red Book*, p. 168.

47 Letter of Sgt Booth dated 14 March 1879. Hope, *The Zulu War and the 80th Regiment of Foot*.

48 Duke of Cambridge to Lord Chelmsford, 11 April 1979. Royal Windsor Archives, VC/Add E1/8624.

49 Wood, *From Midshipman to Field Marshal*, Vol II, p. 39.

50 Emery, *The Red Soldier*, p. 162.

51 The authors have found a variety of spellings for the mountain: Inhobano, Inhlobani, Zlobani, Inzholobawe and Rawani. We have used the modern spelling of Hlobane throughout the narrative to avoid confusion.

52 Lock and Quantrill, *The Red Book*, p. 131. Mrs Rorke was the daughter-in-law of James Rorke of Rorke's Drift, the Zulu wife of his son Michael.

53 Ibid., pp. 130 & 138

54 Wood, *From Midshipman to Field Marshal*, p. 34.

55 Lock and Quantrill, *The Red Book*, p. 131.

56 Ibid., p. 136.

57 Lock, *Blood on the Painted Mountain*, p. 119.

58 French, *Lord Chelmsford and the Zulu War*, pp. 183–5.

59 Lock and Quantrill, *The Red Book*, p. 126.

60 Filter and Bourquin, *Paulina Dlamini*, p. 68.

61 Schermbrucker, WO32/7711 XC6174.

62 Mitford, *Through the Zulu Country*, p. 205.

63 *Port Elizabeth Telegraph and Eastern Province Standard*, circa February 1879.

64 French, *Lord Chelmsford and the Zulu War*, p. 187.

65 Lock and Quantrill, *The Red Book*, p. 138.
66 Knox Leet's report, WO32/7726, pp. 92/103.
67 Knox Leet's report, WO32/7726 XC6174.
68 Dennison, Transvaal Archives, A1889, p. 74.
69 Moodie, *Moodie's Zulu War*, p. 108.
70 Tomasson, *With the Irregulars in the Transvaal and Zululand*, p. 41.
71 Tomasson, *With the Irregulars in the Transvaal and Zululand*.
72 Reyburn, *The Diary of RSM Cheffins*, p. 10.
73 Dennison, Transvaal Archives, Pretoria, A1889, p. 74.
74 Ibid., p. 75.
75 Knox Leet, WO32/7726 XC6174.
76 *The Scotsman*, 17 May 1879.
77 Schermbrucker, *South African Catholic*, circa 1893.
78 Mossop, *Running the Gauntlet*, p. 43.
79 Knight, Ian, 'Kill Me in the Shadows', *Soldiers of the Queen*, Issue 74, p. 10.
80 *London Gazette Supplement*, 6 May 1879.
81 Wood, *From Midshipman to Field Marshal*. Vol II, p. 43.
82 Mr H. Jones has the credit for tracking down the missing chapter. Transvaal Archives Pretoria, A1889.
83 As Dennison's version of events seriously questions Wood's integrity, the authors believe it prudent to review Dennison's background and career. The following details are taken from Creagh and Humphries, *The V.C. and D.S.O.* 'Dennison, Charles George, Captain, was born 21 November 1844, at Cradock, Cape Colony, son of George Dennison, Farmer, Cape Colony, and Mary Dennison (Webber). His father, who was a volunteer, died of wounds received in the Kaffir War of 1851, in Lower Albany, Cape Colony. He was educated at Grahams Town, and says:

"I always, from my boyhood, had a desire to be a soldier. My forefathers have nearly all been in the Army or Navy; my grandfather served through the American War as a Colour-Sergeant in the 55th Regiment, being wounded at Bunker Hill, and also in the Peninsular War. South African boys of my age were born and lived for years in an atmosphere of warfare and inured to danger and hardships, as also subsequently, which has made our South African lads what they are. I have commanded Regulars and troops from New Zealand and Australia, who are all fine and brave men, but none so adaptable, so mobile, as our South Africans, who have done many daring and gallant acts in our South African War. I allude to English and Dutch combined. I first saw active service when I fought at the age of 19 or 20 in the Free State War of 1865, with the Basutos, when I served as a trooper in the Bloemfontein Rangers (O.F.S. Republican Forces). I commanded the Rustenburg Rifles, a local corps raised in Rustenburg, Transvaal Republic, in 1876, with the late Thomas Burgher, the President of the Transvaal, in command of his bodyguard. I was Second-in-Command of the Border Horse, under Colonel Weatherley, under Colonel Sir E. Wood in Zululand in 1879, and when they were practically wiped out and both Colonel Weatherley and his son fell at Hlobane on 28 March, was promoted to the command, with the rank of Commandant and Colonel's pay (Zululand Medal); served under

Sir Garnet Wolseley in Sekhukhuni's Country (in the Boer War of 1891), as Commandant, commanding Border Horse; raised troops on two occasions in Bechuanaland; defeated the natives during the Rebellion of Mashonwing River, Bechuanaland; captured the rebel chief Golishwo – who caused the rising – in the Kalahari Desert, and thus stopped what might have been a prolonged and costly rising to the Cape Government (Bechuanaland Medal); raised Dennison's Scouts, and served with them as O.C., with the Irregular Mounted Forces in the Boer War of 1899–1902. I cannot give particulars as to which particular act gained me the D.S.O. Got the Column – known as the Kimberley Column – out of difficulties on different occasions during the Boer War."

He received the Queen's Medal with five clasps, and the King's Medal with two clasps; was Mentioned in Despatches, and created a Companion of the Distinguished Service Order [*London Gazette*, 31 Oct. 1902]: "Charles George Dennison, Capt., South African Mounted Irregular Forces. In recognition of services during the operations in South Africa." He rose to the rank of Major.

Major Dennison had four grandsons fighting in the European War, two of whom were severely wounded. He is particularly fond of hunting. Most of this has been done in Mashonaland and Matabeleland. He often met the late Major F. C. Selous, D.S.O., the great hunter, and knew him well. He married, 29 August 1867, at Aliwal North, Annie M. Hoffman, descendant on her mother's side of the De Villiers family of French Huguenots, and their children were: Alexander George, who fell in the Boer War; Lillie Elizabeth; Annie Mary; Clifford, who fell in the Boer War; Harold James; Emmie, and Frederick Weatherley.'

(It will be noted that Dennison named his youngest son after Colonel Weatherley – not the sort of thing a man like Dennison would do had Weatherley been a coward. *The authors.*)

84 'Colonel Weatherley was leading his horse with the bridle rein linked in one arm, while with one hand he helped his cripple son.' Dennison, Transvaal Archives, Pretoria, A1889, p. 83.

85 There were two officers by the name of Parminter involved on Hlobane: H. W. Parminter of the Border Horse and W. G. Parminter of Baker's Horse. The former was killed in action on Hlobane 28 March 1879.

86 'He [Weatherley] had lost only six men dead and seven wounded up to this hour.' Wood, *From Midshipman to Field Marshal*, p. 51.

87 Ibid., pp. 50–1.

88 'The attacking forces unconsciously moved into a cleverly laid trap . . .' Schermbrucker, *South African Catholic*, circa 1893, p. 342.

89 Wood, *From Midshipman to Field Marshal*.

90 *London Gazette*, 7 May 1879, p. 3255.

91 *The Foreman Engineer and Draughtsman's Journal*, 1 June 1879.

92 Pickering to Mr Mitchell, 3 April 1879, Killie Campbell Africana Library, Durban.

93 Reyburn, *The Diary of RSM Cheffins*, p. 6.

94 Dennison, Transvaal Archives, Pretoria, A1889, p. 80.

286

95 Ibid., p. 82.

96 Wood, *From Midshipman to Field Marshal*, Vol II p. 111.

97 Mossop, *Running the Gauntlet*, p. 51.

98 Knight, 'Kill Me in the Shadows', *Soldiers of the Queen*, Issue 74, p. 11.

99 Emery, *The Red Soldier*, p. 169.

100 Ibid., p. 168.

101 *London Gazette*, 7 May 1879.

102 Lock and Quantrill, *The Red Book*, p. 186.

103 Schermbrucker, *South African Catholic*, circa 1893.

104 Lock and Quantrill, *The Zulu War Through the Eyes of the Illustrated London News*, p. 98.

105 The quotation is part of his citation for the DCM, for which he was recommended by Buller.

106 *London Gazette*, 7 May 1879.

107 A few weeks later, in May, Smith was 'dismissed with disgrace' from the Frontier Light Horse, having drunk himself into a 'condition of frenzy' and, with a revolver, defied anyone to approach him. Lock and Quantrill, *The Red Book*, p. 213

108 Knox Leet, WO32/7726 XC6174. Private letter written by Knox Leet, dated Kambula Camp 6 April 1879. By kind permission of Mr Richard Stock.

109 *London Gazette*, 7 May 1879.

110 Wood, *From Midshipman to Field Marshal*, Vol II, p. 54.

111 Emery, *Marching over Africa*, p. 78.

112 Emery, *The Red Soldier*, p. 171.

113 Dennison, Transvaal Archives, Pretoria, A1889, p. 87.

114 Private letter written by Knox Leet, dated Kambula Camp 6 April 1879. By kind permission of Mr Richard Stock.

115 *The Scotsman*, 17 May 1879.

116 Lock and Quantrill, *The Red Book*, p. 173.

117 *London Gazette*, 7 May 1879.

118 Montague, *Campaigning in South Africa*, p. 327.

119 *The Graphic*, May 1879.

120 Private letter, 22 April 1932. Courtesy of Mr Paul Naish.

121 Mitford, *Through the Zulu Country*, p. 214.

122 Laband, *Rope of Sand*, p. 270.

123 Ibid., p. 280.

124 McToy, *A Brief History of the 13th Foot in South Africa*.

125 Journal of Colonel Scott, South Africa Public Library, Cape Town.

126 WO146/1 10841.

127 Lock and Quantrill, *The Red Book*, p. 171.

128 *The Scotsman*, 17 May 1879.

129 Captain Woodgate says there were two companies in the cattle laager. All other accounts say one. Emery, *The Red Soldier*, p. 171.

130 *Natal Mercury*, 21 April 1879.

131 Schermbrucker, *South African Catholic*, circa 1893.

132 Trooper Charles Hewitt, private letter to his sister, April 1879. Copy held by the authors.

133 Knight, 'Kill Me in the Shadows', *Soldiers of the Queen*, Issue 74, p. 14.
134 Lock and Quantrill, *The Red Book*, p. 162.
135 *The Friend*, 1 May 1879.
136 Journal of Colonel Scott. South African Public Library, Cape Town.
137 WO32/7726 XC6174.
138 Ibid.
139 Ibid.
140 Ibid.
141 WO32/7726 XC11903.
142 Lock and Quantrill, *The Red Book*, p. 188.
143 Lock and Quantrill, *Zulu Victory*, p. 267.
144 Killie Campbell Africana Library, Durban. 89/9/28/7.
145 Alison, Sir Archibald, Autograph Letters, Brenthurst Library, Johannesburg, MS 165.
146 Ibid.
147 Lock and Quantrill, *The Red Book*, p. 127
148 Strutt, *Life In Natal During The Zulu War*.
149 Wood Papers, Natal Archives, Pietermaritzburg.
150 Lock and Quantrill, *The 1879 Zulu War, Through The Eyes Of The Illustrated London News*, p. 91.
151 Molyneux, *Campaigning in South Africa and Egypt*, p. 125.
152 Dunn, *John Dunn, Cetshwayo and the Three Generals*.
153 Ibid., p. 95.
154 Ibid., p. 28.
155 Dawnay, *Campaigns*, p. 10.
156 Emery, *The Red Soldier*, p. 197.
157 Bourquin, *The Zulu War of 1879*, p. 62.
158 Molyneux, *Campaigning in South Africa*, 1896, p. 127.
159 Dunn, *John Dunn, Cetshwayo and the Three Generals*, p. 101.
160 Molyneux, *Campaigning in South Africa*, p. 131.
161 Dunn, *John Dunn, Cetshwayo and the Three Generals*.
162 French, *Lord Chelmsford and the Zulu War*, p. 172.
163 Lock and Quantrill, *The 1879 Zulu War Through the Eyes of the Illustrated London News*, p. 158.
164 Emery, *The Red Soldier*, p. 200.
165 Molyneux, *Campaigning in South Africa*, p. 131.
166 Tomasson, *With the Irregulars in Transvaal and Zululand*, p. 81
167 Dunn, *John Dunn, Cetshwayo and the Three Generals*.
168 Emery, *The Red Soldier*, p. 201.
169 Knight, *Fearful Hard Times*, p. 199.
170 Molyneux, *Campaigning in South Africa*, p. 139.
171 Ibid., p. 137.
172 Lock and Quantrill, *The 1879 Zulu War Through the Eyes of the Illustrated London News*, p. 114.
173 Emery, *The Red Soldier*, p. 198.
174 Wynne, *A Widow-Making War*, p. 131.

175 Lock and Quantrill, *The 1879 Zulu War Through the Eyes of the Illustrated London News*, p. 114.

176 Main, 'Recollections', Royal Engineers Museum, Chatham.

177 Lock and Quantrill, *The Red Book*, p. 154.

178 Norbury, *The Naval Brigade in South Africa*, p. 275.

179 Wynne, *A Widow-Making War*, p. 154.

180 van der Walt, *Zululand Observer*.

181 Knight, *Fearful Hard Times*, p. 228.

182 WO 30/129 S 6316.

183 French, *Lord Chelmsford and the Zulu War*, p. 338.

184 Dawnay, *Campaigns*, p. 55.

185 Henderson, *The Turbulent Frontier – Biggarsberg and Buffalo at the Crossroads*.

186 Balkema, *Sir Garnet Wolseley's South African Journal*, p. 45.

187 Wood Papers, Natal Archives Pietermaritzburg.

188 Ibid.

189 Alison Letters, Brenthurst Library, Johannesburg, MS 165.

190 Balkema, *Sir Garnet Wolseley's South African Journal*, p. 287.

191 Ibid., p. 28.

192 French, *Lord Chelmsford and the Zulu War*, p. 55.

193 Ibid., p. 60.

194 Alison Letters, Brenthurst Library, Johannesburg, MS 165.

195 French, *Lord Chelmsford and the Zulu War*, p. 213.

196 Alison Letters, Brenthurst Library, Johannesburg, MS 165.

197 WO 32/7795.

198 Balkema, *Sir Garnet Wolseley's South African Journal*, p. 52.

199 Lock and Quantrill, *The 1879 Zulu War Through the Eyes of the Illustrated London News*, p. 208.

200 Alison Letters, Brenthurst Library, Johannesburg, MS 165.

201 Ibid.

202 Balkema, *Sir Garnet Wolseley's South African Journal*, p. 66.

203 Alison Letters, Brenthurst Library, Johannesburg, MS 165.

204 Montague, *Campaigning in South Africa*, p. 101.

205 Alison Letters, Brenthurst Library, Johannesburg, MS 165.

206 Henderson, *The Turbulent Frontier – Biggarsberg and Buffalo at the Crossroads*.

207 Ibid.

208 Wood Papers, Natal Archives, Pietermaritzburg.

209 Balkema, *Sir Garnet Wolseley's South African Journal*.

210 Lock and Quantrill, *The Red Book*, p. 151.

211 Henderson, *The Turbulent Frontier – Biggarsberg and Buffalo at the Crossroads*.

212 Tomasson, *With the Irregulars in Transvaal and Zululand*, p. 34.

213 Lock and Quantrill, *The Red Book*, p. 157.

214 Montague, *Campaigning in South Africa*, p. 132.

215 French, *Lord Chelmsford and the Zulu War*, p. 204.

216 Ibid., p. 276.

217 Ibid., p. 218.
218 Ibid., p. 220.
219 Ibid., p. 222.
220 Ibid.
221 Ibid., p. 225.
222 Ibid., p. 227.
223 Henderson, *The Turbulent Frontier – Biggarsberg and Buffalo at the Crossroads*.
224 Lock, 'Death of the Prince Imperial', *Military History* [USA], August 1998.
225 Deleáge, Paul, *Le Figaro*, 1879.
226 Lock, 'Death of the Prince Imperial', *Military History* [USA], August 1998.
227 Ibid.
228 Deleáge, *Le Figaro*, 1879.
229 Lock, 'Death of the Prince Imperial', *Military History* [USA], August 1998.
230 Kurtz, *The Empress Eugenie*.
231 Deléage, *Le Figaro*, 1879.
232 Deléage, *Trois Mois Chez Les Zoulous et Les Derniers Jours Du Prince Imperial*.
233 Lock, 'Death of the Prince Imperial', *Military History* [USA], August 1998.
234 Ibid.
235 Ibid. The sequence of events after the firing of the first volley has been compiled from the interrogation by Wood, in 1880, of the actual warriors involved. Wood's spelling of Zulu names has been retained. Wood Papers, Natal Archives, Pietermaritzburg.
236 Featherstone, *Captain Carey's Blunder*, p. 108.
237 Grenfell, *Memoirs*, p. 57
238 Slade's letters to his mother, 2 June 1879, National Army Museum.
239 WO 91/48 22382.
240 Main, 'Recollections', Royal Engineers Museum, Chatham.
241 Kurtz, *The Empress Eugenie*, p. 310.
242 WO 91/48 22382.
243 Kurtz, *The Empress Eugenie*, p. 314.
244 Featherstone, *Captain Carey's Blunder*, p. 175.
245 Kurtz, *The Empress Eugenie*, p. 315.
246 WO 91/48 22382.
247 Balkema, *Sir Garnet Wolseley's South African Journal*, p. 126.
248 French, *Lord Chelmsford and the Zulu War*, p. 258.
249 Ibid., p. 200.
250 Alison Letters, Brenthurst Library, Johannesburg, MS 165.
251 Montague, *Campaigning in South Africa*, p. 190.
252 Alison Letters, Brenthurst Library, Johannesburg, MS 165.
253 Ibid.
254 Doncaster, *The Zulu War*, p. 274.
255 *Anglo-Zulu War Research Society*, Vol 3 Issue 1.
256 Montague, *Campaigning in South Africa*, p. 185.
257 Ibid.
258 Dawnay, *Campaigns*, p. 37.

259 Montague, *Campaigns in South Africa*, p. 217.
260 Lock and Quantrill, *The Red Book*, p. 281.
261 Ibid., p. 305.
262 French, *Lord Chelmsford and the Zulu War*, p. 280.
263 Norris-Newman, *In Zululand with the British Throughout the War of 1879*, p. 224.
264 Montague, *Campaigning in South Africa*.
265 *Light*, Houston, Texas, October 1979, with thanks to Ken Gillings.
266 Alison Letters, Brenthurst Library, Johannesburg, MS 165, p. 193.
267 Main, 'Recollections', Royal Engineers Museum, Chatham.
268 Alison Letters, Brenthurst Library, Johannesburg, MS 165.
269 French, *Lord Chelmsford and the Zulu War*, p. 282.
270 Montague, *Campaigning in South Africa*, p. 225.
271 French, *Lord Chelmsford and the Zulu War*, p. 282.
272 WO 32/7795 56333.
273 Vijn, *Cetshwayo's Dutchman*, p. 28.
274 Seven years earlier, Cetshwayo's father Mpande had died at the age of seventy-four of natural causes. Cetshwayo would have remembered his death and the subsequent Zulu traditional ceremony with a degree of anguish. It was Zulu custom that the King's death was not a matter for discussion. Indeed, any questions asked were tactfully responded to by 'Inkosi iyadunguzela' which roughly translates as 'the king is indisposed'. Before rigor mortis could set in a bull was slaughtered. This may well have been a clue to the *amabutho* residing in the *amakhanda* that their monarch was dead. The body was then placed in a sitting posture and the skin of the bull was wrapped tightly around the body leaving the head exposed. This would ensure that the sitting position would, in after life, always be maintained. During this period the king was still 'indisposed'. Heads were shaved and those who kept vigil over the body pushed msuzwane leaves, from a species of shrub, up their noses. The leaves gave off a pleasant odour, thus helping suppress the disagreeable smell of a decaying body.

At kwaNodwengu, Mpande's *ikhanda*, a gravesite was prepared some three yards deep. Today, a monument erected by the National Monuments Commission marks the gravesite. All the monarch's personal effects such as his blankets, sleeping mats, beadwork, eating utensils, and snuff-boxes were placed at his feet. The only exception were his spears, which, if placed in his grave, could one day turn his spirit against his friends and, according to Zulu belief, put them to death. So the spears were taken a suitable distance from the gravesite and buried secretly, thus preventing any potential retribution.

A most gruesome task still awaited the conductors of the ongoing ceremonies. The king was not to repose alone. Servants were necessary to attend to his after life needs. Perhaps two or three royal retainers were led from the *ikhanda* and their legs, arms and necks were broken. In this state they accompanied their king on his journey. Still more was required; in his sitting position and looking down, Mpande should, in accordance with custom, be able to view his closest and most personal servant. The latter, named Makhanda, was aware of his impending fate and wisely fled. One Nhlangano, one of the king's personal advisers, was his unfortunate replacement. The hapless Nhlangano was duly strangled and placed in a lateral position, to be used as a mat on which the king's body was placed. The grave was then covered and in order to ensure that the king and his retinue were well fed, a beast was sacrificed daily for a period of thirty days.

It remained essential that the spirit of the king be well received after its journey and accordingly two or three young maidens of royal lineage were selected for the final act. The method of selection is unrecorded, but great fear and trepidation would undoubtedly have fallen upon the royal household. For a period of a month following Mpande's death, the women would have known that, whoever was selected, those few had not long to live. There could surely have been no volunteers.

In due course the unfortunate duo or trio were marched in silence to the south bank of the Umfolozi River some miles from the royal *ikhanda*, and there a rope was tightened around their necks. Then the rope was stretched taught and the body of the victim held in position whilst a third executioner struck the rope with an *iwisa* or knobkerrie, causing vibration resulting in slow strangulation.

The bodies were then abandoned without burial, left for beasts of prey or vultures to devour. The spirits, known as *abaphansi* or 'the ones below' that lived underground, (Source: Filter and Bourquin) would be pleased, as no blood had been shed, hence the method of execution.

This final ceremony completed the burial of Cetshwayo's father, Mpande kaSenzangakhona. (Source: C. T. Binns).

275 Webb and Wright, *The James Stuart Archive*, Volume 3.
276 Dunn, *John Dunn, Cetshwayo and the Three Generals*, p. 147.
277 Vijn, *Cetshwayo's Dutchman*, p. 47.
278 Ibid., p. 137.
279 Ibid., p. 140.
280 Webb and Wright, *The James Stuart Archive*, Volume 4.
281 Ibid., Volume 3.
282 Ibid., Volume 4.
283 In 1879, the name Ulundi referred to an area on the Mhlabathini Plain. The royal *ikhanda* of Cetshwayo was named oNdini and therefore, strictly speaking, the battle should be recorded as oNdini. Some contemporary sources also refer to the battle as Nodwengu, this being the nearest *ikhanda* to the battle site. To avoid confusion, we have chosen to follow the modern terminology of 'Ulundi'.
284 Mitford, *Through The Zulu Country*, p. 230.
285 Ibid., p. 231.
286 Lock and Quantrill, *The Red Book*, p. 292.
287 Ibid., p. 294.
288 Forbes, *The Bravest Deed I Ever Saw*.
289 Chelmsford Papers, National Army Museum, 6807–386-16-30.

290 Main, 'Recollections'. Royal Engineers Museum, Chatham.
291 Forbes, *The Bravest Deed I Ever Saw.*
292 Lock and Quantrill, *The Red Book*, p. 324.
293 Ibid., p. 295.
294 Harness, Arthur, Autograph Letters, 4 January 1878 – 2 October 1879, Brenthurst Library, Johannesburg, MS 158.
295 Wilkinson, Trumpet-Major William H., 17th Lancers, 'The Fight for Natal', *The Royal* (magazine), 1911
296 Molyneux, *Campaigning in South Africa*, p. 186.
297 Chelmsford Papers, National Army Museum, 6807-386-16-30
298 Lock and Quantrill, *The Red Book*, p. 291.
299 Chelmsford Papers, National Army Museum, 6807-385-16-30.
300 Harness, Arthur, Autograph Letters, 4 January 1878 – 2 October 1879, Brenthurst Library, Johannesburg, MS 158.
301 Tomasson, *With the Irregulars in Transvaal and Zululand*, p. 178.
302 Ibid.
303 'Reminiscences of the Zulu War' by an unidentified young officer of the 58th Regiment, *Medical Services*, 1932.
304 Alison Letters, Brenthurst Library, Johannesburg, MS 165.
305 Ibid.
306 Tomasson, *With the Irregulars in Transvaal and Zululand*, p. 180.
307 Prior, *Campaigns.*
308 Webb and Wright, *The James Stuart Archive*, Vol. 4.
309 Alison Letters, Brenthurst Library, Johannesburg, MS 165
310 Statement of Ndungguna kaNgengene, C.2482.
311 Alison Letters, Brenthurst Library, Johannesburg, MS 165
312 Trumpet-Major W. H. Wilkinson, *Anglo Zulu War Research Society*, Vol. 3, Issue 1.
313 Dawnay, *Campaigns*, p. 69
314 Emery, *The Red Soldier*, p. 237.
315 Chelmsford Papers, National Army Museum, 6807-386-16-30.
316 Filter and Bourquin, *Paulina Dlamini.*
317 WO 32/7795 56333.
318 French, *Lord Chelmsford and the Zulu War.*
319 Lock and Quantrill, *The Red Book*, p. 181.
320 Ibid.
321 Letter, 23 July 1879, addressed to Hermansberg Mission by Pastor H. Filter, by courtesy of Mr T. Engelbrecht.
322 Ibid.
323 Montague, *Campaigning in South Africa*, p. 341.
324 Ibid.
325 Chief of Staff's Journal, W/O 079/2718.
326 French, *Lord Chelmsford and the Zulu War.*
327 Balkema, *Sir Garnet Wolseley's South African Journal.*
328 Ibid.
329 Ibid.
330 *The Graphic*, 20 September 1879.

331 Ibid.

332 *Natal Mercury*, 24 September 1879.

333 Vijn, *Cetshwayo's Dutchman*.

334 Montague, *Campaigning in South Africa*, p. 308.

335 Child, *The Zulu War Diary of Col. Henry Harford*, p. 73.

336 Mitford, *Through the Zulu Country*, p. 203.

337 Ibid.

338 *Sunday Times*, 25 November 1965.

339 Ibid.

340 Montague, *Campaigning in South Africa*, p. 309.

341 *The Graphic*, 4 October 1879.

342 van der Walt, *The Zululand Observer*.

343 'My career in South Africa', Lieutenant-Colonel W. J. Clarke, Natal Archives, A 433.

344 Kurtz, *The Empress Eugenie*.

345 John, *The Prince Imperial*.

346 van der Walt, *The Zululand Observer*.

347 Mossop, *Running the Gauntlet*, p. 98.

348 Ibid.

Bibliography

Unpublished Sources and Private Information

Brenthurst Library, Johannesburg
Alison, Sir Archibald, Autograph Letters, 6 March 1878 – 26 October 1881. MS 165.
Harness, Arthur, Autograph Letters, 4 January 1878 – 2 October 1879. MS 158.

Killie Campbell Africana Library, Durban
Manuscripts and papers as enumerated in the notes.

Local History Museum, Durban
Wood Papers and documents relating to King Cetshwayo's coronation.

Natal Archives, Pietermaritzburg
Sir Evelyn Wood Papers.
W. J. Clarke Papers.

National Army Museum, London
Lt Slade's letter to his mother, 2 June 1879.

Royal Archives, Windsor
Various papers, as enumerated in the notes, by gracious permission of
   Her Majesty Queen Elizabeth II.

Royal Engineers Museum, Chatham
'Recollections', Colonel R. Harrison RE.
'Recollections', Colonel T. R. Main, RE.
Private letter written by Major Knox Leet, dated 'Kambula Camp, 6 April 1879',
   by kind permission M. R. Stock.

Transvaal Archives, Pretoria
Dennison Papers.

South Africa Public Library, Cape Town
The Journal of John Scott. By courtesy of Colonel J. J. Hulme, late Durban
Light Infantry.

UK National Archives, Kew
Various papers, as enumerated in the notes, reference PRO and PRO/WO.

Newspapers, Journals and Periodicals
South Africa
*Cape Argus, Farmer's Weekly, The Friend, Natal Mercury, Natal Witness, Port
Elizabeth Telegraph and Eastern Province Standard, South African Catholic*

Magazine (circa 1893), *Zululand Observer*

United Kingdom

The Foreman Engineer and Draftsman's Journal (June 1879), *Fraser's Magazine, The Graphic, Illustrated London News, Journal of the Anglo-Zulu War Historical Society, Journal of the Anglo-Zulu War Research Society, Journal of the Society for Army Historical Research, London Gazette, Military Illustrated, Medal News, Pearson's, The Scotsman, Soldiers of the Queen* (Journal of the Victorian Military Society), *The Sunday Times, The Times*

United States of America

Military History (August 1998)

Books

Ash, Major, and Wyatt-Edgell, E. V., *The Story of the Zulu Campaign*, London, 1880

Balkema, A. A., *Sir Garnet Wolseley's South African Journal, 1879–80*, 1973

Binns, C. T., *The Last Zulu King – The Life and Death of Cetshwayo*, London, 1963

Bourquin, S., *The Zulu War of 1879, a compilation from the 'Graphic'*, Durban, 1965

Child, D., *The Zulu War Diary of Col. Henry Harford*, Pietermaritzburg, 1978

Clark, John, *The Child of France. The Zulu War and Colony of Natal*, Durban, 1979

Clarke, Sonia, *Invasion of Zululand*, Johannesburg, 1979

———, *Zululand at War, 1879*, Johannesburg, 1984

Cliff, M. M., *Natal Personalities Involved in the War*, Pietermaritzburg, 1979

Creagh, Garrett O'Moore, and Humphries, E. M., *The V.C. and D.S.O.*, London, undated.

Dawnay, Guy, *Campaigns: Zulu 1879, Egypt 1882, Suakin 1885*, Cambridge, 1989

Deléage, Paul, *Trois Mois chez les Zoulous et les Derniers Jours du Prince Impérial*, Paris, 1879

Dunn, John, (D. C. F. Moodie ed.), *John Dunn, Cetshwayo and the Three Generals*, Pietermaritzburg, 1886

Emery, Frank, *The Red Soldier*, London, 1977

———, *Marching Over Africa*, London, 1986

Featherstone, Donald, *Captain Carey's Blunder*, London, 1977

Fenn, C. E., *How I Volunteered for the Cape*, (Fragment, publication place and date unknown)

Filter, H., and Bourquin, S. B., *Paulina Dlamini*, Pietermaritzburg, 1986

Forbes, Archibald, *Barracks, Bivouacs, and Battles*, London, 1892

French, Gerald, *Lord Chelmsford and the Zulu War*, London, 1939

Grenfell, Field Marshal Lord, *Memoirs*, London, 1925

Guy, Jeff, *The Destruction of the Zulu Kingdom*, London, 1979

Henderson, Sheila, *The Turbulent Frontier – Biggarsberg and Buffalo at the Crossroads*, Pietermaritzburg, 1979

Hope, Robert, *The Zulu War and the 80th Regiment of Foot*, Leek, UK, 1997

Intelligence Division War Office, *Precis of Information Concerning Zululand*, London, 1885 and 1894

John, Katherine, *The Prince Imperial*, London, 1939

Johnston, R., *Ulundi To Delville Wood, The Life Story of Major General Sir Henry Timson Lukin*, Cape Town, *circa* 1956

Knight, Ian, *Fearful Hard Times*, London, 1994

———, *The Anatomy of the Zulu Army*, London, 1995

Krige, Eileen Jenson, *The Social System of the Zulus*, Pietermaritzburg, 1957

Kurtz, Harold, *The Empress Eugenie*, London, 1964

Laband, John, and Thompson, Paul, *Kingdom and Colony at War*, Pietermaritzburg, 1990

———, *The Illustrated Guide to the Anglo-Zulu War*, Pietermaritzburg, 2000

Laband, John, *Fight Us In The Open*, KwaZulu-Natal, 1985

———, *Rope of Sand*, Johannesburg, 1995

———, *Lord Chelmsford's Zululand Campaign, 1878–1879*, Stroud, 1994

Lehman, Joseph, All Sir Garnet, London, 1969

Lock, Ron, and Quantrill, Peter, *The 1879 Zulu War Through the Eyes of the Illustrated London News*, Pinetown, KwaZulu-Natal, 2003

———, *The Red Book: a compilation of Natal newspaper reports on the Anglo-Zulu War*, Pinetown, KwaZulu-Natal, 2000

———, *Zulu Victory: The Epic of Isandlwana and the Cover-Up*, London, 2002

Lock, Ron, *Blood on the Painted Mountain*, London, 1995

Mackinnon, J. P., and Shadbolt, S. H., *The South African Campaign of 1879*, London, 1880; reprinted London, 1995

McToy, Edward, *A Brief History of the 13th Foot (P.A.L.I.) in South Africa 1877-8-9*, Devonport, 1880

Mitford, Bertram, *Through The Zulu Country*, London, 1883; reprinted London, 1988.

Molyneux, Major-General, *Campaigning in South Africa and Egypt*, London, 1896

Montague, W. E., *Campaigning in South Africa*, London, 1880

Moodie, D. C. F., *Moodie's Zulu War*, Cape Town, 1988

Morris, Donald, *The Washing of the Spears*, London, 1966

Mossop, P. G., *Running the Gauntlet*, London, 1937

Norbury, H. F., *The Naval Brigade in South Africa during the years 1877–79*, London, 1880

Norris-Newman, Charles, *In Zululand with the British Throughout the War of 1879*, London, 1880; reprinted London, 1988

Preston, Adrian, *Sir Garnet Wolseley's South African Journal, 1879–80*, Cape Town, 1973

Regulations Field Forces, South Africa 1878, example consulted, courtesy of Professor John Laband

Reyburn, Lindsay (ed.), *The 1879 Zulu War Diary of RSM F. W. Cheffins*, Pretoria, 2001

Samuelson, L. H., *Zululand, Its Traditions, Legends, Customs and Folk-Lore*, Durban

Samuelson, R. C., *Long, Long Ago*, Durban, 1929

Strutt, Daphne, *Life in Natal During the Zulu War, 1879*, Pietermaritzburg, 1979

Stuart, James and Malcolm, D. McK., *The Diary of Henry Francis Fynn*, Pietermaritzburg, 1951

Thompson, P. S., *The Natal Native Contingent in the Anglo-Zulu War, 1879*, Pietermaritzburg, 1997

Tomasson, W. H., *With the Irregulars in Transvaal and Zululand*, London, 1881

Tylden, G., *The Armed Forces of South Africa, 1659–1954*, Johannesburg, 1954

Unterhalter, Elaine, *Confronting Imperialism: The People of Nqutu and the 1879 Invasion of Zululand*, Durban, 1979

Vijn, Cornelius, *Cetshwayo's Dutchman*, London, 1880; reprinted London, 1988

War Office (compiled by J. S. Rothwell), *Narrative of the Field Operations Connected with The Zulu War of 1879*, London, 1881; reprinted London, 1907, and 1989

Watkins, Owen, *They fought for the Great White Queen*, Edendale, 1885; reprinted by Newcastle Museum, 1979

Webb, C. de B., and Wright, J. B. (eds.), *The James Stuart Archive*, 5 vols, Pietermaritzburg, 1976

Webb, C. de B., and Wright, J. B. (eds.), *A Zulu King Speaks*, Pietermaritzburg, 1987

Williams, W. A., *Rowlands, VC: The Life and Career of General Hugh Rowlands*, (Privately published) UK circa 1990

Wood, Evelyn, *From Midshipman to Field Marshal*, London, 1906

Wood, Evelyn, *Winnowed Memories*, London, 1918

Wynne, Warren, *A Widow-Making War*, Southampton 1880; reprinted 1995

Young, John, *They Fell Like Stones: Battles and Casualties of the Zulu War, 1879*, London, 1991

Index

Page references in *italics* refer to map and illustration captions.